ISBN 978-1-332-11661-4
PIBN 10286871

For support please visit www.forgottenbooks.com

Similar Books Are Available from
www.forgottenbooks.com

THOS. COOK & SON, 3, BOULEVARD DE LA REPUBLIQUE.

1908.

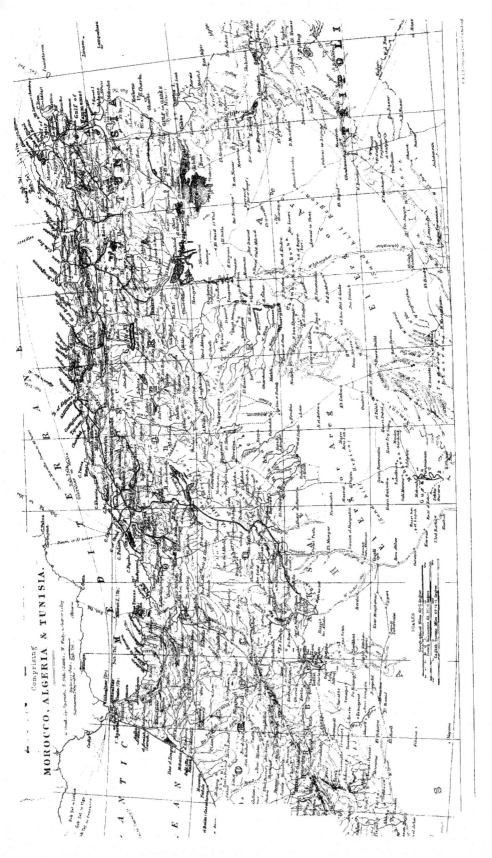

Comprising
MOROCCO, ALGERIA & TUNISIA.

COOK'S

PRACTICAL GUIDE

TO

ALGERIA AND TUNISIA.

With Maps, Plans, and Illustrations.

LONDON:

THOS. COOK & SON, LUDGATE CIRCUS, E.C.

SIMPKIN, MARSHALL, HAMILTON, KENT & CO., LTD.

ALGIERS:

THOS. COOK & SON, 3, BOULEVARD DE LA RÉPUBLIQUE.

1908.

PREFACE.

—◦—

AMONG the several countries that attract the traveller desirous of exchanging the rigours of our English winter for sunshine and health, Algeria and Tunisia easily occupy the first rank.

These countries comprising as they do so many favourable conditions of typical health-resorts, and containing so many varied attractions, are year by year frequented by an ever-increasing number of visitors and tourists.

The climate of Algeria and Tunisia is unique, and eminently adapted to the comfort of those who, whether from necessity or choice, winter abroad; in addition the picturesque aspect of Arab life, of the white cities with their narrow streets; the historical souvenirs of these lands that from time to time have been subject to the Kings of Numidia, to the Roman Emperors, to Arab, Spanish, and Turkish conquerors, afford the learned and enquiring traveller an opportunity to study past civilisations, while the ordinary tourist will experience the enjoyment of a picturesque and beautiful country.

The numerous hotels afford comfortable residence under excellent sanitary conditions; the access to these charming health resorts is easy; and the cost of the voyage to Algiers or Tunis is less than to the Canaries or Madeira, the distance being so much shorter.

a 2

The object of this book is to inform the traveller how to reach Algeria and Tunisia, and where to go when he gets there. Times of trains, steamers, etc., although carefully checked at time of going to press, should be verified on the spot, as they are liable to alteration from time to time.

Concise information is afforded as to the most popular districts and principal places of interest, and the book is printed in clear, legible type, with the important places marked conspicuously, so as to readily arrest the eye.

The Editor will esteem it a favour if those who use this book will kindly point out any inaccuracies they may detect, or alterations they may deem advisable; and any suggestions of a practical nature for insertion in future editions will be gratefully acknowledged.

THOS. COOK & SON.

Ludgate Circus, London, 1908.

Obligations are acknowledged to many authors, ancient and modern, such as Pliny, Strabo, Ptolemy, Apuleius, M. Leroy-Beaulieu, Sir H. Johnston. Sir Lambert Playfair, Père Delattre, V. Guérin, M. Gauckler, Dr. Shaw, G. Charmes.

On pp. 285, 286 will be found a list of Books of Reference concerning Algeria, and on p. 402 a similar list concerning Tunisia.

M. Geiser, MM. Vollenweder and Borgeaud, of Algiers, and M. Garrigues, of Tunis, have allowed us the use of their admirable photographs.

CONTENTS.

—◆—

PART I.

ALGERIA.

PART II.

ALGIERS.

PART III.

THE ENVIRONS OF ALGIERS.

PART IV

THE INTERIOR.

Districts West of Algiers.

Districts East of Algiers.

TUNISIA.

PART I.

Tunisia.

PART II.

Tunis.

PART III.

Excursions from Tunis.

CONTENTS.

Maps and Plans.

Illustrations.

CONTENTS.

ARABIC WORDS AND PHRASES.

ENGLISH — ARABIC.

ANIMALS.

a calf, *ookreeff*
a cat, *kett*
a cow, *beggra*
a dog, *kelb*
a horse, *aood*
a mare, *feress*
camel, *djemel*
cats, *ktett*
chicken, *djedad*
cock, *serdook*
dogs, *klab*
donkey, *hmar*

duck, *brack*
gazelle, *gzal*
goat, *mahza*
goose, *ouaz*
jackal, *deeb*
lion, *sba*
lizard, *deb*
mosquito, *namous*
mule, *beghla*
panther, *nmer*
rabbit, *arneb*
turkey, *serdook el hend*

ARMS.

cannon, *metfah*
gun, *moukahla*
pistol, *kabous*

powder, *barood*
shot, *chatmah*
sword, *seef*

BEDDING.

bed, *frach*
blanket, *ferrachia*

carpet, *bsath*
mattress, *mettrah*

COLOURS.

black, *akhal*
blue, *azrek*
colour, *loon*
green, *akdar*

red, *ahmer*
white, *abiod*
yellow, *sfer*

FLOWERS, TREES, ETC.

date tree, *nakhala*
dwarf palm, *dom*
flowers, *nouarh*
garden, *djenan*
jasmine, *yasmeen*
jujube, *annab*

lily, *sissan*
oak, *zan*
oleander, *defla*
olive, *zeitoun*
pink, *krenfell*
rose, *corda*

FOOD.

bread, *khobs*

butter, *zibda*

coffee, *kaoua*

fish, *hoot*

fowl, *djedad*

honey, *asel*

meat, *lahm*

milk, *hlceb*

mutton, *kebash*

oil, *zeet*

pepper, *felfel*

salt, *melh*

vinegar, *khral*

water, *ma*

wine, *shrab*

FRUITS.

almonds, *looz*

apple, *teffah*

apricot, *mechmach*

bananas, *mooz*

cherries, *habelmlook*

currants, *zebib*

dates, *tmer*

grapes, *ainab*

lemon, *lim-karess*

orange, *tchina*

pear, *nedjass*

MEN.

boy, *ouled*

girl, *bent*

man, *radjel*

old man, *sheikh*

woman. *mra*

boys, *oulad*

girls, *bnat*

men, *redjal*

old men, *shiookh*

women, *nsa*

METALS.

copper, *nhas*

gold, *deheb*

iron, *hadid*

lead, *rsas*

money, *draham*

silver, *fodda*

MISCELLANEOUS.

artichoke, *kernoon*

beak, *menkar*

bridge, *kantra*

east, *cherkh*

eye, *ain*

fez, *chechia*

head, *ras*

horn, *kern*

leather, *djeld*

leg, *redjel*

mountain, *djebel*

north, *dahra*

onions, *bsel*

potatoes. *batata*

river, *ouad*

saddle, *serdj*

sand, *rmel*

sea, *bahr*

skin, *djel*

south, *guebli*

stirrup, *rekab*

stone *hadjra*

tail. *zaka*

tree, *sedjra*

water, *ma*

west, *gherb*

wool, *soof*

NATIONALITIES.

Alexandria. *Skendria*
Algerian. *Dziree*
Arab. *Arbee*
Cairo, *Masser*
Constantinople. *Stambool*
Egyptian, *Chamee*
English. *Veglee*

French, *Frencees*
German, *Alman*
Indian, *Hendee*
London, *Londra*
Moorish, *Mergerbee*
Stranger, *Berrancc*
Turk, *Terkee*

NUMBERS.

one, *ouahed*
two, *zoudj, tneen*
three, *tlata*
four, *arbaa*
five, *kamsa*
six, *setta*
seven, *sebaa*
eight, *temenia*
nine, *tesaa*
ten, *achra*
eleven, *hdash*
twelve, *tnash*
thirteen, *teletash*
fourteen, *arbatash*
fifteen, *kemstash*
sixteen, *settash*
seventeen, *sebatash*
eighteen, *tementash*

nineteen, *tesatash*
twenty, *achreen*
twenty-one, *ouahed ou achreen*
twenty-two, *tneen ou achreen*
twenty-three, *tlata ou achreen*
thirty, *tlateen*
forty, *arbaeen*
fifty, *kamseen*
sixty, *setteen*
seventy, *sebaeen*
eighty, *tmaneen*
ninety, *tesaeen*
hundred, *mia*
thousand, *alef*
two thousand, *alfeen*
three thousand, *tlet alaf*
four thousand, *arba alaf*

USUAL EXPRESSIONS.

a fork, *gharfoo*
a glass, *kass*
a knife, *sekkeen*
a light, *anzel*
a plate, *tebsee*
a spoon, *megherfa*
carriage, *kerrossa*
chair, *kersee*
come here, *adji inna*
get up, *koom*
give, *ara*
give me, *atinee*
go, *machee*
go away, *roh*
God. *Allah*
God bless you, *Allah iselemeck*
good-bye, *slama*
good day, *slama*
good day to you, *slamalik*

good day to you all, *alikoum salam* or *salam alikoum*
good morning, *sbah elker*
how, *kiffash*
how are you, *ashanta* or *ashantina*
how much, *kaddash*
hundred francs, *miat frank*
I have none, *maandish*
look, *shoof*
no, *lala, macache*
no good, *mamennoush*
none, *makansch*
one franc, *frank*
one franc and a half, *frank ou ness*
show me, *ourrinee*
sit up, *erfed*
table. *tabla*

USUAL EXPRESSIONS—continued.

take care, *balck*

thank you. *ketterkher* or *Allah iketter kherrek*

this, *hada*

three francs and a half, *tlata frank ou ness*

three francs, *tlata frank*

to buy, *techree*

to him, *kelloo*

two francs, *zoudj frank*

two francs and a half *zoud frank ou ness*

where, *fayen*

why. *allash*

yes. *hee*

VERBS.

to come. *tedji*

to drink, *teshreb*

to eat. *takkel*

to go, *temchi*

to sleep, *terked*

THE WEATHER, TIME, ETC.

cold, *berd*

day, *nahar*; day of the week, *ioume.*

four years, *arba sna*

Friday. *nahr el djemaa*

heat, *skhana*

Monday, *nahr el tneen*

morning, *sbah*

night. *lil*

one year, *am*

rain. *chta*

Saturday, *nahr el sebt*

Sunday, *nahr el had*

the moon, *el kmer*

the day after to-morrow, *gir geddah*

the stars, *el nedjmat*

the sun, *el chemeh*

three years, *tlet sna*

Thursday, *nahr el kmees*

to-morrow, *gadoua*

Tuesday, *nahr el tlata*

two years, *ameen*

Wednesday, *nahr el arba*

wind, *reh*

yesterday, *elbarrah*

ADJECTIVES AND ADVERBS.

a little, *chouya*

bad, *doonee*

before, *keddam*

behind. *eloora*

cigar or cigarette, *garro*

clean. *nekkee*

deep, *kesheen*

dirty, *moussek*

enough, *barka*

good, *mleh*

here, *innah*

how much, *achal*

large, *kebeer*

left, *chmal*

long, *toocel*

narrow, *deeyek*

near. *keddam*

now, *daba*

on top. *fouk*

outside, *berra*

pretty, *chbab*

right, *imeen*

round. *medooner*

short, *keseer*

small, *segheer*

square, *merbaa*

the middle, *oost*

there, *hnak*

thin, *rekeek*

ugly, *fahesh*

underneath, *taht*

very much. *bezzef*

very near, *kreeb*

ALPHABETICAL LIST OF ARABIC WORDS

IN GENERAL USE.

ARABIC—ENGLISH.

———◦◇•———

Ab, Abo, Bou, father, possessor of

Abd, servant, slave

Abd Allah, servant of God

Abd-el-Kader, servant of the Almighty

Abiad, white. Fem. *Baida*

Adjar, a kerchief which covers all the face, except the eyes

Adrar, mountain

Agha, lord

Ahal, black. Fem. *Kahala*

Ahel, people

Ahmer, red. Fem. *Hamara*

Ain, a fountain

Ain, a spring. Pl. *Ayoun*

Ainba, grapes

Ait. Kabyle for *Beni.* children of

Akhdar. green. Fem. *Khadara*

Alfa, Esparto grass

Allah, God

Amala. province

Amin, chief of a village

Amin-el-Oumena, chief of several douars

Amin Ferkat, the chief of a part of a tribe

Annab, jujube, zizyphus

Aoud, horse

Aradah, earth

Arbäa, four, Wednesday 4th day

Arch, tribal land

Areg, sandhill ; *Beer-el-Areg,* country of sandhills, the desert

Asfel, low. Fem. *Safala*

Ashour, tax

Azel, Government land

Azib, encampment, enclosure

Bab, gate. Pl. *Biban*

Bach-Agha, governor of a certain number of tribes

Badia, country, opposed to town

Baghal, mule

Bahr, sea ; *Bahira,* small sea or plain

Bedoui, bedouin. Pl. *Bedou*

Beit, house ; *beit-esh-shäar,* hair house or tent

Beled, town

Bender, (Mers) harbour

Ben, son

Beni, sons

Berd, cold

Berr, country, region

Beylick, belonging to Government

Bin, Ibn, son. Pl. *Beni*

Bir, well. Pl. *Abiar*

Birket, lake, pond

Blad, more correctly *Belad* country

Bordj, a fort. a castle

Bou, father

Caftan, Turkish dress

Caid, a chief of several douars

Casbah, a fortress, a stronghold

Chaiba, ravine
Chamuch, attendant on Bureau Arabe
Chattaha, a dancing girl
Chebaka, net. Pl. *Chebabik*
Chébec, a large boat of the felucca kind used by pirates
Chechia, a red woollen cap worn under the turban
Cheik, chief, old age
Cheikh, chief, old
Chemal, south
Chergwin, oriental
Cherif, noble
Cherk, east
Chitan, devil
Chott, salt lake
Couscous or *Couscousou*, a farinaceous food. Kabyle, *Seksou*

Dahra, north
Damah, the game of draughts
Dar, stone house; *Dar-es-Sanaa*, manufactory
Daradja, step; *Droudj*, stairs
Defla, oleander
Dekhla, pass, gorge
Deshera, village
Dhara, north
Dhaya, pool, marsh
Dhib, jackal. Pl. *Dhiab*
Diffa, a hospitable repast
Diss, coarse grass
Djama, mosque
Djamäa, village council
Djaneb, side
Djebel, mountain
Djebeli, mountaineer
Djedar, wall. Pl. *Adjdar*
Djedda, shore, littoral
Djehad, war against infidels
Djelad, tanner
Djenan, garden
Djenoub, south
Djerid, palm branch. country of palms
Djeurf, escarpment
Djidid, new
Djir, lime
Djisr, bridge
Djizira, island. Pl. *Djezair*; *el-Djezair*, the islands (Algiers)

Dom, dwarf palm
Douar, group of Arab tents or families
Dowira, small house
Doula, state, government
Draa, mountain chain

El-, The
Erg, pl. *aeg.*, dune

Faras, mare
Fedj, pass, *col*
Ferka, section of a tribe
Fernan, cork tree
Fodha, silver
Fokani, upper
Fondouk, inn. Covered market
Foum, mouth, opening
Fourn, oven

Gandoura, a kind of shirt or frock worn by the Kabyles
Ghaba, forest
Ghar, cave
Gharab, west
Gharsa, plantation
Ghazala, gazelle. Pl. *Ghozlan*
Ghorfa, grotto
Gober, tomb
Goléa, chatelet
Goum, body of Arab soldiers
Gourbi, Arab hut
Guebla, south
Guennar, summit, peak
Gueraa, marsh
Guetar, small wells

Habaya, an Arab shirt
Habs, prison
Hadari, Arab living in town
Haddad, blacksmith
Haddid, iron
Hadj, pilgrim
Hadjara, stone. Pl. *Hadjar*
Hadji, Mecca pilgrim
Hadra, descent
Hafra, excavation
Hai, living
Hait, wall, enclosure

Haïk, a short kind of burnous without a hood, worn by women
Halak, throat, canal
Halfa, esparto grass
Hallouf-el-rhaba, the wild boar
Hamada, plateau
Hamma, warm spring
Hammam, bath
Haouch, farm
Harah, quarter of a city
Hassi, little well
Hedjaz, land of pilgrims
Henchir, farm, Roman ruins
Hezzam, girdle
Hissar, fortress
Hodna, plain surrounded by mountains
Hoot, fish

Ibn, see *bin*
Ighil, Kabyle for ridge
Imam, leader of prayers in a mosque

Kadi, native judge
Kafhr, infidel
Kaid, head of a tribe
Kaläa, fort
Kalig, canal
Khalkals, anklets
Kantara, arch, bridge
Kasr, palace
Kebila, Kabyle tribe. Pl. *Kebail*
Kebir, great
Kedim, old
Kef, hill, mount
Kelb, dog
Keria, borough
Kerma, fig
Khadem, slave, servant
Khalidj, gulf
Khanga, defile
Khaukh, peach
Khazna, treasure
Khaznadar, treasurer
Kheit, thread, rope worn by Arabs as a head-dress
Khenag, defile
Khodja, an adjutant or secretary

Khouans, brethren — a religious order
Kibla, direction of Mecca in a mosque
Kibrit, sulphur
Komer, moon
Korn, horn
Kotan, cotton
Koubba, a dome; tomb of Mohammedan saints
Koudia, small hill
Koum, mound
Ksar, pl. *Ksour*, fortified village
Kubr, tomb. Pl. *Kubour*
Kulb, heart
Kusab, a reed

Lela, lady

Ma, water
Mäaden, a mine
Maaskara, camp
Mabara, cemetery
Mabrouk, blessed
Mafrag, bifurcation
Maghreb, sunset, west
Mahomet, a tuft of hair left to grow on the crown of the head; it is so called after the name of the Prophet
Maïz, goat
Makach, no, not, don't know, not understand
Makam, place
Makhzen, magazine, civil spahi
Malka, confluents
Mansoura, victorious
Marabout,
A person devoted to religion
Marabout, a Mahometan priest.
Marabout, a small temple held sacred, owing to some venerated Marabout being buried in it
Marabout is also a part of the superstructure of an Arab building
Mascara, camp
Matmor, silos
Mechera, ford
Medina, city

Medjez, ferry
Medressa, college
Mehalla, camp
Mekahla, a long barrelled Arab gun with an old-fashioned flint lock
Melah, maleh, salt, *adj.*
Melh, salt, *subs.*
Melk, freehold property
Melouan, coloured
Memleka, kingdom
Menara, minaret
Menzel, place
Merdj, meadow
Meridj, swamp
Mersa, anchorage
Mesjid, mosque
Messaoud, happy
Mezrag, a lance
Mihrab, altar
Mimbar, pulpit
Misr, capital
Moghreb, west; the west country
Mokaddem, head-man; chief of a religious body
Moulai, my Lord
Muezzin, the officiating Marabout who calls the faithful to prayers from the top of the minaret

Nahr, river
Nadour, observatory
Nakhala, date tree
Nam, an ostrich
Nemel, ant
Nemir, a panther
Nhar, fire
Nouba, garrison

Ou, the Berber equivalent of *Ben*, son of
Oued, river, valley
Ouled, tribe
Oum, mother, head of a valley
Oumena, a chief of several villages
Ourida, a little rose, like rosina in Italian
Oust, middle, waist; central court in a house
Outa, a plain

Rahim, merciful
Rahman, compassionate
Raïs, captain
Rakham, marble
Ramla, sand
Ras, head, cape. Pl. *Rous*
Razzia, plundering expedition
Rebia, spring
Rézala, a gazelle
Rhaba, forest
Rhamadan, a Mahometan fast of thirty days
Rharbi, occidental
Roumi, a Christian, derived from *Romanus*. The plural of this word is *rouama* in Arabic, but generally written Roumis by French authors

Säada, happiness
S'ba, the lion
Sabeehad, the beautiful
Sabegha, tribal land
Safar. yellow
Safel, lower part
Sahara, desert plain
Saharidj, cisterns
Saheb, owner, companion
Sahel, coast
Saïd, lord or master, a title given by the Arabs to the lion
Sakia, canal for irrigation
Sebala, fountain
Sebd, lion
Sebkha, salt lake
Sebt, seventh, Saturday
Sedra, jujube tree
Seghir, small
Seïl, torrent
Sekkin, knife
Seksou, Kabyle name for couscous
Sfa, schist
Shaham, fat, grease
Shirk, east
Si or *Sidi*, my Lord
Silos, underground receptacles for corn
Skiffa, vestibule of a Moorish house
Smala, small fort occupied by Spahis
Sof, league, confraternity

Souk, market
Souman, minaret
Sour, rampart
Spaïs, a native cavalry officer in the French service

Täam, food ; couscous
Tamtam, a large flat metallic drum
Tell, plains
Tella, small hill
Temeah, crocodile
Tenia, a defile
Teniet, mountain top, path
Thizzi, a mountain defile
Thuia, a lignum vitæ
Tolbas learned men

Toura, sluice
Towil. long.   Fem. *Towila*

Yatagan, a kind of knife or poignard

Zab.   Pl. *Ziban,* an oasis watered by a river
Zan, an oak
Zaouia, college, convent, or place of refuge for religious mendicants
Zareefeh, the elegant
Zeitoun, olive
Zekka, tax on cattle
Zerb, hedge
Zeriba, cattle enclosure

BRITISH IMPORT DUTIES, DOCK DUES, Etc.

—◆—

BRITISH IMPORT DUTIES.

			s.	d.
Spirits, proof (in cask)	per gall.		11	4
„ „ (in bottle)	„		12	4
Liqueurs	„		16	4
Spirits, perfumed, and Eau de Cologne ...	„		19	1
Tea	per lb.		0	
Coffee	„		0	1½
Cocoa			0	2
„ Raw			0	1
Tobacco			3	10
„ Cavendish, manufactured			4	4
„ Cigars	„		6	0
Wine in cask, not exceeding 30 degrees of proof	per gall.		1	3
„ bottle, „ 30 „	„		2	3
cask, „ 42			3	0
„ bottle „ 42	„		4	0

Articles containing sugar in any quantity are also liable to a small charge for duty, such as :—dried fruits, confectionery, honey, preserved ginger, jams, condensed milk, candied peel, tamarinds, fruit, and vegetables preserved in sugar, etc. All articles subject to duty should be distinctly and specially declared, and it is advisable to place such articles in one package in order to facilitate the Customs' clearance. All dutiable articles, however small in quantity, are liable to duty on entering the United Kingdom, but the Customs' authorities usually allow passengers to bring free of duty :—

Cigars and tobacco	½ lb.
Cordials and perfumed spirits	½ pint.
Spirits	½ pint.

This cannot, however, be claimed as a right. Quantities above ½ lb. of cigars or tobacco, and ½ pint of spirits, are subject to the full duty, no free allowance being made.

All duties are subject to alteration from time to time.

DOCK DUES IN LONDON.

(When baggage is landed direct from Steamer into Customs' shed and examined immediately.)

	Each	d.
Chairs, hat boxes, etc.	0	6
Gladstone bags, gun cases not exceding 56 lbs....		0
Portmanteaux, etc., not exceeding 1 cwt.		6
Packages, not exceeding 1½ cwt.		6
„ 2¼ „		0

PART I

ALGERIA.

———◆◇◆———

INTRODUCTORY.

GENERAL DESCRIPTION OF ALGERIA.

Algeria is bounded on the east by the Regency of Tunis; on the west by the Empire of Morocco; on the south by the Great Desert of Sahara; and by the Mediterranean Sea on the north. Its greatest length from the River Zayne, on the Tunis boundary, to Twent, on the Western frontier, is about 600 miles; its breadth varies from 300 to 400 miles. The chain of the Atlas mountains runs through the whole length of the country. The principal river of Algeria is the **Cheliff,** which has its sources within the borders of the Sahara, south of the Ouarsenis mountains; it reaches the sea near Mostaganem, after a course of 400 miles. During the rainy season it overflows a great tract of country, and sometimes interferes with the road transit between Algiers and the province of Oran. The other rivers are : the **Isser,** to the east of Algiers; the **Zowah,** or **river of Bujeiah;** the **Oued el Kebir** (Ampsaga of the Ancients), which flows into the sea, north of Constantine; and the **Seybouse,** or river of Bône.

The natural divisions of Algeria are three : the **Tell,** the **High Plateaux,** and the **Sahara.** The **Tell** is a narrow strip of cultivated land, hundreds of miles in length, some 30 to 100 miles in breadth, between the seashore and the mountains. The ridges of the Atlas enclose three great plains, the "plaine du Sheleef" (Cheliff), the "plaine de la

Mitidja," and the "plaine du Sahel." The Tell is well watered by important rivers as far apart as the Cheliff, the Macta, the Oued el-Kebir, the Seybouse, and the Rummel, the rich agricultural land being intersected by small mountains and valleys thickly wooded. The grandest scenery and the most interesting population of the Tell are to be found in the mountain district of the **Djurdjura**, inhabited by the Kabyles, between Dellys, Ménerville, and Bougie. The entire extent of the Tell covers, in round figures, 35,000,000 acres.

The **High Plateaux**, running from east to west between the Tell and the Sahara, are uncultivated plains between mountain ranges, some 3,000 feet above sea level. Large quantities of alfa or esparto grass are collected for exportation, and the interminable scrub serves to feed the camels and sheep of the Arabs. During the rainy season, and wherever water is found, cereal crops are eagerly raised. Several small rivers take their rise at the foot of the mountain ranges, and in the plains large salt depressions or lakes called **Chotts** are formed. The High Plateaux extend over 27,000,000 acres. To the south are the vast Aurès Mountains between Batna and Biskra, stretching 75 miles from E. to W., and 40 miles from N. to S.

The **Sahara**, a veritable furnace, is an immense desert extending over 125,000,000 acres, varying considerably in its nature. In some parts, towards Tunis, the soil is a mixture of sand and clay; in others, to the west towards Morocco, are rocky districts and mountains, the rivers rushing from which are utilised to produce the oases by forming dams and canals for irrigation. In other directions the desert is a moving mass of sand-forming dunes.

In various parts of the Sahara are depressions producing immense sheets of water, not very deep, salter than the sea, and sometimes below sea level. These are called Chotts. One of these, on the west or Morocco border of the desert, the **Chott el-Chergui**, between Saïda and Aïn Sefra, is about 100 miles long, and the **Chott El-Melghir**, between Biskra and Tougourt, is 170 miles in length.

DEPARTMENTALLY AND POLITICALLY.

Algeria, under the direction of a Governor-General, is divided into three provinces, administered by Prefects and sub-Prefects—Algiers, Oran, and Constantine,

Algiers, the central province, has five sub-Prefects—at Algiers, Milianah, Médéa, Orleansville, and Tizi-Ouzou.

Oran, forming the western part of the colony adjoining Morocco, has five sub-Prefects, at Oran, Mostaganem, Mascara, Sidi-Bel-Abbès, and Tlemçen.

Constantine, between Algiers and Tunis, has six sub-Prefects—at Constantine, Bône, Philippeville, Guelma, Bougie, and Setif.

In May, 1903, M. Ch. Jonnart was appointed Governor-General of Algeria in succession to M. Paul ¯Revoil, appointed 1901, formerly French Minister in Morocco.

The Commander-in-Chief of the Military Force in Algeria is General G. O. Servière.

The civil Governor-General is the central administrative authority of Algeria. A small extent of territory in the Sahara is still administered by the military authorities, but under the direction of the Governor.

The French Chambers have alone the right of legislating for Algeria, and such matters as do not come within the legislative power are regulated by decree of the President of the Republic.

In December, 1902, a law was passed constituting the Territories of the South under a separate administration, for which an annual subvention is provided in the French budget. The Governor-General will represent the Territories in civil affairs.

The Governor-General is assisted by a council, whose functions are purely consultative.

The Colonial budget is discussed and voted by a Superior Council, meeting once a year, to which delegates are sent by each of the departmental general councils. Each department sends one senator and two deputies to the National Assembly.

CLIMATE.

The climate of the country north of the Atlas is generally healthy and temperate. As a rule, the first rains begin to fall towards the end of October. The early part of an Algerian winter is very enjoyable, viz., that during the months of November and December. January, February, and March have plenty of both sunshine and rain. April and May resemble a fine English summer. The climate of the interior is not so damp as that of the coast, but the heat is much greater. Some towns situated like Médéa and Constantine are extremely cold in the winter. Others, like Orleansville and Biskra, are unbearable in the summer. Generally speaking, the climate on the coast is very healthy and bracing. Those who like Algeria may conveniently prolong their stay at Algiers or Oran as late as June without much fear of extreme heat. The real heat only sets in seriously about the end of July; August, September, and October being very warm months.

There are considerable differences of opinion among medical authorities concerning the geniality of the climate of Algeria, but a glance at the temperature table on p. 7 will at once prove that the average temperature of Algiers is warmer by several degrees than that of the Riviera towns and the western coast of Italy. Again, the superiority of Algiers from a climatic point of view is the evenness of its temperature and the mildness of its atmosphere, which recommend it to the most delicate constitutions. Mr. Alex. A. Knox, who has had the most valuable experience on this subject, declares, in his work " Algeria, or the New Playground," that Algeria is **good for asthma.** Mr. Reynolds-Ball, who has also had an excellent opportunity of testing the comparative advantages of the various towns on the Mediterranean coast, says in his " Mediterranean Winter Resorts ": " Algiers is to be recommended for most forms of pulmonary consumption, for affections of the heart, and for Bright's disease."

As a cure for bronchitis, when open-air treatment is the prescribed formula of the physician, Algiers can claim the first place, because the mildness of its temperature, combined with the dryness of its atmosphere, renders its climate without parallel amongst health resorts. The atmosphere of Algiers allows out-of-door patients to remain in the open air the greater part of the day in the midst of winter. It is not wise, however, to remain out of doors after sunset in the months of December, January, and February, without changing clothes or donning a thick overcoat, as the thermometer records a difference of several degrees between the hours of four and seven. Delicate people should pay great attention to this, and so avoid colds and influenzas, which are frequent in Algiers in winter.

According to recent statistics, the proportion of deaths from pulmonary consumption among the European population of Algeria during a period of six years, was *one in forty,* while the proportion of deaths from the same disease in Paris and London was *one in five.*

No bad fever or other endemic diseases are prevalent in Algeria; in short, the winters are mild and genial, and perfectly appropriate to invalids whose health requires another summer at the expiration of the home season. Dr. Gandil, an eminent French physician, has published (in 1889) a very interesting report on the climate of Algiers. In this report, Dr. Gandil gives the averages of maxima and minima which the thermometer registered during the winter season 1888-89 at Nice, Algiers, Biskra, and Paris. It will be interesting to learn that on no single occasion during six winter months has the temperature of Nice risen to the heat of Algiers, nor has the thermometer at Algiers once gone down so low as it has in Nice. The difference, is on an average, five to six degrees *Centigrade,* with much greater variations in Nice during each twenty-four hours. From November to February Algiers registered the warmest temperatures as compared with those of Biskra, Nice, and Paris.

In February Algiers and the *City of the Desert* (Biskra) are on a parallel; in April Biskra goes to the front and takes an advance, which it keeps right through the summer, and which Dr. Gandil thinks it best for Biskra to retain. Nice comes far behind, and Paris is down at the bottom of the self-recording thermometer. But the most curious remark Dr. Gandil makes is this one: *that there is less difference between the climates of Paris and Nice than between those of Nice and Algiers.*

Rainfall.—In the agricultural districts the rainfall to ensure good crops should be about 36 inches, but in Algiers itself the average is 29·30 inches. Rain falls on 70 to 80 days during the 365, but only a small proportion of these are entirely "wet days," and a considerable percentage of the rain falls during the night.

There is very little cold N.E. wind, and still less *Mistral* during the winter. The prevailing wind bringing rain and cold blows from the N.W., and seldom lasts more than a day or two. Hailstorms occur at intervals, but frost and snow are almost unknown. The desert wind (sirocco), which in the spring or summer may be insufferably hot, is not at all trying even to invalids in winter, and its duration rarely exceeds three days.

Taken altogether, Algiers is the healthiest winter residence within three days of England, but visitors must not expect a tropical and rainless climate—for these they must go further afield to, say, Cairo, Luxor, or Assouan.

The climate of Algiers is warmer and more onic than that of Pau, Cannes, and Mentone, and in cases of phthisis and asthma, bronchitis, and other pulmonary affections, the conditions are most favourable to the invalid.

BEDOUINE.

Average Temperature of Different Twns Compared with Algiers.

Name of Place.	ad.	Feb.	Mar.	April.	May.	June.	July.	Aug.	Sept.	Oct.	Nov.	Dec.
Mgrs	54·0	55·5	57·0	60·9	65·7	71·4	77·5	78·0	74·5	70·0	61·0	53·0
London	37·0	390	42·0	47·0	54·0	59·0	63·0	61·0	57·0	51·0	44·0	39·0
Paris	36·0	390	44·0	50·0	57·0	62·0	65·0	65·0	60·0	52·0	43·0	38·0
New York	38·0	28·0	42·0	52·0	62·0	70·0	74·0	72·0	66·0	52·0	470	41·0
Nce ...	46·0	460	48·0	50·0	66·0	73·0	72·0	71·0	67·0	58·0	52·0	47·0
Naples	44·0	46·0	48·0	54·0	66·0	71·0	74·0	74·0	68·0	64·0	53·0	450
Florence	47·0	45·0	49·0	53·0	68·0	72·0	74·0	73·0	61·0	59·0	510	47·0
Malta	53·0	54·0	55·0	58·0	64·0	72·0	77·0	78·0	74·0	71·0	62·0	54·0
ad.	59·0	59·0	62·0	70·0	77·0	80·0	83·0	78·0	74·0	70·0	620	590
Venice	38·0	37·0	45·0	53·0	68·0	73·0	75·0	77·0	64·0	59·0	47·0	38·0
Rome	42·0	44·0	49·0	55·0	64·0	73·0	75·0	75·0	68·0	63·0	49·0	42·0
Constantinople ...	41·0	370	47·0	58·0	62·0	71·0	76·0	72·0	67·0	64·0	51·0,	43·0
Monte Car o ...	48·0	47·0	50·0	53·0	65·0	75·0	76·0	74·0	69·0	60·0	56·0	48·0
Malaga ...	48·0	47·0	51·0	54·0	69·0	78·0	78·0	76·0	69·0	62·0	58·0	49·0

Average Temperature (Fahrenheit) Registered at Algiers in 13 years.

Compiled from observations made by Algerian Government officials at the Military Hospital.

Thermometer 300 yds. from sea-beach ; 500 feet above sea-level ; six feet from ground.	Hottest day. Highest maximum in 13 years.	Coldest night. Minimum in 13 years.	Coldest day. Lowest maximum in 13 years.	Average maximum in 13 years.	Average minimum in 13 years.	Average temperature in 13 years.	Warmest night. Highest maximum in 13 years.
January	77	32	48	60½	48	54	62
February	75	32½	48	62	48½	55½	63
March	82½	34	51	64	50	57	66
April	95⅓	37	50	68½	53½	61	70
May ..	89½	45½	57	73½	58½	66	72½
June	101	53	66	78½	63½	71	75
July...	102	57½	75½	84½	69	76½	77
August ..	111	56½	75	86½	70	78	82½
September	109	53½	68½	83	68	75½	79
October	97	44	61½	75½	61	68½	79
November	84½	40	53½	66½	54	60½	68½
December	77½	34	50	61½	48½	55	66

During the winter of 1903-4, the most inclement for 40 years, the average temperatures at Algiers for December and January were 58°·4 maximum and 49° minimum, as compared with Nice for the corresponding period, 51°·9 and 39°·2 respectively.

Thermometrical Equivalents.

While Fahrenheit's scale is generally used in England those of Centigrade and Réaumur are used on the Continent.

The following table will show the differences of the three thermometers :—

Fahrenheit.	Centigrade.	Réaumur.	Observations.
212·0	100·0	80·0	Boiling.
203·0	95·0	76·0	
194·0	90·0	72·0	
185·0	85·0	68·0	
176·0	80·0	64·0	
167·0	75·0	60·0	
158·0	70·0	56·0	

Thermometrical Equivalents—*continued.*

Fahrenheit.	Centigrade.	Réaumur.	Observations.
149·0	65·0	52·0	
140·0	60·0	48·0	
131·0	55·0	44·0	
122·0	50·0	40·0	
113·0	45·0	36·0	
104·0	40·0	32·0	
98·6	37·0	29·6	Blood.
95·0	35·0	28·0	
86·0	30·0	24·0	
77·0	25·0	20·0	
75·2	24·0	19·2	Summer.
68·0	20·0	16·0	
59·0	15·0	12·0	
55·4	13·0	10·4	Temperate.
50·0	10·0	8·0	
41·0	5·0	4·0	
39·2	4·0	3·2	
37·4	3·0	2·4	
35·6	2·0	1·6	
33·8	1·0	0·8	
32·0	0·0	0·0	Freezing.

To turn Centigrade into Fahrenheit, multiply by 9, divide by 5. and add 32, thus :—
40 Centigrade × 9 = 360 ÷ 5 = 72 + 32 = 104 Fahrenheit.
To turn Réaumur into Fahrenheit multiply by 2½ and add 32, thus :—
40 Réaumur × 2½ = 90 + 32 = 122 Fahrenheit.

MINERALOGY.

Although the forests of Algeria supply many ornamental woods to the metropolis, the fine marbles and onyx of the country rival the timbers in the delicate beauty of their shades. Ores of iron, copper, lead, zinc, and manganese are worked with advantage ; extensive deposits of rock salt occur, sometimes whole mountains of salt are to be met on the roads of the interior, also large salt lakes and marshes. An English company established at **Beni=Saf** (thirty-two kilometres from Oran) for the exportation of copper and iron ore is doing a very important trade, and is said to pay large dividends to its shareholders. Building stone is plentiful, but some of the best quality is shipped from France and Italy.

AGRICULTURE, HORTICULTURE, Etc.

The fertility for which Algeria was renowned in olden times still continues; in the valleys, which are watered by streams, and rivulets, agriculture and vegetation are extremely flourishing, especially in the Tell, in the provinces of Oran and Constantine. The mould is generally of very dark colour, in some places it is reddish and impregnated with nitre and with salt. The hills are covered with fruit trees of every kind, the quality of the fruit being exquisite.

Cereals.—Wheat is the principal cereal grown in the colony, but notwithstanding the advantages of soil and climate, the result is disappointing. Different systems of agriculture are carried on in different districts, but in all of them there is much room for improvement. The land is not cleared from weeds, little manure is employed, and the ploughing is too superficial. While in England the average produce of the wheat crop is from 22 to 27 bushels an acre, in Algeria it does not exceed 8 bushels. Barley, rye, oats, and maize are grown to some extent. In the 40 millions of acres under cultivation, about 350 million bushels of cereals are produced.

Fruit and Vegetables.—All kinds of fruits and vegetables grow in abundance, many of them available throughout the year. Of fruits may be mentioned plums, apricots, cherries, apples, pears, bananas, pomegranates, melons, and strawberries. Figs thrive almost everywhere, even in the mountains, where they are a common article of food. Tangarines and oranges are as délicious as they are plentiful and cheap, and are exported in large quantities to France and England.

The date tree—of which there are hundreds of varieties—requires great solar heat, and can only be cultivated to perfection in or near the desert of Sahara, affording a most valuable food for the Arabs of that region. The trees flower in March, and the fruit is ripe in October. The trees are between 30 and 40 feet high, are in full bearing when 27 years old, and flourish for 100 years. But when they are dead they are not done with, the wood is used for fuel and for building purposes, the roots for fencing and roofing, and the leaves are made into cord, sacks, mats, and baskets.

Tobacco is cultivated over a large extent of land, and is good in quality, considerable quantities being shipped to

Spain and England. The sugar cane grows, and the cultivation of cotton, although unprofitable to the farmer, is of long standing. Esparto grass or alfa is a valuable natural production of the High Plateaux, where some 16 million acres are covered with this fibre. It is used chiefly for the manufacture of paper, and until recently about 60 per cent. of the total export was sent to England, but now that wood pulp is being largely used in the manufacture of paper in England, the demand for alfa has fallen off.

The most important and successful branch of agriculture in Algeria is undoubtedly vine-growing. M. Dejernon, who was sent by the French Government to examine the subject, reports as follows :—

" In my eyes the vine is a providential plant for Algeria ; it prospers everywhere, in the worst land, on the most burning soil. In the three provinces I have not found a spot which is unfit for it ; everywhere also, but especially on the littoral, I have tasted wine rich in alcohol, and which would have had precious qualities if only it had been better made. The vine will become the fortune of the country. Algeria possesses in its geological structure, in the rays of its sun, in the currents of its air, in its topographical details, those precious qualities which give to the products of the vine their tone, their colour, their delicacy and limpidity. It can produce an infinite variety of wines, suited to every constitution and to every caprice of taste."

Vegetables.—Many and varied are the species of vegetables that grow to perfection in Algerian soil, such as cucumbers, gherkins, gourds, beetroots, lettuces, parsnips, carrots, turnips, green peas, artichokes, asparagus, beans, potatoes, cauliflowers and mushrooms. Onions and potatoes yield two crops yearly. The artichokes, peas, and potatoes are shipped through the winter on a very large scale to France and England. The asparagus from the region of Médéa has acquired a very high and well-deserved reputation.

Trees and Forests.—Leaving out the Sahara, where the ordinary tourist is not likely to visit, the finest forests of date palm trees will be found at El Kantara, Biskra, and El-Aghouat. The india-rubber tree, which was imported from Ceylon in 1863, has become quite acclimatized in Algeria, and in some cases has attained colossal proportions.

Bamboos thrive vigorously in many districts, and, as a rule, every species of Indian, Chinese, or American palms develop splendidly.

The mulberry tree flourishes readily in various parts of the country. The *ricinus* (castor-oil plant) of Japan, and the *eucalyptus globulus* (blue gum tree) from Australia have been introduced with excellent results.

Of forest trees the most valuable are the cork oak, which, when it has reached the age of fifteen years, is stripped of its bark, and this operation is repeated every ten years.

The gum oak, an excellent timber for building purposes, bridges, railway sleepers, etc.

The sweet acorn oak, a valuable tree which grows in almost any soil, and yields acceptable food. The sweet acorns are eaten roasted, or ground into flour and used with " couscous," a favourite national dish of the Arabs.

The Atlas cedar is chiefly to be found in the Aurès Mountains, notably at Teniet-el-Haâd, and at Djebel Tougourt near Batna.

The olive tree grows freely in Algeria and Tunisia, and its cultivation is increasing in both countries. The former produces about $6\frac{1}{2}$ million gallons of olive oil annually and the latter nearly as much.

The Atlas cypress, the mountain ash indigenous to the Atlas, the Aleppo pine, and other species flourish over large extents of land.

It is estimated there are twelve to fourteen million trees spread over some five million acres of land in the three provinces of Algiers, Oran, and Constantine.

FLORA AND FAUNA.

Flora.—With the exception of some indigenous plants such as the dwarf palm, the cistus, the agave, and the tree heath, the flora of Algeria is practically identical with that of Southern Europe. In one field may be seen masses of iris and narcissus ; in another wild hyacinths, violets, and African cyclamen. The flowers usually cultivated in the gardens, and sold in the streets or shops, are roses, carnations, geraniums, lilies, violets, jessamine and various creepers, most of which bloom throughout the winter. There are extensive plantations of **nessri**, or white roses ; these flowers are much larger than those of Europe, and yield the attar of roses essence.

Fauna.—Among the animals of Algeria nearly all those of the domestic kind are to be found. Cows are small, and give but little milk. As a result of the native system of feeding calves on grass a fortnight or so after their birth, and withdrawing milk from their food as soon as it can be done, the veal is tough and black, has no flavour, and is usually of inferior quality. Most of the beef and veal of good quality is imported daily from France, especially in the winter season. Algeria and Morocco are the original countries of the Merino sheep. The flocks of sheep bred on the High Plateaux are a great source of wealth, many thousands being sent to Paris monthly during the summer. Goats are very numerous, and supply the people with milk The horses are well known to be excellent, but except at the military studs, such as the one at Blidah, it is difficult to meet with the pure bred original Arab steed. Asses are very commonly used, but are not such a fine species as formerly. The camel is a most valuable animal to the Arab of the desert, and is considered superior to that of Asia; some very good cheese is made out of its milk. When the animals are old they are fattened for killing, the flesh being wholesome. The interior of the country abounds with wild boars, porcupines, gazelles, and all sorts of game. In the fastnesses of the Atlas Mountains panthers and leopards, and sometimes lions are to be met with but no tigers.

SPORT

In the neighbourhood of Algiers, or, indeed, in the easily accessible districts of Algeria, the shooting is scarcely good, the country presenting an aspect too settled, and those who come out chiefly with a view to sport will generally be disappointed, but in some places not too far from the radius of the Cheliff, especially in the regions of the Hammam R'irha and Cherchell, there are many partridges and woodcocks, hares, and birds of passage (mid-March to mid-April).

No one is allowed to shoot without a licence, which costs 28 francs (22s. 6d.); persons wishing to obtain a licence can do so through their respective consulates. The shooting season opens in August, and closes in February (*see* also p. 129).

As stated on p. 32, the importation of gunpowder or filled cartridges is absolutely forbidden. Empty cartridges with percussion caps may be brought in, but no good houses for filling cartridges are to be found. Neither Harvey cartridges nor good English powder can be bought in Algiers.

Gazelles are generally hunted by Arabs on swift horses, riding them down until they are tired, then firing amongst them at short distance.

Wild Boars are very destructive, and are willingly hunted by the Arabs. Two or three friends, with the help of about 20 Arabs as beaters, can readily organise a party for the chase of these animals, and sometimes kill a number of them.

Falcons are generally found in the Djebel Amour district. When the Arabs have succeeded in taming one, no money in the world would tempt them to part with the bird. *A chasse au faucon*, such as a visitor would wish to enjoy, can be organised with the help of the military authorities in the south of Algeria. At Biskra, a wealthy Arab Sheikh owns a rare collection of falcons.

Well-trained falcons are used for hunting partridges, large birds (such as bustards), and hares.

Ostriches are now becoming very scarce, and are only to be met with on the borders of the Sahara. Their capture is extremely difficult, as they quite easily outstrip the fastest of horses. Ostrich eggs are commonly sold at from 6s. to 12s. each. One has to take care not to be imposed upon with imitations. The best way to detect the fraud is by sounding them with a key. The real ostrich egg is extremely light and thin, although strong and resistant, while the spurious egg is heavy, and sounds dull.

There is a small establishment for breeding and domesticating ostriches in the **Jardin d'Essai** (*see* p. 99).

For the destruction of wild animals, such as lions, hyænas, panthers, and jackals, the Government pays a reward varying from 40 francs to 2 francs. Hundreds of lions, thousands of panthers and hyænas, and tens of thousands of jackals have been killed during the last twenty-five years. Lion, hyæna, or panther hunting is now very rare, the two former animals are nearly extinct, but the panther is still found in several districts, notably between Azazga and Taourirt-Ighil in Kabylia (*see* p. 204), and jackals may be shot in the forests around Hammam R'irha, within four hours of Algiers.

HOT SPRINGS.

In Algeria, as in Tunisia, there are a number of hot mineral springs, the principal of which are those of **Hammam R'irha** (*see* p. 124), **Hammam Melouan** (*see* p. 106), **Hammam Meskoutine** (*see* p. 245), **Hammam Salahin** (*see* p. 240), **Hammam=bou=Hadjar** (*see* p. 180), **Hammam Selama** (*see* p. 162), **Portes de Fer** (*see* p. 221), and **Bains de la Reine,** near Oran (*see* p. 161). These are described at the various pages referred to.

INHABITANTS.

The races that inhabit Algeria are: The **Arabs, Moors, Kabyles, Turks** and **Coulouglis, Jews,** and **Negroes** from the Soudan, exclusive of European settlers, visitors, and speculators.

The native population of Algeria may be separated into two divisions, the Arabs including the Moors; and the Berbers including the Kabyles.

The **Arabs of the Plain** live in tents or in gourbis (huts), and are divided into tribes, changing from place to place as circumstances may require. They are filthy and lazy in their habits, and only trouble themselves about two kinds of work —agriculture and the raising of sheep and cattle. They came into the country from Arabia and Egypt in the 7th and 8th centuries, and occupied the plains, driving the Berbers, their predecessors, into the mountain districts.

The **Moors** constitute the bulk of the Arab population of the towns. They are a very mixed race, sprung from the various nations who have successively occupied the country. The Arabian stock, however, which was engrafted on the population existing at the time of the Mussulman conquest, is supposed to predominate. Their number was much swelled by the Moors who were driven away from Spain. The Moors are farther advanced in civilisation than the Arabs or the Kabyles; they are used to the comforts of the towns; many of them are wealthy, and fond of luxury and pleasure; but their moral character stands very low. They are not deficient in intelligence. All the boys frequent the schools, where they learn reading, writing and arithmetic at trifling cost, elementary instruction having been established at Algiers for ages past on a method somewhat resembling the Lancasterian.

The **Jews** came in great numbers to Algiers on being driven out of Italy, Spain and Portugal in the fourteenth century. They live chiefly in the towns. They are, as everywhere else, brokers, agents, jobbers, retailers, hawkers, etc. ; many of them are rich, and their condition has been greatly improved since the decree of French citizenship conferred upon them by the French Government in 1871. The well-known Hebrew feature which characterises this race is not so prominently marked in the Algerian Jews as is the case with their European brethren. Their features are pleasant and less suggestive of the propensities which are supposed to form the basis of their character. Mr. George Gaskell, in his clever work, entitled " Algeria As It Is," describes them as "industrious, enterprising, and, although fond of money, often satisfied with small profits, to the great disgust of the other traders, whom they sometimes find it good policy to undersell." True, some of them are really despicable, but then so are many of the heterogeneous tribes of Spaniards, Maltese, Arabs, and even French, who constitute the lower orders and classes of Algiers.

The **Kabyles or Berbers** have undergone no change whatever since the French occupation. They were justly described by Sallust as " a race which possesses a robust and healthy constitution, which can resist great fatigue ; they are men who succumb only to age or under the teeth of wild animals." Such as they were a thousand years ago, so they are to-day, compact, and unaltered in all the peculiarities of their race and individuality. *For further description of the Kabyles see Count Stackelberg's account, on p* 205.

The **population of Algeria,** according to the census of 1901, amounted to about 4,700,000 inhabitants for the three provinces, of whom about 4,000,000 are natives (Berbers or Arabs), as follows :—

French	292,000
Spaniards	155,000
Italians	38,000
Maltese	15,000
Arabs ⎱	
Kabyles ⎰ Mohammedans	3,973,000
Mozabites ⎰	
Jews...	57,000
Different Nationalities ...	170,000
	———
Total	... 4,700,000

The **population of Algiers** alone, including the suburbs of St. Eugène, Birkhadem, Birmandreis, El Biar, Agha, Mustapha, and Bouzarea, is composed as follows :—

French	...	...	...	...	65,000
Jews	...	...	...	...	12,000
Mohammedans	...	...	...	...	34,000
Foreigners ...	...	...	...	...	43,000
	Total	...	...	...	154,000

The **Spaniards** are very numerous in Algeria, and especially in Oran and the province of Oran, where they number 120,000. They are subjected to military service in the French army, and granted the benefit of French citizenship, unless they prefer to return to perform their military duties in their mother country, in which case they retain their original nationality.

The **Maltese** element predominates at Bône and the Tunisia frontier. They are subjected to the same regulations as the Spaniards as concerns military duty and nationality.

The **Negroes** are as much Mohammedans in Algeria as they are Christians in the United States. Religion means to them a drum and some money to buy rum with. The free-nigger experiment has been tried by the French in Algiers, not dogmatically, but almost unconsciously, for sixty years. Sambo in Algiers is held by authority to be as good as any other man. The Europeans, the Arabs, the Jews and the Negroes, all enjoy equal rights. The Arabs often intermarry with Negresses. The French Government, and indeed the French settlers, do not entertain the slightest prejudice against the Negro on account of the ebony colour of his skin. They never have done so In fact, the Negro is even popular among the ladies ; he is termed *Boule de Neigr*. The **Zouaves** are arm-in-arm companions of the **Turcos**. The Negro enjoys the full rights of a French subject, and is equal before the law to any other Frenchman. The Negro women often officiate as shampooers in the *Hammams* or Moorish baths, or as peripatetic bakers of *galettes*, or pancakes, and sorceresses.

The Negroes of Algeria nearly all originate from the Soudan, whence they were formerly brought out as slaves and sold in the markets of Algiers. They are an honest and industrious race, self-contented and very fond of singing and music. They are the happiest people in Algeria; they give animation to every Arab fête, with their tambourines, drums, fiddles, and other queer-shaped instruments. Among their other accomplishments they practise a sort of fantastical sword dance.

The **Mozabites** or **M'zabi** are a colony of seven towns spread over adjoining oases in the Sahara, 160 kilometres south of Laghouat, and 600 kilometres from Algiers, the district known as M'zab. This country contains about 200,000 date trees, and a population of about 25,000; it was annexed to France in 1882 (*see* also p. 140).

The towns and oases are **Ghardaïa** (the capital), **Beni Isguen, El=Ateuf, Metlili, Berrian,** and **Guerrara.**

The M'zabi are very industrious and prosperous, engaged in all kinds of commerce, and those of them who come north into the Tell, trade as butchers, grocers, coal dealers, and bankers, and when they have acquired a competence return to their own country, to be replaced by other members of their family.

The **Turks and Coulouglis** are practically extinct as separate races. The Coulouglis are the offspring of Turkish fathers and Arab mothers, but since the French occupation of Algeria, the majority of the Turks have returned to Turkey, and the remainder with their families have been merged in the general population.

COSTUMES.

The **original Arab costume** is undoubtedly the costume of the Arab of the plain, for the costume of the town Arab has degenerated into a mixture of Turkish and Jewish accoutrement, which has no fixed characteristic.

The **Arab of the plain** dresses in haicks and burnouses, and should he be wealthy, wears the most becoming and majestic costume on the surface of the earth. The dress consists first of all of a haick, or long strip of striped woollen gauze, which covers the white felt cap on his head and hangs flat at the back of his head, covering his shoulders and neck, and is fastened on to the belt or sash by a foulard of white or coloured silk material, which prevents the haick from falling to the ground. The haick is kept on the head by a long string of twisted camel-hair of light or dark brown colour, which is rolled round the felt cap some ten to twenty times; only a little part of the haick is allowed to emerge on the forehead, just enough to shade the eyes. The weight of the

ALGERIAN COSTUMES.

burnous and the Mohammedan chaplet keeps it firmly round the neck. On the body the Arabs wear a *gandoura*, or gown of white woollen material striped with silk, and a wide coloured silk sash over it round the waist. Over this, they wear a white

B 2

woollen burnous of very fine texture, and over this burnous again, one or two more burnouses, according to the climate. The rich Arabs wear as a top covering a light or dark plain cloth burnous, braided or embroidered with silk, and tassels of the same colour. The poorer classes wear a camel's cloth—either plain or striped—burnous of such strong texture that one of these garments is supposed to last their lifetime. The cavaliers wear red-top leather boots, which they make use of as stockings, as this boot goes into a shoe, flat heeled, same as worn by all the Arabs of Algeria.

The Arab women are shrouded from head to foot in white haicks and muslin materials, but this is only for out-of-door costume, the only sign of difference of rank being in the fineness of the stuff worn by the ladies, which covers them completely, only the eyes being allowed to be shown. At home this somewhat mythical garment is replaced by a much more gorgeous attire. The baggy trousers, drawn tight about the ankles, are replaced by the *serroual*, or wide trousers of silk or China crêpe, and reaching only mid-leg. The inmost garment is of finest gauze; the feet are in slippers of velvet embroidered with gold; the hair, plaited in long tresses, is knotted behind the head and descends almost to the ground; the head-dress is a dainty little skull cap or *chechia* of velvet, thick with gold and seed pearls, or entirely trimmed with gold coins; it is attached by golden cords under the chin. The upper garment is the *rlila*, or jacket, of brocaded silk, beneath which are one or more vests of gay colours, ornamented with innumerable sugar-loaf buttons. Round the waist is swathed the *fouta*, or manifold sash of striped silk. Add rings and earrings, often of diamonds and emeralds very clumsily cut; necklaces with side rows of fine pearls strung on common string, bracelets for the arms, called *mesis*, and bangles for the ankles, termed *redefs*, and the Mauresque " at home " costume is complete.

The **Town Arab** wears the original Turkish costume of cloth, embroidered with gold or silk of the same colour. This consists of baggy trousers, vest, and coat, somewhat similar to the dress worn by the Zouaves. Where the costume has lost its originality is in the suppression of the huge white turbans and leggings as well as in the shape of the trousers, which has been altered, and is now similar to those worn formerly by the Jews.

The **Jews** have taken of late years to wearing European dress, but they are easily recognised, when wearing native garments, by their dark blue turban, blue stockings, and their long hair. The Jewish dress is somewhat unbecoming, and has lost much of its former character.

The **Kabyles'** dress consists of a piece of white muslin material fastened on a large round white felt cap, with a few yards of twisted camel-hair, and a *gandoura* or dressing-gown of carpet-like material, which is of such resisting texture that they scarcely ever require to replace it by another.

The **Jewesses** are often handsome, but the practice of shrouding the chin in a bandage of linen or muslin gives them the semblance of having a perpetual toothache. Their dress is one of the loveliest costumes worn in Algeria. It consists of a black silk handkerchief fringed with gold which is fastened on the head with gold and diamond pins and next a scarf, often of the most gorgeous materials. Their dresses are gowns of velvet, silk, or stiff brocade, or sometimes cloth of gold or silver, having a stomacher, or breastplate, entirely worked with heavy gold embroidery. This gown is pretty well uniform for all the classes of social standing. The richness of the material and the massive gold embroidery slightly differ, of course. But then the poorest of the poor Jewesses can always boast of a dress worth from £5 to £10, if not more. This gown is fastened round the waist by a sash of silk and gold. The wide sleeves are made of tulle or sprinkled gauze, and are held back on the shoulders. Under the gown, in winter, a caftan with sleeves is sometimes worn. These sleeves are very tightly buttoned, and are of the same material as the caftan: either velvet, gold brocade, or embroidered silk. Another caftan is still worn under the first, a short one buttoning with two buttons, to keep up the figure.

Take away the dash of Arabian Nightism, and they are the same Jewesses whom you may see on the high days and holidays taking their ease in European tight-fitting dresses on the Saint Eugène or Mustapha tramcars, with their red-lipped, moist-eyed children round them.

On gala days and bridal ceremonies, their dresses are of astonishing splendour; a heavy, bizarre, loaded kind of richness, such as in old tapestry hangings representing the Queen of Sheba visiting Solomon, or Esther coming down with Ahasuerus to confound Haman and release humble Mordecai. A real *tableau vivant* of the Ober-Ammergau Pass'on Play.

ARAB MARRIAGES.

The position of the Arab women in Algeria is theoretically much preferable to that of her sex in Morocco or Turkey. The strictly equitable nature of the French rule forbids her being treated with harshness or sold into slavery ; but practically she is not much better off than in other Oriental countries. She is the victim of a stupid and brutalising social code, founded on and bound up in a religion whose theory is pure, but whose practice is barbarous. She is either contemned or maltreated ; a toy to the rich, a beast of burden to the poor. When a child is born to a Moorish woman, she considers it a blessing if a boy, and a curse if a daughter. Directly a girl comes into the world she is baptised in the name of Fathma, which is that of the mother of the Prophet. A week afterwards another name is given to her. The choice of appellatives lies between Nicha, Bedra, Djohar, Halima, Hasuria, Khadidja, Kheira, Zina, Zora, Krenfla Messoudia, Kamra, etc.

If the Moorish girl's parents are poor, they will regard her only as an incubus. Her mother was probably married at ten or twelve years of age ; she ages early, and each accession of maternal cares is to her only a renewed warning that she is no longer fair to look upon. As for the father, it is as much as he knows that he has a daughter till some one buys her of him in marriage. The rich girl is neglected by her mother, and is relegated to a corner of the harem and the care of an old negress. When she is old enough to be married—*i.e.*, sold—the kind of life described by Mr. George Gaskell begins for her.

Beyond these characteristics there is nothing else to add to the social position of the Moorish women in Algiers. Their state of life is, no doubt, very pitiable. The Government can do very little to ameliorate it. They have guaranteed to the natives the possession of the civil law—which is the Koran— and the social code and the civil law are one. They might as well decree that the Arab women should go unveiled, or that the Arabs should leave off their burnouses, as interfere with the domestic arrangements of the Moorish gynæceum. Mr. George Gaskell thus describes in "Algeria As It Is" the Arab marriages :—

As a rule, an Arab marries without having seen the face

of his bride. No doubt some find out by accident whether it be pretty or ugly; and they are occasionally favoured by strategem, for a girl conscious of her own attractions may contrive to make an imprudence of her adjar responsible for what was her own intention. If neither chance nor design befriend them, they must be satisfied with the information given by their parents, who are always allowed to see their future daughters-in-law.

"Generally speaking, an Arab marries early. After ill-treating his wife a few years, he generally sends her adrift, and takes another, whose condition is no better than was that of the one repudiated. Divorce is very common, for it is known statistically that there are nearly as many separations as there are marriages. Marriage, with Mussulmans, is rather more a civil than a religious ceremony, the couple being united in the presence of the cadi or mayor. Some of the more intelligent and less bigoted Arabs, who have observed how much better is the social position of the wife amongst the civilised classes of Europeans, have their daughters married according to the French law. A marriage thus contracted is ever afterwards under the jurisdiction of France. If these examples were more frequent, the improved condition of Arab women would be the result. But as instructing the lower orders is the first step towards civilising them, nothing would so soon and so effectually remedy the evil as compulsory education.

"**The Wives of Arab Chiefs,** and of rich Arabs in general, if they enjoy immunity from labour, have even less liberty than their sisters in humble life. The demon of *ennui* is ever present to these secluded ladies, who are taught to believe that it is a crime to allow their faces to be seen except by their husbands and nearest relations. The adjar, or veil, is not worn in the house; but if a visitor calls, the female part of the family scampers off into the inner apartments. Their only occupation is to paint themselves, dress fine, look in the mirror, cover their persons with jewellery, and pass much time in the bath. Friday, the Arab Sunday, is almost the only day in which a woman of quality leaves her dwelling. She then, accompanied by her female attendants, goes to visit the cemetery, where, shrouded in a cloak of white drapery, many of them seen together look like phantoms wandering about the tombstones."

RAILWAYS.

Seven railway companies are in operation in Algeria and Tunisia, as follows:—

1. The **P.=L.=M.** of **Algeria,** from Algiers to Oran; and from Philippeville to Constantine.
2. The **East Algerian,** from Algiers to Constantine; Ménerville to Tizi-Ouzou; Bougie to Béni-Mansour; El-Guerrah to Biskra; Ouled-Rahmoun to Aïn-Beida and Khenchela.
3. The **West Algerian,** from St. Barbe-du-Tlélat to Ras-el-Mâ and Tlemçen; Oran to Aïn-Temouchent; Blidah to Berrouaghia.
4. The **State Railway,** from (Oran) Arzeu to Figuig and Colomb-Béchar; Tizi to Mascara; Mostaganem to Tiaret; Oran to Arzeu.
5. The **Bône=Guelma et Prolongements,** from Bôue to Kroubs; Bône to Randon; Bône and Souk-Ahras to Tebessa; Bône to Tunis; Pont de Trajan to Béja; Tunis to Bizerta; Tunis to La Goulette; Tunis to Le Kef; Tunis to Kalaât-es-Sénam; Tunis to Kalaa-Djerda; Tunis to Nabeul; Tunis to Menzel-bou-Zelfa; Tunis to Sousse; Sousse to Kairouan; Sousse to Moknine; Tunis to Smindja and Zaghouan; Tunis to La Laverie.
6. The Sfax to Gafsa Company; Sfax to Gafsa and Metlaoui.
7. The **Bone-Mokta—St.-Charles** line, from Bône to Philippeville *via* St.-Charles.

In addition to the above railways there are a number of towns served by light railways (C.F.R.A. Company, Chemins de Fer sur Routes d'Algérie), such as Algiers to Rovigo; Algiers to Coléa and Castiglione; El-Affroun to Marengo; Dellys to the Camp du Maréchal and Boghni.

The seven lines of railway referred to above cover a mileage of 4,500 kilometres, or 2,800 miles.

HOTELS.

Generally speaking, the hotels in the large towns of Algeria and Tunisia, such as Algiers, Oran, Constantine, Bougie, Bône, Biskra, Bizerta, Tunis, and Sousse, also those at Hammam R'irha and Hammam Meskoutine are good; but in the smaller towns and country districts the accommodation for European travellers and the

sanitary arrangements leave much to be desired.   Matters are,
however, improving in this respect.

Those hotels at which THOS. COOK & SON'S *Coupons are*
accepted are indicated in the text referring to the respective places.

HISTORY.

The territory of Algiers includes the several divisions of
ancient Numidia, both of the Massyli and of the Massæsyli,
the kingdoms of Massinissa and his rival Syphax, and afterwards of Jugurtha.   It also includes part of the Mauritanian
kingdoms of Bocchus and of Juba.   It was conquered
successively by the Romans, the Vandals, the Byzantine
Greeks, and lastly by the Arabs, who invaded North Africa
at the beginning of the eighth century, and established
Islamism.   Ferdinand the Catholic, after driving the Moors
from Spain, sent an expedition to Africa under Cardinal
Ximenes and Don Pedro Navarro, which took possession, in
1509, of Oran and Marsa el Kebir, and of Bujeiah in the
following year.

To the general reader the most interesting part of the
history of Algiers commences with the rule of the Turks, and
of the brothers Barbarossa, the famous pirates.

The Moors of Algiers called in the aid of a Turkish
corsair, named Horush, who, after vanquishing the Spaniards,
claimed possession of Algiers itself, where he was killed, and
succeeded by his brother Kheir-ed-Din, the more daring of
the two.   The country in 1519 became a province of Turkey,
governed by a Pacha or Regent appointed by the Sultan.
The first who filled this office was Kheir-ed-Din, the brother
of Horush.   He manned a large fleet, with which he swept
the Mediterranean, striking terror among the Christian
sailors.   Solyman I. called him to Constantinople, and raised
him to the rank of Capudan Pacha, or Great Admiral.

In 1518 the Sultan Solyman equipped an expedition for
the conquest of Tunis.   This was successfully accomplished by
Kheir-ed-Din, who continued his piratical outrages against
Spain and Italy, which caused the Emperor Charles V. to
collect a fleet and army from every part of Europe, and in
July, 1535, the expedition, composed of Spanish, German,
Italian, Maltese, and Portuguese troops to the number of
30,000, set sail in 500 vessels from Cagliari and appeared before

Goletta. Kheir-ed-Din made a desperate resistance, but Goletta was taken by assault, the Emperor's army marched on Tunis, defeated Kheir-ed-Din and liberated 10,000 Christian slaves. Mulai Hassan was placed on the throne as a vassal of Charles V., who, after taking Bizerta and Bône, left for Europe. Kheir-ed-Din escaped to Constantinople, where he died.

At Algiers there was no improvement. Mohammed Hassan Pacha, a Sardinian renegade, who succeeded Kheir-ed-Din, continued to scour the sea and make incursions on the coast of Spain. Consequently, in 1541, Charles V. decided to attack Algiers. An army of 20,000 regular troops, 4,000 volunteers, and 2,000 horse sailed in October, 1541, contrary to the advice of Admiral Dorea on account of the advanced season of the year. A landing was effected near Algiers, where now stands the Jardin d'Essai, but Mohammed Hassan, although he only had about 6,000 troops, refused to surrender. The elements, however, came to his assistance—a violent storm ensued, the invading army, who had no tents, became frozen and wet, were charged furiously by the Moors and Turks, and were obliged to re-embark in the greatest confusion, losing a third of their number and 140 ships.

From that epoch the Algerines thought themselves invincible, and extended their piracies not only all over the Mediterranean, but also into the Atlantic. They seized the vessels of all nations who did not agree to pay them a tribute.

Robert Blake in 1655 first taught the Algerines to respect the English flag by his bold and successful action at Tunis. Louis XIV. caused Algiers to be bombarded in 1682 by Admiral Duquesne, which led to a peace in the following year between France and Algiers. The Spaniards, under General O'Reilly, landed near Algiers in 1775, but were obliged to re-embark in haste and with loss. The Dutch, after several combats with the Algerines, by paying a sum of money, obtained respect for their flag. So did likewise the Danes and Swedes. The Austrian and Russian flags were protected by the special interference of the Porte, in consequence of treaties with the latter. But the Italian States were the greatest sufferers from the piracies of the Algerines and the other Barbary Powers, who not only seized their vessels and cargoes, but made slaves of all on board, who were either sold in the market, or sent, chained, to the public works.

In 1815 the Algerine Power was checked in its lawless exactions by the ships of the United States, which took an Algerine frigate and brig; the Dey was also compelled to conclude a treaty with the Americans, renounce all tribute, and pay them 60,000 dollars as compensation for the ships that had been plundered. In 1816 Lord Exmouth, with a British and Dutch squadron, in execution of the determination taken by the Congress of Vienna, put an end to Christian slavery by bombarding and destroying the forts, the fleet, and part of the city of Algiers, and bringing the Dey to terms on this and other subjects. A better state of things lasted for about eleven years, when an insult offered by Hussein Pacha, the last Dey, to the French Consul, in April, 1827, induced the French Government to send an expedition on a very large scale to take possession of Algiers. This was effected in June, 1830, when an army of 34,000 men, commanded by General Bourmont and Admiral Duperré, landed at Sidi Ferruch (*see* p. 97). Algiers capitulated to General Bourmont; the Dey abdicated, and retired to Europe; and the French took possession of the town, of the fleet, and of the Treasury, where they found above £2,000,000 sterling in precious metals and stores.

Before tracing the further proceedings of the French, it may be as well to remark, that the Turkish chief was known by the several titles of Dey (" Uncle "), Pacha, Effendi, and Baba (" Father ") He was elected by the *bashis*, or officers of the militia, assembled in *dewaun*, or rather by a faction of them, which also frequently shortened his reign by a violent death. Few sovereigns of Algiers for the last two centuries have died a natural death. Any common janissary might aspire to the supreme rank. The Sultan formerly used to appoint the Pacha of Algiers, who was at the same time commander of the forces, and to send men and money for the service of the garrison; but the Turkish militia obtained in the seventeenth century the right of choosing their own commander, and paying themselves out of the revenue of the regency.

By the capitulation of July 4, 1830, the French became possessed " of the city of Algiers and the forts and harbours depending on it." No mention was made of the provinces or of the native tribes, over which the authority of the Dey was little else than nominal. It is from this circumstance that the French have lost so many men and so much money in extending their possessions of the country. The Moors inhabiting the towns of Algiers, Oran, and Bône became sub-

jects of France, but the Arabs and Kabyles of the open
country followed their own tactics, and even the Turkish Beys
of provinces showed a disposition to join with the Arabs and
Kabyles rather than with the invaders. A kind of guerilla warfare ensued, which was carried on with varying intensity for
about seventeen years, marked occasionally by inhuman
atrocities on the part of the Arabs, and by proceedings little
less creditable on the part of their more civilised adversaries.

The most formidable antagonist to the French generals was
the celebrated Arab chief, Abd-el-Kader, the Bey of Mascara,
who exhibited the most stubborn energy, coupled with great
military skill, and inflicted very severe losses upon the invaders of his country. It was not till December, 1847, when
Abd-el-Kader, pressed and hemmed in on all sides, yielded
himself a prisoner to General Lamoricière, that the conquest
of Algeria could be said to be effected, having cost an expenditure of blood and treasure which seemed then out of
comparison with the worth of the colony to France. Abd-el-
Kader was sent to France, and remained there until released
by Napoleon in 1852. He went to Constantinople, and later
on to Damascus, where he died. Even after the removal of
the great Arab chief, numerous outbreaks of the natives
occurred ; and to hold this country, with its native population
of two millions, required as many European soldiers as were
maintained in India by Great Britain. The force kept in
Algeria has seldom been inferior to 60,000 men.

The withdrawal of the French Army for home service in
1870 was the signal for a general insurrection in 1871, which
assumed such unexpected proportions and spread so rapidly
throughout Algeria that it became necessary to reconquer
almost the whole country. As soon, however, as the Franco-
German war was over troops were sent from France, and by
the end of August, 1871, the rising was effectually suppressed.

Since 1871 several insurrections or, rather, revolts have
taken place, notably the revolt of El-Hamri in 1876, and of
the one in the Aurès Mountains in 1879, headed by a Marabout, Mohamed-bin-Abdulla, which was finally suppressed
after a decisive battle at *El-Arbaa*, when the insurgents were
overcome and driven south, large numbers of them dying of
fatigue and hunger in the Sahara.

More serious was the revolt in 1881 of the tribes of Tiaret,
Frenna, Geryville, and Saida, south of Oran, led by Bou-
Amama, a Marabout of the Oulad-Sidi Cheikh family. The

fanatic and his followers were at first successful, and large numbers of Europeans were massacred, but later on General Négrier, with a column composed of Zouaves, Chasseurs d'Afrique, and Legionnaires, inflicted heavy losses on the tribes and drove them to the district of Gouraya, where the insurgents deserted Bou-Amama, and sued for peace.

It 1882 the territory of Beni M'zab, south of El-Aghouat, 700 kiloms. from Algiers, a flourishing district, but the centre for insurrectionary tribes, was occupied by General de la Tour d'Auvergne, and annexed to Algeria. Since then advanced posts have been established in the Algerian Sahara, and in 1900 French troops took possession of In-Sala and of Igli.

There are now signs of tranquility and prosperity everywhere (except in Southern Oran in the south-west corner of Algeria, on the frontier of Morocco, see p. 194), and by the adoption of firm and judicious measures the prejudices of the natives have, to a great extent, been overcome. Algeria, in fact, has entered upon a fairly promising career of wealth and civilisation. It was removed from the control of the War Minister and the *Bureaux Arabes*, and a new organisation was established, comprising all the usual features of the French Civil Government. It is satisfactory to know, in spite of the hundreds of millions of francs which Algeria has cost France, that this nest of pirates and smugglers has been transformed into a really fine colony, with ports, fortifications, public buildings of all kinds, churches, schools, roads, railways, telegraphs, villages, cities, abundance of cleared and fertile land, irrigation works, and mines.

Dr. Bennet, in his " Winter and Spring on the Shores of the Mediterranean," speaks with positive enthusiasm of the care with which the French have built churches and established schools wherever they have founded a colony or a military station :

" The settlement of the French in Algeria, although certainly undertaken and continued for political and military purposes, has also, in reality, a decided Christian character. It is the first grand inroad made on the headquarters of Mohammedan infidelity since the time of the Crusades. The gain is the gain of Christianity and civilisation, and all the Christian nations of Europe ought to feel that they owe a deep debt of gratitude to France for what she has accomplished in Algeria, and be willing to help her in her great enterprise."

PART II.

ALGIERS.

———◆———

Routes to Algiers. The direct route from England to Algiers is through Paris and Marseilles, the journey from London *via* Calais occupying about 22 hours by the Rapide trains, which, however, only carry first class passengers.

From Marseilles to Algiers by the steamers of the Transatlantic Company the voyage occupies 26–28 hours (Monday, Wednesday and Saturday) or 30–32 hours (Thursday).

By the steamers of the Compagnie de Navigation Mixte (Touache), sailing every Tuesday and Thursday (32–36 hours) · there is also another service of the Compagnie Mixte every Saturday from Cette at midnight calling at Port Vendres, due at Algiers on Monday, 6 p.m.

By the Société de Transports Maritimes à Vapeur, Wednesday and Saturday, 6 p.m., due Algiers Friday and Monday, 6 a.m. (*See* also p. 51.)

By the Prosper-Durand Line every Tuesday, noon, returning from Algiers on Saturdays.

Outward bound travellers will be saved much trouble by applying for information and procuring their tickets from Thos. Cook & Son, Ludgate Circus, London, or from their branch offices in London, Liverpool and Southampton, where also Circular Tickets can be obtained for travelling in Tunisia, Algeria, Morocco, etc.

Distance from Liverpool by sea, 1,685 miles. From London, rail to Marseilles, and steamer to Algiers, 1,318 miles.

From *London*, by the P. & O. steamers or Orient-Pacific to Marseilles, thence by sea on the Compagnie Transatlantique; Navigation Mixte (Touache), or Société Générale steamers.

pla
(ne

From *Liverpool* the steamers of the Moss Steamship Co. occasionally call at Algiers, the journey to that port occupying about seven days. The Papayanni Line steamers also call at Algiers at frequent intervals (about fortnightly).

From *Southampton* (from October 1st, 1907) by the North German Lloyd (China and Japan) steamers fortnightly. They also call at Algiers on the homeward voyages fortnightly.

From *Gibraltar* by the Adria Line (three-weekly service); also by the Compagnie de Navigation Mixte to Oran (thence rail) fortnightly.

From *Barcelona* there is a weekly service (Majorca SS. Co.) on Wednesdays, 6.30 p.m., arriving at Algiers Fridays about 7.0 a.m.

From *New York* Algiers is reached by the large steamers of the Hamburg-American and North German Lloyd Companies, about fortnightly during the winter season.

From *Hamburg*, by the steamers of A. C. de Freitas and Co., twice a month.

From *Antwerp* by the German Levant SS. Co.'s steamers to Tunis (monthly), thence rail or sea (Transatlantic Co.).

From *Naples*, by Italiana Gen. Navigation Co.'s steamers to Tunis (weekly), thence rail, or boat of the Transatlantique Company.

Harbour.—A magnificent harbour, well sheltered, able to contain the biggest steamers—capable of holding the French Mediterranean fleet.

Passengers from Marseilles by the Transatlantique Co. land by pontoon without the necessity of taking small boats.

In the case of the Navigation Mixte or Société Générale the traveller has sometimes to hire a small boat in order to land. Fare, 50 centimes per passenger, and 25 centimes each piece of baggage.

Small boats are also necessary for all other steamers coming into port; tariff as above

Cook's interpreter in uniform meets all the principal vessels. Passengers should telegraph to " Cook, Algiers," when the boat is due to arrive before 7.0 a.m. or after 7.0 p.m.

Customs.—Dutiable articles: Tea, coffee, sugar, salt meat, candles, silver goods, cigars, tobacco, spirits, beer, matches playing cards, dried fruits, furniture, soap, etc.; also saddles (new or old), bicycles, tents, arms and ammunition.

Passengers are advised to assist the Customs' officers in the discharge of their duty, as by so doing the work is greatly accelerated, with little annoyance.   Keys of trunks should be produced willingly.

Gunpowder is absolutely forbidden; filled cartridges also.   Empty cartridges can be brought in with percussion cap.   Minister of War, Paris, can give permission for powder and cartridges, but this is seldom taken advantage of.   Neither Harvey cartridges nor good English powder can be bought in Algiers.   No good house for filling cartridges.

Outfit.—Ordinary clothes, including a dress suit, are suitable for large towns such as Algiers, Tunis, Bône, but for travelling up-country or for shooting excursions comfortable riding-breeches, shooting-coats with plenty of pockets *to button up*, strong boots, gaiters or puttees, strong socks, warm under-clothing, a good waterproof and a pair of motor-goggles to protect the eyes against the sand, which is very disagreeable in the desert however light the wind, should be taken.

European tents and materials for camping, if required, can be bought or hired in Algiers.

Railways.—There are two main lines of railway—the Paris, Lyons, and Mediterranean, going towards Oran, and the East Algerian Railway, going towards Constantine.   The same station is used for the departures of trains of both lines. One through train daily in each direction.   Restaurant car. Breakfast, 4f.   Dinner, 4·50f.—wine included.   There is also a night train from Algiers on Tuesdays, Thursdays, and Sundays —*i.e.*, the days of the arrival of the Transatlantique steamers from Marseilles.   In the reverse direction, Mondays, Wednes-days and Fridays.   *During the winter season* the Sleeping Car Co. run a train from Oran to Tunis *via* Algiers, Kroubs (for Constantine) and Duvivier (for Bône).   This train leaves Oran Wednesday evening, arrives Algiers Thursday morning, leaves Algiers on Thursday evening arrives Kroubs Friday morning, leaves Kroubs Friday morning, arrives Tunis Friday, 10.39 p.m.   In the reverse direction the train leaves Tunis Wednesday morning, arrives Algiers Thursday morning, leaves in the evening, and arrives at Oran 6.56 a.m. Friday.   Supple-ment, Oran to Algiers, 16f.; Algiers to Constantine, 20f. *Times and fares subject to alteration.*   Places can be reserved in advance at Cook's OFFICE, 3, Boulevard de la République. There is no restaurant or buffet at the station.

Diligences.—Where practicable private conveyances are recommended in preference to the diligences as these very often leave much to be desired on the score of comfort and sometimes of cleanliness, although matters are steadily improving in this direction.

Money.—Algerian notes pass *only* in Algeria, and travellers are advised to change any such notes for French notes or gold before leaving the country. Although not current in Tunisia, they are generally accepted at Hotels in payment of bills.

French Currency.—

Monetary Unit—the Franc of 100 Centimes.

				s.	d.
Bronze—1 centime.					
„ 2 centimes.					
„ 5 „	. . . . . .	=	0	0½
„ 10 „	. . . . . .	÷	0	1
Nickel—25 „	. . . . . .	=	0	2⅓
Silver—50 „	. . . . . .	=	0	4¾
„ 1 franc .	. . . . . .	÷	0	9½
„ 2 francs .	. . . . . .	÷	1	7
„ 5 „	. . . . . .	÷	4	0
Gold — 10 „	. . . . . .	—	8	0
„ 20 „ The " Louis " or " Napoleon " .		—	16	0

NOTES are issued by the Bank of France for 50, 100, 500, and 1,000 francs, and are the same value as gold.

The silver coins, anterior to 1863, excepting 5 franc pieces, are not current; also all Papal coins and the 50 cent., 1 lire, and 2 lire coins of Italy.

Cabs.—See Tariff below. For excursions or long drives it is well to make a bargain with the coachman beforehand.

Tariff for Public Carriages (for 4 persons).

TARIFF FOR THE DOUBLE COURSE.

From Algiers to destination and return, with liberty to stop on the way or at destination, on payment for waiting of 50 centimes per quarter of an hour.

	fr.	cts.
Alger-Ville (except the caserne d'Orléans, the Cartoucherie, the porte du Sahel and the Prison Civile, Bd. de la Victoire, Casba, Municipal Infirmary), under 2 k. 500 m.	1	—
Alger, Bd. de la Victoire	1	40
Alger, Caserne d'Orléans, 2 k. 700 m. 23'	1	50
Cartoucherie, 2 k. 700 m. 23'	1	50
Casba (Old)	1	40
Cimetière Européen, 2 k. 300 m. 14'	1	25
Cimetière Israëlite, 2 k. 800 m. 16'	1	25
Infirmerie Municipale	1	40
Portes du Sahel, 2 k. 900 m. 23'	1	75
Prison Civile, 2 k. 200 m. 20'	1	40
Tagarins (beyond the walls), 3 k. 600 m. 35'	2	50
Abattoir (Mustapha), 3 k. 900 m. 25'	1	75

	fr.	cts.
Agha (Bains, Carrefour, Gare, Moulin, rue de la Liberté by the rue Michelet), less than 2 k. 500 m.	1	25
Arsenal de Mustapha (by both routes), 3 k. 700 m. 24'...	1	75
Bab-el-Oued (the whole suburb), l'Hôpital du Dey (Salpétrière), 2 k. 500 m....	1	—
Baïnem (Forest), 10 k. 300 m. 1 h. 40'		50
Bains Romains, 8 k. 800 m. 55'		—
Ben-Aknoun (petit Lycée), 8 k. 800 m. 1 h. 25'		—
Belcourt (cimetière musulman), 4 k. 500 m. 30'		—
Beni-Messous (Asile), 11 k. 400 m. 1 h. 45'		—
Birkadem (Mairie), 10 k. 300 m. 1 h. 35'		—
Birmandreis (Mairie), 7 k. 700 m. 1 h. 15'		—
Bois de Boulogne, 5 k. 700 m. 50'		—
Boulevard bon Accueil (viaduct), 2 k. 600 m. 23'		50
Boulevard Bru (North end), 4 k. 600 m. 38' ...		25
Boulevard Bru (middle, South end), 4 k. 300 m. 33'		—
Boulevard Bru (Birmandreis road), 5 k. 300 m. 42'		50
Boulevard Bru Tramway Terminus ...		
Bouzaréa (Mairie) by the El-Biar route or by the Carrières, 10 k. 300 m. 1 h. 45'	6	50
Champ-de-Manœuvres (station of the C. F. R. A.), 2 k. 800 m. 19'	1	25
Champ-de-Manœuvres (Groupe Scolaire), 3 k. 20' ...	1	50
Cap Caxine (Phare, commune de Guyotville), 11 k. 900 m. 1 h. 30'	6	—
Château-Neuf (El-Biar), 6 k. 800 m. 1 h.	4	—
Chemins des Crêtes (Mustapha)	3	50
Chemin Shakspeare (whole length), 5 k. 700 m. 50'	3	—
Chemin Yusuf, Cartoucherie Mustapha, 3 k. 700 m. 27'	1	75
Chéragas (Mairie), 13 k. 700 m. 1 h. 45'	7	
Climat de France	1	50
Colonne Voirol, 5 k. 700 m. 50'	3	—
Dely-Ibrahim (Mairie), 11 k. 400 m. 1 h. 45'	7	—
Deux-Moulins (Commune de Saint-Eugène), 4 k. 500 m. 27'	2	—
Drariah (Mairie), 14 k. 800 m. 2 h. 05'	8	—
El-Achour (Mairie), 12 k. 500 m. 1h. 50'	7	—
El-Biar (Mairie), 5 k. 200 m. 55'	3	50
Frais Vallon (Café Maure) 4 k. 35'	2	50
Fontaine Bleue (Pont). 3 k. 900 m. 30'	2	—
Guyotville (Mairie), 15 k. 300 m. 1 h. 50'...	7	50
Hôpital Civil (Mustapha), 2 k. 700 m. 18'	1	50
Hussein-Dey (Mairie), 6 k. 600 m. 42'	3	—
Hussein Dey (Village St.-Jean)	3	50
Hydra (Café) by the Colonne Voirol, 7 k. 58'	4	—
Jardin d'Essai (route du Ruisseau), 5 k. 300 m. 31'	2	25
Kouba (Mairie), 8 k. 300 m. 1 h. 15'	5	—
Kouba (Vieux), 9 k. 700 m. 1 h. 25'	5	50
Maison-Carrée (Mairie), 11 k. 800 m. 1 h. 30'	6	—
Mustapha (cimetière européen), 4 k. 600 m. 35'	3	—
Mustapha (by the boulevard Bru), 6 k. 48' ...	2	75
Mustapha (by the chemin des Crêtes)	3	20
Mustapha-Supérieur (Palace), 4 k. 30'	2	—
Mustapha-Supérieur (Church), 4 k. 35'	2	—

						fr.	cts.
Notre-Dame-d'Afrique	...	...	...	...	...	3	50
Nouvelle France	...	...	...	...	...	3	—
Oasis des Palmiers, 5 k. 100 m. 33'	...	...	...	...	2	50
Ouled-Fayet (Mairie), 16 k. 2 h. 10'	...	...	...	...	8	50
Petit Séminaire	...	...	...	...	...	4	—
Plateau Saulière (Mustapha), 2 k. 500 m. 17'	...	...	...	1	50
Pointe Pescade, 6 k. 600 m. 45'	...	...	...	...	3	50
Ruisseau (Mustapha), 6 k. 200 m. 40'	...	...	...	...	3	—
Saoula (Mairie), 10 k. 100 m. 1 h. 55'	...	...	...	8	—
Saint-Eugène (Mairie), 2 k. 900 m. 17'	...	...	...	1	50
Télemly (upper end of rues Daguerre and des Fontaines)		1	75
Trappe (la) Monastery, 17 k. 800 m. 2 h. 35'	...	...	...	10	—
Village d'Isly, 2 k. 500 m. 20'	...	...	...	...	1	50

RAILWAY STATIONS AND STEAMERS.

1re Zone.—The rues d'Isly, Mogador, Randon, Marengo, round the jardin Marengo, and all the lower town, 1 f.

2e Zone.—Upper town, and the faubourg Bab-el-Oued, 1f. 50c.

For 5 persons the prices are increased by one-fourth, waiting excepted. Heavy packages are charged 50 centimes extra.

TARIFF BY THE DAY AND BY THE HOUR.

The day of 12 hours	...	...	...	...	...	20 francs.
Half-day of 6 hours	...	...	...	...	...	11 ,,
By the hour	...	...	...	...	...	2 ,,

(Not applicable to Notre-Dame d'Afrique.)

TRAMWAYS.

Electric.—These form a splendid means of seeing Algiers and its environs in every direction, and at a very moderate cost.

Cars leave the Place du Gouvernement for the Colonne Voirol every half-hour, from 6 a.m. to 7.30 p.m.

Cars from the Hôpital du Dey to the Station Sanitaire, or *vice versâ*, every five minutes, from 6 a.m. to 10 p.m.; and every ten minutes from 5 a.m. to 6 a.m. and from 10 p.m. to 11.50 p.m.

Cars for Mustapha Supérieur, Boulevard Bru (for English Cemetery), leave Station Sanitaire every half-hour, from 6.15 a.m. to 7.15 p.m.

Cars for El-Biar leave the Place du Gouvernement every half-hour from 6.5 a.m. to 6.5 p.m. Last departures, 7.5 p.m. and 8.5 p.m.

For the Civil Prison every fifteen minutes, from 6.5 a.m. to 8.35 p.m. Last departure, 9 p.m.

Steam.—Bône to La Calle, a distance of 88 kilometres. Three or four departures daily in each direction. Time on journey, about four hours.

LIGHT RAILWAYS.
Chemins de fer sur Routes d'Algérie (C.F.R.A.).
Steam—
Algiers, L'Arba, Rovigo (37 Kilometres).

6.25 a.m., 1.5 p.m., 5.25 p.m., and on Sunday, Wednesday and Friday, and fête days, 5.5 a.m. Return 5.50 a.m., 12.30 p.m. and 5.10 p.m., and on Sunday, Wednesday, Friday and fête days 9.4 a.m.

Algiers to Coléa and Castiglione, viâ Mazafran.

STATIONS, DEUX MOULINS, POINTE PESCADE, BAINS ROMAINS, CAP CAXINE, GUYOTVILLE.—4.59 a.m., 6.42 a.m., 8.59 a.m., 11.7 a.m., 12.59 p.m., 2.33 p.m., 3.51 p.m., 5.15 p.m., 6.42 p.m.

ALGIERS AND ALL STATIONS TO GUYOTVILLE, CONTINUING TO ZÉRALDA, MAZAFRAN AND COLÉA OR CASTIGLIONE.—6.42 a.m., 12.59 p.m., 5.15 p.m. Algiers, Deux Moulins, Guyotville, Mazafran and Castiglione, 7.59 a.m. Extra trains Sundays and fête days.

El=Affroun to Marengo (20 Kilometres).

Leave ALGIERS (P.-L.-M.) 6.50 a.m., 12.41 p.m., 5.19 p.m. Leave EL-AFFROUN 9.25 a.m., 3.45 p.m., 8.2 p.m. About one hour and a-quarter between El-Affroun and Marengo.

Dellys to Boghni (68 Kilometres)

DELLYS, CAMP DU MARECHAL, MIRABEAU, BOGHNI.— 4.34 a.m., 2.14 p.m. Returning 4.25 a.m. and 2.5 p.m.

Electric—

PLACE DU GOUVERNEMENT TO MAISON CARRÉE. Every twenty minutes from 4.45 a.m. to 8.45 p.m. Extra trains, 9.25 p.m., 10.5 p.m., and 11.5 p.m. Reverse direction from 4.51 a.m. to 9.51 p.m. ; extra trains, 10.31 p.m. and 11.1 p.m.

PLACE DU GOUVERNEMENT TO NOUVEL AMBERT.—Every ten minutes from 4.45 a.m. to 8.25 p.m. ; extra trains, 8.45 p.m., 9.5 p.m., 9.25 p.m., 9.45 p.m., 10.5 p.m., 10.35 p.m., 11.5 p.m. ; special train, midnight, from Square de la République, after the theatre. Reverse direction from 4.52 a.m. to 8.52 p.m. ; extra trains, 9.12 p.m., 9.32 p.m., 9.52 p.m., 10.12 p.m., 10.32 p.m., 10.52 p.m., and 11.22 p.m.

PLACE DU GOUVERNEMENT TO JARDIN D'ESSAI (OASIS DES PALMIERS.)—Every ten minutes from 4.45 a.m. to 9.25 p.m.; extra trains, 9.45 p.m., 10.5 p.m., 10.35 p.m., and 11.5 p.m. Reverse direction from 5.2 a.m. to 10.2 p.m.; extra trains, 10.22 p.m., 10.42 p.m., 11.2 p.m., and 11.32 p.m.

PLACE DU GOUVERNEMENT to JARDIN D'ESSAI (PLATANES).— Every ten minutes from 4.32 a.m. to 8.2 p.m.; every twenty minutes from 8.22 p.m. to 11.22 p.m. Reverse direction every ten minutes from 4.35 a.m. to 8.25 p.m., every twenty minutes from 8.45 p.m. to 9.45 p.m., and from 10.10 p.m. to 11.30 p.m.

PLACE DU GOUVERNEMENT TO RUISSEAU SUPÉRIEUR.— Every twenty minutes from 4.42 a.m. to 8.22 p.m.; extra trains, 6.32 a.m., 6.52 a.m., 7.12 a.m., and 11.12 a.m., 12.32 p.m., 12.52 p.m., 4.52 p.m., 5.12 p.m., 9.2 p.m., 9.42 p.m., 10.2 p.m., 10.22 p.m., 11.2 p.m., and 11.22 p.m. Reverse direction from 4.40 a.m. till 9 p.m. Extra trains, 7.10 a.m., 7.30 a.m., 7.50 a.m., and 11.50 a.m., 1.10 p.m., 1.30 p.m., 5.30 p.m., 5.50 p.m., 9.40 p.m., 10.25 p.m., and 11.5 p.m.; special train at midnight from the Square de la République after the theatre.

PLACE DU GOUVERNEMENT TO ST. EUGÈNE (DEUX MOULINS). —About every ten minutes from 4.51 a.m. to 7.59 p.m.; every thirty minutes from 8.30 p.m. to 11.30 p.m.; special train at midnight from the Square de la République after the theatre. Reverse direction from 5.34 a.m. to 8.34 p.m. Extra trains 5.0 a.m., 5.17 a.m., and every half-hour from 9.0 p.m. to 11.30 p.m.

PLACE DU GOUVERNEMENT TO KOUBA.—Every forty minutes from 5.2 a.m. to 7.2 p.m. Extra train at 10.2 p.m. Reverse direction every forty minutes from 5.22 a.m. to 8.2 p.m. Extra trains at 8.42 a.m. and 10.52 p.m.

PLACE DU GOUVERNEMENT TO THE MARABOUT.—Every five minutes from 5.32 a.m. to 8.2 p.m. Reverse direction from 5.29 a.m. to 7.59 p.m.

Sundays and fête days on all lines extra trains, according to the requirements of the service.

Correspondence between Le Ruisseau and Birmandreïs, Birkadem and Saoula every two hours.

Correspondence between Le Ruisseau and Kouba every hour.

GENERAL INFORMATION.

Cook's Office.—3, Boulevard de la République.

Post Office.—The *General* (Poste Restante) is situated in the Boulevard Carnot at the corner of the Rue Strasbourg. Branch Post Office in the Palais Consulaire, on the Boulevard de France. All ordinary Post Office business, telegrams, registered letters, change of address, are transacted at both these places. There is also a Branch at Mustapha Palace, and one at Mustapha Inférieur.

Parcels (per Parcels Post) are not accepted at the Post Office, but must be sent by one of the Shipping Companies— the Transatlantique, Navigation Mixte (Tonache), and Société Générale de Transports Maritimes. Average time required for parcels from London to Algiers, or *vice versâ*, is about three weeks.

Mails.—The fast mail for Europe is that on Tuesdays, Thursdays, and Saturdays. To ensure departure, letters, etc., should be posted before 11.45 a.m. at the General Post Office. It is desirable, however, to post letters as soon as possible, irrespective of stated times of mails, as advantage is taken of the next boat leaving for despatch of mails at odd times. Letters can be posted on the ship itself if necessary.

No fixed day for New York, China, or Australian letters.

Cycling.—There is a very good track at the Velodrome, Mustapha Inférieur, near the Champ-de-Manœuvres.

Repairs to cycles can be done by M. Gérin or Paul Mayeur, both in the Rue de la Liberté.

Automobilism.—Within the last few years this form of locomotion has increased greatly.

The two principal houses for repairs, sale, hire of these machines are Mayeur, and Gérin, in the Rue de la Liberté. Several huge new garages have sprung up and deserve mention, two in the Rue d'Isly, and one in the Rue de Constantine, etc.

Various automobile excursions from Algiers (occupying from one to eight days), visiting Blidah, Gorges de la Chiffa, Hammam R'irha, Tipaza, Cherchell, Tizi Ouzou, Michelet (Kabylia), Fort National, Bougie, Gorges du Chabet, Setif, Kerrata, etc., have been arranged by Thos. Cook & Son, and particulars can be obtained from their office, 3, Boulevard de la République.

Libraries.—English Circulating, near the English Church at Mustapha ; Bibliothèque Nationale (French), Rue de l'Etat Major, open daily 1 p.m. to 6 p.m. ; University Library, in the École Supérieure des Lettres, Rue Michelet.

The **English Cottage Hospital**, with an **Infectious Ward**, is situated at Mustapha Supérieur (Rue Michelet) in the premises occupied by the late Gardner Home. Treasurer, Rev. E. Arkwright, Télemly, Mustapha.

Sights.—The following are among the most important : Mosque Djema el Djedid, Place du Gouvernement ; Mosque Djema el Kebir, Rue de la Marine ; Mosque Sidi Abder-rahman, Jardin Marengo ; Cathedral St. Philippe, Place Malakoff ; Church Notre Dame d'Afrique ; Jardin d'Essai (tramway), Mustapha Inférieur ; Governor's Winter Palace, Place Malakoff ; Governor's Summer Palace, Rue Michelet, Mustapha Supérieur ; Admiralty, on the Quay ; Archbishop's Palace, Place Malakoff ; Museum, Rue Michelet, Mustapha Supérieur (corner of Chemin du Télemly).

The **Arab Quarters** of Algiers, including the Casbah, are well worthy of at least one day being entirely devoted to them. A guide is necessary, and can be obtained at the office of Thos. Cook & Son, 3, Boulevard de la République.

Governor's Palaces.—These can be visited at any time, on presentation of card, when the Governor-General is away. The winter palace is situated in the town, next to the cathedral. The summer palace at Mustapha Supérieur.

Public Baths.—Bains Michelet, Rue Michelet, on the road to Mustapha ; Bains du Hamma, Rue du Hamma, next to the Theatre ; Bains Parisiens, 36, Rue Bab-el-Oued ; Bains du Palmier, 6, Rue Arago.

Moorish Bath (Bain Maure), in the Arab quarter, 2, Rue de l'Etat Major. From midday till 5 p.m. for women ; from 5 a.m. till midday for men. This is not a Turkish bath, properly so called, and is conducted by Arabs.

Sea=bathing can be had both at Algiers and Mustapha.

Boats.—Rowing boats, about 2 francs per hour. Sailing boats, about 3 francs per hour.

Arrangements can be made at Thos. Cook & Son's office, 3, Boulevard de la République.

Fishing.—Including lines, bait, at 3 francs per hour.

BANKS, CHURCHES, CONSULATES, Etc.

Banks.—THOS. COOK & SON, Bankers, Army Agents, Money-changers, 3, Boulevard de la République.

La Banque d'Algérie, Crédit Lyonnais, Crédit Foncier et Agricole de l'Algérie, Compagnie Algérienne, Crédit Agricole et Commercial Algérien.

Consulates.—British: F. Hay Newton, M.V.O., Consul-General, 6, Boulevard Sadi-Carnot; L. G. C. Graham, Vice-Consul.

United States: James Johnston, Consul, 64, Rue d'Isly; Vice- and Deputy-Consul, L. L. Legembre; Deputy-Consul, T. M. MacGeagh.

Germany: Baron von Tischendorff, 43, Rue Michelet, Mustapha.

Italy: P. Baroli, 9, Rue de Strasbourg.

Portugal: F. M. Burke, 2, Boulevard Sadi-Carnot.

Spain: Mr. Marinas, Consul-General, 31, Rue des Consuls.

English Churches.—Church of England, Place d'Isly, but being rebuilt at Mustapha Supérieur.

Presbyterian Church, Rue Michelet, Mustapha Supérieur.

Scottish Church, Rue Naudot. (*See* also p. 75).

Seaman's Reading Room, Rampe Magenta.

English Physician.—A. S. Gubb, M.D., Club Buildings, Mustapha Supérieur (October to April).

Dentists.—F. Sintes, 4, Boulevard de la République; Décréquy, 1, Rue Littré.

English Chemist.—Licht, Station Sanitaire (close to Mustapha).

Forwarding Agents.—THOS. COOK & SON, 3, Boulevard de la République.

House and Estate Agents.—N. C. Macpherson, 27, Rue d'Isly.

Lloyd's Agents.—Burke & Delacroix, 2, Boulevard Sadi-Carnot.

POSTAL, TELEGRAM, AND TELEPHONE RATES.

Postage on ordinary letters to Algeria, Tunisia, Corsica, and France, 10c. (1d.) per 15 grammes or fraction. To Europe and all countries in the Postal Union (except Italy, 20c.), 25c. (2½d.) for the first 15 grammes, and 15c. for every 15 grammes afterwards (from October 1st, 1907). French postage stamps are used for Algeria, but Tunisia has its own local stamps.

Post Cards to Algeria, Tunisia, Corsica, France, and countries in the Postal Union, 10c. (1d.). Picture post cards for France and certain other countries (not England) may be sent for 5c. if the words " Carte Postale " are struck out and not more than five complimentary words are written on the card.

Letter Cards to Algeria, Tunisia, Corsica, and France, 15c. (1½d.) for 15 grammes; to other countries, 25c. (2½d.).

Cards or Circulars, containing printed matter only, such as Christmas Cards, Wedding Cards, or business announcements, in unfastened envelopes, 5c. for 50 grammes.

Registered Letter fee, 25c. all countries.

Postal Orders, Algeria, Tunisia, Corsica, and France, 5c. up to 10f.; 10c. for 11f. to 20f.

Post Office Orders, Algeria, Tunisia, Corsica, and France, 5c. per 5f. up to 20f.; 25c. for 20f. to 50f.; 50c., 50f. to 100f., etc. Great Britain and Colonies, India, America, Canada, Japan, 10c. per 10f. or fraction.

Telegraph Rates, between two offices in Algeria and Tunisia, or between Algeria and France, 5c. per word; minimum charge, 50c. To Great Britain, Belgium, Switzerland, and Germany, 25c.; New York 1f. 25c. or 1f. 45c.; Italy, Holland, Spain, 30c.; Luxembourg, 20c.; Denmark, 35c.; Gibraltar, 30c.; Malta, 35c.; Bosnia, Bulgaria, 40c.; Norway, 45c.; Russia in Europe, 50c.; Tripoli, 70c.; Greece, 65c.; Canary Islands, 90c.—all per word. Telegrams can be sent cheaply by marking the address London—Calais (or whatever the address and route may be) " Poste Recommandée." Such telegrams are sent at the rate of 5c. per word to the frontier, and thence as registered letters.

Telephone Service, in Algiers and radius of 25 kilometres, three minutes conversation, 15c.; and 40c. outside the above limit. Telephone message to non-subscriber, 50c. not exceeding three minutes.

Telephone Cabins are placed in the post and telegraph offices of the following localities:—Palais Consulaire, Mustapha, Mustapha Palace, Bab-el-Oued, Alger-Port, Hussein Dey, Maison Carrée, St. Eugène, Birkadem, Kouba, Rouiba, Bermandreis, Sidi-Moussa, Blidah, Boufarik, Bir Touta, Mouzaïaville, Arba, etc.

There are several classes of annual subscriptions, the one in general use for business firms being fixed at 200f. (about £8).

TRAM RIDES AND WALKS IN ALGIERS AND NEIGHBOURHOOD.

1. Take electric tram from Place du Gouvernement for Colonne Voirol; on arrival at terminus take first turning to right, and half-an-hour's walk brings one to El-Biar, where tram (electric) can again be taken for Algiers.

Time, 2½ hours.

2. Take electric tram from Place du Gouvernement for El-Biar and Château Neuf (good view on reaching top of town); take turning to the right and walk to Bouzarea; thence turn to the left to Forest of Bainem and down to the shore near Cap Caxine, whence tram for Algiers.

Time, 6 hours.

3. Take electric car from Station Sanitaire to end of Boulevard Bru, walk on till road branches; take path to left leading through the wood downhill to Jardin d'Essai, whence tram to Algiers.

Time, 3½ hours.

4. Take electric tram to Colonne Voirol from Place du Gouvernement. Continue straight on after leaving tram on upper road to Birmandreis, go through village, and take footpath beyond the square on right-hand side of road. Footpath leads to Arab Cemetery and Marabout of Sidi Yahid, and about one mile to another main road. Turn to right on reaching this road and walk on till Colonne Voirol is reached, whence tram for Algiers.

Time, 4½ hours.

Suburb of Algiers.

5. Start from Place du Gouvernement, through Rue du Divan to Rue de la Lyre, thence to Marché de la Lyre, thence by Rue Rovigo and Rue St. Augustin to Chemin du Télemly. Continue on this road till the Hotel Continental is reached, then strike immediately to the right up a narrow path which comes out at El-Biar, then make for Colonne Voirol, thence *viâ* Mustapha Supérieur and Rue Michelet to town.

Time, 5 hours.

CARRIAGE TOURS AND EXCURSIONS IN ALGERIA.

Arranged by THOS. COOK & SON, 3, Boulevard de la République.

The following Carriage Tours and Excursions embrace the most picturesque and interesting points that can conveniently be visited in a short time. Varied as are the tours suggested, other and longer itineraries will be arranged by their agent to meet the wishes of travellers.

The fares for the undermentioned tours vary in accordance with the number of persons forming the party travelling together, and will be quoted on application at any of their offices.

From Algiers.

Brakes leave THOS. COOK & SON'S office as above every Monday (for Sidi Ferruch and La Trappe), Wednesday (for Blidah and the Gorges de la Chiffa) and Friday (for Aïn-Taya and Cape Matifou) at inclusive fares, each excursion occupying a whole day.

Afternoon drives may also be arranged on any day, for parties of not less than six persons, to various points of interest in the neighbourhood; also **automobile** excursions (1 to 8 days), *see* p. 38. Excursions to the Kabylia district, and camping tours and shooting expeditions in the Sahara organised. Terms on application.

From Batna.

Tour I.—Batna to Timgad, 1 day, by carriage; visiting Lambessa on the way. At these two places very interesting Roman remains are to be seen, and are well worthy of a visit. The excavations are still progressing, and archæologists consider these ruins to be quite as interesting as those at Pompeii.

Tour 2.—Batna to Lambessa, half-day. If the traveller has not the time to visit Timgad, Lambessa is well worth a visit. The excursion can be done in two hours from Batna.

Tour 3.—Batna to Cedar Forests, half-day. These are situate in the Djebel Tougourt, the mountain to the north-west of Batna.

From Biskra.

Tour 1.—Biskra, Sidi Okba, and back to Biskra, by carriage; 1 day. This interesting excursion to the oasis, mosque, and shrine can be done comfortably in 1 day in a carriage, and ladies can undertake it.

Tour 2.—Biskra, Tougourt, and back to Biskra, 9 or 10 days' tour; by carriage, horse, mule or camel; 223 kilometres, 139 miles (*see* p. 242).

A visit to Temassin, the holy city, can be decided on at Tougourt. Temassin is one of the most beautiful oases of the desert. This trip will take 1 day more.

Tour 3.—Biskra, Tougourt, El Oued, Souf, and back, *via* Lakes to Biskra, 12 days' tour; by carriage, horse, mule, or camel. The exact itinerary of this tour cannot be given, as, according to the state of the weather and roads, one or another route may have to be taken.

Tour 4.—Biskra, Tougourt, Ouargla, the M'Zab district, and back to Biskra, 25-30 days' tour; by carriage. Itinerary indefinite for same reason as No. 3.

Tour 5.—Biskra, Ziban, Tolga, El Amri, and back to Biskra, 3 days' tour; by carriage or mule.

    1st Day.—Depart Biskra 7.0 a.m. Sleep at Tolga.

    2nd Day.—Visit El Amri and return to Tolga. (Sleep.)

    3rd Day.—Return to Biskra.

Tour 6.—Biskra to Batna (single). Visiting Mount Aures, 4 days' tour; by carriage.

From Blidah.

Tour 1.—Blidah, Ruisseau des Singes, and back to Blidah, 1 day tour.

Tour 2.—Blidah, Tombeau de la Chrétienne, and back to Blidah, 1 day tour. Interesting country and pretty scenery. The "Tombeau" is a monument of important historical interest.

Tour 3.—Blidah to Tipaza, 1 or 2 days' tour.

Tour 4.—Blidah to Cherchell and back. This excursion requires 2 days, but is not in the least fatiguing. Many and interesting Roman remains.

Tour 5.—Blidah to Hammam R'irha. This is a pleasant and interesting drive to the Thermal Baths of Hammam R'irha, far more pleasant than by train. Can be accomplished in 5 to 6 hours.

Tour 6.—Blidah to Coléa, Castiglione, Zéralda, Daouda.

Tour 7.—Blidah to Bains de Rovigo and back, 1 day.

Tour 8.—Blidah to Algiers, *viâ* Coléa or Boufarik, 1 day.

Tour 9.—Blidah to El-Aghouat (or Laghouat) and back, 25 days.

Tour 10.—Blidah to Médéa, 1 or 2 days.

From **Bougie**.

Tour 1.—Bougie to Setif (single) by landau or calèche, 1 or 2 days. Fine view of the Chabet Pass. Or the excursion may be taken in the reverse direction, from Setif to Bougie (*see* below).

From **Miliana**.

Tour 1.—Milianah to Teniet-el-Haâd, 3 days.

Tour 2.—Milianah to Hammam R'irha, or *vice versâ*, 1 day.

Tour 3.—Milianah to Adelia, or *vice versâ*, 1 day.

Tour 4.—Milianah to Affreville, or *vice versâ*, 1 day.

From **Setif**.

Tour 1.—Setif to Bougie (single), by landau or calèche, 1 or 2 days. For travellers coming from Constantine, the visit of the El-Chabet Pass must be made from this point when desiring to see Bougie at the same time, but the finer view is obtained when starting from Bougie (*see* above).

CARRIAGE TOURS AND EXCURSIONS.

Tour 2.—Setif to Kerrata and back; by landau or calèche, 1 or 2 days. For travellers not having time to go to Bougie, and from thence over the Chabet Pass, same can be comfortably visited from Setif on the main line between Algiers and Constantine.

From **Teniet-el-Haâd.**

Tour 1.—Teniet-el-Haâd to the Forest and back, half-day; by riding-horse (about 7 hours).

From **Tizi-Ouzou.**

Tour 1.—Tizi-Ouzou to Mekla, Djema Saharidj, and back to Tizi-Ouzou, 1 day tour. These are villages absolutely in the interior of Kabylia, and composed entirely of natives. Pretty and interesting.

Tour 2.—Tizi-Ouzou to Azazga and back, 1½ days' tour. A very pretty and curiously situated village, easy excursion from Tizi-Ouzou.

Tour 3.—Port Gueydon (Azeffoun) 1½ days' tour. Kabyle village situated on the sea-coast, composed almost entirely of fishermen. Fair accommodation to be had; clean. Roman Remains.

Tour 4.—Tizi-Ouzou to Fort National and back, 1 or 2 days. Fort National is in the heart of Kabylia. Here may be seen the villages where earthenware, pottery, and jewellery are manufactured. Here one gets an insight into real Kabylia life. The large market is held on Wednesdays.

Tour 5.—Tizi-Ouzou to Michelet (Djurdjura), 1 day. Some of the grandest mountain scenery in the whole of Algeria. An excursion to be made comfortably in one day from Tizi-Ouzou, taking in Fort National.

Tour 6.—Tizi-Ouzou to Maillot, or Tazmalt, 2 days. The grand pass of the Djurdjura. Sleep at Michelet. Maillot is the junction for Bougie on the East Algerian Railway. The Djurdjura Pass or Col de Tirourda is magnificent and vies with the Chabet Pass.

Tour 7.—Tizi-Ouzou to Mt. Bellona (Marabout) and back ; by mule, 2 hours. The Marabout is situated on the summit of a mountain, which is inhabited by Kabyles in their little mud huts. From Belloua are grand views of the whole of Kabylia, and on clear days Algiers may be distinctly seen.

From **Tlemçen.**

Tour 1.—Tlemçen to Ain Fezza, or *vice versâ*, 2 hours' journey.

Tour 2.—Tlemçen to Ain Temouchent, 1 day.

TWO SPECIMEN EXCURSIONS.

(For others apply to THOS. COOK & SONS, Algiers.)

I.

1st Day.—Leave Algiers early morning by rail for Tizi-Ouzou. Grand Hotel. In afternoon take mule drive to Sidi Belloua.

2nd Day.—Leave Tizi-Ouzou by private carriage about 8.0 a.m. Arrive Fort National 12.30 p.m. (Hôtel des Touristes) lunch, and continue drive to Michelet. Sleep at Hôtel des Touristes, Michelet.

3rd Day.—Make short excursion towards the Col de Tirourda and back before luncheon. In afternoon return to Fort National, sleep at Hôtel des Touristes.

4th Day.—Drive to Azazga (Hôtel Gebhard), lunching at Fréha (or leave Fort National after lunch direct for Azazga).

5th Day.—Drive to El K'seur (on the line from Beni Mansour to Bougie), lunching at Taourirt-Ighil (Hôtel Lambert), thence train to Bougie. Hôtel de France.

6th Day.—Rest in Bougie.

7th Day.—Private carriage to Kerrata, through the famous Gorges du Chabet-el-Akhra. Hôtel du Chabet.

8th Day.—Continue to Setif by carriage. Hôtel de France.

9th Day.—Leave Setif by rail for Algiers.

The above excursion includes the principal districts of Kabylia.

II.

1st Day.—Leave Algiers by train for Tizi-Ouzou. Lunch at Grand Hotel. In afternoon drive to Michelet (Hôtel des Touristes) *viâ* Fort National.

2nd Day.—Leave Michelet for short excursion towards the Col de Tirourda and back to lunch. In afternoon drive back to Fort National (Hôtel des Touristes).

3rd Day.—Leave Fort National by carriage for Azazga (lunching at Fréha). Hôtel Gebhard, sleep.

4th Day.—Leave Azazga very early, passing by way of the Forest of Yakouren for El K'seur (lunching at Taourirt-Ighil, Hôtel Lambert) in time to catch the train for Bougie. Hôtel de France.

5th Day.—Rest in Bougie. Excursion to Cap Carbon, or other carriage drive.

6th Day.—Leave early by carriage *viâ* the beautiful Gorges du Chabet-el-Akhra for Kerrata. Hôtel du Chabet.

7th Day.—Leave early by carriage for Setif, lunch at Amoucha, and take the last train (about 4.21 p.m.) for El Guerrah. Hôtel Guerrah.

8th Day.—Leave by train for Biskra (lunching at Batna). Royal Hotel, Hotel Victoria or Palace Hotel.

9th Day.—Rest in Biskra. In afternoon take drive to Chetma Oasis.

10th Day.—Day's excursion to Sidi Okba and back.

11th Day.—Drive to the Dunes during the morning. In afternoon take tram drive to the Hot Springs.

12th Day.—Drive to Old Biskra, visit the Jardin Landon and its charming grounds.

13th Day.—Leave for Batna. Hôtel des Étrangers et Continental.

14th Day.—Leave about 8.0 a.m. by carriage or motor-car for Timgad (lunch), *via* Lambessa, and return.

15th Day.—Leave Batna for Constantine. Grand Hotel, Hôtel St. Georges, or Hôtel de Paris.

16th Day.—In Constantine. Visit the Gorges du Rummel Chemin des Touristes, etc.

17th Day.—Leave Constantine early in morning. Lunch at Guelma. Change trains at Duvivier (restaurant-car). Customs at Ghrardimaou. Arrive Tunis about 10.39 p.m. Tunisia Palace Hotel, Grand Hotel, Hôtel de Paris, Hôtel de France. Passengers may break the journey at Hammam-Meskoutine (between Constantine and Guelma), and stay there the night.

18th Day.—In Tunis. Visit the Souks and Arab quarters of the town, the Casbah, Dar-el-Bey, etc. (Hotel supplies guide.) Drive to the Belvedere.

19th Day.—Excursion to Carthage.

20th Day.—Rest in Tunis. Carriage drive to the Bardo.

The above is for a three weeks' Tour, Algeria to Tunis. Other Tours for a shorter or longer time can be easily arranged on application.

COOK'S CONDUCTED TOURS TO ALGERIA AND TUNISIA,

LEAVING LONDON AT INTERVALS DURING THE SEASON.

Including Paris, Marseilles, Tunis, Carthage, Kairouan, Hammam-Meskoutine, Constantine, Biskra, Sidi Okba, Batna, the ruins of Timgad and Lambessa, Setif, Kerrata, Gorges du Chabet, Bougie, excursion by carriage through the Kabylia district, Azazga, Fort National, Tizi-Ouzou, Algiers, etc. Thirty-one days' tour. First-class throughout, including first-class travelling tickets, hotel accommodation, carriage drives and excursions, conveyance between stations and hotels, fees to hotels and railway servants, etc., and the services of a competent conductor.

SHORT SEA ROUTE.

Compagnie Transatlantique.

MAIL SERVICE BETWEEN ALGIERS AND MARSEILLES,
and *vice versâ*.

Marseilles to Algiers.—Departures every Monday, Wednesday, Thursday (slower service), and Saturday, at 1 p.m. Arriving at Algiers next day, between 3 and 5 p.m.; Thursday's boat arrives on Friday about 8 p.m.

Algiers to Marseilles.— Departures from Algiers every Monday at 3.30 p.m., and every Tuesday, Thursday, and Saturday at 12.30 p.m. Arriving at Marseilles between 2.30 p.m. and 4.30 p.m. next day; Monday's boat next day at about 10.30 p.m.

Compagnie de Navigation Mixte (Touache).

Marseilles to Algiers (Rapide). — Departure every Tuesday and Thursday at 6 p.m. Arriving at Algiers on Thursday about 6 a.m., and Friday about midnight.

Algiers to Marseilles.—Departure every Friday and Sunday at noon. Arriving at Marseilles, Saturday about midnight, and Monday about 8 p.m.

There is also a weekly departure from Cette, calling at Port Vendres, as follows: From **Cette**, Saturday midnight, due at **Algiers**, Monday about 6 p.m.; from **Algiers** noon Wednesday, *viâ* Port Vendres, due at **Cette** Thursday night.

Société de Transports Maritimes à Vapeur.

Marseilles to Algiers. — Departure Wednesday and Saturday 6 p.m. Arrive Friday and Monday about 6 a.m.

Algiers to Marseilles. -— Departure Wednesday and Saturday 6 p.m. Arrive Friday and Monday about 6 a.m.

Time tables subject to alteration.

D 2

ALGIERS.

"Mon enfant c'est Alger! C'est la terre promise
Dont je t'appris petite à bégayer le nom!
Son image qu'au fond du cœur je t'avais mise
Etait-cc la chimère au poëte permise
Et t'avais-je trompée?
                          Elle répondit
                                         —Non!

Cet hiver enchanteur, cette Cité prospère,
Ces verts coteaux, ces fleurs, cet azur, les voici!
La douce voix d'en haut qui veut que l'on espère
Je l'entends dans mon cœur . . . . Tu disais vrai mon père,
Et s'il est quelque part, le bonheur est ici!"

                                         MARIE LEFEBVRE.

Algiers (in Arabic **El Djezair**), is the ancient **Icosium** of the Romans, now the capital city of Algeria. It is situated in 36° 49′ N. latitude by 3° 35′ longitude E. of Greenwich. It was first built by Yousuf Zeri, about 935. This Yousuf Zeri was an Arabian chief of the Zerite dynasty, which succeeded that of Agheb in the sovereignty of the country. Algiers has the shape of an irregular triangle, of which one side is formed by the sea coast, and the other two run up a steep hill, which faces the north and the north-east. The houses rise gradually, one above the other, on the declivity of this hill, so that there is scarcely one that has not a view of the sea from its terrace.

The **Town** is divided into two distinct quarters—the old and the modern town.

The **Native Quarter,** or the old town, is chiefly populated with Arabs and Jews. It extends from the streets which form the basis of modern Algiers up to the Casbah, the old palace of the Deys of Algiers. The streets are very narrow and irregular, and the houses are so near to each other from one side to the other of the street, that it is sometimes hardly wide enough for a person to pass through. The houses are nearly all painted white or pale blue, and very closely resemble each other, the only apparent distinction being the carvings of the street door, and the more or less elaborately carved marble or stone of the arcade encircling the door. The Moorish houses are airy and cool, and all have an open square court inside, surrounded on the

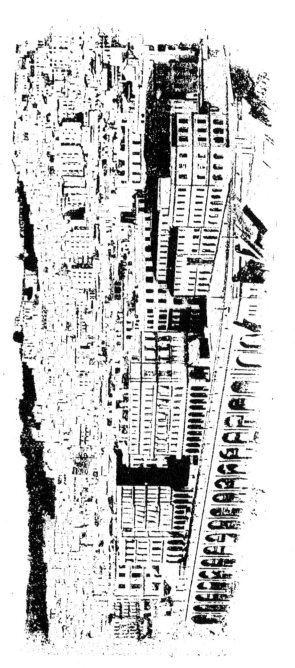

ALGIERS FROM THE SEA.

four sides by a gallery of arcades, with pillars supporting the
upper gallery. The private apartments are situated on the
floor above, which is similar to the basement, the only difference being that the gallery round is encircled by a balustrade of
elegantly carved wood, just high enough to allow a person to
lean on. All the houses are flat-roofed, and the tops round
the central court (which is an open-air yard) are used as
terraces, especially for the private exercise of the women.
These seldom leave the house, at least never during the year
following immediately their marriage. In ordinary times
their peregrinations outside their dwellings are confined to the
Moorish baths, and very limited visits to parents and sick
members of the family. Moorish women, although strictly
secluded from the outside world, are very freely accessible to
ladies of other nationalities.

There are many loungers and so-called Arab guides hanging
about the hotels, to entice visitors into putting so many francs
a head to get up a Derba in the Kattaroudjil. Tourists who
wish to enjoy a Mauresque fandango, should secure a respectable guide to take them **Chez Fathma**. This Fathma is
actually the professional beauty of Algiers. When she is no
more, there will be another one to take her place, for the
post of **Belle Fathma** is pretty nearly hereditary in Algiers.
She lives in a very quaint and genuine Moorish house, and is
said to be very wealthy. She carries an enormous amount of
jewellery, and goes about veiled the same as the respectable
Moorish ladies, but you may detect her by her white leather
shoes. She is, in fact, a personage. She boasts of presents
and jewels given to her by many an illustrious guest. She
condescends to offer coffee to visitors, and unveils herself in
her private apartments.

"The houses of old El Djezair," says Augustus Sala, "are
as white as brand-new dice, and the little peepholes of
windows in them stand for the pips. I question if there ever
lived such a nation of inveterate whitewashers as the modern
Moors, who have been incited, perhaps, to a profusion in the
use of the double-tie brush by their French masters. Inside,
as well as outside, the Moorish dwellings are thickly covered
with glaring white distemper paint. At least six times a year
every wall and every ceiling are whitewashed: to the horror
and despair, one would think, of the fleas. The Moors white-
wash their inner courts and living rooms persistently, often
to the concealment, beneath heavy layers of body colour, of

the most exquisitely beautiful sculpture and tracery, the work of less enlightened but non-whitewashing ages.

" Algiers is not only a healthy resort for the consumptive and for the dyspeptic, but there is not a healthier, brighter place between the Gut of Gibraltar and the Dardanelles, and though the number of English tourists is yearly increasing, the colony residentiary of our countrymen ought to increase in equal proportions. There are charming villas, handsome hotels, new, cheap, and scrupulously clean, waiting for English patronage ; there is a fund of amusement for idlers, of sketching ground for artists, of materials for study and research, for linguists and archæologists. The country is crammed with Roman relics. There is the East, again—the sunshiny, mysterious, dreamy East—as glowing and picturesque as you could wish to have it, but swept and garnished and kept in order by an efficient police and a large European garrison. And all within three days' journey from Charing Cross! Nothing can be more comfortable than the railway from Paris to Marseilles. The steamers of the Transatlantique Company are swift and serviceable, the journey across the Mediterranean occupying less than thirty hours ; the arrangements on board are admirable. The Custom House officers at Algiers, when you produce the keys of your trunks, make you a low bow, and dispense with the ceremony of examining your luggage ; there is nobody to worry you about passports ; the Arabs have been too well disciplined by the French to bother you for backsheesh. The city is well drained and well lighted with gas. The sirocco does not blow oftener than once a month, and the locusts and grasshoppers don't ravage the country more than once in two years. It is never too warm and never too cold. Food is cheap, vegetables and fruit abundant."

" The **streets** in the old quarter are a continual subject of observation. The contrast of the French and Arab element creates a perpetual interest—the Frenchman is good humoured, eager, full of bustle and expectancy, as if he thought Fortune might be just round the next corner ; and the son of the desert strides by with clear-cut face, full of passion and character, yet with no sign of life, as if he thought that Fate was coming to meet him, and that it was unnecessary to hasten a step to find her. Our civilisation seems a frivolous thing of yesterday when you meet those deep-set Arab eyes, that look at you as if nothing temporal was of moment to those who learn in the desert to 'see life steadily.' No doubt this

modern Lazarus is as keen a hand at a bargain, and by
no means above the minor immoralities, but his ancestors
'walk' in him—he inherits the stamp of 'Kismet,' and
the Forty Thieves, to be met with in every street, have the
eyes and face which, if all had their rights, belong to the
first warriors of the Prophet.

"The streets seem a curious rendezvous for Old Testament
patriarchs and the actors in the Arabian Nights; the idlers on
the floor of the Moorish café, over their coffee and draughts,
group themselves like a picture of Joseph's Brethren; it might
be Abraham or Isaac who is driving the flock of brown goats
and asses which push you off the pavement. You turn up
some steep alley with the houses meeting overhead, and some
lovely old brass-worked door opens, and Morgiana flits out,
veiled in white, with her copper water jar on her shoulder,
giving you a momentary glimpse of cool courtyards with
slender pillars and bright tiles. Across the sunlit opening at
the top of the alley passes a slim, handsome boy, all in
white except for a long soft mantle of grass green, the colour
of Mahommed, as of Thomas the Rhymer. Then you meet
a Jewess in her black skull cap, and then a dandy in
slashed blue satin over a gold vest. It is quite a relief
to turn out of the sunshine into the solemn gloom of the
mosque, where the only sound is the nasal monotonous chant
of the reader, or the plashing of the fountain in the courtyard.

"The intensity and reverence of Abraham's prayer seem to
live again as you watch these fifty or sixty business men
praying in business hours; had it been some all-important
commercial transaction each man could not have seemed more
impressed with the intense importance to himself, personally,
of how he spent his time there. Perhaps there still lingered
something of the spirit of the great Arab teacher, **Malek**, who
used to pray in that Mosque 800 years ago. The story says a
list of forty questions was given to him one day, and to thirty-
eight of them he replied, 'I do not know.' The comment of
his Moorish biographer, who records his immense learning, is,
'that only a man who cared more for God's glory than his
own would have confessed to so much ignorance.' He wept
on his death-bed, to the surprise of his disciples, who knew his
holy life, and he explained his grief by saying, 'Would that
I could now receive stripes for every decision which I have
given according to my own opinion; I could then better meet
my God.'"

The **Environs of Algiers** (fully described further on)
are some of them very beautiful and enjoyable, especially
those of which **Mustapha Supérieur** and **El Biar** may
be considered the centres. Well supplied with furnished or
unfurnished villas and hotels situated in gardens gay with
orange, lemon, and banana trees, or with flowers of various
kinds, and favoured with lovely views of sea and mountain,
they are very popular with English or American families

ARAB COMMENCING PRAYER.

passing the winter in Algiers. Good roads for walking or
driving lead to villages and rural retreats through country
lanes whose hedges are clothed in creepers, roses, honeysuckle,
and blue bells, mingled with aloes and cacti.

The **Arab Restaurants** have this difference compared with
the European establishments of similar kind, that it is the
kitchen that is exposed to public view, while the dining-
room is hidden by a piece of material hanging from a bamboo

pole.   Behind the screen the *couscous* is absorbed in large quantities, and in Rhamadan time, all sorts of cakes and sweetmeats are added to the otherwise uniform menu. This *couscous* is the national dish.   It consists of semolina and water, cooked by steam, and has very much the appearance of raw tapioca.   As for the national drink of the Arabs, it ought to be water, according to the prescription of the Koran, but it is very often replaced by absinthe, aniseed, and other alcoholic beverages.   For the faithful, milk is indulged in during holiday time, especially at Rhamadan, when every Mohammedan is supposed to become pious.

The **Rhamadan,** or Mussulman Lent, is the severest of fasting Lents, as it adds the most complete abstinence to the most absolute continence.   That is, during thirty days the good Mussulman is forbidden to eat, drink, or smoke from sunrise to sunset.

True, the faithful indiscriminately make up for loss of time during the night, and sometimes go beyond the limits of good living, but Allah is great, and Mohammed is more than ever His prophet.   Paradise, with its streams of milk, its shady palm trees, and fascinating houris await them ; for paradise has not been created for the use of Christian miscreants who eat at fixed hours and walk not in Moslem paths.   The Mussulman who falls a victim to his religious zeal and the sacred precepts of the Koran, will smoke in paradise the golden *chebli* in an enchanted pipe, lighted for him by a black-eyed Khadidja.

The **Arab Cafés, or Cafés Maures,** are there in a majority.   The **Café Maure** consists of a narrow room, a few benches and mats, and a cooking-stove, round which a few coffee-pots and cups are hung.   The walls are decorated with very ordinary chromos, and some Koran maxims imprisoned in capricious arabesques, lions, or fantastical Ottoman fleets, or some City of the Arabian Nights, abounding with cupolas and minarets.   Here, hanging from a colossal nail, a tiny little mirror, and there, a little bird in its cage ; on some brackets, miniature **hachish** pipes, awaiting the smokers of *keef*.   The stove, continually lighted, throws out an unbearable heat ; the customers for that reason take their coffee outside in the street, on stools, benches, or more commonly on mats that are spread on the ground against the café, or on the opposite side of the street, if there be a bare wall. Each café possesses special clients. One is patronised solely by Moors from Morocco, the other receives the water-carriers, generally Kabyles from Biskra. Another is especially affected to the use of fishermen. There are some others which are frequented by veteran soldiers, invalids from the corps of Spahis and Turcos, living on their pensions. Many Arabs, for the most part workmen, end there their day's work.

Numbers of these Arab workmen possess neither roof nor family. Their chief resort is the Arab café, which constitutes their home. They bring a few onions and a piece of bread, and delight in a jugful of water, after which they drink a solitary cup of coffee, and deliver to Allah a prayer of praise and thankfulness. When night sets in they wrap themselves up in their burnous (if they possess any) and sleep on the vacant benches, or if it be summer, on the mats outside in the street.

In the **Shops** behind the Rue Bab-Azoun and the Rue Bab-el-Oued, leading up to the old town, and in the native quarter itself, all kinds of Arab specialities may be seen in course of manufacture. One man will be hammering a design on copper or brass vessels; another will be embroidering ladies' slippers or men's waistcoats. In one " hole in the wall " the shoemaker will be turning out coloured leather slippers, which are slippers indeed; in another the working jeweller will be busy making earrings, or rings or brooches with his gold and silver thread or wire. Other shops abound, offering to the visitor a sight of very novel interest. Nothing in these dark and narrow recesses, in these tortuous streets bordered by mysterious Arab homes, recalls to the mind the European town of Algiers, and one might easily fancy himself a thousand leagues away from Europe, although Algiers is but forty-two hours from Paris and fifty-one hours from London. The streets in the old town worth a visit are the Rues du Chameau, Médée, Des Maugrebins, Ben Ali, Des Sarrasins, Des Abencerrages, De la Casbah, Porte Neuve, De la Gazelle, Sidney Smith, Des Abderrames, Staouéli, Du 4 Septembre, Sophonisbe, Akermimouth, Lalahoum, Sidi Ferruch, De la Giraffe, Sidi Abdalla, Des Pyramides, Sidi Hallel, Heliopolis, De la Grenade, Des Janissaires, Kattaroudjil, Du Locdor, Sidi Ramdan, Des Pithyses, Du Sphinx, Tombouctou, Lahemar, and du Scorpion.

Contrary to the general opinion of the visitors, the Casbah,

or Arab quarter of Algiers, is perfectly safe in every respect in the daytime, and anyone might venture through
its various labyrinths without any fear for his own safety.
However, an inspection of the Casbah at night should only
be attempted by a party of men. One or two buildings in
the Arab quarter deserve a cursory inspection, such as the
old mosque of **Djama Sidi Ramdan** in the Rue Sidi
Ramdan, the mosque of **Djama Safir,** in the Rue Kléber,
and the two Arab schools which are held in the mosques of
Djama Sidi Bou Gueddour and **Djama Sidi Abdallah**.

The **Old Town** of Algiers has not suffered any great
changes since the days of the Turkish domination. The dirty
lanes are pretty much as they were, save in so far as the
French and foreign element has penetrated. Four large
mosques are left, but the many bagnios have disappeared. One
was near the Admiralty, in the barracks now occupied by the
artillery, called **Jetée Khair ed-Din**; another somewhere in
the Rue d'Etat Major, in one of the dependencies of the
Djenina, or Bey's palace and Government offices; another
at the Bab-Azoun Gate, near the Fort. A propos of these
bagnios, there is an interesting story of a Spaniard's imprison-
ment in and escape from Algiers in Chapters XXXIX–XLI,
Part I, of Don Quixote. Dr. Shaw, who was chaplain to the
British factory at Algiers about the beginning of the eighteenth
century, and who, of course, saw the place as it then stood,
gives the following description of it :—

"This place, which, for several ages, has braved the
greatest Powers of Christendom, is not above a mile and a
half in circuit, though it is computed to contain about 2,000
Christian slaves, 15,000 Jews, and 100,000 Mohammedans,
of which thirty at most may be renegadoes. It is situated
upon the declivity of a hill that faces the north and north-
east. The walls are weak, and of little defence, unless
they are further secured, chiefly at the gates, by some additional fortifications. The Casbah, or citadel, built upon the
highest part of the city, toward the south-west, is of an
octagonal figure, each of the sides in view having port-holes,
or embrasures, defended with cannon. A ditch formerly surrounded the city to the landward, which is at present almost
entirely filled up, except at the west and south gates, where
it is still of little consequence for defence. But towards the
sea it is better fortified ; the embrasures in this direction are

all employed; the guns are of brass, and their carriages and other utensils in good order. The battery of the Mole Gate, upon the east angle of the city, is mounted with several long pieces of ordnance, one of which has seven cylinders, each of them three inches in diameter. Half a furlong to the west-south-west of the harbour is the battery of Fisher's Gate, or the Gate of the Sea, which, consisting of a double row of cannon, commands the entrance to the port and the road before it.

"The port itself is of an oblong figure, a hundred and thirty fathoms long, and eighty broad. The eastern mound of it, which was formerly the island which gave the name to the city, is well secured by several fortifications. The Round Castle, built by the Spaniards whilst they were masters of the island, and the two remote batteries erected within this century, are said to be bomb-proof, and have each of them their lower embrasures mounted with 36-pounders. But the middle battery, which appears to be the oldest, is of the least defence. Yet none of these fortifications are assisted with mines or advanced works; and as the soldiers who are to guard and defend them cannot be kept to any regular course of duty and attendance, a few resolute battalions, protected by a small squadron of ships, would find little difficulty to take them.

"The hills and valleys round about Algiers are all over beautiful with gardens and country-seats, whither the inhabitants of better fashion retire during the summer season. They are little white houses, shaded with a variety of fruit-trees and evergreens, which, besides the shade and retirement, afford a gay and delightful prospect towards the sea. The gardens are all of them well stocked with fruits of every kind, and enjoy a considerable command of water from the many rivulets and fountains which everywhere abound in this station. The water made use of at Algiers is universally esteemed."

The **Casbah** or **Citadel** is the old palace of the Governors or Deys of Algiers, and was defended by 200 guns. These Deys, as is well known, were invested with the governorship by the "Porte," and in spite of their allegiance to the Ottoman sovereignty, they were almost all of them pretty nearly independent. In fact, the Porte was often content with investing with the Imperial Firman the Governor who was elected, by way of terrorism and usurpa-tion by the followers of the Usurper.

This Casbah, in the good old days of Algerian predomi-nance, was a magnificent palace fitted with all the luxury and refinement of the epoch. The palace was used for general Government offices, as well as for the Courts of Justice. Some parts of it were affected to Inquisition rooms, others to State prisons. A separate building was reserved for the Dey's harem and household.

The whole building was enclosed with magnificent gardens, and a mighty wall encircling it overlooking the " White City " and all its lovely surroundings. To-day the road connecting the Rue Rovigo with the Rampe Valée, cuts through the gardens and streets of the old Casbah, and entirely separates the palace from the town. The Casbah is now being used as barracks for a regiment of artillery, and its lofty and spacious council rooms have seen themselves trans-formed into mere *Cantines*. The place, however, is worth a careful inspection, as most of its principal structure remains untouched and in a very good state of preservation, the outer walls being two metres in thickness.

Indeed, the military authorities have gone so far as to repair some of its finest halls and have taken great pains to preserve their authentic aspect. In the Casbah can be noticed many very fine specimens of Arabic painting and engraving, some of the marble inscriptions being worth any amount of money. There are rooms which have remained almost as new as if they had only been finished a year or two back. The ceiling of the State room is a marvellous work of art, and the *patios*, or central yards of some minor buildings belonging to the original palace, are real gems of the kind, with their gracefully twisted marble pillars and arched galleries of pure Moorish design. The Casbah is worth a good afternoon's inspection, as it is one of the few historical and instructive buildings that the French conquest has respected.

On the right-hand side of the entrance inside the Citadel is the pavilion where the celebrated " episode of the fan " took place between the Dey of Algiers and the French Consul (April 30, 1827), which ultimately brought about the conquest of Algiers by the French. In the central court of the Casbah, on the right of the large entrance gate, is a room with a magnificently painted ceiling; this was the throne room where the Dey held his assizes. A chain is suspended right across; on this chain used to be exposed the heads of the beheaded Christian and other slaves for twenty-four hours, then the chain was lowered, the heads unfastened, and the Turkish soldiery indulged in some football distraction with these bloody relics. From the terrace of the Casbah can be enjoyed a splendid view of the Bay of Algiers, harbour, the Cape Matifou, and mountains of Kabylia.

Lower down the road still, on the right-hand side from the Casbah, is the celebrated

Mosque of Sidi Abd el-Rahman et Thalebi; this build ing overlooks the **Jardin Marengo.** In the mosque can be seen the tombs of the former Deys and Pashas of Algiers, including that of the venerated **St. Sidi Abd el Rahman,** who was buried in 1741; also that of **Ahmed,** the last Dey of Constantine, and **Khader Pasha.**

The Casbah standing as it does at the very top of the old town, a portion of the Arab quarter must be passed through to reach it, so that it is quite convenient to combine a ramble through the old town with a visit to the Casbah. It is not absolutely necessary to take a guide, but the narrow streets and alleys are so bewildering it is advisable to engage a competent guide from Cook's Office. or from the hotel.

Cards for visiting the Casbah can be obtained on application to the office of the *Etat-Major*, 11, Rue de la Marine.

The most interesting quarter after the Casbah is decidedly the **Admiralty,** and the two large mosques of Algiers, the **Djama el Djedid** and the **Djama el Kebir.**

The **Inner Harbour of Algiers,** constructed by Christian slaves under the reign of Khair-ed-din in 1518, is the one situated between the Grecian-looking establishment of the **Direction du Port** and the mole on which stands the lighthouse of the **Peñon.** This lighthouse was built under the reign of Hassan Pasha in 1544, on the old Spanish fortress. The marvellous doorway in the building called the **Bureau de la Marine,** is an exquisite work of the seventeenth century, one of the rare specimens of Arab art which have been preserved in Algiers. It is carved out of white marble, and bears Arab inscriptions and tigers, coloured in red, green, and blue. These tigers are all the more wonderful, for the Mohammedan laws forbid the reproduction of

ALGIERS INNER HARBOUR AND LIGHTHOUSE.

living species of animals and human beings. It is explained in this way : that the carver was a Moslem of Persian creed, who decorated the arch as best he could, and once the work was finished it was found so beautiful that it was allowed to remain.

The house of the Turkish Raïs, or Commander of the Harbour (Captain Pasha), is a very interesting sketch for an artist, and is at present the dwelling of the French Admiral commanding the navy in Algiers. It is a perfect model of Arab architecture. The little fountain at the side is also equally artistic, bearing Arabic inscriptions most exquisitely carved in the whitest of marbles. It has preserved unto this day a *cachet local*, which excites the admiration of true artists. There were many fountains of this kind in Algiers, but they have been tampered with, most of them having been sold by the Direction of the Museum, together with many very valuable carved marble pillars, inscription plates, carved wooden doors, verandahs, moucharabiehs, etc. The damage done is deeply regretted, and in this case one must reverse the proverb and say, " *It is too late to mend.*"

The Mosque of **Djama el Djedid** (the new mosque), on the Place du Gouvernement, is built in the shape of a Grecian cross, with a large central cupola and four smaller ones. The entrance is from the Rue de la Marine. It was built in 1660. The interior is very plain, being bare and whitewashed, with straw matting on the floor and round the columns and walls to a height of about four feet. The minaret (square) tower with an illuminated clock is a hundred feet high. The mosque contains a magnificent manuscript of the Koran, a present of the Sultan to one of the Algerian Deys.

The Mosque of **Djama el Kebir** (the great mosque) is the most ancient of Algiers, and is said to have been built in the year 409 of Hedjira, or 1018 of the Christian era. The minaret of this mosque, which is at the corner of Rue de la Marine, was completed between Sunday, 27th Doul Kada, 722, and the 1st Redjeb, 722, according to an inscription near the staircase, by Tachfin, Sultan of Tlemçen. That places the date of this construction from October, 1322, to March, 1323. The mosque covers an area of 2,000 square metres. The interior is a large rectangular hall, divided into several smaller courts, arcaded and pillared. The floor is covered with straw matting, which is likewise fastened round

E

the pillars and the lower part of the walls. The appearance is rather bare, the only decoration being a few lamps and the **mimbar,** or pulpit for the imam. The exterior is far more handsome ; the façade in the Rue de la Marine presents a gallery of fourteen arcades, all of them exquisitely dented and supported by magnificent white marble pillars of about two feet in diameter. In the middle of the gallery a larger arcade discloses a magnificent black marble fountain, surrounded by a double row of arcades supported by pillars in pairs, Alhambra fashion. Badly damaged by the successive bombardments of the Christians, the mosque of **Djama el Kebir** has been partly reconstructed ; it is now affected to the worshippers of the Maleki rite.

The oldest religious order now existing in Algeria is the Mohammedan order of **Abd el Kader el Djelali,** better known as **Moulai Sidi Abd el Kader.** This saint was born at Bagdad, where he was interred, after having travelled a great deal. He is the patron of travellers, of thieves, and, above all, of beggars.

The **Mosque and Tomb of Sidi Abd er Rahman et Thalebi** (p. 63), near the Jardin Marengo, is open to Europeans on Monday, and Tuesday, from 8 a.m. to noon, and from 2 p.m. to 3 p.m. With the exception of the Djama el Kebir (p. 65) this is the oldest religious building in Algiers, and the oldest in Algeria except the *7th century tomb of Sidi Obka, near Biskra* (p. 244). The marabout Abd er Rahman et Thalebi was born in 1387, and died in 1471. The mosque was built between these dates, and contains his tomb, over which are hung silk banners, ostrich eggs, etc., and on which lights are kept burning.

At the top of the Rue Kléber in the old town is the

Djami Safir, a small mosque with roof supported by six marble columns ; but the interior is otherwise bare, with the exception of the mimbar and mirhab.

Close by, in the Rue Caton, is the

Djami Sidi-Abdullah, its minaret ornamented with old tiles. And in the Rue de Tanger is a mosque belonging to the tribe of the Beni M'zab.

The composition of the staff of a Mohammedan mosque is as follows :—

An **oukil,** manager of the funds and donations; a sort of collector and paymaster.

A **chaouch,** or assistant **oukil.**

An **imam,** or chaplain for the daily common prayers, which are five in number.

A **khetib,** who recites the prayer for the chief of the Government on the Friday of each week.

An **anoun,** who carries the sceptre of the **khetib.**

Two **muddenin** (plural for **mueddin**), who call the faithful to prayer from the top of the minarets.

Two **hezzabin,** readers of the Koran.

Two **tolbas** (plural for **taleb**), readers of litanies and religious commentaries.

And a **mufti,** interpreter of the law.

Many of the handsomest Moorish houses are used by the French as Government offices or public buildings. Some of these are real gems of Arab architecture. As a matter of fact, every stranger that visits Algiers takes the first opportunity to view the Archbishop's Palace, the Library, and the Governor's Palace. Besides these, there are other houses which deserve a thorough inspection. In this class may be noted the house occupied by the "**Conseil Général**" behind the Prefecture, No. 5, Rue de la Charte, and the fine building now occupied by the "**Commandant du Génie,**" on the Boulevard des Palmiers. This house, or more really a palace, although not a genuine Arab house from the time of the Turks, is nevertheless a marvel of magnificence. It presents from the outside the ordinary plain appearance of all Arab houses. But the interior is a fine illustration of native construction, and does honour to the French architect who built it. The "**Direction des Domaines**" furnished the "Engineer Authorities" with all the materials, and the valuable *débris* of the bombardment, such as old tiles, delicately carved banisters, finely chiselled iron gates, bolts, knockers, twisted marble arches, carved doors, and porticoes, etc. It is in fact built of the genuine materials of Arab make. The house is erected on some rocks outside the tracing of the Boulevard des Palmiers, the waves dashing furiously at its foundations, and on stormy days sometimes penetrating through the open windows.

The Moorish house of No. 5, Rue de la Charte is the only one in Algiers which has twisted marble pillars, all in one piece, that are undoubtedly of Moorish origin. Indeed, the house is genuinely Arab in every respect, and has undergone few repairs. There are no cards to be obtained for viewing these houses ; the best way to obtain admission is to apply privately or by letter to the "**Commandant du Génie Militaire**," Boulevard des Palmiers, for the one, and to the "**President du Conseil Général**," Rue de la Charte, for the other.

The islet on which the lighthouse of the harbour now stands is better known by the name of

The **Peñon**, and deserves a detailed description, being one of the chief historical buildings of the Algiers of the past that has remained untouched by the French. The interest attached to this very remarkable construction resides in its history, and is by no means exaggerated if one remembers that the present Peñon and its stony foundations are the same in every respect as stood in the time of the Turkish Dey, Khair ed Din. The tower which forms its basis is the old bastion of the fortress built by the Spaniards in 1510. The lighthouse and the present jetty connecting it to *terra firma* date from A.D. 1544. This lighthouse is the only construction that has preserved unto this day its original structure, together with the several Turkish buildings of the **Behira**, or inner harbour of Algiers. While all the Mosques and Arab palaces have either been screened by modern buildings, repaired or pulled down, this particular tower still displays its bold and graceful profile on the ever-changing shades of the turquoise sky of Algiers. Everything is surprising in this strange monument— its position, its shape. It is built on a circular platform, the original and only remains of the Spanish fortress, above the entrance of which can still be seen the coat of arms of Spain carved in the stonework. The whole edifice projects boldly into the sea, braving the fury of the waves and the north-westerly gales, the most dangerous on that part of the coast.

In olden times nothing, it must be remembered, existed on this part of the coast which characterised the work of man— neither tower, lighthouse, nor building of any sort. Nothing stood there but a few abandoned rocks, called **El Djezair** (the islands). The largest of these rocks, which was seized by the Spaniards in 1510, in the course of a dispute with the

Algerines, was utilised as a foundation for their fortress. It was one of the links of a long fortified chain that extended from **Melilla** to **Tripoli**, by way of **Oran, Cherchell, Algiers, Bougie, Bône,** and **Tunis.**

Soon after the conquest of Granada, Spain found herself obliged to carry the Holy War outside the radius of the Peninsula. The Moors that were driven out of Spain took refuge on the north coast of Africa, wherefrom they carried a piratic warfare most prejudicial to Spanish commercial and maritime interests. They made frequent raids on Valencia and Malaga, which they often pillaged, and carried away the inhabitants as slaves. To put an end to this unbearable situation, Cardinal Ximenes organised a powerful expedition, commanded by himself, and seized on the towns of Oran and Bougie, after desperate fighting. The fall of these two cities spread a great terror throughout the African world. The Algerines felt particularly uncomfortable, and commenced erecting huge batteries on the coast. It was then that the Spaniards, to keep an eye on their doings, seized the islet in front of Algiers, on which they built the **Peñon**. This was in 1510. The Algerines seem to have respected this fortress during nineteen years. It was not until the death of Ferdinand d'Aragon that they resolved on capturing the Spanish fort, which interfered greatly with their movements. Khair ed Din and his brother, Baba Aroudj, were entrusted with the siege operations, and soon life became unbearable for both the Spanish fort and Algiers. The Spaniards, hardly pressed, cannonaded the city, destroying the mosques, minarets, palaces, and houses. The enemy sometimes wishing to compromise, supplied the Spaniards with the necessary victuals At other times the Turks would brave the Spanish cannon, and the Peñon was reduced to very pitiable extremities, obliged to look to Spain for provisions. If the ships that bore the supplies were unfortunately seized by the Algerines, the garrison were deprived of shot, powder, food, and water, and obliged to undergo the greatest privations. Still, they held on; and this state of things lasted till the year 1529, when at last the most formidable preparations were set up by Khair ed Din to storm the fortress. During fifteen days an incessant and infernal fire was kept up by the Moorish batteries and flotilla, more than one hundred cannon battering the Peñon on all sides. The gallant little garrison of 150 men resisted during a fortnight the most terrific bombardment on record, besides supporting all kinds of hardships and privations. At last the Peñon was taken, and its commander, Martin de Vegas, and the twenty five survivors, were put to death. Khair ed Din pulled down the Spanish castle, and joined the fortress to the coast by a jetty; 20,000 Christian slaves were employed building it. On the only tower that was spared the present lighthouse was erected. The most formidable defensive works of the north coast of Africa were then constructed, and armed with a continual flow of cannon. During three centuries the Peñon protected the pirates, resisting the numerous attacks of the Christian fleets. Sometimes lost to view in the midst of the storm of battle, the Peñon disappeared in the smoke and the noise, to appear again after the fight, the high tower superbly gleaming in the azure sky as the insurmountable barrier separating the barbarian from the civilised world. The barrier has now been wiped off; civilisation has set its firm footing on the land of piracy, and transformed this nest of smugglers into the most hospitable of cities.

Both the **Library** (*see* p. 71), and **Museum** of Algiers, were formerly in the Rue de l'Etat Major, but the **Museum** has been transferred to Mustapha Supérieur, in a building on the main road nearly opposite the Governor-General's Summer Palace, and contains, amongst other valuable curiosities, the casting of **San Geronimo**, obtained by Mr. Latour from the original block of chalk in which that martyr was buried alive.

The **Odyssey of San Geronimo** is sufficiently known; but for those readers who should happen not to be acquainted with it, the following poetical account, by "A. O. M.," an anonymous poet of great talent, who has written a history of Geronimo's life, will give an idea of his captivity and martyrdom :—

> " In time of Spanish wars an Arab child
> Was captive taken from his native wild,
> When Christian people brought him to the font;
> Geronimo they called him, on his front,
> This infant forehead bore the sacred cross
> In pearly dross for weal, or care and loss.
> When but a child of eight he fell once more
> Into his parents' hands, for nigh a score
> Of years with them he lived, and then returned
> To Oran with a high resolve he burned

To live a Christian, who to Christ was brought,
And in the sacred precepts had been taught.
And yet, again, unchristian hands their prey
Seized, and in pirate vessel fast away
They carried him as slave to Algiers' strand.
That nest of pirates and accursèd land.
No power of word or threat could change the Saint
From his resolve. No words of mine can paint
The horrors of his death, when, flung away,
Into a block of concrete there he lay,
And his firm spirit braved the martyr's death
And won the palm branch and the martyr's wreath,
Amid the jewels of his Father's store
He shines a glittering star for evermore."

A. O. M.

There are many pieces of ancient sculpture in the Museum, statues, sarcophagi, mosaics, also pottery, bronzes, enamel vases, tiles, etc., medals and coins, many of them in gold. There is also a complete collection of Algerian coins, and the Chkoti collection of coins used by the French Company of Bône in its transaction with the Arabs. The *chkoti* was nothing else than a Spanish piastre, cut in different sizes, corresponding to the different weights and values of the *rial-boujdou*, the standard monetary coin of the Algerine Government. Open free every day except Monday, from 2 p.m. to 5 p.m. in summer; and 1 p.m. to 4 p.m. in winter. Catalogue.

The **Library**, Rue de l'Etat Major (Bibliothèque Nationale d'Alger), is in a palace erected in 1799 for Mustapha Pacha, who was murdered in the Mosque of the Djenina, in 1806. The Library contains 35,000 volumes, and a considerable number of Arab, Turkish, and Persian manuscripts. Open daily 1 p.m. to 6 p.m., except Sunday and fête days.

The **Governor-General's Winter Palace** is open to the public every day, in the absence of the Governor-Général, on presentation of card (*see* p. 39). The real entrance of the palace was in the Rue du Soudan; the entrance and façade are now in the Place du Gouverneur. It needs hardly any description, all the interest residing in the richness of the decorations. The entire front of the building on the Place Malakoff was constructed by the *génie militaire*, thus adding considerably to the old palace of Hassen Pacha.

The **Archbishop's Palace**, opposite the Governor's Palace, is the finest Moorish palace now in existence in Algiers. Can be visited; small fee to attendant. It was formerly the residence of the Sultan's daughter (Dar Bent el Sultan).

The old **Secrétariat du Gouvernement**, the former residence of **Ahmed Pasha**, was part of the celebrated **Djenina**, or old palace of the Deys of Algiers. This **Djenina** extended from the building now occupied by the Post Office, on the Place du Gouvernement, up to the Rue Socgémah, including all the buildings right and left of the Rue Bruce, the beautiful house now occupied by the First President of the Court of Appeal in the Rue Socgémah, the house of **Mustapha Pasha** in the Rue d'Etat Major, No. 12, lately occupied by the Museum (now removed to Mustapha), and Library and several other buildings of less importance.

The **Cathedral**, which was formerly a mosque, is situated in the Place du Gouverneur, next to the Palace of the Governor of Algeria. It has undergone very extensive repairs, and ranks now as one of the most conspicuous buildings in Algiers. A handsome flight of steps leads up to the front entrance and its magnificent arched doorway, crowned by two high towers. The interior is a large arched hall, supported by marble pillars in the Oriental style. Some devices of the Koran, in gold letters painted on a black ground, are perceptible round the cupola over the high altar, which is turned towards the *west*.

In the chapel on the right-hand side on entering is the white marble tomb containing the bones of St. Geronimo. The fort in which Geronimo suffered martyrdom in 1569 was demolished in . 1853, and among the ruins in a block of concrete the skeleton of Geronimo was found. The bones were collected, and removed to the Cathedral. A perfect model of the body was taken from the mould in which it lay so long, and this model may be seen in the Museum at Mustapha Supérieur. (*See* p. 70.)

The **modern**, or **French town**, is very handsome and imposing, looking from the sea, but in reality it resembles any modern European city in its general appearance, although most of the principal streets are lined with arcaded houses.

Directly facing the harbour are the palatial houses of the Boulevard de la République, built on arches 40 feet above the quays and the railway, which are reached by inclined roads skilfully constructed. This great work was carried out by Sir Morton Peto between 1860 and 1866, and the whole of it, including the inclined roads, quays, vaults, and warehouses, was conceded by the City of Algiers to an English company—The Algiers Land and Warehouses Company Limited—in

1863, for a term of ninety-nine years. There exists certainly no finer street in any seaport town of Europe than this magnificent boulevard, which excites the admiration of all new-comers.

It is intended to continue this broad thoroughfare westward past the Porte de France and along the sea coast. To the eastward beyond the Square de la République fine blocks of houses and public buildings have sprung up of late years, and building operations on a large scale are still going on.

Close by the west end of the Boulevard de la République is the principal square, ´

The **Place du Gouvernement**, a large, badly-paved and kept space, with double rows of plane trees on three sides, surrounded by mosques, hotels, and cafés, and the great central point for the departure and arrival of the many electric car services.

On the north side of the square is the New Mosque (Djama el Djedid), the entrance to which is from the steps leading down to the fish market Close by, in the Rue de la Marine, is the Grand Mosque (Djama el Kebir). The west side of the square is occupied by the old-established Hôtel de la Régence, in front of which, surrounded by clumps of palms and bamboos, the flower market is held daily.

An equestrian bronze statue (erected 1845) of the Duke of Orleans, former Governor of Algeria, stands in the centre of the square. This statue is the work of Marochetti; it was cast out of the cannon taken from the Arabs at the conquest of Algiers.

The excellent band of one of the Zouave regiments performs on the Place du Gouvernement in winter twice a week, on Thursdays and Sundays, in the afternoon, generally from 3 till 5 (weather permitting). But the time is subject to alteration according to the length of the days.

The **Rues Bab=Azoun and Bab=el=Oued** start from the Place du Gouvernement, south side, in exactly opposite directions.

The **Rue Bab=Azoun** is THE fashionable street of Algiers; it contains the finest shops, and is the habitual promenade of the Algerian population.

The **Boulevard de la République** is the handsomest and best situated thoroughfare of Algiers. The architecture of its lofty, solid buildings, containing palatial banks, hotels, and shops, compares favourably with the best Paris boulevards.   It has cost the city of Algiers, together with the harbour, quays, &c., two hundred million francs (eight millions sterling).

The **Square de la République** (late Square Bresson) is a garden of recent construction; it is situated between the Place de la République and the Boulevard de la République, overlooking the sea; in the garden, planted with many species of trees of wild Algeria and the Far East, is a bandstand, where concerts are given occasionally.

The **Municipal Theatre** stands opposite this square, in the most central situation.   It is a very spacious and elegant building, fitted with the latest theatrical appliances and machinery, and affords the greatest facility of egress in case of fire.   The *troupes* are generally well selected, as the Algerian population is never disposed to tolerate the employment of artists of inferior talent.   The plays are alternately composed of dramas, comedies, vaudevilles, grand operas, opera-comiques, and opera-bouffes.

The **Rue Bab-el-Oued, Place Bab-el-Oued, Rue Bab-Azoun, Rue de Constantine,** and several other streets are paved with wood.

The **Rue de la Lyre** is chiefly inhabited by Jewish retail and wholesale traders.   There are, however, in this street several Mohammedan shops for the sale of local curiosities and Algerine ware.

The **Rue de Constantine** is another beautiful street, in which are situated the **Law Courts**, a magnificent building of stately dimensions.   All the houses in this quarter of Algiers are the *nec plus ultra* of modern construction.   The cost of building in lower Algiers is very heavy.   First of all, the best stone has to be shipped from France and various remote parts of the coast.   Secondly, the land is very expensive, owing to this particularity: that, being level ground, it is many times more valuable than in the sloping quarters. Consequently, a house on the Boulevard de la République, Rue Bab-Azoun, Square de la République, or Rue de Constantine costs a proprietor very nearly as much as a house in the Rue de Rivoli or Boulevard Haussmann in Paris.

The **Rue d'Isly** is a very commercial street, chiefly patronised by English residents, it being the main road to

Mustapha Supérieur, the head-quarters of the British colony in Algiers.

The fortified wall that girded Algiers with its massive stonework, which had become a perfect nuisance, as it interfered greatly with the wide extension of the city, has been removed, and detached forts have been erected on the surrounding hills and armed with powerful ordnance. The Bab-el-Oued Gate and the celebrated Porte d'Isly have been taken down to make room for finer and better ventilated thoroughfares. The Municipality of Algiers has expended large sums of money for the improvement and enlargement of Algiers.

CHURCHES.

The **Church of the Holy Trinity (English)**, Rue d'Isly, was built in 1870 by public subscription, and consecrated in 1871 by the Bishop of Gibraltar. It is wholly supported by voluntary contributions and offerings. One-half of the seats are free, the other half are let at the charge of £1 per seat per season.

The exterior is built on the same plain and unattractive model which is customary in English Protestant churches. The interior is, however, very interesting. The walls are covered with tablets of different shades of Algerian marble, some of them very handsome indeed. Many memorial inscriptions are engraved on these marble slabs, some in reminiscence of British subjects deceased at Algiers as far back as 1580, some in record of historical deeds, etc. One of the principal tablets, called the Jubilee tablet, bears the following inscription : " This tablet is erected, June 20, 1887, by citizens of the United States, grateful for the privilege of associating this commemoration of their countrymen with the Jubilee of that illustrious Sovereign Lady, Queen Victoria, who has made the name of England dear to children's children throughout all lands." In connection with the church is a good lending library, subscription 3f. a month or 10f. for the season.

The **Scotch Presbyterian Church**, erected by the late and much regretted Sir Peter Coats at Mustapha Supérieur, is built on the same principle as the latter. It was left by Sir Peter Coats to the Scotch community of Mustapha.

The Cathedral of St. Philippe (Roman Catholic), formerly the Mosque of Hassan. Modern exterior, portico with six black marble columns. Interior dark, some stained glass windows, etc. (*See* p. 72.)

Notre Dame d'Afrique, on Mount Bouzarea, overlooking the sea. Built in the Roman-Byzantine style. Interior walls covered with votive offerings. (*See* p. 97.)

NOTRE DAME D'AFRIQUE.

The **Church of Notre Dame des Victoires**, in the Rue Bab-el-Oued, is a very plain building, its only interest being its antiquity. It is the mosque that was built in 1622 by Ali Bitchnin.

The **Church of Sainte Croix**, opposite the Casbah, is likewise an old mosque (Djama el Kesba Berranee) built in 1817.

The **Church of St. Augustin,** in the Rue de Constantine, was built in 1878, in the Roman style ; it is situated opposite the Law Courts. The three large halls in the interior are supported by magnificent white marble pillars, monoliths of 17 feet.

The **French Protestant Church,** Rue de Chartres.

Jesuit Church, Rue des Consuls, and the

Jewish Synagogue, Rue Randon, complete the list of religious buildings of importance in Algiers.

PRISONS.

There are three prisons in Algiers and one at **l'Harrach,** some twelve kilometres from Algiers. The **Prison Civile,** or civil prison, is situated at the Casbah, and the military prisons are situated, one in the old Arab fort called Fort Neuf, near the Place Bab-el-Oued, the other at the Fort Bab-Azoun, in the original Turkish fortress of that name. The prison of **l'Harrach** is utilised for prisoners who are to be transported.

Maison Centrale du Lazaret, Faubourg de l'Agha (for women.)

Maison Carrée.—*See* p. 103.

FORTIFICATIONS.

Algiers is a strongly fortified place, but, on account of its particular situation, is a fortress very difficult to defend. The town extends in amphitheatre form, and consequently is exposed to the enemy's shells, besides being open on the north side and north-east side. The walls, ditches, and gates (recently demolished) would have been of no avail in the event of a serious attack by sea ; the isolated works crowning the hills overlooking Algiers are far more formidable.

Of the old fortresses

The **Fort de l'Empereur,** built in 1545 above the Casbah, is now a military prison. It was here that General Bourmont received the capitulation of the Dey in 1830.

The **Fort Bab-Azoun,** built in 1581, is also a military prison.

The **Fort des Anglais,** near St. Eugène, built in 1825, is used as a powder depôt.

The **Battery of Notre Dame d'Afrique** is armed with six heavy ordnance cannons; the **Battery of the Casbah** has four guns of 34 centimetres; the **Battery of the Mole** and that of the **Arsenal** are likewise armed each with six 26-centimetre guns. The **Battery of Cape Matifou,** commanding the entrance of the bay, is armed with 34 centimetre heavy guns. There are besides other batteries on the heights of **Bouzarea, El Biar,** and **Sidi Ferruch,** which are closely guarded from public view.

SCHOOLS, COLLEGES, Etc.

There are in Algiers four superior schools, constituting the **University,** viz.:—

Ecole de Droit, law school, with ten professors.

Ecole des Lettres, school of letters, with fifteen professors.

Ecole de Médecine, school of medicine, with fifteen professors, and

Ecole des Sciences, school of science, with nine professors.

There is also a large college, or **Lycée,** for boys, Europeans or natives, on the Place Bab-el-Oued; and a **Petit Lycée** at Ben Aknoun, for youngsters; and many public schools in every quarter of the city, either on the secular or Catholic systems.

There is a very good convent, called the **Couvent des Sœurs de la Doctrine Chrétienne,** in Rue Rolland de Bussy. Another convent, called **Sacré Cœur,** is situated at Mustapha Supérieur. A third, that of the **Sisters of the Holy Trinity,** a very superior educational establishment, is installed in the Boulevard Gambetta.

The **Zoological Institution,** situated near the Admiralty, is a branch of the École des Lettres, and is liberally equipped for the use of students. The electric light is available for microscopic photography, there is an excellent zoological library, and a well-furnished aquarium.

OTHER PUBLIC BUILDINGS.

There are in Algiers four large barracks for quartering the troops, which consist of a section of almost every corps in the army. A whole regiment of **Zouaves** (the 1st) is located in the barracks of Tagarins, at the Casbah. The Engineers are lodged on the Place Bab-el-Oued, in the **Caserne du Génie.** The **Intendance, Gendarmerie,** and **Artillery** have likewise very spacious buildings affected for the quarters, most of these buildings having served for the same purpose under the Turks. The **Douaniers** possess very handsome barracks in the Rue de Constantine, and the **Cavalry (5th Chasseurs d'Afrique)** is quartered entirely at Mustapha Inférieur. There is an **Arsenal** at Mustapha, admission to which is very seldom granted.

The **Hôpital du Dey,** or **Military Hospital,** stands in the **Faubourg Bab-el-Oued,** outside the city. It was the former residence of the last Dey of Algiers. Permission to visit it is very easily obtained from the local authorities. It is a wonderful establishment, fitted with the most perfect sanitary arrangements, and well deserves inspection. In the various buildings 700 patients can be accommodated. Smoking rooms are provided for the convalescent, and comfortable quarters for a large staff of officers and attendants. The gardens are full of tropical vegetation, and kept in admirable order.

The **Hôpital Civil,** is situated at Mustapha Inférieur, and contains 500 beds. Patients are well cared for by French physicians or surgeons, and by Sisters of Charity

The **Central Market,** in Place de la Lyre, is a spacious building where meat, game, fruit and flowers can be bought very early in the morning, the earlier the better ; there is another Market, in the **Place de Chartres,** where flowers, fruit, and vegetables can also be bought early every morning. The afternoon is reserved for the sale of hosiery, furniture, and fancy goods.

The **Fish Market** is held in the arches underneath the Boulevard de la République, near the Mosque Djama el Djedid and the Place du Gouvernement.

The **Bureau Central Météorologique**, or **Observatory**, is installed at the **Mairie**, Boulevard de la République.

The **Palais Consulaire**, or Chambre de Commerce, is a stately building situated on the Boulevard de France at the branch Post and Telegraph Office, corner of the Place du Gouvernement. It contains a library, the Tribunal Consulaire, or County Courts, and is the central resort of the Board of Trade. It is also called the **Bourse**, which corresponds to the English appellation of Stock Exchange, as stock transactions are carried on there.

CLUBS AND SOCIETIES.

There are several clubs in Algiers—

The **Cercle Militaire** (for officers only), in the Square de la République (*see* below); the **Cercle d'Alger**, the **Grand Cercle Algérien** (both in the Rue Combe); the **Cercle Républicain d'Alger**, in the passage Duchassaing; the **Club Gymnastique**, Rue Michelet; the **Cercle d'Escrime**, 6, Rue d'Isly; the **Automobile-Club et Cercle des Sports**, 23, Boulevard Carnot; and the **English Club**, at Mustapha Supérieur, Rue Michelet prolongée.

There are also Tennis and Golf Clubs.

The **Société Hippique d'Alger** has its seat at No. 2, Rue Arago. Mr. F. Altairac is the president.

The **Comité Algérien de Propagande et d'Hivernage** has its headquarters at 1, Rue Combe. (*See* p. 86.)

The **Société des Beaux-Arts** is situated No. 4, Rue du Marché (Isly). It has a fine gallery of pictures; open to the public from 2 p.m. to 4 p.m. on Thursdays and Sundays. It gives private concerts every fortnight, which are very highly appreciated.

The **Atlas Section of the Club Alpin Français** is at the Lycée.

The **Military Academy** is installed in the old Janissary Barracks, in the Rue Médée. The principal entrance is by the Military Club, Square de la République. It possesses a very complete library, a large conference hall, where the pictures of the different Governors of Algeria are exposed; chemical and other laboratories, etc., fencing and billiard rooms, and restaurants. During the season several balls and parties are given by the officers, and these fêtes are usually brilliantly attended.

The **Société de Tir d'Alger**, 4, Rue Champlain, has a shooting stand installed outside the Bab-el-Oued gate on the military zone of the fortifications.

The **Société Philharmonique** and **l'Harmonie d'Alger**, are the leading musical societies of the town. There are also several minor societies which it is not necessary to mention.

Société protectrice des Animaux, 36, Rue d'Isly.

CEMETERIES.

The cemeteries of Algiers are situated at St. Eugène. They consist of the **Catholic**, the **Protestant**, and the **Jewish Cemeteries**. The **English Cemetery** is a part of the Commune Cemetery of Mustapha Supérieur at **Fontaine Bleue**, near the Boulevard Bru. It is very carefully tended by the English community of Algiers. There are also two Arab Cemeteries, one near the Civil Prison at the Casbah, and the other at Mustapha. On Fridays these are only open to ladies.

Excelsior HOTELS. *Al. arrd 3/6/10 -2*

The success and value of health resorts depend not only on the climate, but on the comfort, cleanliness, position, and sanitary arrangements of the hotels. In these respects the hotels of Algiers and Mustapha leave little or nothing to be desired, and may challenge comparison with European hotels. Most of those in the town are very central, and overlook the harbour, while those on higher ground at Mustapha Supérieur are, many of them, surrounded by magnificent gardens, affording delightful land and sea views. Situated at an altitude of several hundred feet from the sea, the climate at Mustapha Supérieur is more bracing and healthy than in the town, and the sanitary arrangements have, in many cases, been carried out under English supervision. The food and cooking, as a rule, are excellent, and the charges, which in the first-class hotels are pretty much the same, are moderate. (*See* also p. 24).

F

The following brief notice of the principal hotels and pensions will be found useful :—

The **Hotel St. Georges**, at Mustapha Supérieur, is in a very healthy situation, overlooking the Bay of Mustapha. The house is built in true Moorish style, and very comfortably furnished. The Hotel St. Georges combines first-class living with very moderate prices, an acceptable departure in the rule of first-class hotels. Cook's Coupons, Series C only, accepted.

The **Hotel Continental** has the great advantage of being at a stone's-throw from Algiers and yet quite in the country ; and considering the frequent communications (tramways every ten minutes), it is well adapted for visitors making but a short stay at Algiers. It was built in 1887, considerably enlarged in 1889, and has since been provided with a hydraulic lift of the most improved system. Mr. Hildenbrandt is the proprietor and the personal manager of one of the best hotels in Algiers. Cook's Coupons, Series A, B and C, accepted.

The **Hotel Alexandra**, late **Kirsch**, splendidly situated at Mustapha Supérieur, is a very old-established hotel, first-class in every respect, comfortable, clean, and managed in best English style. Excellent cuisine. The proprietors speak English. Cook's Coupons, Series A, B and C, accepted.

The **Mustapha Palace Hotel** (formerly the Hôtel Splendide, is a stately mansion of English appearance, built in the style of the fifteenth century. The interior is completely Moorish in architecture. The central court or Arab *patio* is a magnificent lounge of 70 feet square, entirely paved with marble, and surrounded by graceful arches and pillars. It is luxuriously fitted and handsomely furnished throughout. There is a spacious and well-stocked library, a billiard room with a full-sized English table, large drawing-rooms and dining-rooms. Situated on the highest part of Mustapha Supérieur. the views from the hotel are admirable. Cook's Coupons, Series C only, accepted.

The **Hotel de la Régence**, an old-established house on the Place du Gouvernement, is in the very centre of the promenade. Very comfortable hotel, well and obligingly managed, good cooking, moderate charges. The rooms on all the floors are lofty and spacious. Hydraulic lift to each floor on the most improved system. Cook's Coupons, Series A, B and C, accepted.

The **Hotel des Étrangers** is situated on the Place de la République, facing the Square de la Ré_lublique, and in full view of the sea. This central, comfortable hotel is much frequented by English and Americans. The proprietor is Mr. Glogg, who has a well-deserved reputation amongst his numerous clients. Cook's Coupons, Series A, B and C, accepted.

The **Hotel de l'Oasis** has had for years past the reputation of being a good hotel. Situated in the centre of the Boulevard de la République, it overlooks the harbour. The hotel is managed in a business-like manner, is comfortable, clean, and private. The charges are moderate and the cooking excellent. Restaurant on the ground floor. Modern lift to every floor. Cook's Coupons, Series A, B and C, accepted.

The **Hotel Beau Séjour,** opposite the Presbyterian Church, in the Rue Michelet, Mustapha Supérieur, is a very healthy place, commanding a most magnificent view of Algiers, the bay, and the surrounding hills. Cook's Coupons, Series R, accepted.

The **Hotel Oriental** adjoins the Hotel Continental, and has the same advantages of position, being close to the Station Sanitaire Terminus of the tramways, and yet surrounded by large and shady grounds with good views. The hotel is well managed by Swiss proprietors, and the cuisine leaves nothing to be desired. Baths and modern sanitation. Moderate charges. Cook's Coupons, Series R, accepted.

The **Grand Hotel** is one of the finest hotels established on the Mustapha slope, between the Hotels Continental and Alexandra. It is under entirely new management, and newly furnished throughout. It commands a lovely view. Cook's Coupons, Series R, accepted.

The **Hotel Pension l'Olivage Birmandreis** is situated on the highest part of Mustapha Supérieur, near the "Bois de Boulogne." It is an old Moorish villa transformed into a comfortable modern hotel, and surrounded by magnificent gardens of ten acres. The view and site are admirable ; the air balmy and pure. English spoken. Cook's Coupons, Series R, accepted.

F 2

The **Hotel Pension Victoria,** in the Rue Michelet, Mustapha Supérieur. M. Kipfer, proprietor. Cook's Coupons, Series R, accepted.

Furnished Villas can be obtained in the best quarter (Mustapha Supérieur), but are very expensive, ranging in price from 3,500f. up to 10,000f. for the season of six months. Less expensive villas are met with in the village of Isly, Mustapha Inférieur, or Saint Eugène, but these districts are not so healthy, and the houses are not so large or comfortáble.

RESTAURANTS.

Restaurants are plentiful in Algiers. Mention may be made of the **Taverne Grüber;** London House attached to the **Hotel de l'Oasis;** all of which are good. There are also second-class and homely restaurants, such as the **Restaurant de Nice,** Place de la République; and the **Restaurant Jaumon,** 2, Rue Dumont d'Urville.

The **Restaurant Cassar** (for a fish dinner) is situated at the " Poissonnerie," at the bottom of the street leading from the Place du Gouvernement to the " Pêcherie," by the side of the Mosque of Djama el Djedid. It has another entrance by the side of the Palais Consulaire, on the Boulevard de France.

There are restaurants in many of the hotels where non-residents are well catered for.

The **Hotel Continental** supplies luncheons to **non-residents** at the uniform charge of 3f. 50c., and 5f. for dinners, exclusive of wine.

The **Hotel des Etrangers,** in the Square de la République (late Square Bresson). Luncheon 3f., dinner 4f. The chef is considered one of the best cooks in Algiers.

The **Hotel de la Régence,** Place du Gouvernement. Luncheon 3f., dinner 4f.

The **Restaurant Galian,** a small hotel and restaurant, at **El Biar,** near Algiers, is very comfortable and clean.

The **Café Restaurant du Petit Château=Neuf** at **El Biar** is also a good place for a private dinner. The garden is very pretty, and the guests are served either in the dining-rooms or in the grounds.

CAFÉS.

There are, of course, many *cafés* in Algiers. The principal are the **Café Grüber**, 7, Boulevard de la République; **Café d'Apollon**, on the Place du Gouvernement; the **Café de Bordeaux**, Place du Gouvernement; the **Taverne Tanton-ville**, 7, Place de la République; the **Brasserie de l'Étoile,** Rue de la Liberté; the **Brasserie Suisse**, 11, Rue de la Liberté; and the **Bar Glacier**, 2, Rue de Constantine. The **Café de Bordeaux**, Place du Gouvernement is under the control of a French company of beer manufacturers. The **Brasserie Terminus**, Boulevard Carnot, is in a good summer quarter. The **Café Tantonville**, being situated next to the theatre, is very animated on winter nights. The **Café** or **Taverne Grüber** sells the famous Strasburg beer, and the **Brasserie Suisse**, retails the beer of Lyons from the famous and world-renowned brewery known as the Brasserie Georges. The establishment is kept on the Swiss and German principle—sauerkraut, Frankfort sausages, West-phalian hams, etc., to be had there, the same as in Germany. The **American Bar** of the Hotel de l'Oasis is the only one of the kind in Algiers.

There are other *cafés*, such as the **Brasserie du Phénix,** in the Rue de la Liberté, and also *cafés* and restaurants of minor importance, scattered over the secondary thoroughfares.

There is a very good little Turkish restaurant in the Rue Mahon kept by Dziri and Oulid Aïssa.

The Moorish and Arab *cafés* are to be found in almost every street. The charge for a cup of black coffee is a half-penny. They also retail sahleb, Arab tea, lemonade, etc. The most picturesque Moorish *cafés* are in the Casbah quarter.

AMUSEMENTS, Etc

Algiers does not offer the same distractions as Nice, Monte Carlo, Cannes, or the winter resorts of Italy, and those in authority do little or nothing to increase the popularity of the town among European visitors or winter residents. The chief attractions of Algiers are its climatic advantages.

The **Theatre**, subsidised by the Municipality for opera, opera comique, drama, comedy, six nights a week in the season, is centrally situated in the Place de la République; and close by (Rue d'Isly) is a large Music Hall, generally called the **Casino,** but in the ordinary acceptation of the word there is no Casino, though one has long been talked of. Restaurant and Brasserie attached. On Sunday and Thursday the band of the 1st Zouave Regiment plays on the Place du Gouvernement, and in the Museum gardens, Mustapha Supérieur, the first and third Wednesday of the month, always in the afternoon. **Kursaal,** in the Rue Bab-el-Oued, comedies and operettas occasionally. **Popular Theatre** and **Velodrome** at Mustapha Supérieur, comedies and operettas at intervals.

The newly constituted **Comité d'Hivernage,** in the Rue Combe, are making praiseworthy efforts to provide fêtes and amusements both for French residents and for visitors, but the funds at their disposal are very limited. A room on the ground floor of the offices is supplied with newspapers, and a small library for the free use of visitors. Programmes of proposed entertainments are issued in December each season, and the obliging Secretary-General is always anxious to see callers, and to give information.

The programme of the Algiers Fêtes Committee generally includes Arab fantasias, Mauresque and Spanish fêtes, carnival festivities, torchlight processions, races, veglioni, etc., and on the second and fourth Wednesday of each month Classical Concerts (free) are given at the Hôtel de Ville.

In the course of the season 1907-8 (December–May) arrangements have been made for the following events :—

December.--Automobile Races, Moorish Fêtes, Sports Fête.

January.—Jackal Hunts, Paper Chases, Cross-Country Rides, Moorish Fêtes.

February.—Battles of Flowers, Veglione, Native Fête.

March.—Battles of Flowers, Horse Races, Carnival.

April.—Bull Fights, Spanish Fair, Battles of Flowers, Veglione.

May.—Regattas, Motor-boat Races, Naïlia Fête.

The hotels at Mustapha also arrange dances, concerts, and even private theatricals have been indulged in, to pass away the otherwise monotonous evenings. For Clubs *see* p. 80. Concerts are also given at the Beaux Arts, 4, Rue du Marché (Isly), and the Petit Athénée, Rue d'Isly.

During the carnival season many and varied official and private balls take place, those of the Governor-General, the Commander-in-Chief, the Admiral, and of the French clubs in the Theatre being the most noteworthy.

The Governor-General's ball, which is given about the middle of March, is a very fashionable gathering; it offers the means of studying the local society of Algiers, and also—and this is the more interesting from a European point of view—it affords the facility of contemplating the Arab Sheiks and Aghas in the full glare of their gaudy and dashing costumes. The Caïds, with their red burnouses, are there in overwhelming numbers. Visitors can obtain invitations through their consuls.

Overlooking the bay is the **Théâtre du Soleil,** or open-air theatre, inaugurated in May, 1907, special performances being given in honour of the occasion. This enterprise is due to the initiative of M. René Garnier of the *Revue Nord-Africaine.*

There is an English Club at Rue Michelet prolongée, Mustapha Supérieur. Parks or well-ordered public gardens, such as are always to be found in European health-resorts or popular seaside stations are conspicuous by their absence.

An occasional review of the troops by the Governor-General, golf at Birmandreïs, lawn tennis at most of the hotels, afternoon concerts in others, boating and bathing complete the list of Algerian attractions.

Visitors to Algiers should not miss viewing the Sacrifice of the Hen, which can be seen in the winter, every Wednesday morning. Take the Saint-Eugène road as far as the second kilometre, and stop at the **Rocher de Cancale**. The cere mony takes place on the sea beach, and is very curious.

The " Fête des Fèves," or the fête of the beans, is a special negro performance. It takes place every year on a Wednes day in April (any negro will tell you the day) on the seashore, near the marabout of Sidi Bellul, between the Jardin d'Essai and the village of Hussein Dey, four kilometres from Algiers (*see* also p. 103). To get in, you must pass through the workshops of the P.-L.-M. Railway.

The **Aissaoui** fanatic religious performances are held in the native quarter by followers of Sidi bin Aïssa. In these, after a maddening dance continued until exhaustion ensues, the fanatics, regardless of pain, inflict on themselves all kinds of torture, such as eating live scorpions, branding with hot irons, forcing out their eyes—altogether a revolting spectacle.

LUGGAGE.—Porters' Official Tariff.

First Zone.—From the landing place or the railway station to the Bd. Laferrière, the Rue St. Augustin, the Rue Randon, the lower part of the Boulevard Valée to the Rue Randon, the Bd. General Farre, and the Rue Rovigo as far as No. 29, the charges are:

Not exceeding 25 Kilogs. .	0f.30
25 to 50 ,,	0.50
50 ,, 100 ,,	1.00

per article.

Second Zone.—From the landing place or the railway station to the Hôpital Civil, the Pâté, the Hotel Continental, the Cité Bisch, Boulevard de la Victoire, Pont du Beau Fraisier:—

Not exceeding 25 Kilogs. .	0f.60
25 to 50 .,	1.00
50 ,, 100 ,,	2.00

per article.

Third Zone.—From the landing place or the railway station to Jardin d'Essai, Fontaine-Bleue, Colonne Voirol, Chemin des Aquéducs, Sahel Gate, Saint-Eugène (Deux-Moulins):—

Not exceeding 25 Kilogs. .	1f.
25 to 50 ,,	2f.
50 ,, 100 ,,	3f.

per article.

For the above rates porters are bound to carry up the luggage to the indicated floor without extra charge.

The small hand-luggage, such as umbrellas, sticks, rugs, shawls, etc., are not considered as luggage. Three of these articles will be counted as a single package of less than 25 Kilogs., and only charged as for that weight.

BAGGAGE SERVICE ESTABLISHED BY THE COMPAGNIE GÉNÉRALE TRANSATLANTIQUE.

Departures.—On receipt of verbal orders, letter, or telephone message at the Offices of the Company, 6, Boulevard Carnot, or at the Secretary's Office on the Quay, baggage will be collected at the residence of passengers, or at the railway station, transported to the steamer and registered on production of the Passage Ticket.

Arrivals.—A special employé wearing an armlet with the words "Bagages C. G. T." is authorised to collect the baggage tickets on board and on the landing stage, and as soon as the baggage has been examined by the Customs' Officials it will be transported to any address required, or to the baggage office of the Company, or of the Railway Company.

The Compagnie Transatlantique authorises (but without any responsibility) a number of porters to come on to the landing stage, to assist passengers with their hand baggage.

An office for the reception of baggage of all kinds which cannot be delivered immediately has been opened at the Company's warehouse on the Quay. The prices charged are the same as those prevailing at the railway stations.

OFFICIAL TARIFF.

The Company's charges for collecting or delivering baggage as described above are as follows, and vary according to the Zones (or districts) :—

1st Zone.—1f. 50 per 100 Kilos, minimum				0.75
2nd Zone.—2f.	,,	,,	,,	1.00
3rd Zone.—2f. 50	,,	,,		1.25

Limit of Zones referred to above :—

First Zone.—From the Custom House and the warehouse of the Company (or *vice versâ*) to the Isly town gate, the Rue Saint Augustin, the Rue Randon, the lower part of the Boulevard Valée as far as the Rue Randon, the Bab-el-Oued gate, and the Rue Rovigo as far as No. 29.

Second Zone.—From the Custom House and the warehouse of the Company (or *vice versâ*) to No. 34 of the Rue de Constantine (Agha) to Boulevard Victor-Hugo, Plateau Saulière, the village of Isly, the Avenue Gandillot, the Rue Rovigo as far as the Rue Montpensier, the Rampe Valée, the Hôpital du Dey.

Third Zone.—From the Custom House and the warehouse of the Company (or *vice versâ*) to the Civil Hospital, the Pâté, the Hotel Continental, the Cité Bisch, Boulevard de la Victoire, Pont du Beau Fraisier, the Cemetery.

(*Beyond these districts the charges must be fixed by arrangement with the Company.*)

PART III

THE ENVIRONS OF ALGIERS.

———◦◊◦———

1. Mustapha Agha, Mustapha Supérieur, Colonne Voirol.

2. Birmandreïs, Birkadem.

3. El Biar.

4. Bouzarea, through El Biar.

5. Dely Ibrahim, Douéra.

6. St. Eugène, Pointe Pescade, Cap Caxine, Guyotville.

7. Staouéli and La Trappe (Monastery)

8. Notre Dame d'Afrique, Vallée des Consuls.

9. The Frais Vallon.

10. The Jardin d'Essai.

11. The Ruisseau, Hussein Dey.

12. Maison Carrée.

13. Fort de l'Eau, Cape Matifou.

14. Rovigo, Baths of Hammam Melouan.

The environs of Algiers have already been briefly alluded to on p. 57.

1. Algiers to **Mustapha Agha.** Start from the **Place du Gouvernement**; tramcar every five minutes for Station Sanitaire; **Mustapha Supérieur** and **Colonne Voirol** every half-hour; electric tramcar to Mustapha Inférieur, Belcourt, and Jardin d'Essai every few minutes. The road to

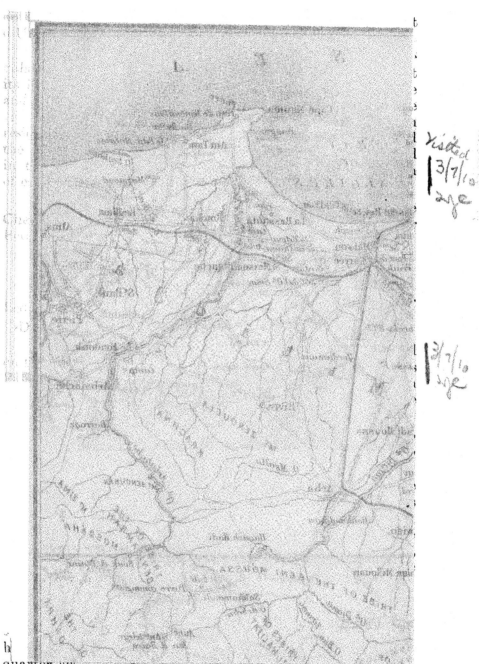

quarter shortly after the French occupation. From there
the tourist can drive to

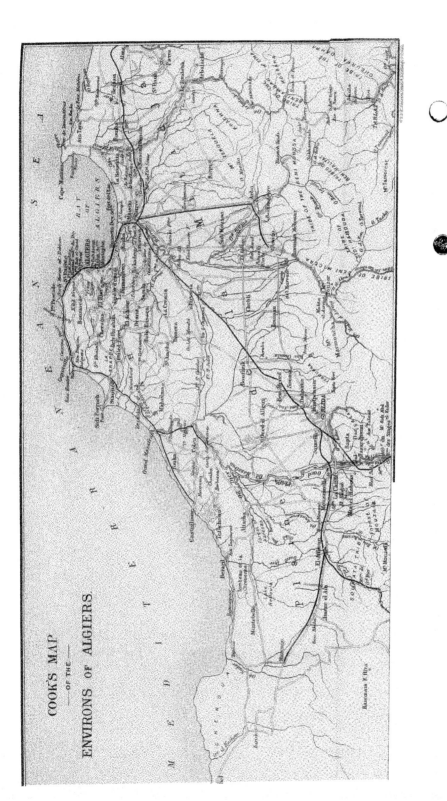

COOK'S MAP
— OF THE —
ENVIRONS OF ALGIERS.

Mustapha Supérieur is by the Rue Bab-Azoun, or Boulevard de la République, Square de la République, Rue Dumont d'Urville, Rue d'Isly, and the Rue Michelet.

Mustapha Supérieur stands on the long range of the Sahel Hills. It is about 600 feet above the level of the sea at its highest point. On Mustapha Hill are several comfortable and really good hotels (*see* p. 81), and numerous handsome villas in beautiful gardens, many of them belonging to English residents. Amongst the prettiest villas are the **Bardo,** and the Governor-General's summer palace, which can be visited in the absence of the **Governor=General** on presentation of card. (*See* pp. 39 and 71).

Next comes the magnificent **Campagne du Sahel,** on the **Chemin des Aqueducs,** the residence of the late Sir Peter Coats.

The **villa Mustapha Rais.**

Campagne Télemly.

Chateau d'Hydra, the residence of the late Mr. E. Ledgard.

Djenen Ali Rais.

The **Museum** of Algerian art and antiquities is situated on the Mustapha main road before arriving at the Governor's Palace (*see* above). A military band plays twice a month in the gardens of the museum, first and third Wednesdays in the month.

Continuing beyond the hotels, and the Bois de Boulogne, the trams stop at their terminus at the Colonne Voirol *see* pp. 35 and 42.

2. Algiers to **Birmandreis** and **Birkadem.** Start from the Place du Gouvernement : Electric tramcars every 20 minutes for the Ruisseau. Then walk, or carriage 4f. to Birmandreis, 5f. 50c. to Birkadem. Pass through the Rue Bab-Azoun, Square de la République, Rue de Constantine, Champ de Manœuvres, Jardin d'Essai, and follow the road to Hussein Dey to **Le Ruisseau,** p. 37. There leave the main road and take the one called **Chemin de la Femme Sauvage,** which cuts the main road at right angles. This leads direct to

The Ravine of the Femme Sauvage, so named after a handsome lady who used to keep a café-restaurant in that quarter shortly after the French occupation. From there the tourist can drive to

Birkadem (the well of the slave), 11 kilometres from Algiers, where there is a military prison in the fort above the village, and a female orphan asylum on the road leading to **Kouba** (13 kilometres). Here a **Séminaire** or ecclesiastical college for boys and older students may be visited. The building, situated in extensive grounds, is remarkable for its immense dome. In the village of Kouba has been erected the statue of **General Margueritte**, by Albert Lefeuvre.

The road follows up from the Ravine to **Birmandreis** and thence to **Colonne Voirol**.

Birmandreïs is a little village 8 kilometres from Algiers. It can also be reached by a short cut starting from the main road at a place called " Villa King," about a hundred yards above the Hotel Alexandra. On leaving the pretty little village square, just turning at right angles, opposite the Kilometric post No. 7800, there is a lovely road shaded with beautiful plane trees, siding an orange grove. This is the road to the Marabout of Sadi Yahia, one of the most charming drives of the region.

The road from Birmandreïs follows on to

Colonne Voirol (5¾ kilometres from Algiers). It takes its name from a column, which has been erected at the side of the road, in commemoration of its construction by the **Légion Étrangère**, under command of General Baron Voirol, in 1833, when France decided to remain in possession of Algiers. The walks and drives around here are of the most enjoyable description.

3. Algiers to **El Biar**. Tramcars every half-hour from the Place du Gouvernement. The route is by the Rue de la Lyre, Rue Rovigo, winding up to the Sahel Gate, and following by the *route* d'El-Biar. It is a most picturesque road, abounding with pretty landscapes. Once past the **Auberge du Panier Fleuri**, one gets the view of the sea from both sides of the road, with magnificent inland scenery. The **Villa Olivier**, a fine Moorish mansion, is situated at the entrance of the village of El-Biar.

The **village** of **El Biar** (the wells), 5 kilometres from Algiers, is a prolongation of the Commune of Mustapha as far as the **Colonne Voirol**, approached from the road above Mustapha Supérieur. It contains the most charming villas of the British Colony, among which is that of H.B.M.'s Consul-General. In this healthy and delightful suburb and district are several schools and religious establishments, such as the Convent of the *Bon Pasteur* for young girls, also an orphanage directed by the sisters of *St. Vincent de Paul.*

Outside the village is the Maison Couput, where the final surrender of Algiers was agreed to, through the mediation of Mr. St. John, the British Consul General. An account of this will be found in Sir Lambert Playfair's "The Scourge of Christendom." There is a small hotel in the village, where, as also at the Restaurant of le Petit Château-Neuf, lunch (déjeuner) can be obtained.

El Biar can also be reached by a curious and picturesque lane accessible to horses and mules. This pathway, called the **Chemin Romain**, starts straight up like a ladder, at the back of the Hotel Continental, on the Chemin des Aquéducs; it is one of the prettiest walks in the environs of Algiers, and discloses most exquisite views.

4. Algiers to Bouzarea through El Biar.—The drive to **Bouzarea** is one of the best in the suburbs. The road passes through the **Casbah** and the **Sahel Gate** of Algiers, leaving on the right the site of the **Fort de l'Etoile**, built in 1568 by **Moustapha**, a Sicilian renegade, under the reign of **Mohammed ben Sala Rais**, and blown up by gunpowder through the jealousy of one of the wives of the **Agha** commanding the fort.

The road then circles round the **Fort de l'Empereur,** built in 1545 by **Hussein Dey**, successor to **Khair-ed-Din**, on a hill called by the Turks **Koudiat-es-Saboon** (the soap hill). On the 4th July, 1830, the Turks tried to blow up this fort, but only succeeded in destroying the round castle, which contained the gunpowder. This fort was the headquarters of General Bourmount, and here it was that the capitulation of Algiers was signed in 1830. It is now used as a prison.

A pretty lane leads from El Biar to **Birmandreis** (p. 92), where it joins the main road near Colonne Voirol. About half-way up this lane, a narrow pathway takes you to a charming little spot, where an Arab café, called the **Café Hydra**, is found nestling under a wide-spreading fig-tree. A good cup of Arab coffee may be indulged in here for a half-penny. The lane is public, but not accessible to carriages.

Continuing from El Biar through delightful country roads the drive ends at

Bouzarea, a favourite suburban resort, 1,240 feet above sea level. The view from the village is one of the loveliest, a perfect panorama including **Djebel Chénoua**, the **Harrach Valley**, the **Sahel**, and in front the Mediterranean.

Situated about a thousand yards from Bouzarea is the pretty little **Mosque of Sidi Nouman**, with the Koubas, shaded by palm-trees.

The best road for returning to Algiers would be to drive first to the **Observatory**, from the cliffs of which a splendid view can be enjoyed, next to the **Hospice des Vieillards**, and then, through the **Vallée des Consuls**, to Algiers.

5. Algiers to **Dely Ibrahim and Douéra.**—Electric trams from Algiers to El Biar from the Place du Gouvernement (*see* p. 35), with omnibus connection four times a day to Dely Ibrahim, and for Douéra twice a day. Carriage 20f. The road passes through El Biar, Ben-Aknoun, and then through

Dely Ibrahim, 11 kilometres from Algiers, 1,800 inhabitants. This village was founded in 1832, with a nucleus of 416 Alsatians, who had set out on a travel to America, but who, for some reason, were prevented from proceeding to the end of their journey. They were eventually persuaded to settle in Algeria, where the French Government granted them allotments of land in the vicinity of Algiers. They formed the two centres of Dely Ibrahim and Koubba. A statue of Marshal Pélissier has been erected in front of the village church, and beyond a charming view of the Mediterranean there is nothing to detain the visitor.

Baba Hassan, 19 kilometres from Algiers, is met on the road to

Douéra (in Arabic, the small house), about 4,000 inhabitants, a pretty little agricultural town, surrounded by a wall. Its principal street, shaded with stately trees, which is, by the way, the main road to Algiers, affords all the aspects of a promenade. It is very animated and busy, and contains all the principal establishments—a church, the old military camp and barracks, and several steam mills of a certain importance. Douéra possesses, as well as a Protestant church, a civil hospital with 300 beds, an asylum for old and crippled paralytics, and a military penitentiary.

6. Algiers to St. Eugène (Deux Moulins), Pointe Pescade, Cap Caxine, Guyotville.

—Electric tramcars start from the Place du Gouvernement every ten minutes for St. Eugène (Deux Moulins), 20c., thence steam car (frequently) to Pointe Pescade, 30c. and 45c.; Bains Romains, 40c. and 55c.; Cap Caxine, 55c. and 70c.; Guyotville, 70c. and 95c.

The route is by the suburb of Bab-el-Oued and along the sea front, past the **Fort des Anglais** and the European and Jewish cemeteries to

St. Eugène (Deux Moulins), a large suburb of 4,000 inhabitants, with numerous villas and small houses, chiefly inhabited by Jews, Spaniards, Maltese and French people. Continuing parallel to the sea for three kilometres

Pointe Pescade is reached, where a beautiful old Moorish fort, built in 1671, and restored later, projects into the sea on a reef of rocks. Fish dinners can be obtained at a restaurant. An aqueduct at Pointe Pescade supplies the neighbouring houses, gardens, and roads with soft water.

The **Bains Romains**, so called, are about 600 yards to the south, but the Roman bath has disappeared, owing to the railway operations on the line to Coléa. Boating and fishing parties are frequently held in summer at the Hotel des Bains.

Cap Caxine, 12 kilometres from Algiers, has a lighthouse of the first order with a revolving light, visible 20 miles. A road near the village leads to the forest of **Aïn Beïnen**, planted with eucalyptus, acacia, cork oak, casuarina, Aleppo pine, and other trees by the Department of Woods and Forests. Several hundred acres have been thus planted.

Guyotville, 15 kilometres from Algiers, is a well-laid-out village of 2,500 inhabitants, in a very productive district, much frequented by Algerians. The village is named after Comte Guyot, who was Minister of the Interior from 1840 to 1846. Close by is the prehistoric grotto of the **Grand Rocher**, and at Beni-Messous a large number of **dolmens** may be seen, while in another direction are the ruins of a Roman aqueduct. Staouéli is 7 kilometres, and Sidi-Ferruch 11 kilometres from Guyotville. (See p. 96.)

7. Algiers to **Staouéli** and **La Trappe (Monastery)**
(35 kilometres there and back).—This excursion along the
coast is one of the most interesting in the environs of Algiers.
The road passes through the villages of St. Eugène, the Pointe
Pescade, Cap Caxine, and Guyotville, already described. A
private carriage there and back costs 20f., the drive occupying
four hours, exclusive of the time spent at the Monastery.
The return journey, if preferred, can be made by way of
Cheragas, Château-Neuf, and El Biar. Steam trams start
from the Place du Gouvernement for Staouéli three times a
day, at 6.42 a.m., 12.59 p.m., and 5.15 p.m. ; fare there and
back, 2f. 55c.

La Trappe de Staouéli is about a mile and a quarter
south of the village of Staouéli, where, on 19th June, 1830, the
Moslem army was camped, and a battle was fought in which
the French completely routed the Turks.

The French Government granted to the Trappists 2,500
acres of land on the plains of **Staouéli**, on which the Trappists
settled on August 19, 1843, under the care of their holy
Superior, the Reverend Francis Regis. The first stone of the
abbey was laid on a bed of shells and balls found on the
battlefield. It is a rectangular and spacious building of fifty
square yards, with a garden in the centre. The chapel occupies one wing, the refectory, kitchen, and dormitories occupy
the rest. Some inscriptions in this style, " *S'il est dur de vivre
à la Trappe qu'il est doux d'y mourir,*" ornament the walls.
In the grounds are large farms, granaries, wine-cellars, cattle
stalls ; beyond are extensive vineyards and orchards.

The Monastery contained 120 monks (Trappists), and some
250 men, including those at work in the mills, and in the
distillation of essences, the manufacture of liqueurs and wine,
were employed, but only the conventual buildings now exist,
the monks having been expelled by the Government in 1904.

In the library are some Roman mosaics and pottery, but
the most interesting curiosity is the table on which was signed
the abdication of Hussein Dey, and the cession of Algeria to
France in July, 1830.

The vines of Staouéli produced annually large quantities
of excellent wine, which brought in an immense revenue to
the Trappists. The wine is now made by Spaniards who have
occupied the monastery since the expulsion of the monks.
There was also a forge, a bakehouse, and various workshops,

such as wheelwright's, carpenter's, etc. There are two corn mills and an aqueduct.

About six kilometres to the westward of the Monastery is situated the village of

Sidi=Ferruch, named after a marabout held in great estimation by the Algerians, and rendered celebrated as the landing place of the French army on June 14, 1830, previous to the battle in which the French completely defeated the Moslem, as related above. The village itself was founded fourteen years later. The barracks, capable of holding 1,500 men, is a large building in the fort. The principal entrance bears the following inscription on a marble slab :

Ici
Le XIV Juin, MDCCCXXX,
Par l'ordre du Roy Charles X.,
Sous le Commandement du Général de
Bourmont
L'Armée Française
vint arborer ses drapeaux
Rendre la liberté aux mers
Donner l'Algérie à la France.

In a chapel built by the Romans was found the following inscription :

HIC EST JANVARI
I ET FILII EJVS MEMORIA,
QVI VIXIT ANNIS XLVII MENSIBVS. V
DISCESSIT IN PACE VI   ANNO PROVINC
CCCCX

8. Algiers to Notre Dame d'Afrique and the Vallée des Consuls. Electric cars from the Station Sanitaire, and the Place du Gouvernement, by the Bab-el-Oued, and the Hôpital du Dey, then a steep walk or drive (omnibus or carriage) to the Church, from which is obtained a magnificent view over land and sea.

Private carriage 3f. 50c., and 50c. per quarter of an hour for waiting.

Notre Dame d'Afrique is a church especially attended for the worship of the Virgin by the sailors of Algiers. It is built on the top of the Bouzarea hill, and is the most conspicuous building visible from the steamer when nearing Algiers. The church was commenced in 1858, and consecrated in 1872 by Cardinal Lavigerie. The building is very effective from the outside, having a gigantic central dome and two Romano-Byzantine wings of the most pleasing appearance. But the interior does not correspond to the outside effect. Save the showy plastered stucco on the whitewashed walls, and the solid silver statue of the Archangel Michael, presented by the Union of Neapolitan Fishermen, there is nothing very substantial in its architecture or in the decoration which deserves a particular notice. " Notre Dame d'Afrique " is personified by the statue of a black Virgin above the altar. Round the apse there is this motto: " Notre Dame d'Afrique, priez pour nous et pour les Musulmans." Every Sunday, at 3.30 p.m., the officiating clergy perform in the open air, on a point of vantage overhanging the sea—a touching and very imposing ceremony—the blessing of the sea for the souls of the sailors who perished in the storms. Beyond Notre Dame d'Afrique is the

Vallée des Consuls, which takes its name from having been the quarter affected by the foreign consuls in the time of the Deys. The neighbouring country is very beautiful, but rather lonely and neglected. The road is likewise in a very dilapidated state, having been little improved since the time of the Deys. The Saint Eugène road, which is the main road from Algiers, has been lately very much improved with wood pavement.

9. Algiers to the **Frais=Vallon.**—Electric cars from the Station Sanitaire and the Place du Gouvernement. Carriage 2f. to the Café, plus 50c. per quarter of an hour for waiting. The road passes through the **Bab=el=Oued Gate,** and the **Cité=Bugeaud,** an old suburb of Algiers, and then, leaving the **Hôpital du Dey** on the right, turns abruptly westwards near the powder-magazine. The route follows the bushy ravine of the Bouzarea, creeping along the mountain slopes until the **Frais=Vallon** is reached. From this point the rent in the mountain side is narrower, and delightfully shaded with trees. An old Arab pathway, which has been rendered accessible to carriages, takes you to the Arab Café, a celebrated pilgrimage of the tourists, situated at an altitude of 2,300 feet. The carriage drive to the Frais-Vallon is most delightful, and for pedestrians it affords a most agreeable promenade. A tolerably good walker will find it a very pleasant stroll to the top of the glen, where will be found the house of a celebrated Arab doctor who is supposed by the Arabs to be endowed with unlimited curative powers. The little Arab village, in which are the waters of **Aioun Srakna**, is very interesting to visit. In it are several **koubbas**, or tombs of Arab saints or **marabouts**. The principal one is that of the most venerated **Sidi=Medjebar**, the patron of divorced Arab women. Tradition has it that whenever a divorced Mohammedan lady makes three pilgrimages to this koubba she is sure to marry again. The **waters** of **Aioun Srakna** are ferruginous, alkaline, and carbonated, and recommended as a remedy for many complaints. But the sources are not public, and have not been, up to the present, conceded to any company. Visitors can view the grounds in entire liberty, and even taste the waters. The **Frais=Vallon** can also be reached by the road starting from **Sahel Gate**, the **Ravine of Bir=Traria**, and the **Fontaine du Dey**.

10. **Algiers** to **Jardin d'Essai**. Electric trams start from the **Place du Gouvernement** every 10 minutes, carriage 2.25f., and 50c. per quarter of an hour for waiting. The route is by the Boulevard de la République, the Champ de Manœuvres (or Drill Ground) of Mustapha, and to the Jardin d'Essai, either through Belcourt (north side), or through the Abattoir (south side) bordering the sea. The northern road is more picturesque and less dusty. The electric tramcar conveys passengers from town to the Jardin d'Essai by the southern route.

The **Jardin d'Essai** is one of the most interesting gardens in existence. Each alley is planted with trees of the rarest species, carefully cultivated in Algiers. Here is an alley of Japanese palm trees, which is one of rare beauty, there an avenue of African palm trees. India-rubber trees, which were imported into Algiers for the first time some twenty-five years ago, can be seen in all their glory, and the alley of **Ficus Roxburghi**, or pagoda fig-trees, as the india-rubbers are termed here, resembles the Indian scenery near the gigantic forests that surround the pagodas of Pegu and Benares. One of these trees has a height of eighteen metres and a circumference of six metres.

Another specimen, **Ficus nitida**, dominates with its enormous growth a little eminence sloping down towards a diminutive water-pond crowded with bamboos, China sagittaries, and Madagascar cypresses. Its roots cover the ground over a surface of twenty metres. In the middle of the alley, a splendid fountain reflects the graceful groups of the innumerable exotic trees that surround it. In the centre of the fountain, on a small platform, are a few banana trees, phylodendrons, and the jewel of the Jardin d'Essai, namely the **Juarez cocoa tree**, an emerald green tree of the strangest and wildest appearance, a splendid specimen of Mexican vegetation that has excited on many occasions the admiration of learned horticulturists.

Amongst celebrated palm trees and others of the same species that have been reared at the Jardin d'Essai at the expense of the most careful training and attention, are the **Royal palm tree** (*palmito de Cuba*), with a plain trunk 12 yards in height, its pretty bouquet of vivid green leaves at the top, resembling somewhat a gigantic feather-broom ; the **white cocoa tree**, the **dwarf cocoas** from the Island of St. Marguerite, the priceless **Java palm tree**, of which there is no specimen in Europe ; the **Tabal** of Havana, with its blue leaves ; the **wild date trees** from Southern Africa ; the **Indian Caryota**, and the massive and powerful **Jubea** from Chili, whose trunk measures one metre and a half in diameter, a remarkable colossus, which carries at a height of ten metres an enormous crown of graceful leaves.

Nowhere can be found grouped together such a complete and valuable collection of the vegetation of the old and the new continents. Nowhere can these majestic hosts of the virgin forests of distant lands be watched under more favourable conditions, with flower and fruit, and an extraordinary amount of vitality, as if they had brought with them the embalmed and pure air of their original country. The celebrated **Yuccas** from Carolina, Brazil, and Texas are also very curious specimens of American vegetation. There are many of them here ; in fact, quite a little forest. One of them, the **Yucca draconis**, is a representative of a very rare species, almost extinct. It has a flat trunk, several yards in height, and curves down like a camel's back at its summit, the branches hanging almost to the ground.

The **Strelitza** and the **Strelitza regina** are also remarkable species of Cape banana trees. The **Ravanela**, from Madagascar, which is called in its country the traveller's fountain, reserves for the thirsty traveller a provision of water at its root. This tree originates from a forest where roads do not exist, and where man can only proceed with fire and axe through the densely packed trunks of its innumerable trees.

Without further indication the visitor will see for himself that there is to be found at the Jardin d'Essai almost every kind of Eastern vegetation. The palm-trees are cultivated on a large scale within its precincts and are shipped wholesale to almost every part of Europe ; and their sale brings to the Compagnie Générale Algérienne a revenue of no less than £4,000 a year. Nearly all the pots of palm trees that are sold in the flower markets of Paris, such as La Madeleine, and at Covent Garden in London, are shipped from Algiers.

The tangerine-trees are also exported in great quantities. The banana-tree, so pretty, with its large leaf of amber colour, has a special space reserved for its development under the care of experienced gardeners, the younger banana trees being all sheltered by means of bamboo netting.

The avenue of Japanese and African palm trees planted alternately form an admirable and unequalled sight, the avenue commencing at a circle planted with eucalyptus and india-rubber trees, with a handsome waterfall in the middle, and ending literally in the sea.

Outside the garden, bordering the sea, is an oasis of palm trees, called the " Oasis Sainte Marie."

Attached to this part of the Jardin d'Essai is a very comfortable café and restaurant, -

The **Café Restaurant Français de l'Oasis des Palmiers**. Luncheons are served at fixed prices or *à la carte*. Tea, coffee and milk, English beer, champagnes, Algerian and French wines of all kinds, sandwiches, etc., are obtainable at very moderate prices.

Directly outside the Mustapha gate of the garden is a picturesque Moorish café, renowned for its delightful, shady, and almost unique situation, and bordered on the right-hand side by a very curious fountain of Moorish structure, built about 300 years ago, a little marvel of its kind. The architecture of this fountain is of the purest Arab style, and it has preserved up to this day its original outlines and features. The fountain is shaded by trees of every description, which hang from the hill over its arched roof and give a resemblance to the entrance of a Moorish palace.

This fountain has been immortalised in a painting by Fortuny, the great Spanish artist, who was an enthusiastic admirer of Arab art, and also by Fromentin.

The painting, which was in the possession of Defoer Bey, has now returned to the Museum of Amsterdam with the celebrated gallery of that famous *collectionneur*, who made the munificent donation of his works to the museum of his country—works that took him all his life to collect.

The Jardin d'Essai was commenced by the Government in 1832, and kept up at a great expense. Later on it was passed over to the Société Générale Algérienne in 1865, at a nominal rent of 1,000f. a year. This company, with a capital of a hundred million francs, was bound to employ its capital in the development of agricultural works, mines, forests, canals, etc., for which the Government gave them 25,000 acres of land, at a nominal rent of 4d. per acre per annum. Instead of this, the company entered into financial operations at great loss, and was liquidated in 1878. A new society took its place under the title of the Compagnie Générale Algérienne, and under the management of this company the Jardin d'Essai is now carried on.

11. Algiers to the **Ruisseau** and **Hussein Dey.**—Electric trams start from the Place du Gouvernement every twenty minutes. Carriage, 2f. 75c., plus 50c. per quarter of an hour for waiting. Hussein Dey the second station on the Algiers-Constantine Railway can also be reached by train (ten daily).

The route is by the Boulevard de la République, then through the busy suburb of **Agha Inférieur**, an annexe of the commune of Mustapha, and along the populous district of **Mustapha Inférieur**, which reaches as far as the sea. The barracks of the 5th Regiment of **Chasseurs d'Afrique** are close to the **Champ de Manœuvres**, a vast piece of ground used for the exercise of the cavalry regiments, and also, in the winter season, for the Algiers races and equestrian displays.

Four kilometres further on the road is the **Koubba of Sidi Mohammed Abd er Rahman Bou Kobrin**, a marabout or saint, from the Djurdjura Mountains, who came to Algiers in 1798, and remained till 1805. He founded a powerful religious caste in the territory of the **Beni Ismail**, which counted numberless adherents and fervent apostles. His body was brought back to Algiers after his death, and buried at the village of **Hamma**, the present spot occupied by his tomb, or **Koubba**. The Kabyles of the Djurdjura, and the tribes of the Beni Ismail, on hearing that his body had been transported to Algiers, became much irritated, but soon calmed down when they had verified that his body still remained in the original burial-place. The story of the saint's body existing in duplicate at **Hamma**, gave rise to the current belief that the saint had been miraculously doubled, and rested in both tombs.

Thus was he named **Bou Kobrin** (the man with two tombs). The religious order of **Sidi Mohammed Ben Abd er Rahman** is the most powerful of Algeria after that of **Sidi Okba**.

The **Koubba** is visited every Friday afternoon by multitudes of Moorish women.

The **Ruisseau** (six kilometres from Algiers), p. 37, is reached by a lovely shaded road, and the walk or drive is continued towards the sea to

Hussein Dey, a pleasant village which derives its name from **Dey Hussein,** the last ruler of Algiers, who possessed there a magnificent villa, which has since then been turned into a tobacco dépôt. Visitors to Hussein Dey should ask Mr. Trottier's permission to visit his splendid gardens, which contain the largest eucalyptus trees in Algeria.

A few hundred yards from Hussein Dey, on the sea-shore, is a little Mussulman cemetery, called **Topphanat el Moudjhadin** (Turkish dialect, signifying **Battery of the Champions of the Holy War**). This cemetery commemorates the great victory of the Turks, the Beys of Constantine, over **O'Reilly**, a Spanish general, who was entirely routed and cut to pieces, with his army. (*See also p. 87.*)

12. From Algiers to Maison Carrée.—Electric trams from the Place du Gouvernement every twenty minutes, The route as far as Hussein Dey is the same as that given above for No. 11. Ten trains a day to and from Maison Carrée on the P.-L-M. and East Algerian Railways; single fares, 1f. 25c., 90c. and 70c.

The station and village of **Maison Carrée** (12 kilometres from Algiers) take their name from a Turkish fort built in 1721 by Mahomet V., Dey of Algiers, and enlarged in 1826 by Agha Yehia. The present building, one storey high, is used as a native penitentiary and dépôt for prisoners waiting to be deported.

The great attraction for visitors to this purely native village (population about 7,000) is the large early market on Friday. To witness this interesting assembly the Oran train leaving Algiers at 6.50 a.m. (due at Maison Carrée 7.13 a.m.) should be taken.

The large buildings near the sea, surrounded by trees, contain an orphan asylum for young natives, and the **Monastery of St. Joseph,** a missionary order wearing the Arab costume, and called the White Fathers. Some of the fathers have been sent as missionaries to Lakes Tanganyika and Nyanza, others to Uganda and to Timbuctoo ; the Monastery contains a small museum of natural history and other objects brought by the fathers from their distant missions.

Close to Maison Carrée is an Agricultural School established in 1905.

13. Algiers to Fort de l'Eau and Cape Matifou.—The route to Fort de l'Eau is by electric tramway or railway as far as the Maison Carrée (as given above, No. 12), and then by the diligence to the Fort. Cape Matifou is about 9 kilomètres from Fort de l'Eau ; but another route is from Algiers to Rouiba, on the East-Algerian Railway, five trains a day, 1f. 60c., 2f. 20c. and 2f. 90c., thence diligence to Aïn-Taya, two miles from the Cape.

Fort de l'Eau (18 kilomètres from Algiers) is a fortress built in 1581, by **Djafar Pasha**, for the defence of the Bay of Mustapha. It is inhabited chiefly by Mahonese from the Balearic Islands. From Fort de l'Eau can be enjoyed the most magnificent view of Algiers and the Bay of Mustapha. The old Turkish fort is very interesting to visit. It is now occupied by a detachment of **Douaniers** (Customs' soldiers). The village is remarkable for its extreme cleanliness, and is noted for its Mahonese restaurant, where *soubresade*, a sort of Spanish sausage, is supplied. The women are mostly pretty, with oval, regular features. The views in the neighbourhood are lovely, and the country around, thanks to irrigation and labour, is a succession of highly cultivated market gardens. A Casino has lately been built.

Unless the traveller pays a separate visit to Cape Matifou from Algiers to Rouiba, as explained above, he will continue from Fort de l'Eau *via* Rassauta, L'Oued, Khamis, and Rusgunia, where ruins of an old Roman city of considerable extent may be seen,

Cape Matifou or Ras Temenfous, on which there is a first-class lighthouse at some little distance from the village, and the old Turkish Fort of Matifou, built by Ramdan-Agha under the Pashalik of Ismaïl in 1661, and restored under Mezzo-Morto-Dey in 1685, after the bombardment of Algiers. At the present time the fort is the property of M. de la Villegontier.

It was at Matifou in 1541 that Charles V. re-embarked after his disastrous attack on Algiers, when, owing to tempestuous weather, the large army that had been landed, where now stands the Jardin d'Essai, was compelled to retreat and re-embark as best as they could at Cape Matifou. One hundred and forty vessels were wrecked by the tempest, and a third of the army perished.

At rather more than two miles from Cape Matifou is

Aïn=Taya=les=Bains, a charming, shady, little village with a beautiful sandy beach and pleasant walks in the country. A modest meal can be obtained at the well-kept little inn.

14. Algiers to Rovigo and the Baths of Hammam Melouan.

—Visitors can reach Hammam Melouan from Algiers by electric or steam tram as far as Rovigo (19 miles), fares 2f. 45c. and 1f. 85c., thence by some other conveyance, 4 miles, to the Baths; by rail (5 trains daily) as far as the P.-L.-M. railway station, Gué-de-Constantine, where an omnibus is in attendance; or by carriage direct to the Baths, which is the most convenient plan, 20f.

The road passes through Mustapha Inférieur, the Ruisseau, Koubba, and descends into the **Mitidja** plain, in the midst of numerous villas and farms belonging to French and Turkish settlers. The Turkish *haouchs*, or farms, are an illustration of the old Arab farms from the time of the Deys. Sometimes the French building combines the old Arab house, when it does not completely replace it.

Beyond Gué-de-Constantine, the road crosses the Harrach.

Sidi Moussa (22 kilometres from Algiers), an agricultural village, standing at the junction of the **Boufarik, Rovigo**, and **Aumale** roads.

Rovigo (30 kilometres) takes its name from the Duc de Rovigo, who was Governor-General of Algeria from 1831 to 1833. It is a village built near the **Harrach**, at the foot of the **Atlas Mountains**. It is chiefly remarkable for its beautiful orange groves, and two quarries of cement and sand, very much appreciated in the manufacture of glass and porcelain.

Two miles from Rovigo, on the left bank of the Harrach, is the site of a camp, built at the same time as the **Camp de Fondouk**. A mile further south are the baths of

Hammam=Melouan. — When nearing the baths the visitor will observe a bamboo hut, the dwelling of the **Kaid of Hammam-Melouan**, which serves as a Moorish café as well.

The name of Hammam-Melouan signifies in Arabic **the Coloured Baths**, so called from the red deposits of iron in the water, and partly perhaps from the divers specimens of coloured stones that line the bed of the Harrach. The baths are surrounded by several acres of park, in which, during the season May, June, and October, scores of tents are inhabited by visitors, Europeans and natives.

There are two springs, one of which flows through a small rough bath in the celebrated **Koubba** of Sidi Sliman. The other flows into a wooden hut. The **Koubba** is a parallelogram of about six yards square, constructed in heavy thick mud walls. The hall that precedes the inside bath, situated in a kind of recess, with scarcely any light, does not inspire a prepossessing idea of the place at first sight. However, once the eye gets accustomed to the comparative darkness, and begins to perceive the clear water of the bath, surrounded on the four sides with a bench of masonry, the somewhat depressing aspect of the interior gloom soon vanishes, and is replaced by a sentiment of confidence in the pure and wholesome waters, that are credited with so many beneficent qualities. Both baths are small, and leave much to be desired on the score of cleanliness.

The actual supply to both sources of Hammam-Melouan amounts to 200 litres per minute ; and, according to the estimate of the Captain of Engineers, Rayral, the output could be extended to 600 litres per minute with only a trifling expense.

Hammam-Melouan is the habitual resort of a great many Algerians and Jews, and during the season the average number of visitors amounts to 150 daily. Indeed, the virtues of the hot waters are by no means exaggerated, and wonderful rheumatismal cures are authenticated that could not have been effected by ordinary medication.

The temperature of the baths is, on an average, from 85° to 105° Fahrenheit. Analysis has proved that a great quantity of salt (as much as 26 grammes in every kilogram of liquid) enters into the composition of these waters, which in this respect may be compared with the baths at Nauheim.

A small hotel is situated near the Baths, but as the bed-room accommodation is very limited, visitors should secure rooms in advance.

The waters of Hammam-Melouan are recommended to all persons suffering from any kind of neuralgia, paralysis, or rheumatismal indisposition.

PART IV

THE INTERIOR.

——◆——

DISTRICTS WEST OF ALGIERS.

—————

ALGIERS TO BOUFARIK, BLIDAH, AND THE GORGES DE LA CHIFFA.

Trains start from Algiers to Boufarik and Blidah several times a day. The fastest is the Oran train, which leaves Algiers at 6.50 a.m. Omitting Boufarik, a favourite excursion from Algiers is to leave by the 9.55 train due at Blidah 11.42, lunch at the Hotel d'Orient, drive to the Gorges de la Chiffa, and return in time to take the 4.41 train to Algiers. (Train times subject to alteration.)

Boufarik is a flourishing little town of about 9,000 inhabitants, of which about 5,000 are Europeans, 37 kilometres from Algiers on the main road to Blidah. It is considered a very promising agricultural centre, composed of modern farms with a rural population, almost exclusively European. "In 1830 Boufarik was an uninhabitable compound of marsh and jungle, swarming with hyenas, jackals, and panthers. A few bridle-paths traversed the combination of thicket and quagmire, converging at an expanse of somewhat more solid earth in the form of a hillock, and crowned by a well, which was over shaded by three tall trees. From the branches of these trees floated permanently sundry hempen ropes, and to these ropes were not unfrequently suspended human bodies, the corpses of true believers, who, to their own ill-luck, had come into collision with the criminal code as administered by the Moorish judicial functionaries."—*George Augustus Sala.*

For many years the malaria or pestilential fever killed the settlers almost as fast as they came, and the vast camp which General d'Erlon had built there, and which is now used for the Monday market, was baptised "Le Cimetière." However, to-day Boufarik is one of the healthiest spots in Algeria; its lofty trees and pretty gardens render it an unusually attractive little place. The water is pure and good, and the prosperity of the district is yearly increasing.

The public garden is both shady and pleasing, being densely planted with trees and flowers of all kinds. It contains a magnificent Chinese palm-tree and many maritime stone-pine-trees.

A great many plane and poplar-trees are seen in all directions, and though they have been planted only about thirty years, they have attained to fabulous heights. In summer the district is comparatively cool, owing to its numerous trees and the abundance of water. There are a great many Jews in the town, as everywhere else in Algeria where money is to be made. They are peaceful, frugal, and persevering, and most of the trade is in their hands.

The **Monday market** for which Boufarik is renowned, is one of the most important in Algeria. Past the public garden, and on the way to the market, is a large piece of ground shaded by plane-trees of splendid growths. The road to the market and the road from the station are bordered with olive, acacia, eucalyptus, and plane trees. In the central place there is the statue of **Sergeant Blandan,** the hero of the **Beni=Méred** encounter (April 11, 1841) when 25 French soldiers held their ground against 300 Arabs for three hours, until help arrived, when only five of the plucky little troop were found living. The following inscription is on the pedestal: "*Courage, enfants; défendez-vous jusqu'à la mort!*" (Courage, boys; fight to the death!) These were the last words Blandan was heard to say, for his body was among the slain (*see* also p. 143).

The best hotel at Boufarik is the **Hotel Nemoz,** greatly frequented by English and American tourists. Carriages at the station. The **Hotel Benoît** is the oldest established, and well spoken of.

From Boufarik to Blidah the train proceeds S.W. through the Mitidja plain, and the approach of Blidah is announced by orange groves, which are, indeed, real forests of orange

trees.   From Blidah station to the town (one kilometre)
the 'bus fare is 2d. (20 centimes), or 1 franc for a private
carriage.

Blidah, 51 kilometres from Algiers, is a prosperous town,
situated 260 metres above the level of the sea.   Its population
amounts to 29,000 inhabitants, of which 9,000 are Europeans,
chiefly French colonists.   It stands in 0° 30′ longitude W.,
by 36° 20′ latitude N., on the **Oued=el=Kebir,** a tributary
stream of the **Chiffa,** at the foot of the **Atlas** range of
mountains.   The town is abundantly supplied with water, and
is chiefly remarkable for its numerous and important orange
groves, and extensive and well-cultivated gardens.   There are
two public gardens ; one, the Jardin Bizot, is well laid out
and carefully maintained, and here a military band plays
several times a week in summer ; in the other garden, called
the Bois Sacré, are a number of large olive trees, and the
Koubba of a Marabout, Sidi Yakoub.   The town is surrounded
by a wall 4 metres high, (pierced with musket-holes) in which
are six gates : The **Algiers,** the **Camp des Chasseurs,** the
El Zionia, the **El Rabah,** the **Es Sebt,** and the **El Kebia,**
or **Bizot** Gates.   Coming from the railway, the town is
entered by the Es-Sebt Gate.

Hotel : Hotel d'Orient, comfortable well-managed and
clean (Cook's Coupons, Series, A, B, and C, accepted).

The **Fort Mimich,** situated on a hill 400 metres high,
completes the defensive works of Blidah.

Blidah was destroyed in 1825 by an earthquake, and the
present town was built at some little distance from the ruins.
Another earthquake caused considerable damage to the new
town in 1867.   But the modern French buildings stood the
shock better than the Arab constructions, which serves to
illustrate that the damage to property in cases of earthquakes
is very often checked by solidity of construction.   The streets
are lined with very neat and pleasant-looking houses, nearly
all built of bricks, painted white.

The **Place d'Armes** is a cheerful-looking square, bordered
with a double row of plane-trees and arcaded houses.   In the
middle is a pretty fountain, over which in winter a temporary
bandstand is erected, and concerts given by the regimental
band.

The **Barracks,** which can accommodate 2,000 soldiers,
deserve an inspection, as well as the

Cavalry Barracks and **Stud.** These occupy a whole quarter of the town, and have good stabling for 300 stallions. Many fine specimens of the best existing Arab races are there to be seen. Syrian thoroughbreds and Sahara stallions are represented in their handsomest productions.

The famous **Orange Groves,** situated to the north, are noted for their beauty and numbers. There are, one may say, millions of oranges and lemons of all the known sorts, of every shape, size, and flavour, large quantities of which are bought by dealers from Algiers for exportation to France and England. The most interesting places to be visited are as follows :—**Within the Walls:** La Place d'Armes, Djama el Turk, Rue des Coulouglis, Le Dépôt et la Remonte, the Hospital, the Arab market, the Arab quarter, the Protestant Church, Hammam Kaïd Dira, the Catholic Church, the St. Charles' Church, the College, the Cavalry barracks, the barracks of the Turcos, the Avenue Trumelet. **Outside the Walls :**—Square Bizot, Fort Mimich, Bois Sacré, Kouba of Sidi Yakoub, Blad Djedida, orange groves, Oulad Sultan, Sidi Abd el Kader, Propriété Gonin, etc.

Blidah is a good centre from which to make excursions, the most popular being that to the **Ruisseau des Singes** and the **Gorge de la Chiffa,** 14 kilometres by road. A diligence leaves Blidah every day, but by carriage this delightful excursion and the return to Blidah railway station or to Blidah town can be made under four hours. Carriages in any number may be ordered from **Mr. Artusio,** Blidah, either personally or by letter or telegram in advance.

The road by the gate of Bab-es-Sebt, parallel to the railway, passes near the village of La Chiffa, on the right, and runs alongside the **Oued Chiffa,** a small river in a rent of the Atlas mountains. The gorge extends a distance of seven miles, the road at one place being cut out of the solid rock, and at another carried over the bed of the Chiffa, with peaks of the Atlas towering five or six thousand feet above. A halt is generally made at the Ruisseau des Singes, where there is a small, unpretentious, but cleanly-kept inn, called the **Auberge du Ruisseau des Singes.** Good beds can be procured there, and a tolerably good service for tourists who may wish to spend a day or two in the midst of this grand scenery of a portion of the Atlas mountains. In the inn is a picture of a number of monkeys, but the real article is becoming comparatively rare in the neighbourhood.

About a hundred yards from the inn on the other side of the road there is a stalactite grotto, which can be visited on applying to the Auberge du Ruisseau. An entrance fee of 50c. each for one or two visitors, or of two or three francs for a party, is expected. It is also worth while to go up the rough path at the back of the inn to visit the waterfall, garden, and luxurious vegetation. Here wild monkeys, large and small, may occasionally be seen.

Resuming the excursion, the drive is continued about three kilometres until the second waterfall is passed, and then the return journey is made to Blidah. Or a pleasant variation may be made by continuing (6 kilometres only from the Auberge) to the railway station at Camp-des-Chênes, whence train may be taken to Blidah. Fares 1f. 60c. and 1f. 15c.

A capital whole day's excursion is the ascent of

Beni Salah, 5,400 feet, affording a fine view of the Atlas flanks and ridges. Leave Blidah by Bab-el-Rabah, pass through the village of Imama Rita, Glacières Laval (1,206 metres altitude), the Two Cedars (altitude, 1,453 metres), then the excursion can be extended along the ridge, which is broad and carpeted with turf, as far as the **Koubba** of **Sidi-Abd-el-Kader El-Djilani,** returning to Blidah from the west. Mules can be hired, 5f. each ; guide 3f.

Other excursions are also very interesting—for instance, to the

Oued Sidi el-Kebir, where, at the head of the beautiful ravine, are the Koubbas of Sidi Ahmed el-Kebir (1560) and his two sons ; to the **Tombeau de la Chrétienne** (see p. 121), carriage 20f. ; to the finely-situated town of **Médéa,** 3,100 feet above the sea, 30 miles from Blidah by rail. The town is essentially French and has no feature of interest except its situation, but the neighbourhood is rich in well-cultivated vegetation. A permanent garrison was established here in 1840. Market on Thursdays and Fridays (see also p. 136).

ALGIERS TO MARENGO, CHERCHELL, TIPAZA, AND THE "TOMBEAU DE LA CHRÉTIENNE."

This is one of the most interesting and enjoyable excursions to be made from Algiers, and as there are several ways or routes open to the visitor, the following particulars will be found useful :—

Cherchell and Tipaza (*via* Marengo) can be comfortably explored in two days.

If the "Tombeau de la Chrétienne" be included, then three days will be required.

The "Tombeau de la Chrétienne" can be visited at any time from Algiers in one day *via* Coléa, or *via* Marengo.

Supposing only Cherchell and Tipaza are decided upon, the route is as follows :—

From **Algiers** to **El Affroun** by rail, 6.50 a.m., 69 kilometres. The journey takes about two hours and a quarter.

From **El Affroun** to **Marengo** there is a steam tramcar of the **Société des Chemins de Fer sur routes d'Algérie,** 20 kilom , 1 hour and 10 minutes. Fares : second-class return, 2f. 70c. Trains start from El Affroun for Marengo at 9.25 a.m., 3.45 p.m., and 8.2 p.m. ; returning from Marengo to El Affroun at 6.6 a.m., 1.40 p.m., and 5.40 p.m., in correspondence with the P.-L.-M. trains to and from Algiers—viz., 6.50 a.m., 12.41 p.m., 5.19 p.m. from Algiers, and 7.40 a.m., 3.44 p.m., 7.33 p.m. from El Affroun for Algiers. (Times subject to change.)

An extension of the light railway from Marengo to Cherchell is contemplated.

Arrive Marengo 10.39 a.m., lunch at **Hôtel d'Orient,** engage break with two horses, 25f. for the round—(2 days) Marengo, Cherchell, Tipaza, Marengo—leave for Cherchell 11.30 a.m., arriving there 2 p.m. ; visit, dine and sleep at the **Hôtel Nicolas,** a large, new, and quite comfortable hotel.

Leave Cherchell 6.30 to 7 a.m., arrive Tipaza (22 kilom.), 9 a.m., visit ruins, lunch at comfortable and scrupulously clean **Hôtel du Rivage,** leave for Marengo 12.15, arriving there in time for steam tramway (1.40) for El Affroun, and P.-L.-M. train (3.44) for Algiers. (2 days.)

For description of route from Algiers to the Tombeau de la Chrétienne, *via* Coléa, *see* p. 120.

H

If the Tombeau de la Chrétienne be added, the better itinerary would be : Marengo to the " Tombeau," " Tombeau " to Tipaza, sleep ; Tipaza, after lunch, to Cherchell, sleep ; Cherchell to Marengo, etc., Algiers. (3 days.) For this round a carriage (2 horses) from Hôtel d'Orient, Marengo, would cost 35f.

A good idea of the fertile district of the Sahel is afforded by the journey from El-Affroun to Marengo by the light railway, especially if the traveller has not previously visited the interior of Algeria. The train passes directly through the agricultural villages of

Ameur=el=Aïn (6 kilometres) and **Bourkika** (8 kilometres), surrounded by miles of well-cultivated farms and valuable vineyards, some of which produce as much as 80 hectolitres of wine per feddan of $2\frac{1}{2}$ acres.

Marengo is an important village and commune of 5,000 inhabitants, where the Wednesday market (Souk el-Arba) is largely attended, and deserves to be seen. **Hotel:** Hôtel d'Orient (Cook's Coupons, Series R, accepted). Thousands of natives, including **Kabyles**, from all parts of the region meet on that day to sell and buy their supplies. The rich land of the district is well watered by the **Barrage of Oued Merad** (10 kilometres from Marengo) a solid piece of work 17 metres high, covering a valley of 130 metres in width. This immense cistern, which is continually filled up by the river, contains a provision of about 850,000 cubic metres, and supplies 200 litres per second.

The road to Cherchell leaves Marengo by the western avenue, and passes through a delightful agricultural country with picturesque views of hills and valleys, and crosses the **Oued=el=Hachem** to

Zurich, a small village of 600 inhabitants, where the public conveyances halt for a quarter of an hour. Zurich was built in 1848 on the site of a Roman villa. Thursday is market day.

The route is continued through a splendid avenue of lime trees for several kilometres, then along the side of the vast **Djebel Chénoua** and through the valley of the **Oued=el= Acheur,** where, on the left, are the ruins of the aqueduct, which conveyed the water from the mountain into Cæsarea. Some of the arches are still complete, but the upper rows are partially or entirely destroyed. Beyond this point the sea soon comes into view, and during the next four kilometres the road skirts the blue Mediterranean on one side and delightful vegetation on the other as far as **Cherchell** (117 kilometres from Algiers), situated at the foot of a hill on the seashore. It was originally the Phœnician colony of **Jol.** Juba II. enlarged it and gave it the name of **Cæsarea**, the capital of Mauretanian territory. It was designated, according to numerous inscriptions discovered in the ruins of Cherchell, "Splendissima Colonia Cæsariensis," and covered a space of 1,200 acres, with a population of over 100,000. When Ptolemy, son of Juba II., was assassinated, his kingdom was incorporated with the Roman Empire. Later it was destroyed by the Vandals, rose again under the Byzantines, and after many changes, it was destroyed by an earthquake in 1738, and reduced to its present size. In 1839, the inhabitants of Cherchell having plundered a French wreck in Cherchell Straits, the French occupied the town on the 15th of March of the following year. It is now the centre of a military circle, belonging to the Division of Orleansville.

Cherchell is now a quiet town of about 10,000 inhabitants, pleasantly situated between the hills and the sea, amidst rich lands and luxurious vegetation, with interesting ruins in every direction, a charming country for either the archæologist, the artist, or the tourist. Some persons will be disappointed at the absence of *important* ruins of palaces, temples, amphitheatre, and other public buildings, but no pains have been taken to preserve them; and most of the monuments have been destroyed for the sake of their stone, and many of the smaller objects removed to various museums; still there are sufficient evidences in all directions to show to what dimensions and magnificence the city of Cæsarea had attained more than 2,000 years ago.

Cherchell contains no buildings of any magnificence or originality, except the **Grand Mosque**, which the axe and spade of conquest have spared. It has, however, been converted into a military hospital. The roof is designed in horseshoe arches, supported by eighty beautiful green granite columns, which formed part of a Roman temple.

Of the ancient Roman palace behind the Museum, overlooking the sea, only some of the party walls, some pillars, with beautiful capitals and injured mosaic pavements now remain. The cisterns, which are very large, still exist, and

H 2

supply the city with water as they did twenty centuries ago.
Nearly all the other Roman buildings have fallen to the
ground and disappeared through neglect. The site of the
seats round the old Roman amphitheatre can still be traced.
This was the place where St. Marcian, the martyr, was de-
voured by wild beasts. The centre is now a ploughed field.
The theatre where St. Arcadius was cut to pieces for admitting
his belief in Christ is in a very dilapidated state, it having
been used for a long time as a stone quarry. The port, which
was very important at the time of the Roman occupation, is
now only a small harbour of about 2 hectares. Recent excavations have discovered a variety of Roman vases and curiosities,
a Roman barge 11 metres long by 4½ metres wide, which was
full of pottery, and a black basalt statue, the lower half of
an Egyptian divinity bearing the cartouche of King Thotmes
III. (now in the museum). This statue is supposed to have
been sent as a present from Egypt, her native land, to Juba's
wife, Cleopatra Selene, who was the daughter of the famous
Cleopatra.

In the modern Roman Catholic Church adjoining the Hotel
Nicolas is a handsome floor of mosaics recovered from the
ruins.

There is a small **Museum** (recently restored) in the town,
created by MM. Lhotellerie and Waille, where some very fine
ancient statues, which have been found to be copies from the
originals in Rome, can be seen. These statues have evidently
been brought there by Juba. There are many pillars,
capitals, cornices, pottery ware, tiles, mosaics, vases, etc. One
of these vases, of very elegant shape, bears an inscription, a
dedication to Bacchus, with the name of the town, thus—
" Resp. Cæsarea." Catalogue published in Algiers.

About 2 kilometres outside the Western Gate on the Ténès
road a retired French officer, M. le Commandant Archambeau,
has an interesting little museum of antiquities found in his
own garden during the last seventeen years. The collection
consists of several hundred objects of pottery and glass, principally relating to the burial rites and customs of the Romans,
vases, cups, urns, lamps, plates, tear bottles, inscriptions,
amphoræ, oil jars, etc., and some broken portions of remarkably
delicate mosaics. The Commandant is always pleased to show
his collection to visitors, and possibly would be willing to
dispose of it to an antiquarian or collector.

Another collection of antiquities may be visited by applying to **Mr.** Romain, jeweller, nearly opposite the town museum. This collection is not so large as that of the Commandant Archambeau, but it contains statues, vases, urns, mosaics, and bronzes.

Tourists should be in no hurry to leave Cherchell. The place is full of Roman relics, and affords great archæological surprises. Its environs are very beautiful. The site of Cherchell is a splendid one, the views on the seashore are delightful, the district abounds in copper, iron, marble, clay, etc., all of which, with a larger harbour and railway facilities, would increase its prosperity.

From Cherchell an excursion can be made on horseback or by carriage to the village of **Gouraya** (30 kilometres), the headquarters of a commune containing 25,000 inhabitants. (Diligence twice a day from Cherchell, 3 hours, 1f. 50c.) This is the best point from which to make the ascent of **Djebel=Gouraya** (4,700 feet), on which dwell the formidable tribes of Beni-Menasser (Kabyles).

The journey from Cherchell to Tipaza can be made on foot, or on mule over the famous **Djebel=Chénoua,** inhabited by sturdy Kabyles, who mix little with the Arabs of the district, seldom quitting their mountain homes except to carry their produce, tissues, or pottery to Tipaza, Marengo, or Cherchell. They are, however, well disposed to visitors, and travelling among them is perfectly safe. The routes are easily found, but it is desirable to be accompanied by a guide. The views from the summit over sea and land are of incomparable beauty.

Leaving Cherchell for Tipaza (26 kilometres) in the usual way by carriage (or diligence in about $2\frac{1}{2}$ hours), the route follows for some distance the road to Marengo along the side of the **Djebel=Chénoua,** past the aqueduct referred to above, then turns to the left on the road to Algiers through a cultivated district to the village of

Desaix, the ancient **Nador,** a good starting point from which to ascend the Djebel-Chénoua. About 4 kilometres further on the sea near Tipaza comes into view, and then on each side of the road are seen walls and loose stones which once formed part of the ancient city.

Tipaza is now a small seaport and village charmingly situated on rising ground just off the main road. To the west there is a fine sandy beach for bathers, the country round is rich in excursions, such as to the "**Tombeau de la Chré-tienne,**" 10 kilometres; the ascent of the **Djebel-Chénoua** *viâ* Nador (already mentioned), time required 7 to 8 hours, mule and guide 6f., provisions must be carried : to the forest of **Sidi-Sliman,** along the Oued Nador, on the road to Marengo.

Small steamers leave Algiers at least weekly calling at Tipaza, and a diligence leaves Marengo for Tipaza (14 kilo-metres in about 1½ hours) in connection with all trains, so that supplies of all kinds are easily procured. There is also a diligence service between Castiglione and Tipaza (24 kilo-metres in about 2½ hours). And as previously mentioned good accommodation and cooking can be obtained (for twenty-five or thirty persons) at the Hotel du Rivage, pleasantly situated close to the sea.

The ancient city of Tipaza was built on three hills, Ras-ez-Zarur to the east, Ras-el-Knissa to the west, and Ras-Bel-Aishe in the centre, where the brazen serpent was worshipped. The old harbour was at the east end ; the present small harbour and village are in the centre just within the ancient line of ramparts.

The history of Tipaza is not very circumstantial, but Phœnician remains have been found, so that it was in-habited by the Carthaginians, falling afterwards into the power of the Kings of Mauretania. Soon after the Emperor Claudius made it a Latin colony and city, which prospered, and is believed to have numbered 20,000 inhabitants. Later the Vandals by their cruelty drove a large proportion of the population to Spain, and those of them who remained and refused to be converted to the Arian heresy had their tongues cut out and their right hands cut off. After the Arab conquest the city was abandoned.

The public buildings of Tipaza were numerous, including churches, theatre, amphitheatre, baths, etc., but the ruins are in a lamentable state, many of the monuments having served as quarries.

The most interesting monument which has been partly excavated lately under the direction of M. Gsell, professor of archæology at the Ecole des Lettres, Algiers, is the

Basilica of St. Salsa, on the summit of the eastern hill, to the north of which is the ancient harbour. The history of this large church is too long for insertion here, it will be found in the writings of M. Gsell referred to below.

The **Ramparts** are in a dilapidated state, but it is just possible to trace their circuit.

The **Baths** in the centre of the town are scarcely visible, buried as they are in the ground.

The **Amphitheatre** is equally difficult to be traced.

A Nymphæum to the west of the amphitheatre has been cleared out by M. Trémaux, the proprietor of the land.

The **Theatre** is merely a mass of ruins. The principal church on the western hill,

The **Great Basilica** was an important edifice with a chapel, a baptistery, and other dependencies, in very bad condition, having served as a quarry. Near the cemetery on the western hill, outside the ramparts, is

The **Basilica of Bishop Alexander,** containing stone coffins covered with mosaics.

Many of the ruins have been explored by M. Pierre Gavault, and a full description of the district will be found in " Recherches Archéologiques en Algérie, Paris, 1893, by M. Gsell. with plans and illustrations by M. Gavault.

M. Waille, professor at the Ecole des Lettres, Algiers, has devoted himself to the study of Cherchell, and by his writings has given much historical interest to the ruins of this ancient city.

Adjoining the Hotel du Rivage, which was built by the late M. Trémaux, a wealthy proprietor, is the family villa with extensive gardens and shrubberies, where, in various directions, will be found a number of valuable and interesting objects recovered from the ruins by M. Trémaux. The collection includes large marble sarcophagi, with well-preserved carved figures, capitals of pillars, portions of marble cornices, fragments of mosaics, tumulary inscriptions, and large amphoræ. Visitors are kindly welcomed, and from the grounds the ruins on the western hill can be reached.

Visitors returning to Algiers without going to the " Tombeau de la Chrétienne " will leave Tipaza, as shown on p. 113.

It is, however, possible to go to the Tombeau and thence to Marengo, arriving there in time for the 5.40 p.m. steam tramway departure for El-Affroun, and P.-L.-M. train 7.33 p.m., due at Algiers 9.51 p.m., but this involves a very long day of fifteen hours, and is not recommended.

ALGIERS TO COLÉA (CASTIGLIONE) AND THE "TOMBEAU DE LA CHRÉTIENNE."

This excursion and return to Algiers can easily be made in a day.

Leave Algiers by the Chemins de Fer sur Routes d'Algérie (light railways) at 6.42 a.m., arrive Coléa 9.29 a.m. Carriage to the "Tombeau de la Chrétienne" and back to Coléa, 44 kilometres, 20f. Train from Coléa 4.35 p.m., due at Algiers 7.27 p.m.

Or, if it is preferred not to make so early a start, leave Algiers 12.59 p.m., due Coléa 3.51 p.m.; visit the town, and take carriage to Castiglione (7 kilometres), sleep there and proceed by carriage next morning to the Tombeau (15 kilometres), thence to Coléa (22 kilometres); cost of carriage for the round 30f. Train from Coléa, 4.35 p.m.; due Algiers, 7.27 p.m. For the first route, leave the Place du Gouvernement by electric tramway at 6.42 a.m. (or 12.59 p.m. as preferred) for the Deux Moulins, and there change into the steam tramway for Coléa. The train, passing close to the shore, goes through the villages of Pointe Pescade, Guyotville, Staouéli, etc., see p. 96, and, leaving Sidi-Ferruch on the right, arrives at Zéralda, crosses the River Mazafran (junction for Castiglione) passes Daouda, a prosperous village, to **Coléa** or **K**oléa (44 kilometres from Algiers), a pretty little town of about 6,000 inhabitants, perched up on one of the hills of the Sahel range, looking over the Mitidja Plains towards Blidah, at 130 metrés altitude. It is surrounded by vineyards and orchards, and has an abundant supply of stream water. It is celebrated as the residence of the Marabout Sidi Ali Embareck, who is said to have performed many miracles.

The **Mosque** and the **Koubba** of **Sidi Embareck** is considered by the Arabs as the Mecca of Algeria. It contains a palm-tree, and a cyprus tree, of which the seed is said to have been brought by Moslem pilgrims from Mecca.

Coléa was destroyed by an earthquake in 1825, and has been entirely rebuilt. It was attacked by the French in 1832, for the first time, and was definitely secured in 1843. The aspect of the town is decidedly European, the Mosque itself having been converted into a military hospital. The Koubba alone has been respected, and still preserves its original appearance.

The **Jardin des Zouaves,** at the lower end of the town, deserves a visit and also the **Cercle des Officiers,** where is preserved the celebrated flag of the 2nd Regiment of Zouaves. The Jardin des Zouaves is, in fact, the great attraction of Coléa. It is not a stiff and formal piece of ground, like most French gardens generally are, but covers the ravine which separates the military quarter from the town. There are tall and shady trees, frequented by a multitude of singing birds, such as the nightingale, that make this garden truly delightful. It is one of the most picturesque gardens in Algeria, and the most beautiful and extensive, after the Jardin d'Essai.

The barracks, for 1,200 soldiers, and the camp are situated on an eminence outside the town. An Arab market is held in the Rue-es-Souk every Friday, and the ordinary market in the same street daily.

Coléa is the starting point for visiting the remarkable edifice called Tombeau de la Chrétienne, or, in Arabic, Kbour-er-Roumia, tomb of the Christian woman.

The **Tombeau de la Chrétienne** is a tomb of circular form, standing on a hill 792 feet above sea level, the great sepulchre of the Mauretanian kings, erected 26 B.C. The building is about 100 feet high, of which the cylindrical portion is 36 feet, and the pyramid 64 feet. The base is 198 feet in diameter, and forms a zone presenting a vertical wall, with sixty Ionic columns, surmounted by a cornice. Above the cornice are thirty-three steps, decreasing to a point towards the summit, assuming the appearance of a pyramid. The entire edifice is placed on a platform 64 metres square.

The Emperor Napoleon gave permission for the tomb to be opened and explored, and in May, 1866, the necessary entrance was made. Long passages and many vaulted chambers were discovered, but no traces of the bodies for whose reception the tomb had been erected, thus leading to the conclusion that the tomb had been entered in search of treasure at a very early period.

The entrance to the tomb, closed by a gate, is below the basement to the east. A small door gives access to a vaulted chamber (on one of the walls a lion and lioness are roughly sculptured) from which, by a flight of steps, is entered the large gallery, nearly 9 feet in height, and 6 feet in breadth, running round the whole of the monument, with a passage leading out of it to the centre, where are two sepulchral chambers, one

14 feet 6 inches by 10 feet 6 inches by 10 feet 6 inches, and the other 12 feet by 4 feet 6 inches by 8 feet 6 inches, separated by a passage from the outer passage by stone doors. The passages, vaults, and galleries measure together 1,450 feet.

Antiquarians differ as to the origin of this vast tomb, but the balance of opinion points to its having been built by Juba II., and, if so, it is probable that the sepulchral chambers above described were the tombs of Juba and his wife, Cleopatra Selene.

The Arabs, who believe that treasure exists in all buildings or monuments, the origin of which they are unable to explain, have the following tradition concerning the "Tombeau." An Arab named Ben-Kassem, made a prisoner of war by the Christians, was carried off to Spain and there sold as a slave. One day his master, an old savant, hearing him lamenting his enforced absence from his wife and children, offered him his liberty, promising that he should return to the bosom of his family if he would swear to carry out, on the fourth day after arrival, what was required of him. The instructions were that he should proceed to the Tomb and there burn a scroll of paper in a brazier. He was not to be astonished at anything that happened, and return home. No sooner had the flames touched the paper than the Tomb opened and thousands of gold and silver pieces issued from it and flew over the sea towards the land of the Christians. Recovering from his his surprise, Ben-Kassem arrested the flight of a few of the pieces with his burnous, and the stream of money ceased immediately. The charm was broken and the tomb shut.

News of Ben-Kassem's marvellous adventure having reached the pacha himself, labourers were sent to demolish the tomb for the treasures it might contain. At the first blow struck the phantom of a woman appeared on the summit, exclaiming in a loud voice, "Alloula! Alloula! come to my help!" At this appeal the lake Alloula, then situated at the foot of the hill, poured forth a cloud of enormous mosquitoes, driving the workmen incontinently from the spot.

Other monuments, nearly similar, are found in Algeria; the Djedars, near Tiaret, in the province of Oran, *see* p. 184, and the Medrassen, near Batna, in the province of Constantine, *see* p. 223.

The key of the tomb is kept at a farm on the opposite side, and a guide will conduct visitors through the interior.

A model of the Tombeau de la Chrétienne, on the scale of

1 centimetre for 1 metre, can be seen at the Bibliothèque Museum of Algiers. It was made by Mr. Latour, of Algiers.

For those who wish to travel more leisurely to the Tombeau passing a night at Castiglione the route is the same as far as Coléa.

Leaving Algiers at 12.59 p.m., Castiglione is reached at 3.53 p.m., or a carriage can be hired at Coléa (*see* p. 120) for Castiglione where the night can be spent and the "Tombeau" visited next morning. The road from Coléa to Castiglione (7 kilometres) is pleasant and well-wooded, passing through the village of Fouka, and Saidia the charming property of the Rev. E. Arkwright, of Mustapha Supérieur, Algiers.

Castiglione is an excellent bathing station, much frequented in summer by the inhabitants of Coléa, Blidah, and other districts. The village is shaded. by trees, and very healthy The small harbour is chiefly used by Italian fishermen. There are several small hotels, such as the Tapis Vert and the Hotel de Paris.

From Castiglione next morning the carriage drive is continued to the Tombeau de la Chrétienne (taking provisions from the hotel). The drive, 15 kilometres, is along the sea-shore, through the villages of Tefeschoun, and Bérard, a small bathing place; then for a short distance the road to Tipaza (p. 117) is followed, as far as the Farm of Kandouri, where, turning to the left, you proceed to the foot of the hill on which the Tombeau is situated.

After visiting the tomb, return direct to Coléa, 22 kilometres, in time for the 4.35 p.m. train to Algiers.

Or train may be taken to Castiglione, leaving Algiers at 6.42 a.m., reaching Castiglione at 9.34 (the 12.59 p.m. train from Algiers reaches Castiglione at 3.53 p.m., too late to return same night), whence drive to the "Tombeau" (*see* above), returning to Castiglione. Train to Algiers 4.30 p.m., due there 7.27 p.m.

Time tables subject to alteration.

ALGIERS TO HAMMAM R'IRHA.

Trains from Algiers on the Algiers-Oran line run three times a day to

Bou Medfa (viz., at 6.50 a.m., 9.55 a.m., and 5.19 p.m., in about three hours) the station from which the

Hotel and Thermal Establishment at **Hammam R'irha** is reached. An omnibus from the hotel awaits passengers by these trains, and takes them to the establishment at a charge of 2f. 50c. per person, luggage extra. Carriages can be obtained by giving notice the previous day to the manager of the hotel, the usual charge being 14f. for three or four persons.

From Bou Medfa the road crosses the Oued Djer and the railway line, and, leaving the Miliana road on the left, proceeds by the left bank of the **Oued=el-Hammam** through a succession of zigzags to **Hammam R'irha**, which is reached in one hour and ten minutes. The elevation of Hammam R'irha is 1,900 feet above the sea level, looking S.W.

The **Grand Hotel and Thermal Establishment (Hotel des Bains)** is now in the hands of a financial company. Extensive improvements have been made, both in the hotel accommodation and embellishment of the place. The cuisine and service are very superior, and the wines first class. There is also an excellent orchestra. The bedrooms have been newly furnished, and the sanitary arrangements are modern. The establishment is open from January 1st to April 30th (*see* p. 128). Cook's Coupons, Series A, B, and C, accepted.

The walks in the park are both numerous and shady, and afford, in themselves, excellent and delightful recreation. All sorts of outdoor games and gymnastics can be indulged in. A fine large tennis court has been added, also a ground for croquet.

Riding-horses and mules, with good English saddles, are kept on the premises. Carriages, such as landaus, brakes, English dog-carts and donkey-carts can be had at all times of the day and at most reasonable charges. Excursions are organised to Miliana, Teniet el Haâd, and the Cedar Forest, *see* pp. 131-135.

The approach to the entrance of the hotel is through well-kept grounds planted with the beautiful flowers one is accustomed to see in that climate, as well as date palms, aloes, orange, tangerine, fig, eucalyptus, pine and other trees. From this entrance the building runs right and left, the entire

Hammam R'irha.

edifice being in the form of a hollow square, the wings extending backwards at right angles. From the entrance hall the staircase ascends to the upper floors, and corridors run either way, with doors opening into private rooms, to the S.E. and S.W. corners. The large dining-room and lofty drawing-room are situated on the level of the entrance, and the spacious bath rooms are installed on the underground floor.

The **Baths** are really two large swimming baths, each 30 feet by 15 feet, one containing water at a temperature of about 95° Fahr., the other water at 110°, the temperature at the source being 130° Fahr. The process of taking the baths is commenced by first entering into No. 1. After remaining in it for about ten minutes, the bather proceeds to No. 2, in which, upon first placing his feet, a feeling of scalding is produced, which makes the bather hesitate about going into it further, but he gradually becomes accustomed to the heat, and is enabled to immerse the whole body.

Immediately after the application of the hot douche, the bather is wrapped in a blanket and laid upon a couch in a dressing-room, and covered up to the neck with four or five more blankets to promote perspiration, which soon becomes profuse, and is kept up for twenty minutes, after which the attendant uses vigorous friction with a rough towel or flesh-glove for some time longer, and the process is completed.

When commencing the baths, there is a sense of weariness and fatigue for the first few days, after which time it passes off, and a feeling of lightness and elasticity is established. The water of *Hammam R'irha* resembles that of Bath in many respects, both being of high temperature, as well as belonging to the class of thermal salines.

Adjoining the two large baths are rooms fitted with all modern appliances for hot or cold shower, spray, needle, or hip baths, also private baths with *ordinary water* for visitors in the hotel.

The charges are as follows :—

In the large baths	...	...	...	...	1f. 50c.
„ private baths	...				2f.
Douche only	...	...	...	...	1f. 50c.
„ with massage	...	...	...	...	2f. 50c.
Massage, local	...	...	...	...	2f.
„ complete	...	...	...	...	4f.

It may be stated generally that these baths are beneficial, not only in chronic rheumatism and gout, both articular and muscular, but in certain diseases of the nervous and cutaneous systems, periostitis, painful cicatrices, prostatitis, vesical catarrh, some chronic uterine affections, néuralgias, and some forms of paralysis.

In the **Belle Vue Hotel,** a short distance from the Grand Hotel (*see* p. 129), are two swimming baths, in which the temperature is about 104°, which, however, are not so comfortable as those described above; and situated immediately below the Bellevue are still other baths exclusively for the use of Arabs. More than 15,000 natives resort annually to Hammam R'irha.

In addition to the hot spring, there is at Hammam R'irhà a cold chalybeate spring, which is of great importance, and constitutes a most refreshing drink.

This chalybeate spring is about a mile distant, and the water is conducted to Hammam R'irha by pipes. It is by no means disagreeable, and is drunk by many at meals, either pure or mixed with light claret, the presence of carbonic acid being decidedly an advantage. This water is useful in anæmia, chlorosis, and allied affections. It is said to be of much service in cases of dyspepsia, chronic hepatitis, and other affections of the liver, and also in malaria and cases of renal calculus—probably in the latter because of its slightly diuretic action. There can be no doubt that this water is of great service in the treatment of chronic rheumatism, many cases of which are frequently associated with anæmia.

The great charm of such an establishment is its situation. It occupies the edge of a plateau at a considerable elevation above the sea level. It is opposite a pretty little village called Vesoul-Benian, from which it is distant about eight kilometres by road, but separated by a deep ravine, the valley of the Oued Hammam, running east and west. Beyond the opposite eminences, towards the south, the ranges of the lesser Atlas rise, whilst towards the west the summits of the Zakkar stretch upwards above Miliana. To the east, the high peaks of Berrouaghia and Ben Chicao are seen. From nearly all parts of the grounds beautiful panoramic views are beheld, and the eye never wearies of admiring the charming scenery. To those who are fond of sport, and who are well enough to enjoy it, there is ample opportunity afforded for gratifying their tastes, for in the pine forest of 1,800 acres there is a great abundance of game, including red partridges, hares, rabbits, wild boars, jackals, etc. There are numerous beautiful walks, and for those who are unable to walk far, many pleasant excursions can be made on ponies, mules, or donkeys. It may be of interest also to state that for the antiquary there is a varied field opened up calculated to delight the heart of an enthusiast. To prove how much the surroundings are interesting, it is only necessary to mention that the Hammam R'irha of to-day is in the same situation as the **Aquæ Calidæ** of the Romans, a town which flourished under the reign of the Emperor Tiberius about A.D. 32. It is recorded that many patients suffering from various disorders gathered there on account of the benefit to be derived from its waters.

Climate.—The climate of *Hamman R'irha* renders it a suitable **winter resort** for cases of pulmonary disease, as well as for rheumatism and gout. It is most useful in cases of phthisis occurring in persons of a lymphatic or strumous diathesis, and it is especially serviceable when dyspeptic complications are present.

The mean temperature at Hammam R'irha in winter ranges from 53° to 60° Fahr. in the morning, and 65° to 70° at mid-day. In the event of wet weather, invalids have the use of the splendid and extensive corridor, which may be considered one of the great features of the establishment. Leaving aside now all question of the curative virtues of the waters nothing more picturesque than the situation of Hammam R'irha can be easily conceived. The best time for visiting Hammam R'irha is from December to May, but it is also a summer resort (*see* below). The Thermal Establishment rivals those of a similar kind in Europe, *and is one of the very few places where a course of baths can be taken with safety in winter.* It unites in one and the same spot the three most desirable items—viz., a medium altitude, a favourable climate, and the extensive installation of wholesome thermo-therapy. The establishment is divided into two separate hotels, distant 150 metres one from the other. They are called the Grand Hôtel des Bains and the Hôtel Belle Vue.

The **Grand Hôtel des Bains** is a building of colossal proportions, measuring 110 metres by 90 metres. The grand saloon and the dining saloon are each 20 metres square, and the bedroom accommodation is sufficient for 200 guests. The hotel is supplied with all the latest appliances and necessaries

—post office, telegraph, telephone, billiard-rooms, reading-rooms, lawn tennis, etc., and, as previously mentioned, with carriages of every description.

The **Belle Vue Hotel,** of quite another style and disposition, reminds one more of an English cottage villa. The view from the windows is exceedingly beautiful. The service at the Belle Vue is not so rich, and consequently the prices are lower. This hotel is open all the year round (under the same management as the Grand Hôtel des Bains, *see* p. 124).

The **Military Hospital,** close by, is a group of buildings adjoining each other with only a ground floor. The central building contains thirty-four soldiers' berths, a room for the non-commissioned officers, and four small rooms for officers.

In December, 1887, Sir Morell Mackenzie visited R'irha. He was very much impressed with the place, and in his opinion it is "in every respect suitable as a winter health resort." Hamman R'irha is especially suitable for persons suffering from consumption (at an early stage), chronic rheumatism and gout, bronchitis, neuralgia, dyspepsia, and affections of the stomach.

Sports.

Shooting over a forest of 1,800 acres may be indulged in by visitors to the hotel free of charge. Partridges, hares, rabbits, and quails when in season afford good sport, with the help of Arab beaters. A licence must previously be obtained at the Prefecture of Algiers, or at the sub-prefecture of Miliana. It costs 28f.

Jackals are plentiful in the neighbourhood of Hammam R'irha. Hyenas are occasionally seen, and sometimes panthers are shot.

As already stated on p. 32 the importation of gunpowder into Algeria is absolutely forbidden. Empty cartridges, with percussion caps, can be brought in and filled in one of the large towns. Neither Harvey cartridges nor good English powder can be bought in Algiers.

Excursions from Hamman R'irha.

Numerous walks and excursions can be made in the neighbourhood of Hammam R'irha.

First, to the **Tombeau de la Chrétienne** (*see* p. 121),

a pleasant drive of three hours.   Carriage there and back, 25f. to 30f.

Second, to **Miliana** (*see* p. 132), a very fine and picturesque drive of about three hours (about 30 kilometres)   Special carriages for long distances cost 35f. ; but many carriage-drives and organised parties start almost daily from the Hôtel des Bains at a very moderate cost.

Third, to the top of the **Zakkar** mount.   This can be done either from here or from Miliana, but it is advisable to ascend the Zakkar from the latter place (*see* p. 132).

The **pine forest of Chaiba,** in the environs of Hammam R'irha, affords many pleasant walks and charming scenery. The forest and the neighbouring slopes abound in game of all sorts.   Sporting parties are often organised either for small or large game.

The **Ravin des Voleurs** (16 kilometres south) is also a nice drive.   The *Auberge Gaspard* is the *rendezvous de chasse*, where an excellent breakfast may be had.

ALGIERS TO MILIANA, TENIET EL HAÂD, AND THE CEDAR FOREST.

Table of Distances from Algiers.

Stations.	Distance in kilometres from Algiers.	Stations.	Distance in kilometres from Algiers.
Algiers	—	El-Affroun ..	69
Agha	2	Oued Djer ..	78
Hussein Dey ...	6	Bou Medfa ..	91
Maison Carrée ...	11	Vesoul-Benian ...	98
Gué de Constantine ...	15	Miliana-Margueritte (Adélia)	110
Baba Ali ...	20		
Bir-Touta ...	26	**Affreville**	120
Boufarik ...	37	*By Road.*	
Beni Mered ...	45	**Miliana**	132
Blidah	51	**Teniet el Haâd** ...	181
La Chiffa ...	58	Cedar Forest ..	195
Mouzaïaville ...	63		

Distance from Affreville.	Distance from Affreville.
Teniet el Haâd	59
Cedar Forest (Rond Point) ...	73

The best train is the one to Oran, leaving Algiers at 6.50 a.m. for **Affreville**. Omnibuses meet all trains, and carry passengers t.) **Miliana** in one hour and a half. The fare is 1f. for each passenger, or by private carriage ordered from the Hôtel du Commerce, Miliana.

Affreville (buffet) is a small town of about 5,000 inhabitants (market on Thursdays) situated at the entrance of the **Cheliff plain,** at the foot of the **Mounts Zakkar.** **Hotels:** Hôtel de Vaucluse, Hôtel de l'Univers. Both accept Cook's Coupons, Series R. It is not necessary to remain there, even if the traveller does not wish to go to Teniet the same day. The best plan is to visit and sleep at Miliana, and start next morning for Teniet el Haâd and the Cedar Forest. From Affreville to Miliana by road occupies about 1½ hours ; diligence, 1 fr.

The road from **Miliana-Margueritte** (Adélia) (one station before Affreville) is a little shorter, if one is in a hurry to reach Miliana, but the Affreville road affords much finer scenery, and is better and more frequented. Tram worked by the Zakkar miners, from Miliana-Margueritte in ½ hour; car starts on arrival of trains.

Miliana, 132 kilometres from Algiers, is a fortified town (population about 8,000) situated at an altitude of 2,300 feet above the level of the sea on the side of one of the **Zakkar** range of mountains. It commands a magnificent view of the **Cheliff plain** and the surrounding country. It is encircled by a wall pierced with musket holes, in which are the **Zakkar and Cheliff** gates. At Miliana is a branch of the Blidah remount dépôt.

Miliana was occupied by the French troops in 1840, but the garrison left there was besieged by Abd-el-Kader, and suffered such privations that out of 1,200 men only 100 were effective when General Changarnier relieved the garrison.

The route from Affreville to Miliana is a very picturesque one. It follows the side of the mountain, reaching the summit by a succession of zigzags in the midst of scenery of great beauty. Fruit-trees of all kinds grow plentifully in well-watered gardens, the vegetation of northern climates alternating with tropical plants and foliage. Olive-trees, eucalyptus, palms, fig-trees, etc., are there intermingled with plane and chestnut-trees, poplars and pine-trees. On reaching Miliana the streets will be found delightfully shaded, and cool with running streams. The garden opposite the Zakkar gate is laid out with great care and taste. The roads and public gardens are kept in excellent order ; the town itself is unusually clean, and lighted throughout by electricity, the dynamos being worked by water power. In the middle of the Central Place is a Moorish minaret entirely shrouded with evergreens, and now being used as a clock tower. The town is completely French ; very few of the original Arab dwellings have retained their former appearance, but those remaining are in the western portion of the town.

Of the numerous mosques that adorned Miliana, only two remain ; the one deserving a visit is the **Koubba of Sidi Ahmed Ben Yussuf,** a poor but virtuous saint, who was still more remarkable for his epigrammatic and sarcastic poetry than the example of his life. Many of his writings have been handed down to Arab posterity as proverbs. His severity against the Miliana women, "who," he said, "usurped the place of men, and commanded when it was their duty to obey," is an Arabic illustration of the "Women's Rights Question" mooted in this out-of-the-way region some 400 years ago! The mosque was adorned with a double row of arcades of the pure Moorish architecture, decorated with handsome open-work tiles. There was a very curious marble fountain in the middle of the court. The mosque itself was decorated in the interior with lovely coloured tiles, with a great deal of red, the secret of the manufacture of which has been lost for three centuries, and is not likely to be recovered for some time. The ceilings were handsomely painted and decorated with golden devices. The doors were of bronze, with big copper nails. Of all this nearly everything remains, save that the tiles have lost their brightness, the carvings and paintings are getting yearly more dilapidated, and seem, in fact, what they appear to be—the relics of another age.

One of the favourite walks of visitors is undoubtedly the beautiful terrace overlooking the valley, especially at eventide, when the setting sun is lighting up the **Ouarsenis,** with its high peaks covered with snow and lost in the azure of the sky. This is the great landmark of the country, but other and many beautiful views are to be met with on all sides.

However, one must not look for many specimens of typical Arab buildings or dwelling-houses, for, as already mentioned, the town is essentially French. In fact, save the **Mosque of Sidi Ahmed Ben Yussuf,** there are no Arab buildings of any importance.

The quantity of water which Miliana derives from Mounts **Zakkar** is very large, amounting to no less than 120,000 gallons an hour. The water, rushing in a stream, is pure and clear, and the motive power derived from this force is utilised in many ways—to light the town by electricity, to work tile, corn mills, and other factories, etc. The country round is most intensely green and fresh-looking, delighting the eye with sights of the finest emerald scenery imaginable.

The **Hôtel du Commerce** is at the bottom of the central street to the left. (Cook's coupons, Series A, B, and C, accepted.)

It is very cleanly kept, and supplies excellent beds. The cooking is very good ; call on Mr. Matte, the proprietor, who is now one of the most important farmers in the district ; he has gained a renown in Algeria and abroad for his excellent wines. His **Clos Zakkar 1878,** which he keeps for connoisseurs, can be highly recommended.

Tourists wishing to proceed from **Algiers** to **Teniet=el= Haâd** DIRECT, without going to Miliana, can wire to the Hôtel de Vaucluse, Affreville, where carriages, or seats in the automobile-diligence, can be obtained for Teniet-el-Haâd (or wire for seats to Margot, Affreville or Martin, Buffet de la Gare, Affreville). The automobile-diligence (proprietor M. Margot) leaves Affreville for Teniet-el-Haâd at 11.30 a.m. daily, arriving at Teniet 5.30 p.m. Fares, coupé 5f., cabriolet 4f. This journey requires two whole days, and necessitates sleeping at Teniet-el-Haâd (Hôtel du Commerce, Cook's coupons, Series A, B and D, accepted). The road from Affreville to Teniet is a very good one; it affords no sudden steep ascents, and, though a little tortuous during part of the journey, is on the whole excellent. It follows a straight course across the **Plaine du Cheliff,** and then winds round the many crevices of the **Oued Massin.** The scenery, though not so striking as in the Miliana district, is never-theless very picturesque, and gets very interesting after the **Caravanserai of the Oued Massin** has been reached, situated in the midst of splendid oak and pine trees.

The road shortly after reaches the **Camp des Chênes,** where breakfast may be had, and crossing through very wild and rocky passes, Teniet-el-Haâd at length is reached.

Teniet-el-Haâd, 59 kilometres from Affreville, is a village situated in a woody and picturesque plain, at an altitude of 3,917 feet above the level of the sea. It is a very animated and lively place (important market on Sundays) well shaded with plane and pine-trees, commanding by its situation a very important pass of the Atlas, communicating with the **High Plateaux** and the **Ouarsenis.**

The only good hotel here is the **Hôtel du Commerce,** where horses and mules can be obtained for the excursion to **the Cedar Forest.** The price is 5f. for one horse for the journey. The price of a guide is also 5f. ; but if the tourists start in any number a guide is not required, as the main road leads straight to the forest, and there cannot be any risk of losing one's way. The ride occupies two hours, and the same time to return. At about 5 kilometres distance from Teniet, the trees are already very numerous. But the real object of the journey is the

Rond Point des Cedres (14 kilometres), a rustic little place, looking somewhat like a Swiss cottage, surrounded by a semicircle of imposing cedar-trees. Though the cedars of Teniet are not so large as those of the Lebanon range, they are much more numerous, but unfortunately have been subject to the frequent devastations of the Arab incendiaries. However, in recent years the Forest Department has taken measures for the protection and regeneration of the forest ; young trees have been planted, and the unique beauty of the district will be maintained. Some of these cedars, such as the **Sultane,** (110 feet height, 8 feet diameter) have attained enormous dimensions. The forest extends over a surface of about nine thousand acres, including a large extent of fine oak trees. The cedars cover an area of 2,300 acres.

Tourists who wish to enjoy a really magnificent view of the surrounding country should climb to the crest of the glen, wherefrom the cedar forest itself looks like a distant speck. The ascent occupies about half an hour on foot. The double row of mountain ranges is plainly visible, the high peak of the **Ouarsenis** standing out much higher above the others. To the south the magnificent **Plaine du Cheliff,** with the fortress of Miliana shining brightly in the sun, surrounded by its wall, gives a vague appearance of a Monaco perched up in the clouds. The particular peak from which this view is enjoyed is simply a continuation of the pathway that takes you to the Cedar Forest; it is called in Arabic **Aïn-ed-Denia,** or the " eye of the world."

The winter in this part of the region is sometimes as bitterly cold as in the coldest parts of Scotland. Excursions to Teniet-el-Haâd and the Cedar Forest are best made early in November or else in April, and even then visitors should not neglect to take a good supply of plaids, shawls, overcoats, etc.

ALGIERS TO LAGHOUAT (EL=AGHOUAT).
By Rail and Road.

This interesting journey of 443 kilometres requires at least four days, of which 135 kilometres are by rail, and 308 kilometres by diligence.

The first day the traveller should leave Algiers for (change at Blidah) Berrouaghia by train, 6.50 a.m. (135 kilometres), and proceed from Berrouaghia by diligence at 1 p.m. to Boghari, 43 kilometres, 4f., in about 4 hours.

The second day, Boghari to Guelt-es-Stel by diligence, 91 kilometres, 14 hours.

The third day, Guelt-es-Stel to Ain-el-Ibel by diligence, 100 kilometres, 16 hours.

The fourth day, Ain-el-Ibel to Laghouat by diligence, 74 kilometres, 12 hours.

From Algiers to Blidah (and the Gorge de la Chiffa), see p. 111.

From Blidah to Berrouaghia the line runs between orange gardens and vineyards, and follows the Mitidja plain, pierces the **Mouzaïa** by a long tunnel, and passes the end of the Gorge de la Chiffa at Camp des Chênes, crosses and recrosses the Chiffa, and continues to Lodi, a cultivated country at the foot of the **Dakla** on to

Médéa, boldly situated on a plateau 3,000 feet above sea level, on the site of the Roman **Ad Medias.** The town was occupied by Abd-el-Kader in 1835, and submitted to the Duc d'Aumale in 1840. Médéa is now a thoroughly French town, the headquarters of a military sub-division. Its population is 4,000, and that of the commune 15,000. The Place d'Armes and the Boulevard are planted with trees, and the gardens are well supplied with water from the **Djebel-Nador.** The principal buildings are the hospital, a mosque used as a Catholic church, the barracks, and other military edifices. To the east of the town is an ancient aqueduct.

The surrounding district is very healthy and prosperous. Cereals, olive, chestnut, and fruit trees of all kinds flourish abundantly, the wines have an excellent reputation, and Médéa carries on a large business in wool and cattle. **Hotel** Hotel d'Orient. (Cook's coupons, Series A, B and C accepted.) Arab market on Thursdays and Fridays.

A delightful excursion, requiring only four hours to go and return, can be made to the

Piton du Dakla or **Nador** (3,674 feet), the view from which is, of its kind, one of the most beautiful in Algeria, embracing as it does the Mouzaïa, the Zakkar, the Boghar, Beni Salah, the Djurdjura, and other mountains, the Sahel, and a glimpse of the Mediterranean.

A still finer view is obtainable from the summit of Ben-Chicao (4,325 feet) reached on foot in about an hour from Ben-Chicao Station, that before Berroughia.

Leaving Médéa, the line rises gradually, three insignificant stations are passed, and the narrow valley of the **Chitane** leads to

Berrouaghia, the terminus of the railway.

The town contains a population of 2,300, but the commune, which extends over a large and well-cultivated district, numbers 35,000. There is a separate quarter for Jews in the village, and an agricultural penitentiary close by, where more than a thousand of the inmates are occupied in farming and vine culture on land specially provided for the purpose. Market on Wednesdays.

The village is supposed to be built on the site of the ancient **Tanaramusa Castra,** and numerous Roman remains are seen.

Hotel.—Hotel de France.

Those who are not making a stay at Berrouaghia may proceed at once by diligence (*see* p. 136) to Boghari, 43 kilometres in 4 hours ; fair accommodation at the Hôtel Célestin.

From Berrouaghia the diligence follows the road which passes between the valley of the Hammam and the Cheliff, and beyond the inn of Aïn-Maklouf some fine mountain views are obtained ; a long plain planted with pines is entered as far as the former Camp des Zouaves, where the valley of the Cheliff, several kilometres in length, leads to the **Oued Hakoum.** At this point the road crosses the river near some sheep farms, and continues by the river Cheliff to

Boghari, a place of some commercial value, arising from its situation between the Tell and desert. Market on Mondays. The village contains 3,000 inhabitants (with hotel, telegraph office, baths, etc.), and the commune, about 30,000 inhabitants. The **ksar,** on a spur of the hill, is built and fortified like any of the villages of the Sahara. Here in the evening may be witnessed interesting native dances by the women of the Ouled-Naïl and other tribes (*see* p. 139).

To the west of Boghari, on the side of a mountain, is **Boghar,** a military station, where the fort was built by Abd-el-Kader, and destroyed by the French in 1840. It is now an important military position, and the redoubt contains barracks, officers' quarters, hospital, commandant's residence, etc. Arab market on Thursdays.

Situated 2,970 feet above sea-level, and commanding a splendid view over the Tell, the Cheliff, and the Hauts Plateaux, Boghar is called the **Balcon du Sud.**

The next stage is from Boghari to Guelt-es-Stel (91 kilometres), sleeping at the caravanserai, which is fairly comfortable.

About 25 kilometres from Boghari a railway from El-Krachem to El-Aghouat, distance of 250 kilometres, has been commenced but abandoned.

Leaving Boghari by the Cheliff plain, the diligence proceeds by a good road through the hills to **Aïn-Saba,** and 10 kilometres further on to the caravanserai of

Bou-Ghazoul, where good accommodation can be obtained, but the diligence stops for *déjeuner* about 30 kilometres further on at

Aïn-Oussera, another caravanserai, not so comfortable, but more equidistant, between Boghari and Guelt-es-Stel.

For the rest of the journey there is nothing of interest to be seen ; nothing but miles of alfa on both sides of the road until arriving at

Guelt-es-Stel, where the caravanserai is comfortable (dine and sleep).

Leaving Guelt-es-Stel for **Aïn-el-Ibel,** a long stage of 100 kilometres, the road gradually ascends a valley to a sandy plain, and later on passes salt lakes many miles in length to a caravanserai at **El-Mesran;** here the road descends for some distance to the Oued Melah, and after crossing this, to the caravanserai of the

Rocher de Sel, where at a small inn a stay is made for *déjeuner.*

The Rocher de Sel is a mountain of salt about a mile and a-half in circumference, through which trickle rivulets which are covered with crystals of salt. The sides of the rock are strewn with iron pyrites, gypsum, and stones of various colours, altogether a curious object of interest.

Owing to the action of the atmosphere and the salt being dissolved by the underground water, large portions of the mountain fall in from time to time, leaving fantastic hollows and crevices in many of which thousands of pigeons find a home.

Beyond the caravanserai the route lies over the Djebel Sen-el Lebba (the lion's tooth), passing the caravanserai **Cazelle,** surrounded by a fruit garden, then another caravanserai, and further on a small inn at **Aïn-Ouerrou,** then a Government mill, to

Djelfa, situated 3,770 feet above sea-level, very cold in winter and hot in summer. The village has a population of 1,100, and two principal streets. The official house in the bordj is occupied by the Bach-Agha (or Governor) of the **Ouled-Naïls,** of whom Djelfa is the centre. The Ouled-Naïls belong to the great tribe of Zoreba, and occupy a very large district from Bou Saâda to the Ziban and to the Djebel Amour.

The district of Djelfa furnishes large numbers of sheep and camels. In the forest of Tadmitz a military post is maintained. Roman remains have been found in the neighbourhood and a number of megalithic tombs.

There is a diligence every second day from Djelfa to Bou-Saâda, 120 kilometres, fifteen hours. Provisions should be taken.

From Djelfa the road crosses the **Col des Caravanes** to the caravanserai of **Oued Sédour,** and 15 kilometres beyond is the caravanserai of

Aïn-el-Ibel, close to which is the Hôtel du Roulage, where the traveller dines and sleeps.

During the next and last stage of 74 kilometres, the route is over a barren plain for many miles, until the **Mokta-el-Oust** is crossed, near which is a caravanserai and a café, and soon a stay is made for breakfast at **Sidi-Maklouf,** situated on a shelf of rock overlooking a ravine, at the foot of which is a river, in which are a species of trout.

The road now winds over ridges where nothing enlivens the scene, and passes to the left of **Djebel Zebecha** to

Metlili, a small caravanserai, where a short rest is taken.

For some distance there is no improvement in the monotony of the route, until, on approaching Laghouat, by the side of the **Oued Mzi,** signs of cultivation and palm trees are seen, the military quarters and establishments outside the town are passed, and the traveller arrives at

Laghouat or **El-Aghouat,** a considerable military station and town, built on two spurs of a mountain nearly 2,500 feet above sea-level in the form of two amphitheatres, with a forest of 30,000 palm trees in front.

Laghouat has seen many masters, having in turn belonged to Morocco, and to the Turks; it was first occupied by the French in 1844, taken by Abd-el-Kader, and finally retaken by the Maréchal Pélissier in December, 1852, with heavy losses on both sides.

The reconstructed town is built quite in the French style, with a fine square, the Place Randon, surrounded by civil and military buildings, such as the Military Club, the Post Office, and the General's residence; straight streets are bordered by European houses, while the native portion of the old town is confined to the south-east quarter.

The entire town numbers 4,500 inhabitants, and a garrison of 1,500 soldiers, shut in by walls, and defended by forts on the highest points. Laghouat is the base for operations further south, and is the connecting link between the provinces of Oran and Constantine; and the centre of routes to the M'zab, the Ouargla, the Ziban, and to Biskra.

The town has good native baths, and there are three cemeteries, two Arab and one Catholic.

Hotel: Grand Hotel du Sud. (Cook's coupons, Series A, B and C, accepted.)

The oasis of Laghouat is delightfully rich in vegetation, and in addition to the thousands of date trees, the pomegranate, fig, peach, apricot, vine, and other fruits flourish luxuriantly.

Best market day, Friday.

An agreeable and short excursion of two miles can be made over the mountain to the **Col de Sable**, from which there is a good view of mountain and oasis.

Longer excursions can be easily accomplished on horseback in a day to the oasis and ksouri of **El-Assafia** or Tajemout, situated on the side of the Djebel-Amour, between Laghouat and Géryville.

About 160 kilometres south of Laghouat is the important and prosperous district of the M'Zab, which was annexed to Algeria as recently as 1882. A brief account of this interesting colony and its inhabitants appears on p. 18. Further details will be found in M. Edward Cat's "A travers le Desert"; or in a pamphlet by M. le Commandant Robin, "Le M'Zab et son annexion à la France," Alger, 1884.

ALGIERS TO ORAN AND TLEMÇEN BY RAIL.

Stations.	Distance in kilometres from Algiers.	Stations.	Distance in kilometres from Algiers.
Algiers	—	Pontéba	203
Agha	2	**Orleansville** ...	209
Hussein Dey ...	6	Oued Sly	224
Maison Carrée ...	11	Charon (Bou-Kader) ...	232
Gué de Constantine		Le Merdja ...	243
(junction) ...	15	Oued-Riou (Inkermann)	254
Baba Ali	20	Djidiouïa (St.-Aimé) ...	263
Birtouta-Chebli ...	26	Les Salines (for Ferry)	283
Boufarik	37	**Relizane** (junction,	
Beni Méred	45	buffet) ...	296
Blidah (junction) ...	51	L'Hillil	315
La Chiffa	58	Oued Malah	332
Mouzaïaville ...	63	Sahouria ...	340
El Affroun (junction) ...	69	**Perrégaux** (junction)	346
Oued Djer ...	78	L'Habra...	360
Bou Medfa ...	91	**St. Denis du Sig** ...	370
Vesoul-Benian	98	L'Ougasse ...	376
Miliana Margueritte ...	110	Mare d'Eau ...	381
Affreville (buffet) ...	120	Ste. Barbe du Tlélat	
Lavarande ...	124	(junction) ...	395
Les Aribs (Littré) ...	134	Arbal	404
Duperré	146	Valmy	411
Kerba	154	**La Sénia** (junction)...	416
Oued Rouina	160	**Oran**	421
St. Cyprien des Attafs ...	170	*From Oran.*	
Les Attafs-Carnot ...	173		
Temoulga-Vauban ...	183	St. Barbe du Tlélat ...	26
Oued Fodda	186	Sidi Bel Abbès	78
Le Barrage	195	**Tlemçen** ...	165

The railway from Algiers to Oran was the first railway constructed in Algeria. It is in the hands of the P.-L.-M. Company, and is very well managed. There is only one train during the day, starting either way, which leaves Algiers at 6.50 a.m., and reaches Oran at 7.5 p.m. On this train there is a restaurant car, *déjeuner* 4f., including wine. By taking the train at the station of **Agha,** some minutes are saved to the dweller of Mustapha Supérieur, but it is better to enter the train at the town station in order to secure good seats. *Time tables liable to change.*

For those who wish to avoid the fatigue of this long journey during the day, there is a night train three times a week to Oran—Sunday, Tuesday, and Thursday—leaving Algiers at 8.11 p.m., due at Oran 6.56 a.m. the following day.

During the Winter Season, from December to May, there is a " Train de Luxe " once a week from Oran to Algiers, Constantine, Tunis, and *nice versá.* This train leaves Algiers on Tuesday, at 8.11 p.m. for Oran, due there at 6.56 a.m. It is exclusively composed of sleeping car carriages, and carries only first-class passengers paying a supplement of 16f. for the journey between Algiers and Oran.

The journey from Algiers can be made by sea on several days of the week to Ténès, Mostaganem, Arzeu, and Oran, either by the steamers of the d'Hauteville Co., the Nord Co., the Havraise Péninsulaire Co., or Prosper Durand, but this should only he undertaken in fine weather. Consult time tables, etc.

Leaving Algiers from the P.-L.-M. station on the Quay the train soon arrives at the passenger and goods station at **Agha,** the nearest point to Mustapha Supérieur, then following the shore through railway works and between large buildings of various mills and manufactories, stops at

Hussein Dey (6 kilom.), a district of well-cultivated market gardens. *See* p. 103.

The line then leaves the sea, and turning inland crosses a bridge over the river **Harrach,** arriving at

Maison Carrée (11 kilom.) junction of the East Algerian line to Constantine, a considerable village, noted for its Friday market and for a large prison. *See* p. 103.

The line now turns south-west, and soon enters the **Mitidja plain** between the Atlas and the Sahel, a vast agricultural district tenanted by thousands of Europeans. Crossing the Harrach, the approach is made through plantations of eucalyptus to

Gué de Constantine (15 kilom.), surrounded by farms, whence Arba and Rovigo are easily reached by omnibus to Sidi-Moussa. There is nothing to note between the next stations,

Baba Ali (20 kilom.), and **Birtouta** (26 kilom.), until the luxurious plantations of plane trees, acacias, and eucalyptus are passed on approaching

Boufarik (37 kilom.), a thriving town of about 9,000 inhabitants. Here the most important market of the commune is held every Monday, attended by some 4,000 Arabs coming from the surrounding villages for the sale or purchase of produce and cattle. Boufarik, which as late as 1832, when occupied by the French, was nothing but a deadly pestilential swamp, is now a healthy, clean town, with fine streets, surrounded by woods, orange and lemon groves, and gardens. In the square is a bronze statue of Sergeant Blandan (*see* below) ; and in various streets are distilleries of perfumes.

At a short distance the aspect of the country changes, the willow, the cypress, and the plane tree give place to the cactus, the aloe, and the prickly pear. Coléa and the Tombeau de la Chrétienne (*see* p. 121) can be seen in the distance.

Beni=Méred (42 kilom.), a village of 550 inhabitants, engaged in the cultivation of cereals, cotton, fruit, and the vine. Here it was that in April, 1841, Sergeant Blandan, who with twenty soldiers occupied a blockhouse, was attacked by 300 mounted Arabs. This small band maintained a stubborn defence until help arrived, but Sergeant Blandan and fourteen of his men were killed. An obelisk over a fountain was erected in memory of this tragic event (*see* above, also p. 109).

The line gradually approaches the slopes of the Atlas mountains, and passes through forests of orange trees, tangerines, and lemons, to the important and pleasant town of

Blidah(51 kilom.), *see* p. 110. (Branch line to Médéa and Berrouaghia.) Changing its direction the railway makes a considerable descent parallel with the river Chiffa, which it crosses to the village of

La Chiffa (58 kilom.), entirely destroyed by the earthquake of January, 1867. This is the station from which the Gorge de la Chiffa and the Russeau des Singes can be visited, but it is preferable to do so from Blidah, *see* p. 111.

Mouzaïaville (63 kilom.), an important village of 5,000 inhabitants, completely rebuilt after having been destroyed by the earthquake of January, 1867, which also did serious damage at Blidah, and destroyed La Chiffa (*see* above). The country around Mouzaïaville is very productive, being well irrigated ; and there is a largely-attended market on Saturday. At a short distance from the village are some Roman ruins, where a tumulary bas-relief of Bishop Donatus, A.D. 493, and a statue of Bacchus have been found—now in the Museum at Algiers. In the neighbourhood are deposits of iron, copper and quicksilver.

A capital whole day's excursion can be made to the **Pic of the Mouzaïa**, 5,262 feet (guide 5f., time there and back nine hours).

El Affroun (69 kilom.), a pleasant village bordered by the *Oued Djer*. Steam tramway to Marengo, diligence or carriage, thence to Tipaza and Cherchell, *see* p. 113. El Affroun also suffered severely from the earthquake of 1867, when many persons perished.

Passing over the Oued Djer the line leaves the Mitidja plain, and enters into charming valleys, wooded with olive, carobs, cypress, oak, and other trees, to

Oued Djer (78 kilom.), a hamlet devoted to the making of charcoal, the neighbourhood producing good wine and cereals, and where small game is fairly abundant.

Bou Medfa (91 kilom.), the station where passengers alight for the **Grand Hotel and Baths of Hammam R'irha,** *see* p. 124.

Vesoul=Benian (98 kilom.), the village of the same name being three miles from the station, on a high plateau overlooking the river Hammam. The history of this model village is very interesting. It was founded in 1853 by Marshal Randon, when 43 families were sent from **Vesoul,** in the Haute Sâone, with 270,000f., or about 6,230f. (£251) each family, to whom was made a grant of 1,300 acres of land, being 30 acres per family, and the experiment has proved highly successful.

Miliana=Margueritte (Adélia) (110 kilom.). Tram to Miliana (*see* p. 132.) From this point the line descends rapidly and crosses the *Oued Boutan.*

Affreville (120 kilom.), an important commune, named after an archbishop of Paris, with 4,200 inhabitants, producing excellent wheat, oats, barley, and flax, as well as oranges and grapes. Diligence service from **Affreville** to **Miliana,** also to Teniet-el Haâd, *see* p. 134.

After Affreville the line enters the great plain of **Cheliff,** which extends to Relizane, a distance of 176 kilometres, a very hot and fatiguing journey in summer, the country around being parched and burnt up, but in winter and spring the earth is in verdure clad, and covered with wild flowers. The next station is

Lavarande (124 kilom.), named after a French general killed at Sebastopol.

Les Aribs (Littré) (138 kilom.), a prosperous village of 1,000 inhabitants, situated at the foot of the **Zakkar** chain.

Between Les Aribs and the next station the line crosses the river Cheliff by an iron bridge of splendid workmanship, not far from the remains of a Roman bridge. The **Cheliff** frequently met with in this district is the longest river in Algeria, taking its rise in the **Djebel Amour**, in the Sahara, and falling into the sea near Mostaganem after a course of over 400 miles.

Duperré (146 kilom.), named after the French Admiral who commanded the Fleet in 1830, when the army landed at Sidi-Ferruch and defeated the Moslem army at Staouéli (*see* p. 96). Cereals and the vine are largely cultivated, and a well-supplied market is held weekly (on Tuesdays). The village owes its origin to a number of French families who settled there in 1859.

Oued Rouina (160 kilom.), a small village on the bank of the river *Rouina* (which joins the Cheliff), on which a *Barrage* is being built to irrigate a large tract of adjoining land.

St. Cyprien des Attafs (170 kilom.), a small village, St. Cyprien, composed of Christian Arabs who were collected together during the famine of 1867 by Cardinal Lavigerie, Archbishop of Algiers. It is a prosperous agricultural village under clerical management. A large and commodious Hospital was also built for the neighbouring Arab tribes.

Les Attafs=Carnot (173 kilom.), where every Wednesday an important Arab market is held. Ruins of a Roman camp, **Djebel Temoulga,** also the remains of an aqueduct and ramparts.

Temoulga-Vauban (183 kilom.).

After crossing the *Oued Fodda* (silver river), in view of the **Ouarsenis** mountain, where the river takes its rise, and passing through a well-cultivated country the train reaches

Oued Fodda (186 kilom.), a prosperous village, producing wheat, beans, and high-class vines. Market on Mondays.

Diligence to **Lamartine** (12 kilom. distant) in the neighbourhood of which the gorges of the Cheliff are very picturesque.

Le Barrage (195 kilom.), near which a large and important dam or barrage has been constructed some three miles from the junction of the rivers Cheliff and Fodda, for the purpose of irrigating many thousands of acres on both sides of the river as far as Orleansville.

Ponteba (203 kilom.). Between here and the next station, Orleansville, are some Roman remains.

Orleansville (209 kilom.), founded by Marshal Bugeaud in 1843, has become a town of importance, with a population of 12,000 inhabitants. It is about half-way between Algiers and Oran. **Hotel:** Hôtel des Voyageurs. (Cook's Coupons, Series R, accepted.) Owing to the great heat in summer and the cold winds of winter it is anything but an agreeable residence for Europeans. The Woods and Forest Department has planted eucalyptus and pine trees in and around the town, thus affording some welcome shade. The town, surrounded by eight gates, contains barracks for 3,000 men, a military hospital with 500 beds, a theatre, palace of justice, etc. A very large Arab market is held every Saturday, attended frequently by 10,000 natives from the Dahra, Ouarsenis, and other districts.

Orleansville was built on the site of the Roman *Castellum Tingitanum*, and numerous antiquities have been discovered, such as the remains of a canal, and the mosaic floor of the **Basilica** of **St. Reparatus,** and an inscription giving the date of the Saint's burial as in the 436th year of the Mauretanian era, corresponding with A.D. 475. The mosaic measures 120 feet by 50 feet.

A very fine excursion can be made from Orleansville to the **Ouarsenis** (L'Œil du Monde), by diligence (3 times a week in about 10 hours), or carriage to *Beni-Endel,* 59 kilom. whence the ascent of this grand mountain, with its triple peaks, affords views of surprising extent and beauty.

Orleansville to Ténès is an interesting journey of 53 kilometres, by diligence or carriage. Diligence in about 5½ hours. A railway is contemplated.

As far as Aïn-Beida, Les Cinq Palmiers, and Kirba, the route is dreary, then the road passes through valleys and wooded glens by the river *Allala,* on to *Montenotte,* then through a wild gorge to **Old Ténès,** surrounded on three sides by a deep ravine, inhabited by Arabs, and once a resort of bandits and pirates. This village, said to be very ancient, is well worth a visit, as it still preserves its native character. There are remains of some Berber ramparts and an old bridge.

About a kilometre beyond is

Ténès, a new town of 5,000 inhabitants, founded in 1843, situated on the coast midway between Mostaganem and Tipaza. It is built on a plateau, the site of the Phœnician, and then the Roman town of

Cartenna. There remain some cisterns still used by the inhabitants, portions of ramparts and some rock-cut tombs. The streets are conveniently large and planted with trees, surrounded by gardens, and encircled by four large gates. The harbour, nearly a mile from the centre of the town, is large and well protected except from the east wind. Ténès was formerly the port for the export trade of the Cheliff plain, and is in fact the only shelter for vessels for a distance along the coast of about 180 miles, but was injured and isolated by the railway from Oran to Algiers. It is now, as the French say, a *ville morte*, but, from its position on the coast, if ever it is served by a railway it may again become an important commercial and military station. A railway is contemplated to connect it with Orleansville. Ténès may also be reached by local steamers (*see* p. 142).

Roman tombs, Roman and Phœnician wells, coins, and other remains have been found from time to time. (Hotel St. Paul.)

Oued Sly (Malakoff) (224 kilom.), on the boundary between the provinces of Algiers and Oran, a small village of 240 inhabitants, cultivating the vine and cereals, is situated on the river *Sly*. A large financial establishment of Algiers has been instrumental in causing a Barrage to be constructed, by which some 10,000 acres of land will be irrigated.

Charon (Bou-Kader) (232 kilom.).

Le Merdja (243 kilom.), the first station in the province of Oran, surrounded by marshy land (from which it is named) on which birds, including bustards, are found.

Oued=Riou (Inkermann) (254 kilom.) on the river *Riou*, running into the Cheliff. Near the station is a populous and prosperous village situated at the foot of rocky hills, which supply excellent stone for building purposes. Market for cereals and cattle every Wednesday.

Excursions can be made by omnibus to **Ammi=Moussa** (25 kilom.) where many interesting Roman ruins are met with; also to

Mazouna, via Renault (34 kilom.), the chief town of the wild mountainous district of the Dahra. Renault is a highly prosperous French village, founded in 1845. Mazouna is inhabited almost entirely by Arabs, with the exception of a few Europeans including the village schoolmaster, a Frenchman. The suburb on the opposite side of the ravine is famous for the cultivation of every species of fruit.

Djidiouïa (St. Aimé) (263 kilom.), a modern village of about 1,000 inhabitants, and a manufactory of bitumen. Close by is the river *Djidouïa*, and about four miles away is a

K 2

very solid dam or barrage, long, broad, and deep, capable of holding up about 100,000 cubic metres of water for the supply of neighbouring villages and the irrigation of large tracts of land. It formerly held more but has been partly filled up with mud.

Les Salines (Ferry), (283 kilom.), the station for the transport of salt obtained from salt hills, and from the immense salt lake of *Sidi-Bou-Zain*. The village of Ferry is about 3 kilom. distant.

Relizane (296 kilom., buffet at the station); junction for Tiaret and Mostaganem, p. 183.

Relizane, built on the ruins of the Roman city **Mina**, is a French town, with large streets and a population of about 7,000. The Mussulmans and the Jews have their separate streets, shops, and baths. The adjoining land being impregnated with salt requires to be well watered. At the river Mina, two miles away, a barrage with sluices has been built to furnish 1,500 cubic metres of water per second, which irrigates thousands of acres in the plain, and supplies the inhabitants. The land thus irrigated produces excellent cereals and high-class vines. All around the town gardens and fruit orchards abound. An important fair of cattle and cereals is held every Thursday. Not far from the barrage are traces of the ancient Roman city.

Les Silos (Clinchant) (305 kilom.).

L'Hillil (315 kilom.), a small but prosperous village in a well-cultivated valley, on the river *Hillil*, on which there is a small dyke for irrigating the district. Diligence daily to Mostaganem (40 kilom.).

An interesting excursion can be made to the remarkable Berber town of

Kaläa (11½ miles south of L'Hillil), which had never been visited by an Englishman until Sir Lambert Playfair went there in May, 1877. An omnibus leaves L'Hillil every morning for Kaläa, returning in the afternoon; or a carriage may be taken from either L'Hillil or Relizane. The following is Sir Lambert Playfair's account of this little-known town :—

Kaläa is a town of Berber origin 17 kilometres south of L'Hillil and 36 kilometres north-east of Mascara, picturesquely situated on the south-west slopes of Djebel Barber, which descends almost perpendicularly to the Oued Bou-Mendjil. It occupies the mountainous centre of that *massif* situated between the Mina and the Habra, which was at one time occupied by fractions of the great tribe of Houara. The village is divided into several portions, each situated on a projecting spur of the mountain, and separated from the next by a deep ravine. The houses are of stone, but in a dilapidated condition. The place is celebrated for its carpets, which resemble those usually obtained from Smyrna ; nearly 3,000 are made every year, and they are everywhere held in high esteem ; the cost of them on the spot is about 10f. a square metre. They are made by the women ; the process is most curious, but it will be difficult for the *male* stranger to obtain access to a house where they are being made. At the bottom of the hill, along the banks of the river, are beautiful gardens of fruit trees, especially oranges and lemons. The population is about 300. The only European in the village is a schoolmaster, who, as at Mazouna, is sent to teach the children French. They are most apt pupils, and some of their exercises are quite astonishing.

It is uncertain whether this was ever a Roman station, but the remains of two cisterns still visible are wonderfully like the work of that people.

The place is said to have been built by a chief of the Houara tribe, Mohammed bin Ishak, about the middle of the sixth century of the Hejira, and after the extinction of that tribe it fell into the hands of the Beni Rachid, a branch of the Zenati, from Djebel Amour. It eventually submitted to the sovereigns of Tlemçen.

The Spanish occupation of Oran commenced about the beginning of the sixteenth century, and the Beni Rachid became in turns their allies and their tributaries. This state of things continued till 1517, when Baba Arouj, who had already taken Algiers, appeared at the head of a Turkish Army. The Mehal, under one of their most celebrated chiefs, Hamid el-Abd, were defeated ; Ténès and Kaläa fell into the hands of the Turks, and Tlemçen opened its gates to Arouj and recognised him as its sovereign. The Sultan Abou Hammom, dispossessed of his country and put to flight by the corsair, sought the aid of the Spaniards, who, having all their commerce cut off by the Turks, gladly sent a force to replace their old ally on his throne. It was commanded by Don Martin d'Argote, who eventually marched on Kaläa, which was defended by Ishak, elder brother of Arouj, with 500 Turkish infantry. After a spirited resistance he agreed to capitulate, on condition of being allowed to leave with arms and baggage, but no sooner had the Turks surrendered the place than the Spaniards fell upon them and put them all to death. The Spaniards then continued their march to Tlemçen, took that town, and pursued Arouj to the Rio Salado, where he and all his people were killed.

Kaläa became subsequently annexed to the regency of Algiers, and so continued till the French conquest. After the fall of the Turks, the people refusing to recognise the Emir Abd-el-Kader, he attacked the town, and after a siege of three days he took it and gave it up to pillage. It submitted to the French in 1842, joined the insurrection of Bou Maza in 1845, was retaken by the French with considerable loss, since when it has remained tolerably quiet. Kaläa was used by the Turks as a place of deportation for all their most turbulent soldiers, and at the present day there are two distinct sections of the population, the Kouloughlis or descendants of Turkish fathers, and the native race, a mixture of Berber and Arab.

There are three other similar villages in the neighbourhood. *Tliouanet* on the banks of the stream bearing the same name, 4 kilometres east of Kaläa. The word signifies *coloured*, on account of the perpetual verdure of the place. [Here are petroleum wells.] *Debba*, 800 metres south of Kaläa, on the same river as that town; and *Mesrata*, 2 kilometres south-west, on the lower part of the Oued Bou-Mendjil. It was at one time of considerable importance, but was greatly destroyed by landslips in 1845. The traveller will not fail to remark the great number of koubbas or tombs, of local saints in every direction.

[El-Bordj, another native village, is about 8 kilom. from Kaläa.]

Oued=Malah (El Romri), (332 kilom.) a hamlet situated on the river *Matah*.

Sahouria (340 kilom.).

Perrégaux (346 kilom.; Buvette); junction for Arzeu *viâ* Damesme for Mascara, Saïda, Aïn Sefra, Duveyrier and Colomb-Béchar on the Franco-Algerian State railway. Perrégaux, founded in 1858 by the General of the same name, is a large and prosperous commune of about 9,000 inhabitants. Important Arab market every Thursday. (Hôtel des Colonies.) Eleven kilometres from Perrégaux is the famous **Barrage** of the **Habra**, or the *Oued Fergoug*, at the junction of three rivers: the Fergoug, the Terzoug, and the Habra. The length of the dam is 440 metres (more than a third of a mile), the thickness at the base 40 metres (124 feet), and it forms a lake capable of holding fourteen million cubic metres of water.

In December, 1881, the barrage suddenly in the night gave way, losing all the water. More than 400 persons and numbers of cattle were drowned, dwellings and railway embankments swept away. It was reconstructed at a cost of five million francs (£200,000).

L'Habra (Bou-Henni) (360 kilom.), a small village on an eminence, surrounded by a forest.

St. Denis=du=Sig (370 kilom.), a large thriving town of 10,500 inhabitants, situated in a plain of extraordinary fertility, producing wheat, barley, oats, colza, cotton, flax, tobacco, and vines. The streets and public squares are well built and planted with trees, the private and public gardens are delightfully cultivated. There are several flour-mills and cotton-ginning factories. A largely attended Arab market is held every Sunday.

The richness of the land is due to artificial irrigation. From the time of the Turks, barrages have been constructed on the river *Sig*, but they were small and insufficient. In 1884, however, a very large barrage was completed, holding up several million cubic metres of water. In 1885 this structure collapsed, flooding the country, carrying away bridges, houses, and inundating farms, but no lives were lost. The barrage was reconstructed, and has been working for nearly twenty-five years, and when full contains eighteen million cubic metres of water.

From Perrégaux, Mascara is easily reached either by rail, or road.

L'Ougasse (376 kilom.), an unimportant hamlet, pleasantly situated on a stream.

La Mare d'Eau (381 kilom.), a small village near the forest of *Moulai-Ismail*, extending over 12,000 hectares (30,000 acres), planted with cypress, olive, and pine trees. Here it was that in 1707 Moulaï-Ismail, the Moroccan chief, was defeated and his army destroyed.

Sainte Barbe du Tlélat, Buvette (395 kilom.). Junction and terminus of the West Algerian line for Sidi-Bel Abbès (buffet), Tabia (junction for Ras-el-Mâ), and Tlemçen (*see* p. 166).

Ste. Barbe du Tlélat is a pretty village on the *Oued-Tlélat*, in a fertile district, producing cereals, olive, mulberry, and other fruit trees. An Arab market is held every Tuesday.

Arbal (404 kilom.). In the neighbourhood of the village, situated in the hills, several kilometres from the station, are many Roman ruins.

Valmy (411 kilom.), situated on the site of the *Camp du Figuier*, celebrated in the history of the conquest of Algeria. The present village, population 900, was founded in 1848, and is situated at the eastern extremity of the Sebkha of Oran, a large salt lake.

La Sénia (416 kilom.), the last station before arriving at Oran. Junction for the West Algerian line to Aïn-Temouchent (thence diligence to Tlemçen) *viâ* Aïn-Kial and Pont de l'Isser.

Oran (Karguentah) (421 kilom.).

ORAN

is the chief city of the province of Oran, and the residence of all the superior chiefs, civil and military, of the province. Its population amounts to about 88,000 inhabitants, divided as follows:—

French	41,500
Other Europeans (nearly all Spanish)	22,500
Mohammedans	13,500
Jews	10,500
	88,000

Oran is situated in 35° 44′ lat. N. by 2° 58′ long. W. at the head of the gulf of the same name, 220 miles E. of Gibraltar, 120 miles S. of Carthagena, 240 miles S. of Port Vendres, and 600 miles S.W. of Marseilles.

The old harbour has only an area of twelve acres, but a new outer harbour has been completed with spacious breakwater and quays in accordance with the commercial importance of the port, at present the most important commercial centre of Algeria. Close by are the various consulates, the custom house, marine stores, warehouses, electric tramways, etc. The safe natural harbour of **Mers-el-Kebir** (*see* pp. 158 and 161), five miles from Oran, is reserved for the naval and military requirements of the government.

The department of Oran contains 105,000 square kilometres of territory, of which 39,000 are in the Tell and 66,000 in the Sahara. The civil territory is administered by a Prefect; the military territory is under the administration of the general and officers of the army exercising judicial, police, and administrative functions. The city contains schools, libraries, museums, hospitals, and theatres.

Post and Telegraph Office.—Place de la Bastille. Branch offices at Boulevard Malakoff, Eckmühl, St. Eugène.

British Vice-Consul.—T. Barber.

United States Consular Agent.—A. H. Elford. **Belgian Consul.**—C. Geraud. **Italian Consul.**—Russi.

Banks.—Banque d'Algérie; Crédit Lyonnais; Crédit Foncier et Agricole; Compagnie Algérienne.

Hotels—Continental, Grand Hotel Victor, Hotel Metropole, at all of which Cook's Coupons, Series A, B and C, are accepted.

ORAN.

Library.—At the Mairie, Place d'Armes.

Clubs.—Cercle des Etrangers, 1, rue St.-Denis; Cercle du Sport, 14 rue d'Arzeu.

Automobiles and Garages.—Grignon, 21, Boulevard Malakoff; Serviès, 48, Boulevard Séguin; Schmitt, 60, rue d'Arzeu.

Theatres.—Rue de Turin, near the Promenade de Létang. French company, Sunday, Tuesday, and Thursday, in winter Spanish company, Sunday, Monday, Tuesday, and Thursday in summer. A new theatre is being built in the Place d'Armes.

Summer Theatre and Circus, Boulevard National.

Hippodrome at St. Eugène.

Cab Fares.—Within the walls, single course, 1f. by day, 1f. 50c. by night. Double course, 1f. 50c. and 2f. Suburbs, 1f. 50c. and 2f. Double course 2f. and 2f. 50c. By the hour, in the town, 2f. and 3f., outside the town, 2f. 50c. and 3f. 50c. By the day 16f., half-day 8f.

Electric Trams.—Seven lines leave the Place d'Armes every five or ten minutes, from 6 a.m. or 6.30 a.m. until 9 p.m. or 8.30 p.m., according to the season. The routes are

1. To the Custom House Quay.
2. To the Ste. Thérèse Jetty.
3. To Eckmühl-Noizeux.
4. To the European Cemetery.
5. To the Railway Station (Karguentah).
6. To St. Eugène.
7. To Gambetta.

Fare, 10c. from the Place d'Armes to the end of any one line, and 15c. with correspondence from one line to another.

Syndicat d'Initiative de l'Oranie.—At the Office of the Syndicat, in the Hôtel de Ville, visitors are invited to apply for information calculated to assist in making their stay in Oran agreeable, and to make free use of the reading and writing room.

Steamer Communication.—Steamers of the Compagnie Générale Transatlantique leave Marseilles for Oran Thursday and Saturday 5 p.m.; leave Oran for Marseilles Tuesday and Thursday, 5 p.m.

Steamers of the same company leave Oran for Carthagena, Monday, 11 p.m., returning Tuesday, 8 p.m.

Steamers of the Compagnie de Navigation Mixte leave Marseilles Wednesdays for Oran; due Oran Fridays, about midnight. Leave Oran Friday night; due Marseilles Monday afternoon.

Steamers of the Prosper Durand line leave Algiers for Oran, Arzeu and Mostaganem, weekly.

Steamers of the Cie de Navigation Mixte leave Oran Saturday midnight, for Nemours due Sunday morning or afternoon and Tangier, due Tuesday (or Wednesday) morning; leave Tangier Tuesday or Wednesday afternoon, due Oran Friday evening (fortnightly during summer).

Steamers of the Société de Transports Maritimes à Vapeur leave Marseilles for Oran Tuesday, 5 p.m.; leave Oran for Marseilles Saturday, 5 p.m.

Time tables subject to alteration.

The climate of Oran is cool in winter, very hot in summer, and there is an absence of country suburbs with villas and gardens, such as are found in Algiers.

Oran is a disappointment for the true lover of realistic Orientalism. The hand of the modern builder has been busy here; and, except a couple of old towers, with here and there an old piece of wall and an escutcheon bearing the Spanish coat of arms, there are no remnants of its old splendour left. The streets are wide, Frenchified, and commonplace; the barracks are very dismal looking. Oran is more of a French town than any other city in Algeria.

Oran was founded in 903 by Mahomed Ben Abdoun. In the course of half a century Oran was governed by no less than nine different rulers of several nationalities. The city was burnt in 1055, but rose again, attaining great prosperity under the Beni Zujan or Zean of Tlemçen. According to Alvarez-Gomez, there was in Oran in the year 1437, 6,000 houses, 140 mosques, a number of schools worthy of the famous colleges of Cordova, Granada, and Seville. In 1509 Oran was attacked and stormed by the Spaniards, under the leadership of Cardinal Ximenes. More than one-third of the Mussulman population was put to death, and the remainder carried away to Spain as captives, or imprisoned. The town was pillaged, and a considerable amount of money and booty fell into the Spaniards' hands. The headquarters of the Province of Oran were then transferred to Mascara. In 1708 the Dey of Mascara, **Mustapha Bou Chelarem,** succeeded in driving the Spaniards out of Oran after a memorable and bloody assault. In 1732 Philip V. of Spain sent an army of 25,000 men to the coast of Africa to retake Oran from the Moors. The place capitulated after only six hours' resistance, and formed henceforward an integral part of Spanish territory for sixty years.

In 1790, after a terribly disastrous earthquake, which destroyed most of the buildings and houses of Oran, and caused considerable loss of life and property, **Mohammed el Kebir,** Dey of Mascara, laid siege to the place and invested it closely for fourteen months, until, in 1791, an arrangement having been entered into between the regency of Algiers and the Spanish Government, Oran capitulated, with the honours of war. The Spaniards delivered the town to the Turks, and were themselves allowed to retire with their guns, treasures, and property. The troops and inhabitants were transported to Carthagena.

Oran was occupied by the French for the first time in 1831. Marshal Clauzel, in the name of the French Government, ceded the town to the Bey of Tunis, but this arrangement not having been ratified by the French Parliament, Oran was taken possession of a second time on the 17th August, 1831, and has ever since remained in the hands of the French.

The principal sights of Oran are

The **Cathedral of St. Louis.**

The **Great Mosque** (Djana-el-Bacha) in the Rue Philippe.

The **Mosque of Sidi El Haouri.**

The **Museum Demaeght.**

The Mount **Mourdjadjo,** at the summit of which is the **Fort Santa-Cruz,** the **tower,** and the **Chapel of the Virgin**

The **Casbah.**

The **Promenade de Létang.**

The new **Military Hospital.**

The new **Jewish Synagogue,** not yet (Jan. 1908) finished.

The **Cathedral** of **St. Louis,** close to the Military

Hospital, was an ancient mosque, which was first transformed into a monastery by Cardinal Ximenes, and eventually into a church dedicated to " Our Lady of Victories." From 1709 to 1731 it was used as a synagogue, and then fell into ruins until restored by the French in 1839. In the choir roof is a valuable fresco, representing the entry of St. Louis into Tunis. Near the Place d'Armes (Boulevard Magenta) a new Cathedral is now (1908) being built.

The **Great Mosque** in the Rue Philippe (La Grande Mosquée, or Mosque du Pacha) is a charming building, with an exquisitely carved little minaret. A marble court, with a handsome fountain in the middle and an arcade round, with a double row of columns, form the entrance hall. This court leads into the mosque, which is in pure Moorish style, and very richly decorated.

The **Mosque of Sidi el Haouri** is situated at the foot of the hill on which stands the Cathedral of St. Louis. This mosque was built in 1800 by **Bey Othman,** son of Mohammed El Kebir, Bey of Mascara. Its minaret, decorated with a treble row of delicately carved arcades, dominates the koubba or dome of the mosque still affected to the Mussulman worship. Wonderful miracles are related about El Haouri. This is one of the most popular legends which is told in reference to this saint :

A very pious woman whose son had been taken prisoner by the Spaniards, was carried off as a slave to Malaga. El Haouri told the woman to worship God with faith several times a day, and also to bring him a dish of beef-tea with meat in it, which was eventually done. El Haouri gave the broth to his favourite dog, a superb greyhound, who was at the time suckling her little ones. The dog started at once, and got on board a vessel bound for the Spanish coast. She met the young man in question in Spain, and as soon as he saw the dog he recognised her as belonging to the saint. He followed the dog to the vessel, which was preparing to return to Oran. He concealed himself among the cargo, and succeeded in landing safely on his native shores. The dog returned to her master and her young ones, and the poor mother narrated all over the city how, by the prayers of the saint and the intelligence of the dog, her son had been miraculously restored to her.

The **Museum Demaeght,** 9, Rue Montebello (open free

from 1 to 5 p.m.) is the most important in the colony, inaugurated 1886. It contains Roman antiquities from St. Leu, including some splendid mosaic pavements. Also collections of natural history, pottery, medals, and coins. Under the Presidency of Commandant Demaeght all the antiquities found in the department will be installed in the Oran Museum.

The steep and beautiful walk to

Santa-Cruz a spur of **Mount Mourdjadjo,** should be undertaken; it is not by any means so formidable as it looks from below. There is a good and well-defined path which leads up from the Porte del Santa, behind the cathedral. Those who wish to ride up to it can obtain horses for the purpose. The fort of St. Gregoire can be visited on the way, also a little chapel erected in 1849 after a severe visitation of cholera. Close by is a tower 75 feet high, surmounted by a statue of the Virgin. The foot of Santa-Cruz is perched on the highest point of the mountains behind the town, and commands a view over the whole country and the seaboard; so that on clear days the coast of Spain can be distinguished. The splendid panorama from the top amply compensates the sightseer for the trouble of the climb. The ascent occupies about an hour, the distance being only two miles. Its highest elevation is 580 metres—that is, about 200 metres higher than the Bouzarea at Algiers. On the summit of the Mount Mourdjadjo is a well-equipped observatory. (For permission to visit apply to the Syndicat d'Initiative de l'Oranie at the Hotel de Ville, Oran.)

The City of Oran is far from being as handsome, architecturally speaking, as Algiers; neither is it half as picturesque from an Eastern point of view. Of late years the harbour has been completed, but the only safe anchorage on the coast, as already stated, is the harbour or natural bay of **Mers el Kebir,** five miles north of Oran (*see* p. 161). This bay, in its shape and the security it affords to large-size vessels, resembles very much the celebrated bay of Villefranche near Nice. The town is well supplied with water from the springs at Ras-el-Ain and Brédéa.

Oran is about two-thirds as large as Algiers, but of its eighty-eight thousand souls, only about fourteen thousand are Arabs. The rest are Jews, Italians, Biscris, and anybodies from anywhere, and many Spaniards. These may be reckoned the last descendants of Spaniards settled here for centuries, and others are emigrants who are continually flocking over from

Spain, the nearest point of which to Oran, Carthagena, is but ten hours steaming. It must not be forgotten that for centuries Oran has been a kind of political challenge-cup. Half a dozen nations have in turn fought for it, conquered it, lost it, conquered and lost it again. Roman medals, belonging to different epochs, have been found in abundance in the neighbourhood, and archæologists are at issue as to whether Oran stands on the site of the Quisa Xenitana of Pliny. All, however, are agreed on this point—that the present modern village of Mers el Kebir is on the very spot where stood Portus Divinus; also that the Oued el Malah, or Salt River, in the environs of Oran, which the Spaniards still name El Rio Salado, is the Flumen Salsum of the Romans.

The old Spanish forts and walls of Oran are considered, even to this day, fine specimens of masonry; they exhibit a solidity which has defied earthquakes and cannonadings without number. They were nearly all built by convicts. The public works at Oran do not seem to have ruined his Catholic Majesty, for at the eastern end of the Casbah may still be read this remarkable inscription :—

En el Ano 1589
SIN. COSTAR. A. SU. MAGESTAD.
MAS. QUE. EL. VALOR. DE. LAS. MADERAS.
ESTA. OBRA.
Don Pedro de Padilla so Capitan General
Y. JUSTICIA. MAYOR. DE. ESTAS. PLAZAS.
POR. SO. DILIGENCIA. Y. BUENOS. MEDIOS.

("In the year 1589, without costing his Majesty any more than the value of the timber and scaffolding, this has been erected by Don Pedro de Padilla, H.M. Capitan-General and Grand Justiciary of these parts, by his diligent aid and good services.") The convicts got the stones from the quarries and built the Casbah. On the postern gate (la Porte d'Espagne) near the Casbah there are still to be seen curious but superb Spanish escutcheons.

Oran was for many years the port of deportation of the Spanish kingdom.

The **Casbah** must have taken a great many years to build, or else the convicts must somehow have contrived to get the Arabs to do their work. This would not be altogether incredible if one bears in mind that the citadel was always crammed full with prisoners taken at the various encounters outside the gates of the city. There was a garrison of 6,600 men, and about 5,000 *puridarios*, or felons. There were but 3,000 Spanish inhabitants. Between the military, the convicts, and the population reigned the most delightful *entente cordiale*. The soldiers let the thieves do pretty well as they liked, and when there was a *Capitan-General* who turned rusty and talked of the cat-o'-nine-tails, the rogues took themselves gaily off to Morocco, where to this day there are whole towns peopled by their descendants. Many of the exiles, being banished for political reasons, bore aristocratic names, and had plenty of money; they brought with them the fashions and manners of the Spanish Court. Oran was in fact one of the most jovial, most rollicking and luxurious places it is possible to imagine. It gained the *sobriquet* of *La Corte Chica*, "The Little Court." Night and day there was nothing but balls, collations, and festivities, wine-quaffing, cigarette-smoking, guitar-strumming, bull-fighting, love-making, and gondoling. It was a *presidario* of pleasure, but every now and then the Arabs or the Turks would come thundering at the gates, and there would be a mighty fight by way of diversion.

The **Promenade de Létang** (named after a French general), planted with palm-trees, pines, etc., commands a very fine view : on the north, the harbour and roadstead ; on the west, the lower part of the town, the Mourdjadjo (with Santa Cruz and the Chapel of the Virgin), Mers-el-Kebir ; on the east, the cliffs, Canastel and the Pointe de l'Aiguille and the Djebel-Kahar (Mountain of Lions).

Oran is now a very prosperous town, and rapidly becoming, commercially speaking, more important than Algiers. The trade with England is considerable, chiefly in alfa and cereals. The ravine which separated Oran has been of late years nearly all filled up, and the **Mosquée** and **Karguentah** quarters joined to Oran proper. The principal thoroughfares are the **Boulevard Oudinot, Place d'Armes,** monument erected 1898 in memory of the fight at Sidi-Brahim near Nemours in 1845 (*see* p. 187) **Boulevard National, Place de la République, Place Kléber, Boulevard Malakoff, Rue Philippe, Boulevard Séguin,** etc.

The band of the Second Regiment of Zouaves plays twice a week on the Place de la République. Amusements are few and far between, and the ordinary tourist will scarcely spend more than two or three days at Oran, the town affording but very little interest from an Eastern point of view. A visit should be paid to the Negro quarter (between the Boulevard d'Iena and the Tlemçen and Mascara Gates).

The **Bains de la Reine** (Hammam Sultana) are situated 3 kilometres from Oran, on the road to Mers-el-Kebir. An hotel and a café are attached to the establishment. These are the thermal springs of Jane, daughter of Queen Isabella of Castille, which are still used by the Arabs and Europeans, especially for cutaneous diseases. At the end of a narrow path, scarcely wide enough to allow one person to pass at a time, is a grotto, in the heart of the quartz rock, from which the waters (temperature 130° F.) rush out into a cistern at the rate of 300 litres a minute. The water is rather salt, but very clear and pure. The Thermal Establishment below is divided into bathing-rooms, with private baths, and also douches and separate bathing places. These waters, are most beneficial in cases of rheumatic affections and all kinds of cutaneous diseases, neuralgia, and gout.

The small town of **Mers=el=Kebir** (5 kilometres beyond the Bains de la Reine) contains about 3,000 inhabitants (nearly all of Italian origin) and is picturesquely situated on the slope of the rocky point to the west of the citadel overlooking the bay (see pp. 152 and 158). The drive to Mers-el-Kebir will be found a pleasant excursion from Oran (carriage 5f. for the double journey; or by omnibus in 1 hour, 50c.). It is a magnificent anchorage, protected from the fury of the winds on all sides save one, where the soil has been artificially extended by a jetty. The harbour and village are strongly protected by forts.

A drive to the **Ravin Vert,** or Oued Rehhi, is a most pleasant one, as well as an excursion to the **Camp des Planteurs,** and to several prosperous Arab villages if time permits.

L

HAMMAM SELAMA.
(Near Oran.)

Two hours by train from Oran on the Oran-Arzeu-Saïda Railway, and at 2½ miles from the station of **Port=aux= Poules** (55 kilom.), much frequented in summer, are the baths of

Selama, overlooking the Mediterranean. The "spring" was discovered when boring for petroleum at a depth of 900 feet, and the pressure at the mouth of the well is equal to 80 s.p. on the steam gauge. The water is highly mineralised, warm, and beautifully clear; the carbonic acid gas mixed with it causes it to rise in a sparkling jet of 12 to 40 feet above the ground.

The water has been proved to be very beneficial for gout, rheumatoid arthritis, eczema, throat, kidney, stomach, and intestine troubles.

Attached to the baths is a small hotel, very comfortable, and quiet. Pension terms, 10f. a day, and no extras.

Rough shooting, including wild duck, snipe, hares, and partridges, is obtainable in the district, and sea fishing from the rocks and boats is within easy reach.

A variety of drives and picnics may be enjoyed by visitors.

Taken internally, the water is slightly laxative, and an excellent diuretic.

Hammam Selama can be reached in less than four days from London, via Paris and Marseilles, thence steamer, Tuesday, Thursday, and Saturday, to Oran; or from Paris, via Madrid and Carthagena, thence steamer (nine hours) to Oran.

(For fares and dates of sailings, which are subject to alteration, consult time tables.)

ALGIERS OR ORAN TO SIDI BEL ABBÈS AND TLEMÇEN BY RAIL.

Stations.	Distance in kilometres from Oran.	Stations.	Distance in kilometres from Oran.
Oran	—	**Sidi Bel Abbès** ...	78
La Sénia ...	5	Sidi Lhassen (Détrie)	84
Valmy	10	Sidi Khaled (Palissy)	90
Arbal ...	17	Boukanéfis...	97
St. Barbe du Tlélat Junction }	26	**Tabia Junction** for Ras-el-Mâ-Crampel	101
St. Lucien ...	32	Taffaman ...	114
Lauriers Roses	42	Aïn Tellout	125
Oued Imbert	55	Lamoricière	134
Les Trembles ...	62	Oued Chouly	144
Sidi Brahim (Prudon)	68	Aïn Fezza ...	156
		Tlemçen ...	165

The railway communication between **Oran** and **Tlemçen** was completed in 1899, and is very convenient for tourists, who previously hesitated to go to this most interesting place on account of a long and tedious journey in the uncomfortable diligence. The extension from Tlemçen to Turenne is expected to be opened shortly (*see* p. 176).

The through train from **Algiers** to **Tlemçen** leaves Algiers at 6.50 a.m., arriving **Ste. Barbe du Tlélat** at 6.15 p.m., where passengers for Tlemçen change carriages, and arrive at Tlemçen at 11.5 p.m. same day. Many travellers, however, prefer to go on to Oran, a short run of fifty minutes, spend two or three days there, and proceed from Oran to Tlemçen by one of three trains, the best being the 1.0 p.m., due at Tlemçen 7.25 p.m.

There is another route from Oran to Tlemçen, viz. :—Oran to Aïn Témouchent by rail (76 kilom.) *and thence to Tlemçen by diligence.* (See p. 180.)

Leaving by the Sainte Barbe du Tlélat route several small stations are passed, but as no tourists are ever likely to call there is no need to describe them. Their names are given in the table at the head of this chapter.

Sidi Bel Abbès is the only important station on the line between Oran and Tlemçen. It is 78 kilometres from Oran, and well deserves a visit. Population, about 25,000, including about 6,000 French, 12,000 Spanish and 7,000 native inhabitants. **Hotel:** Hôtel d'Orient. (Cook's Coupons, Series A, B and C accepted.)

Sidi Bel Abbès is built in the shape of a rectangle, surrounded with walls and bastions on the four sides. Four gates give access to the city—the Gates of Oran, Daya, Tiemçen, and Mascara. The town owes its rapid development and prosperity to agriculture, being situated in one of the most fertile districts of Algeria.

The principal street, the **Rue Prudon** (name of a distinguished officer of the French army), cuts the town into two distinct portions, the military quarter and the civil quarter.

The military quarter is situated west. It contains the different barracks of the troops stationed at Sidi Bel Abbès, the **Commissariat,** the **Hospital,** and the **Military Club**—a cheerful house, surrounded by handsome gardens, where the famous band of the **1st Légion Étrangère** plays six times a week. It is well to remind the reader that the Légion Étrangère is a regiment composed, as its name indicates, of soldiers of foreign nationality, who serve in the French army without being naturalised French citizens. The bulk of this regiment is composed for the greater part of Alsatians and foreigners, mostly Poles and Germans, many of whom are talented artists. It gives very often string concerts, and has acquired the reputation of having, with the Garde Républicaine, the most perfect band in the French army.

The **Rue de Tlemçen** is the principal street of the military quarter.

The town proper, situated east of the Rue Prudon, contains very decent modern buildings, such as the Theatre, the Mairie, the Tribunal de Police Municipale, the College, the Church, a Mosque, and a Synagogue. The chief streets are the **Rue Montagnac, Rue de Jérusalem, Rue de Mascara,** and the **Rue des Ecoles.** The **Place des Quinconces** is a fine square, with the Palais de Justice and Prison adjoining it.

Sidi Bel Abbès has several **faubourgs** outside its walls. They are:—

The **Mekerra,** the **Village Nègre,** the **Village Espagnol** (or Spanish quarter), **Faubourg des Palmiers,** and the **Faubourg Thiers.**

The **Promenade Publique** is a magnificent promenade shaded with beautiful trees. Other parts of the town and the suburbs are fortunately sheltered by numerous stately trees which serve to procure agreeable shade during the great heat of summer.

Sidi Bel Abbès is chiefly a garrison town, the troops at all times quartered there amounting to 6,000 men. It has however, a considerable trade, especially in alfa fibre, wheat, and barley and is one of the chief inland dépôts of the Province of Oran. Water is plentiful, being derived from a river, and a tributary stream of excellent quality

The **Roman Fountain,** in the **Mekerra** quarter, well deserves a visit ; it is an exquisite mixture of Roman and Arab architecture.

Sidi Bel Abbès enjoys the inestimable advantage of having no history worth speaking about. It takes its name from the marabout or koubba of Sidi Bel Abbès, one of the innumerable holy men of Algeria, whose shrine adjoins the redoubt erected for the defence of the place. The town is about the same calibre as Blidah or Miliana, or scores of similar towns, more than half French, formerly picturesque, but now undergoing the ruthless metamorphosis of civilisation. There is a theatre where the good old stock vaudevilles are played ; a **café chantant,** several good hotels, and a **military club** (*see* p. 164).

Four stations beyond Sidi Bel Abbès, at Tabia (where the line turns off to Tlemçen), a railway continues through the valley to **Chanzy** (thermal springs and numerous Roman remains), through a district of thickly planted forests, along the river Mekerra to **Magenta,** surrounded by mountains. The line then enters the region of the High Plateaux and of the alfa grass, and ends at **Ras=el=Mâ-Crampel,** the terminus, at the foot of **Djebel Beguira** (4,622 ft.). A great contrast is afforded by the view from the summit. On the north are the forests of Daya and Majenta, and on the south the sea of alfa grass, an expanse without a single tree.

Two stations beyond Tabia the train arrives at

Lamoricière, 31 kilometres from Tlemçen, an important village of about 2,000 inhabitants, called after the general of the same name. Near it are the remains of a Roman camp. The Arab market is on Monday. This is the territory of the tribe of the **Ouled Mimoun,** renowned for their agricul-

tural capabilities, and is one of the most fertile in the province
of Oran. It is well cultivated, and brings in very good
revenues to its owners. The site is one of the finest in
Algeria. The fertile valley at the west is bordered by a
chain of small mountains, over which the sunset effects are
incomparably grand.

From Lamoricière the character of the scenery changes, the
country is more wooded, and the various views of the Lella-
Setti mountain are a great delight to the somewhat tired
traveller. Then, on nearing Tlemçen, the railway passes over
the beautiful cascades of **El Ourit** (*see* p. 177), crosses the
Saf Saf ravine, and traversing numerous plantations of olive,
fig, and other fruit trees, arrives at

Tlemçen. Population about 30,000. This is the antique
Pomaria of the Romans, then **Agadir,** one mile from the
town. It was a Roman camp, with a body of occupation of
cavalry, whose duty was to watch the movements of the
neighbouring warlike tribes of natives. Tlemçen, the Moorish
capital of Western Algeria, was founded by the Beni Ifren;
it was successively under the yoke of different dynasties, such
as the Idrissides, the Almohades, the Abd el Ouadites, the
Turks, and lastly the French.

The glorious reign of Tlemçen as the brilliant capital of
Algerian Magreb was at its climax under the domination of the
Abd el Ouadites. The Sultan Abou Moussa II. contributed
greatly to its magnificence. Its population amounted then,
according to trustworthy Arab historians, to 125,000 souls;
its maritime connections extended to the most remote ports of
the Mediterranean.

Tlemçen was the city of light and genius . . . . its
kings were lovers of arts, science, and literature. The
Court was numerous and brilliant; the army was disciplined,
brave, and well commanded; they coined their own money,
had their police, judges, etc. In a word, Tlemçen was one
of the most civilised towns of the world about 1553, when
the different nations of Europe were hardly awakening from
their long lethargy.

Under the Turks, Tlemçen was a pashalik of the Turkish
odjak or province. It was afterwards made an aghalik; it
was in a state of anarchy and revolution for a succession of
years (1553–1830). After the surrender of Algiers the
Emperor of Morocco tried to capture Tlemçen, but was

baffled in his enterprise by the obstinate resistance of the Koulouglis (Turkish descendants), who first fought on their ruler's account, and last on behalf of the French. The French occupied it, and handed it over by treaty to Abd el Kader. Later on, Marshal Clauzel took possession of it again in 1836. In 1839 the French gave it to Abd el Kader for the second time. This Arab chief sought in vain to make Tlemçen the capital of a flourishing province, and restore to it some of its ancient splendour.

After several years' trial the town was taken possession of definitely by the French (1842), and became an integral part of French Algeria.

"The town of Tlemçen, the ancient capital of the Magreb, 'the Key of the West,' as it was called by the Turks, with its picturesque mosques, crenelated walls, high Moorish minarets, its circular koubbas and delicately carved archways, sparkles," says Lady Herbert, "like a diamond in the rising sun." Its monuments, with the exception of the Grande Mosquée which is somewhat older, date from the 13th and 14th centuries, and are of great artistic interest and worthy of comparison with those of Granada. Cf. " Les monuments arabes de Tlemçen." Paris, 1903.

Tlemçen is now a very prosperous town, doing a large trade with Europe. The chief exports consist of olive oil, wool, figs, flour, and corn, cattle, carpets, and other manufactured goods. A great quantity of alfa from the province is packed at Tlemçen. Many-coloured haïcks and blankets are manufactured, and also red haïcks or shawls worn by Jewish ladies and used for mourning; red is the mourning colour for the Jews of the province of Oran.

The principal hotel at Tlemçen is the **Hôtel de France** (Cook's Coupons, Series A, B and C, accepted), and if this leaves something to be desired it must be remembered that Tlemçen has not yet reached the degree of civilisation which would entail the adoption of modern usages in hotels and dwelling-houses. The completion of the railway and the natural influx of visitors, which will be its immediate consequence, cannot fail to improve this state of things in the future.

Tlemçen is destined to develop into well-frequented winter quarters, for although it is the only shining star in the province of Oran, it sparkles brightly enough to attract the tourists in its orb, and to keep them there for some considerable time.

The climate of Tlemçen is exceedingly healthy, but although the atmosphere be clear and the sky bright blue, the air in winter is often sharp and frosty, and shawls and wrappers are much needed.

The chiefly interesting buildings of Tlemçen are its mosques, which at one period are said to have numbered seventy. The principal one is Grande Mosquée or

Djama el Kebir, on the Place d'Alger. The saint **Ahmed Ben Hassan el Ghomari** is buried here ; every native who passes the little oratory which gives access to the mosque kisses the grating. Above the door is an Arabic inscription, the translation being :

" The virtues of this sanctuary spread themselves abroad,
Like the light of the morning, or the brilliancy of the stars,
O ye who are afflicted with great evils, he who will cure them
for you
Is this son of science and profound nobility, AHMED."

The mosque is a spacious building, about 180 feet square, supported by seventy-two columns. It is entered by eight doors, and the large court surrounded by arcades is a spacious and grand specimen of Arab architecture, built of massive onyx, with a fountain in the centre. The interior of the building is dark and sombre, and the eye has to get accustomed to this obscurity, coming from a brilliant and dazzling sunshine.

The **mihrab** is very imposing, looking, as usual, towards Mecca. The recess, lighted from the roof into which it stands, is an elaborately carved archway ornamented with arabesques. The date of the foundation of the mosque is carved on it ; it is given as A.D. 1136, or 530 of the Hejira. There is also a handsome chandelier, the gift of **Sultan Ghamarazan** in 1255.

The minaret, built of brick, is 112 feet high, and is a very notable object, no matter from which side Tlemçen is approached. It is decorated with little pillars, square in shape, and sparkling glazed tiles add a great deal to its artistic profile.

At a few yards from the Grande Mosquée, at the west side of the Place d'Alger, is the small

Mosque of Sidi Ahmed Bel Hassan el Ghomari commonly called the mosque of **Aboul Hassan.** It scarcely looks like a mosque from the exterior, were it not for its minaret, with the usual little pillars and mosaic work. It was founded A.D. 1298, as is testified by the inscription in the centre of the third arch. The *mihrab* is the finest specimen of Arab work in the world; the view of it alone is, according to the expression of learned Orientalists, worth the journey to Tlemçen. The hand of man has scarcely ever attained this perfection. The interior of the mosque is very highly decorated, three rows of horse-shoe arcades dividing it into three large halls. The roofs are all made of fine cedar, with lovely designs and paintings still remaining, supported by six columns of Algerian onyx. This mosque is said to have been founded in honour of the Emir **Abou Ibrahim Ben Yahia,** but the name was really given to commemorate the virtues of the eminent lawyer and Arab *savant,* **Abou Hassen Ibn Yaklef el Tenessi.** Mr. Alex. A. Knox says, in " The New Playground " : "All I can say is, that there has never been a lawyer in the world who has had such a splendid monument to his memory. I will go back from London to Tlemçen to have another look at the *mihrab.*"

The mosque has been turned into a museum of antiquities. Key can be obtained of the concierge at the Mairie close by.

The Museum contains architectural fragments, inscriptions, and other interesting objects. Adjoining is another museum, the **Musée Brevet,** with important geological collections, presented to the town by a curé named Brevet.

The **Mosque of Sidi Ibrahim,** behind the barracks of Gourmellat, contains nothing to attract attention, and is scarcely worth a visit if time be of consequence. The tomb of the Saint is in a koubba outside the mosque, in which are four iron arches covered with arabesques.

Near the Porte de Fez is a small mosque, the

Djama=Oulad=el=Imam, with a rectangular minaret 55 feet high, the sides covered with well-preserved glazed tiles.

These are all the mosques of ancient Tlemçen that remain *within the walls.*

The mosque of
Sidi=el=Haloui, the confectioner saint, lies immediately outside the walls (open 9 to 11 and 1.30 to 2.30). This saint

was born at Seville, in Spain, where he was a kadi. He started on a pilgrimage to Sidi Okba and came back to Tlemçen, where he settled as a sweetmeat baker. The sweetmeats made by him are called **Halouat** in Arabic, and the name **El Haloui** was given him on that account. He used to preach to the children, and as a great crowd of spectators collected round his bon-bon stall, soon the whole town got to know him and worship him. The Sultan, hearing of his great popularity, called him to the palace as tutor to his three sons. This appointment, however, gave umbrage to the Grand Vizier,

Mosque of Sidi Haloui, Tlemçen.

who had him tried as a sorcerer, condemned and beheaded outside the gates. The evening of the execution, which had aroused the public mind to exasperation, the following miracle is said to have taken place : The **Bouab**, or doorkeeper, was crying as usual to the infidels to come in before the doors were closed, when a sepulchral voice was heard exclaiming : " Close thy gates, Bouab ; there is no one without, save El Haloui the oppressed ! " For seven days the same voice was heard uttering the same sentence. The people openly murmured. The Sultan came himself to the gates of the mosque, and returned to the

palace, saying : " *I wished to hear ; I have heard !* " The next
morning the Grand Vizier was put to death on the very spot
where El Haloui had been beheaded; his treatment was to
be buried alive in a block of mortar, like San Geronimo,
the Spanish martyr. To appease the spirit of the saint,
the beautiful mosque of **Sidi-el-Haloui** was built, which exists
to this day. Close by is a negro village, and just beyond
El-Haloui's tomb is another mosque with a graceful minaret.

The mosque is a smaller edition of the Djama-el-Kebir. The
court and the interior are decorated with arabesques, the ceiling is of carved cedar wood, and the arches of the aisles rest
on magnificent onyx columns, with exquisite capitals. The
minaret, 60 feet high, is rectangular, the sides divided into
compartments with arcades decorated in tiles.

The beautiful portal of the mosque bears the inscription
754 of Hedjira, or A.D. 1353, the date of its foundation.

The **Mechouar,** or Citadel, in the southern part of the
town, was the official residence of the Sultans of Tlemçen,
including the governors of the Almohades, and the kings of
the Abd-el-Ouadites. It was a gorgeous residence, attended
with all possible luxury and splendour. There was in a
splendid gallery, paved with marble and onyx, a silver tree,
erected by Sultan **Abou Tachfin,** on which stood all the
species of singing-birds in existence, made of gold and silver.
The celebrated clock of this palace, which excited the wonder
of all visitors, was built 200 years before that of Strasburg,
and 300 years before the gift of Sultan **Aroun el Rachid** to
Louis XIV. of France. There now remains of the Mechouar
but the mosque **Djama el Mechouar,** or rather the minaret,
which was the most prominent part of that mosque, and a
marble column which lies in the museum of Tlemçen (*see*
below). The minaret is 98 ft. high, entirely built of red
bricks, and offers no particular interest. This vast edifice is
now adapted as a hospital, barracks, prison, commissariat and
stores. The adjacent building is used by the French authorities as a military chapel. The magnificent old walls and
gateway are in a tolerable state of preservation, but have
no particular features, and are nothing else but what they
purport to be.

In the **Museum** there is little to be seen except the marble
columns of the Mechouar and of the mosque at Mansoura,
and a collection of glazed tiles, which are unimportant when

compared with the beautiful Hispano-Moorish tiles, with metallic reflection, of the Alhambra and Alcazar of Seville and Granada.

The **French Church** on the Place Cavaignac, erected in 1855, is rather a handsome building in the Roman-Byzantine style, with a high tower and steeple. The font is of porphyry and onyx from the ruins of the mosque of Mansoura.

Excursions in the neighbourhood of Tlemçen.

The excursions round Tlemçen are numerous and interesting, the country in every direction being one of great beauty, well shaded with large trees and abounding in waterfalls.

Carriages to hold four persons can be hired for 16f. the day, or 8f. half a day, or an arrangement can be made at the Hotel de France for a good carriage, with guide and interpreter, including his own and the driver's fee, and the expenses of sight-seeing, for 25f.

A very interesting drive and walk of about 2 hours is to

Agadir (ancient fortifications), and the **Bois de Boulogne.** Leaving Tlemçen by the Abattoir gate you soon come to the beautiful minaret, the only portion left of the **Mosque of Agadir**, built in 173 of the Hedjira, A.D. 789. A little further on the remains of the fortifications are seen, and the tomb of Sidi Daoudi, the patron saint of Agadir, before the time of the Sidi Bou Medin. Beyond is the valley of the *Oued Kalia*, and the commencement of the Bois de Boulogne, a delightful promenade, with shaded walks and flowing rivulets, interspersed with koubbas more or less in ruins.

The return drive can be made through the valley, thus obtaining another view of the fortifications.

Half a day should be devoted to a visit to **Mansoura**, 1½ miles to the west of Tlemçen, and a whole morning to **Sidi-Bou-Médine**, 1¼ miles to the S.E.

Mansoura was built by **Abou Yakoub** in the thirteenth century, when he besieged Tlemçen. The siege lasted seven years, the Sultan Yakoub taking advantage of the leisure hours of his combatants by building Mansoura in the meanwhile. It was a great city, with baths, mosques, and all the appliances of Eastern civilisation. The fortifications enclose a rectangular space of 300 acres. The walls or ramparts were 5 feet thick, and 39 feet high, with towers at intervals of 125 feet, built of concrete, and the portions remaining are still very imposing. However, when Tlemçen yielded to his troops and was occupied, the new Mansoura was abandoned. Abou Yakoub was himself assassinated by a slave before the surrender of Tlemçen.

The following translation from **Ibn Khaldoum's** works on Tlemçen is interesting, coming as it does from a contemporary, and will help to form an idea of the place as it stood in 1302 :—

" In the very spot where the army had pitched its tents, a palace was erected for the residence of the Sovereign. This vast site was surrounded by a wall and was filled with great houses, immense edifices, magnificent palaces, and gardens traversed by streamlets. It was in the year 702 of Hedjira (A.D. 1302) that the Sultan caused the circuit of the walls to be built, and that he thus established a town admirable not ·only for its extent and its numerous population, but also for the activity of its commerce and the strength of its fortifications. It contained baths, caravanseraïs, and a hospital, as well as a mosque where service was performed on Fridays ; its minaret was of extraordinary height. The town received from its founder the name of El-Mansoura, or the victorious. From day to day its prosperity augmented, its market overflowed with provisions, and merchants flocked to it from all countries. It soon took the first place among the towns of the Magreb."

When the dynasty of the Abd el Ouadites took possession of Tlemçen in 1359, Mansoura was allowed to fall to ruins, the Arabs themselves helping to its destruction.

The tomb of Sidi Yakoub at Mansoura is in good repair, whitewashed every Thursday, and decorated with brocade, flags, ostrich eggs, etc. . . . It is wonderful to see in what a perfect state of preservation is the surrounding wall of Mansoura after five centuries of destruction. The beautiful horseshoe arch known as **Bab el Khamis**, which was a gateway in this famous wall, has been allowed, however, to fall to pieces, the French contributing a great deal to this calamity. The celebrated **minaret** or Tower of Mansoura, which was built of hewn stone, remains unmoved unto this day, and still preserves its bold appearance. It stands 125 feet high,

and is the finest Moorish monument in all Algeria. At the
bottom of it the mosque was accessible through the handsomest of Moorish arches. The front side of the minaret is
perfect, but the three other sides, although faultless in
appearance, have been considerably repaired and strengthened
by French engineers. Of this, however, no one can complain.
It is, as usual, divided into three arched storeys, panelled
with glazed tiles and carved onyx pillars. The interior is
lighted by windows of coloured glass. Nothing remains of
the mosque, but ruined walls open to the heavens.

On the road to Mansoura, outside the Fez gate, is

The Saharidj, a reservoir 660 feet long and 330 feet broad,
built by Abou Tachfin, the last king of the Ouadites, for his
wife to sail boats on. It is now out of repair, and dry.

The present village of

Bou Médine, or **El=Eubbad**, is situated about a
mile and a half from Tlemçen. The road starts from the
Oran gate of Tlemçen, through the Arab cemetery and a succession of olive groves, passing the koubbas of Sidi-Yacoub ·
and es-Senucci, until it reaches a spot where carriages can proceed no further. One is obliged to alight here and walk up a
rough path amongst half-ruined houses. At the end of this
steep bit of climbing there is a wooden porch with patent
arabesques in a stone wall encircling the **Koubba** of the Saint
Sidi Bou Médine. On the right is the **Mosque**, with its graceful minaret ; a little further on is the **Medressa**, a dependency
of the mosque. The Koubba of Sidi Bou Médine is reached
by several steps to a court or **patio** surrounded with arcades
supported by marble columns. In the centre is a beautiful
onyx fountain, and to the right and left are tombs of persons
connected with the mosque.

From the court one enters the koubba, on the doors of
which it is recorded that after a fire in 1792 the building was
restored by Sidi Mohamed, Bey of Oran. From the centre of
the arches hang fantastic lanterns, and numerous cages filled
with singing-birds are suspended on the walls, which are
decorated with Arab inscriptions, illuminated Moslem draw-
ings, and views of holy places of the Islam. The Tomb of the
saint is in carved wood, covered with the richest gold and
silver brocade and damask materials. From the dome above
hang all sorts of flags, ostrich eggs, sculptured ornaments and
lamps. The ceiling, doors, and generally all the woodwork

is carved in the most elaborate style, many of the paintings still preserving their freshness and delicacy of tint. The handles, hinges, locks, grates, window bars are made of bronze or wrought iron of beautiful workmanship, revealing the Hispano-Arab origin of the workman.

Sidi Bou Médine was born at Seville, in Spain, in the year 520 of the Hedjira (A.D. 1126), under the reign of the Sultan **Ali-Ibn Youssef-Ibn-Tachfin,** the same Sultan who built the mosque of Tlemçen. His real name was **Choaib-Ibn-Hussein-el-Andalosi.** He studied in the schools of Seville, Granada, and Fez, then visited Tlemçen, El-Eubbad, and Mecca, where he met the celebrated **Sidi Abd el Kader el Djelali.** He afterwards gave lectures at Bagdad, Bougie, Seville, and Cordova, and was finally invited to settle down and lecture to the Court of **Yakoub el Mansour,** at Tlemçen, where he died at the age of 75 years, after having expressed a strong wish to be buried at **El-Eubbad.** The Sultan **Mohammed el Nasser,** the successor of Sultan **Yakoub el Mansour,** had a magnificent mausoleum and tomb built for Sidi Bou Médine, which was subsequently embellished and ornamented by the successive Sultans **Yarmoracen Ben Zeyian,** and **Aboul Hassen Ali.**

By the side of the tomb of Sidi Bou Médine is the tomb of Sidi Abd-es-Selam-et Tounin, a disciple of the saint, who came to die near his venerated master ; and to the right of the staircase are interred several privileged persons of high birth or eminent piety.

The **Mosque** is rich in tile mosaics, some of which are said to have been made in Spain, others in Morocco. A row of steps leads to a portico, beyond which by massive cedar wood doors, adorned with solid bronze of decorative workmanship, the open court paved with tiles gives access to the mosque. A short description of the beautiful mosque will suffice. It is divided into four naves decorated with very fine work, somewhat similar to the delicate tracery of the mihrab in the mosque of Aboul Hassan (p. 169). The portico and walls of the building are covered with sculptured ornaments. The mimbar (wooden) was given by Abd-el-Kader to replace one in marble that was broken, and the mihrab is of great beauty and value.

The minaret placed at the right of the porch is covered with tiles, thus completing the general effect of the façade. It will repay the visitor to ascend the 72 steps to the belvedere for the sake of the splendid panoramic view of an intensely interesting country.

At a little distance from the mosque is

The **Medressa**, or college for the higher class studies founded in 747 of the Hedjira, A.D. 1347, by Aboul-Hassan le Merinide. Before the building was ruined by the infiltration of water from the rocks against which it stands, the Medressa suffered nothing by comparison with the koubba and the mosque. The tile mosaics at the entrance are of the finest possible quality. The grand hall with a domed roof, which was utilised both as a college and a mosque, was ornamented with artistic plaster carvings and sculptured wood, all of which have been irretrievably damaged.

If Mansoura, with its sudden appearance and disappearance, is like Aladdin's Palace, Sidi Bou Médine is an Eastern version of the Sleeping Beauty. The magnificent mosque, tomb, and college of the Black Sultan, are as fresh and sparkling in all their beauty of tiles and arabesque as when he built them, five hundred years ago. The great doors of the mosque still boast their bronze work, of a pattern so beautiful and intricate that only Ghiberti's gates can be named beside them. In the courtyard the water still flows from fountains, carved in Algerian onyx, where the faithful have performed their sacred ablutions all these centuries. But the place is dead, except for here and there some marabout, or holy man, with long white beard, who pauses in his prayers to see that infidel shoes do not profane his sacred places, and then "plunges in thought again."

The mud Arab village which encases this sleeping beauty's palace accentuates the feeling of enchantment and "apartness."

The West-Algerian Company are extending their line westwards from Tlemçen to Lalla-Marnia (a distance of about 25 miles). The portion from Tlemçen to Turenne is expected to be opened in a few months. From Lalla-Marnia to the Moroccan frontier is only 15 kilometres and from that point there will ultimately be a connection with the projected line to Tangier and Fez (see p. 400).

Excursions should also be made to the cascades of

El Ourit, about three miles from Tlemçen, leaving the Bou-

Médine gate, on the road to Sidi Bel Abbès, passing through gardens and olive grounds to a bridge, from which a good view of the falls is obtained. These are not remarkable for their volume, but for their surroundings of precipitous red rocks springing from green sloping banks, covered with wild cherry trees. The fall from the top of the cliffs to the ravine below is over 1,300 feet, but the cascades are broken into series of falls of some 100 feet each.

CASCADE OF EL OURIT, TLEMÇEN.

The circus of El-Ourit is one of the most lovely spots that it is possible to conceive. Imagine a wall of high rocks arranged in the form of a circus, thickly covered with plants and shrubs of all kinds. Down these rocks plunge cascades of water, and the vegetation is so dense that the water, so to speak, filters through it until it reaches the base.

M

On Easter Monday, when the cherry trees are in bloom, the inhabitants of Tlemçen hold a great fête at El-Ourit.

Travellers wishing to visit some stalactite caves can do so at

Beni Aad. This involves a drive of about 10 kilom. along the Sidi-Bel-Abbès road to Aïn Fezza, thence 8 kilom. on mules to be obtained from the Arabs to reach the caves, 5 kilom. from the road.

The main grotto, which has not yet been thoroughly explored, is two-thirds of a mile in length, and no doubt other caves exist in the neighbourhood. Stalactites in every size and form surround the visitor as he passes under arches, or between groups of tinted columns of exquisite design and finish. It is a splendid but costly spectacle to see the grottoes lighted up by the Arabs with torches. A good plan is to take some magnesium wire for the purpose.

A longer excursion can be made by diligence or carriage to **Sebdou** (38 kilom., diligence daily in 5 hours from Tlemçen *viâ* Terny) and the mountains of **Beni Snous,** 40 kilometres.

Twelve eminences to the north of the plain of Sebdou have been surnamed " the Twelve Apostles."

Tlemçen to Nemours. Diligence at 5 a.m. daily, 96 kilometres in 12 hours, 10f.

Passing the ruins of Mansoura (p. 172) through an uncultivated district, and several unimportant villages to Hennaya, a prosperous agricultural commune, the **Oued Zitoun,** and **Sidi Brahim,** the road crosses the river **Tafna,** to **Hammam-bou-Khara,** an efficacious sulphur spring, where gardens and olive trees suddenly appear, to **Lalla=Marnia,** a prosperous village, the headquarters of a military post, nine miles from the frontier of Morocco. Railway in course of construction from Tlemçen (*se* p. 176). The village, protected by a redoubt constructed in 1844, has an important market on Sunday, where cattle, horses, wool, wine, and cereals are disposed of. The presence of Moroccans at these markets adds considerably to their interest for travellers. The entire commune of Lalla-Marnia covers an area of 335,000 acres, with a population of about 30,000.

Excursions can be made to **Gar Rouban** (34 *kilom.*) *and to* **Oudjda** (25 *kilom.*) *near the frontier of Morocco. At the first named are valuable silver-lead mines. These places being in Moroccan territory, permission should be obtained and enquiries should be made at the* bureau arabe *at Marnia before undertaking either excursion.*

The road now goes north, crosses the river **Mouia,** through a pleasant country up the range of hills of **Bab Tazza,** which commands a fine view over the plains of **Nedroma** and the mountains of Morocco. The descent passes through valleys to the thirteenth-century Berber town of

Nedroma, in an admirable situation surrounded by gardens, orchards, and olive trees; the town and suburbs occupy a space of 5,000 acres; population 5,000, of the commune 30,000. There are manufactories of carpets, haïcks, burnous, and Berber pottery. A largely attended market is held on Thursday.

The date of the origin of this town is uncertain. Remains of old walls flanked by four towers still exist. There are ten mosques, the oldest of which dates from 1082 A.D. according to an inscription now in the Algiers museum.

To the south east and within a short distance of the village are some interesting grottoes.

Leaving Nedroma by the plain of **Mézaourou** the road leads through the fertile valley of **Saf Saf,** passing before rocks with caverns which were formerly inhabited, and through gardens to

Nemours, *see* p. 186.

·ORAN TO TLEMÇEN BY AIN=TEMOUCHENT.

To Aïn Temouchent by rail, 76 kilom. Aïn-Temouchent to Tlemçen by diligence, 66 kilom.

Stations.	Distance in kilometres from Oran.
Oran	—
La Sénia...	6
Misserghin	20
Brédéa	31
Bou-Tlelis	36
Lourmel	47
Er-Rahel	56
Rio Salado	64
Chabet-el Leham	70
Ain-Temouchent	76

There are three trains a day from Oran to Aïn-Temouchent at 6.35 a.m., 12.25 p.m. and 5.25 p.m. For the first few kilometres the train passes over the Oran-Algiers line to La Sénia (junction), then branches off on the West-Algerian line, passing an immense salt lake to

Misserghin, a charming village of more than 4,000 inhabitants, the nucleus of which was conceded, in 1851, to the Abbé Abram, who established an orphanage and an asylum for old men. The inmates cultivated the land and raised their own fruit and vegetables, wine and liqueur, for all of which they found a ready sale ; so that families were attracted to the district, which has now become a source of supply to Oran.

At a distance of 4 kilom. from Misserghin is the " Ravine of the Virgin," a lovely spot, the source of the streams to which Misserghin owes its verdure.

At the next station,

Brédéa is one of the sources from which Oran derives its water supply.

Other stations are passed, and the train reaches

Er-Rahel, where passengers alight for the **Thermal Establishment** of **Hammam-bou-Hadjar,** known to the

Romans, the waters of which rush out of the ground in a column a yard high, at a temperature of about 165° Fahr. They are greatly used by the Arabs, and an hotel has been opened for the accommodation of Europeans. (Hôtel des Bains.)

Diligence three times a day in each direction between Er-Rahel and Hammam-bou-Hadjar. Fare 75c.

Chabet-el-Leham (the Defile of the Flesh) is said to have been the scene of a terrible disaster in 1535, when a body of Spaniards, going to the relief of Tlemçen, were slaughtered, and thirteen only escaped to tell the tale.

Aïn-Temouchent, the terminus of the line, is a busy, prosperous town of about 7,000 inhabitants, built on the ruins of Roman **Timici,** where numerous bas-reliefs, statues, portions of columns, coins, etc., have been found. The town is planted with avenues of trees, the gardens and orchards are well cultivated, being watered by the river **Senan.** The vineyards are of the very finest description. Aïn-Temouchent was one of the places attacked by Abd-el-Kader in 1845. **Hotel:** Hôtel de Londres (Cook's Coupons, Series A, B and C accepted).

From Aïn-Temouchent the journey to Tlemçen must be continued by diligence (66 kilom.) passing Aïn-Kial (14 kilom.), Pont de l'Isser (33 kilom.) and Saf Saf (61 kilom.) From Aïn-Temouchent at 8 p.m. daily and on Sundays, Tuesdays and Thursdays at 10 a.m., time occupied 8 hours, coupé 6f., other places 4f. The only noteworthy objects *en route* are the quarries of **Algerian Onyx**, near **Aïn-Tekbalet,** at a farm named **Joignot,** from which is obtained a splendid view of the valleys of the **Isser** and **Ouled Abdeli,** as well as of the plains and distant mountains, on a spur of which are seen **Bou Médine** and Tlemçen.

The road descends rapidly by the river Isser to **Pont de l'Isser,** a commune of 3,800 inhabitants, when soon are seen white mosques, minarets, and towers, by which the traveller knows he is arriving at Tlemçen, *see* p. 166.

ORAN TO MOSTAGANEM, MOSTAGANEM TO TIARET BY RAILWAY (MASCARA).

Coasting steamers from Oran to Algiers, and *vice versâ*, call at Mostaganèm twice a week, and a steamer of the Navigation Mixte takes passengers from Oran for Marseilles once a week.

Oran to Arzeu (*see* p. 188).

Mostaganem, about 18,000 inhabitants, is on the sea-coast road, eight or ten hours' drive by carriage or diligence *viâ* Arzeu, La Macta and La Stidia, from Oran, 5f.; or it can be reached by rail by the direct Oran-Algiers line, changing carriages at **Relizane** junction (*see* p. 148) or rail to La Macta, thence diligence (*see* p. 191).

It was an Arab town, and one of the most curious, they say, before the conquest; but it has experienced the ordinary fate of Arab towns under French rule, and its few Moorish streets can now be counted on the fingers. The European quarter is broad, clean, well ventilated, monotonous, and healthy, surrounded by large gardens and orchards.

It is thought to have been a seaport, **Portus Magnus**, in the time of the Romans, and in the reign of the Emperor Gallienus, it is recorded, the whole of this part of Africa was visited by a tremendous earthquake. One of these convulsions may account for the astonishingly bizarre form borne by the rocks behind Mostaganem. They are of all shapes and sizes, and anything more terribly abrupt it is difficult to picture. The hot and salt streams found in the vicinity, among which the chief is **Aïn Sefra** (Yellow River) dividing the European portion of the town from the native portion, are also attributed to earthquakes. The Arab historians of the seventeenth century describe Mostaganem as a charming city, full of mosques, bazaars, baths, etc. To what extent this might have been true we cannot ascertain, though another historian, our satirical friend, **Ahmed Ben Youssouf,** of Miliana, had said of the Mostaganese "that they have added heels to their slippers, in order to be able to run faster after their prey, and away from their pursuers." In slippers without heels, of course, one can only shuffle.

The town was seized by the French in 1835, to prevent its falling into the hands of Abd-el-Kader, but it was allowed to be governed by a native Bey until 1840. Mostaganem is now an important trading centre, and the chief district of an admirable agricultural country. The harbour is not well sheltered from the north and west winds.

Near Mostaganem are the Caves of the

Ouled Riah, in which a horrible massacre of natives took place, under the order of Colonel Pelissier, in April, 1845, when, to suppress an insurrection of the Dahra, nearly 1,000 Arabs were burnt to death in one day—a deplorable tragedy which caused a tremendous sensation in Europe at the time. A full account appears in *L'Afrique Française*, by P. Christian, Paris, 1846.

The race-course is about 2 kilom. from Mostanagem, close to Le Haras, the remount dépôt established by General Lamoricière (may be visited).

A pleasant drive of eight miles from Mostaganem can be made to the French village of **Aïn-Bour-Dinar,** above the valley of the *Cheliff*, where the river is seen 500 feet below flowing to the sea.

There are two hotels at Mostaganem, the Grand Hotel and the Hôtel de France.

From Mostaganem to Tiaret is a journey of 197 kilom. by rail, changing carriages at **Relizane Junction,** on the main Oran-Algiers line. One through train a day at 8.55 a.m., due at Tiaret 6.15 p.m.

Travellers who do not propose going to Mostaganem, but wish to visit the extraordinary monuments called the **Djedars,** near Tiaret, can do so either from Oran or Algiers by rail as far as **Rélizane Junction,** thence train 121 kilom. to Tiaret, where diligence, carriages, or horses are to be obtained for visiting the pyramidal monuments and tombs, some 30 kilom. from the town, on the road to Frendah. There is also a diligence service between Rélizane and Tiaret (96 kilom.) daily in about fifteen hours (15f.).

Between Relizane and Tiaret will be seen tombs and koubbas of local saints, Roman ruins, etc., and at

Méchéra Sfa (Prévost-Paradol), about four miles from the station, are a number of megalithic monuments, or stone slabs, called *Souama*, which were taken from the rocks already shaped for use, and which served in their natural state for walls or roofs of houses or for tombs. (These can be visited in a day from Tiaret.)

Tiaret (Hotels: de la Gare, d'Orient) is built on the site of the Roman city of **Tingurtia.** It stands on an elevation of

1,083 metres above sea level. or about 3,500 feet, on the slopes of the **Djebel Guezoul,** between two ravines; the panoramic view from the Military Club is superb. The town (population about 6,000) is surrounded by a bastioned wall with three gates, and the country abounds in ruins of small Roman dwellings. A **stud farm** and a **Smala of Spahis** stand on the east of the town, the district being famous for its breed of Arab horses. A very important fair is held every Monday.

No one would travel to Tiaret who did not intend to visit The **Djedars** (distance about 30 kilom.) and this will occupy the whole of a very long day by carriage, without, however, involving more than two miles walking. There are two groups of monuments, and the first of these nearest Tiaret consists of three Djedars built on, three peaks of the hill *Djebel el Adjdar.* These can be entered, and the sepulchral chambers explored. Very little is known as to the origin and history of the tombs. which are mentioned by only one historian of the tenth century. In the opinion of M. R. de la Blanchère, the sepulchres date from the fifth to the seventh century, and are the tombs of a native dynasty, Catholic in religion, which was swept away with the Arab invasion.

Some of the Djedars are in a fair state of preservation, and the general form of all of them is the same. They are built of cut stone on a square base 10 or 12 feet high, and 100 or 110 feet square, surmounted by a pyramid, of which the first step is very much deeper than the others. On the east side a flight of steps led up to the platform, in the centre of which a door gave access to the pyramid. A wide straight passage led to the sepulchral chambers, which were roofed with stone and shut off from each other by stone doors.

Travellers wishing to explore the second group of Djedars at **Frendah** (50 kilometres from Tiaret), can, if so disposed, continue by road to Mascara, 111 kilometres, a long and tiresome journey, with no public accommodation *en route.*

Mascara can be more conveniently reached by returning from Tiaret to Rélizane Junction, there taking the main line to Perrégaux Junction, and joining the Arzeu-Ain-Sefra line as far as Tizi, thence branch line about eight miles to Mascara (P. 191).

From Oran the communication is more direct. viz., Oran, change at Perrégaux, Tizi, Mascara.

Mascara is situated at an elevation of 1,834 feet on a mountain of the **Beni Chougran,** called in Arabic **Choua-reb el Rih** (the Lips of the Wind). Population about 20,000.

The ground and the climate of Mascara are equally favoured by nature; it has before it, no doubt, a great industrial and commercial future. The cultivation of the vine has made great progress in the vicinity, and the vineyards now cover an area of between 3,000 and 4,000 hectares. The wine of Mascara is noted, and fetches as high a price as the Miliana produce, being bought freely by agents of Bordeaux firms. There is a large trade done in oil and cereals.

The sheikh **Sidi Ahmed Ben Yussuf,** of Miliana, has not spared the inhabitants of Mascara in his sarcastic appreciation of the different Algerian localities. He thus defines the Mascarian gentlemen:

" I was leading several thieves prisoners under the walls of Mascara, and they took shelter in the houses of that town, where they found themselves at home." And further: " If thou meetest some one, fat, proud, and dirty, be sure it is an inmate of Mascara." . . . . " A counterfeit coin is less false than a man from Mascara."

This judgment is rather harsh on the poor Mascarians, and no doubt must have been inspired by a strong personal dislike of the saint against the inhabitants of that unhappy city.

Mascara was the residence of Abd-el-Kader in 1837, and there in the Mosque of Aïn-Beida, now a grain store, he preached the holy war. The town was taken by Marshal Bugeaud, May 30, 1841, and later Abd-el-Kader retired to Morocco.

The town is divided into two distinct quarters by the **Oued Toudman** (a ravine converted into a public garden), which is crossed on four bridges. One part of the town, east of the Oued Toudman, is called **Mascara;** the other part is called **Argoub=Ismail.** The suburb of **Bab=Ali** is outside the walls. The neighbourhood is very imposing and picturesque. The ground, most fertile everywhere, is shaded by very noble-looking old trees; the scenery is backed on all sides by hills and mountains of great elevation, rocks and peaks covered with gardens and windmills. Water flows liberally; cascades, rivers, and streams are met in many parts of the country. An important market is held three times a week.

Hotels. Grand Hotel, Hotel du Luxembourg, de Bretagne.

Saint Hippolyte, on the road to the **marabout of Sidi Daho,** is situated in one of the loveliest spots near Mascara, the scenery along the banks of the **Oued=Sidi-Daho,** which falls in cascades on the sides of the mountains of **Beni Chougran**, being refreshingly beautiful. The **pépinière** (or nursery) at the entrance of the **Egris Plain**, extends over a distance of 15 kilometres, and fully deserves inspection.

ORAN TO BENI-SAF AND NEMOURS.

By Sea.

The steamer service between Oran and Nemours is very irregular, but about weekly (C$^{ie.}$ de Navigation Mixte). The voyage along the coast occupies about seven or eight hours, and in fine weather is very interesting.

The steamer passes before Mers-el-Kebir (p. 152), rounds Cape Falcon, passes Capes Lindles, Sigale and Figalo, and, weather permitting, calls fortnightly at

Beni=Saf at the mouth of the river *Tafna* (*see* below).

Beyond Beni-Saf the coast is more monotonous as far as Cape Noé, and then becomes rocky until arriving at

Nemours (*see* below).

Beni=Saf, situated opposite to and sheltered by the *Island of Rachgown*, is a town of about 7,000 inhabitants, which has sprung up entirely owing to the rich iron deposits in the neighbourhood.

The valuable iron mines of **Mokta=el=Hadid**, close to the sea (*see* also p. 283), belong to a company which has constructed at its own expense a commodious harbour (Mersa-Sidi-Ahmed) with a depth of 23 feet, and moles at which the ore is loaded. Private vessels have to pay dues to the company, and eventually the French Government has the option of claiming the harbour.

About 400,000 tons of ore are annually extracted from the mines, and the company have applied for a concession for a railway between Beni-Saf and Tlemçen (*see* p. 166).

Nemours, the Ad Fratres of the Romans, the Ghazouat of the Arabs, and a nest of robbers and pirates under the Turkish government, is a bright little town of about 3,000 in habitants, founded in 1844 chiefly as a military post on the frontier of Morocco, from which it is only 22 miles distant.

The streets are large, shaded with trees, and well kept. The climate is temperate, and on the shore is a splendid sandy beach.

Hotel. Hôtel de France.

There is no harbour, and the bay being exposed to the N.W. wind, communication with the shore is often difficult. Steamers for Morocco, Oran, and Spain call, weather permitting. Cereals and alfa are largely exported, and in the immediate neighbourhood are deposits of iron, calamine, and lead waiting to be explored and worked. About seven and a-half miles to the S.W. is the koubba of Sidi-Brahim, where, in 1843, Col. Montagnac and 416 soldiers were entrapped by Abd-el-Kader into an ambuscade, and all but a dozen men annihilated. A monument to their memory has been erected by the government in the **Vallée des Jardins**, about a mile from Nemours (*see* also p. 160).

ORAN TO BENI=SAF AND NEMOURS.

By Rail and Road.

The journey to Beni-Saf is made by rail as far as Aïn-Temouchent (*see* p. 181), thence by diligence (daily) at 9 a.m., 31 kilom. in 4 hours, to Beni-Saf, passing the villages of

Les Trois Marabouts, peopled by Protestants sent from Lyons in 1880, and

Guiard, founded in the same way in 1891

Beni=Saf (*see* p. 186).

The road from Beni-Saf (distance about 70 kilom.) to Nemours lies along the coast, but there is no public conveyance. Arrangements must be made for horses or mules (the muleteer will act as guide), and the journey can, if necessary, be accomplished in one day, but it is better to devote two days to it, passing the night at Rhar-el-Maden. From Beni-Saf it is sometimes possible to reach Nemours by sea in about four hours, but, as already mentioned, this means of communication is only available weather permitting.

ORAN TO ARZEU, TO MASCARA, SAIDA, AIN SEFRA, AND COLOMB-BÉCHAR.

By Rail.

Stations.	Distance in kilometres from Oran.
ORAN	—
Saint-Rémy	8
Sidi-Chami	11
Assi-bou-Nif	14
Assi-Ameur	18
Fleurus	20
Saint-Cloud	28
Renau-Kléber	34
Sainte-Léonie	36
Damesme	42
ARZEU	47

Stations.	Distance in kilometres from Arzeu	Stations.	Distance in kilometres from Arzeu.
ARZEU	—	Les Eaux Chaudes ..	159
Saint-Leu ...	8	Nazereg ...	167
Port-aux-Poules ...	18	Saïda ...	172
La Macta ...	22	Aïn-el-Hadjar ...	183
Débrousseville ...	39	Bou-Rached (Halt)	191
Ferme Blanche ...	43	Tafaroua (Halt) ...	207
Perrégaux	52	Kralfallah ...	216
Barrage (Halt) ...	62	Muley-Abdelkader	225
Oued-Fergoug ..	63	El-Beida	231
Dublineau	72	Modzba	239
La Guetna (Halt) ...	81	Tin-Brahim ...	249
Bou-Hanifia	89	Kreider ...	272
Tizi (for Mascara) ...	101	Bou-Ktoub ...	286
Froha	108	El-Biod	324
Thiersville ...	114	Méchéria	353
Taria	128	Naâma	386
Charrier	141	Mékalis	421
Franchetti	146	AÏN-SEFRA ..	455

Stations.	Distance in kilometres from Aïn-Sefra.
Aïn-Sefra	—
Tiout	11
Aïn-el-Hadjadj	24
Rouïba	35
Dra-es-Saâ	46
Moghrar	54
Oglats	64
Dayet-el-Kerch	76
Djenien-bou-Resq	85
Hadjerat M'Guil	100
Duveyrier	118
Béni-Ounif de Figuig ..	145
Mérirès	164
Bou-Aïech	180
Ben-Zireg	206
Hassi-el-Haouari	233
Colomb-Béchar	257

From Oran to Colomb-Béchar is a long journey of 749 kilometres, or 465 miles, viz.: Oran to Damesme, 42 kilometres; Damesme to Tizi (junction for Mascara, *see* p. 184) and Aïn Sefra, 450 kilometres; Aïn-Sefra to Colomb-Béchar 257 kilometres.

From Oran to Arzeu the traveller, if so disposed, can go by sea, either by the Compagnie de Navigation Mixte (Touache), or by a coasting steamer, once a week.

There are three trains a day from Oran to Arzeu, two trains a day from Arzeu to Saïda, but only one through train from Arzeu to Aïn-Sefra, and one train from Aïn-Sefra to Colomb-Béchar on Tuesday, Thursday and Saturday.

The journey from Oran to Colomb-Béchar (Franco-Algerian railway) occupies three days, sleeping at Saïda and Aïn-Sefra.

Leave Oran 7.15 a.m., arrive Saïda 5.10 p.m.—sleep; leave Saïda next morning 7.20, arrive Aïn-Sefra 6.24 p.m.—sleep;

Leave Aïn-Sefra 6.47 a.m., arrive Colomb-Béchar 4.50 p.m. on Tuesday, Thursday and Saturday;

Leave Saïda 1.5 p.m., due Colomb-Béchar 6.55 p.m.

Another arrangement allows the traveller to leave Oran on Monday, Wednesday, and Friday at 5.10 p.m., and arrive at Aïn Sefra at 9.19 next morning, reaching Colomb-Béchar at 6.55 p.m., thus occupying about 26 hours.

If the tourist has not visited Mascara, he can do so coming from Oran or from Arzeu (or from Algiers), by stopping at Perrégaux (junction, *see* p. 184), sleep at Hotel des Colonies, visit Mascara early next morning, changing trains at Tizi, arriving back at Perrégaux

4.4 p.m., joining the through train leaving Oran at 5.10 p.m. on Mondays.

Return tickets available for eight days are issued from Oran for Aïn-Sefra, or for stations beyond seven days longer. *Consult time table, as trains are liable to alteration.*

The short line from Oran to Arzeu passes at the foot of the **Djebel Orous,** and between the railway and the sea are several small villages. The stopping place **St. Rémy** has no station; further on are the prosperous villages of St. Cloud and Ste. Léonie; at Kléber are the celebrated marble quarries of Djebel-Orous or Arousse, and passing **Damesme** (where the narrow-gauge État line branches off for Perrégaux, Saïda, Aïn-Sefra and Colomb-Béchar) the line ends at

Arzeu, a considerable town of 5,700 inhabitants, founded in 1845 on the site of the Roman **Arsenaria** (*see* also p. 155).

British Vice=Consul, M. A. Gautray.

Hotel, Hotel des Bains.

The town is regularly built, and surrounded by walls with two gates. A citadel was erected in 1863. There is a splendid natural harbour of 350 acres protected by a break-water, and it is soon about to be furnished with quays and appliances in keeping with the considerable business derived from the districts of Saïda, Mascara, Rélizane, and the alfa monopoly of the Société Algérienne.

In 1831 Arzeu was taken by Abd-el-Kader, retaken by the French in 1833, and became French by treaty in 1837.

Many important ruins are found in the immediate neigh-bourhood, and about ten miles south is the salt-lake of **El= Malah,** covering 10,000 acres.

The railway that the traveller takes on leaving Arzeu for Aïn-Sefra and Duveyrier was constructed by the Compagnie Franco-Algérienne under a concession granted by the govern-ment in 1873, in consideration of valuable privileges and a subsidy. It was first made as far as Aïn-Sefra, but has lately been extended to **Figuig** and Colomb-Béchar in Morocco, and it is expected that some day the railway will be continued to Timbuctoo, a distance of 2,383 kilometres, or 1,490 miles.

The first station after leaving Damesme (Arzeu) is

St. Leu, near which is the Berber village of **Old Arzeu,** where very interesting Roman ruins have been collected, some of which are in the Museum at Oran.

At **La Macta,** where the river *Macta* is crossed, is one of the few districts in which the sportsman will meet with a fair amount of game, such as wild duck, partridges, and bustard.

Diligence from La Macta to Mostaganem (28 kilometres) in two and a-half hours. Railway in contemplation.

Perrégaux is the next station of any importance, *see* p. 190; also p. 150.

About 10 kilometres from Perrégaux is

Le Barrage, an account of which is given on p. 151.

The line now enters a fertile plain, and touches at small stations of no special interest until

Bou Hanifia is reached. Close by are the **Hot Springs and Baths** of the same name, frequented chiefly by Arabs. The water issues at a temperature of 136° Fahr., and there are baths for Europeans, but the accommodation for visitors is very incomplete and uninviting.

The railway continues to

Col Tizi (the junction for a short line of 12 kilometres to **Mascara,** *see* p. 184).

Resuming the journey from Tizi, the valleys of the **Oued Saïda** and the **Oued Traria** are entered, then the prosperous villages of **Franchetti** and **Nazereg,** rich in all kinds of fruit trees, are reached, the latter having near the station a fine stalactite cavern 300 metres long, at the end of which runs a river. A few kilometres beyond the train stops at the busy station of

Saïda, a fortified town of about 6,500 inhabitants, owing its rise and prosperity to the railway. It is situated on two rivers, about two kilometres from the borders of the **Hauts Plateaux,** where Abd-el-Kader held the old Arab Saida. A column, inaugurated in 1901, has been erected here by the Foreign Legion in memory of the encounter with Abd-el-Kader.

Some charming excursions can be made in the neighbourhood of Saïda, and to those spending a day or two in the town a drive can be recommended to **Aïn=Tifrid,** 28 kilometres, where in a lovely wooded gorge expanding gradually to a delightful valley are the imposing waterfalls of **Tifrid,** around which the sportsman would not be disappointed with either the rod or the gun.

Another excursion can be made to the ravine of **Sidi Salim,** an old fortified camp, interesting to those fond of exploring Roman remains.

Leaving Saida, the Engineers of the railway encountered their most difficult task. The line makes a very steep sudden ascent, and passes around a series of curves until it reaches the Hauts Plateaux and the station of

Aïn=el=Hadjar, the alfa dépôt of the Franco-Algerian Company, where thousands of tons are pressed into bales for exportation annually. The town, situated 1,024 metres above the sea, is all built on the same model (small houses and gardens), and the entire property has an air of comfort and prosperity. Twelve kilometres beyond, the line, at **Tafaroua,** rises to a height of 1,150 metres or 3,770 feet, thence descending to

Kralfallah, where occurred in 1881 the terrible massacre of Spaniards by the rebels, led by the marabout Bou-Amama.

At this point there is a road crossing the **Chott=el-Chergui** on to the military station and small growing town of **Géryville.**

At **Modzbah,** the Franco-Algerian Company has an immense territory covered with alfa, then passing the village of **Sidi Khalifa,** whose people claim to be descended from the Prophet, the train continues to

Kreider, a veritable oasis of the desert, with thousands of aromatic trees, planted by the soldiers. The well-kept little village is on the borders of the Chott-el-Chergui, an immense basin, 140 kilometres in length, covered with sand, saline deposits, etc.

Crossing a portion of this depression for a distance of about 12 kilometres, the line passes through a barren country to

El=Biod, a fortified post well supplied with water, commanding the passage of the **Chott-er=Rarbi,** and rising gradually the railway again attains the height of 1,150 metres at

Méchéria, an abandoned village, now an important military post, with a number of native dwellings, situated at the foot of the **Djebel Antar.**

Leaving Méchéria the country becomes more barren and

rocky, with scarcely coarse grass enough to feed the large flocks of sheep scattered over the yellow desert. In this way, with nothing but the stations of **Naâma** and **Mékalis** (the highest point of the line 1,314 metres) and the mountains of Morocco in the distance, the line continues for about 70 kilometres to

Aïn Sefra, the largest military station in this part of Algeria, with barrack accommodation for 5,000 soldiers. But Aïn Sefra is more than this, it is the first *ksar*, or native village, one can visit in the date country of the Sahara. The inhabitants belong to the tribe of the Amour, each village of which has its own administration. The houses are of bricks dried in the sun, with one living room, and one small sleeping room for everybody and everything, such as donkeys, goats, fowls, children. The men do nothing but smoke or eat, the women make haïcks and burnous for sale to the tribes.

The village is built on the side of a hill, beneath which flows the **Oued Sefra** (Saffron River). The houses have smart gardens planted with fig and pomegranate trees, and beyond are the date trees.

In October, 1904, the European portion of the village was inundated and entirely ruined by a sudden rise of the Oued Sefra, separating it from the redoubt.

Hotels.—Hotel Plasse, Hotel Pascal. Excursions can be made to the oases of **Tiout** and **Moghrar**, but more conveniently by rail, *see* below.

Continuing the journey to Duveyrier, etc. (*see* time table), the first station is

Tiout, a small *ksar* of narrow streets with mud-dried dwellings, in the midst of the desert, a delightful oasis with large vines and palms, peach and almond trees, watered by a small lake. In the neighbourhood are curious coloured rocks, on which various animals, hunters, etc., are carved.

From here the line descends between the **Djebel Djara**, and the **Djebel-Mekter**, and after three stations reaches

Moghrar, an oasis well watered by the **Oued Nammou**, producing an ample vegetation and 30,000 date trees.

It was from this village that the insurrection of Bou Amama in 1881 set out (*see* p. 192).

Leaving Moghrar, the line, passing at some distance from the **Djebel-Mekter** and the **Djebel-Zaraf**, continues for some 30 kilometres through a flat desert to **Djénien-bou-**

N

Rezg, a charming contrast of varied scenery; and 33 kilometres further arrives at

Duveyrier.

Duveyrier itself has nothing of interest for the tourist; it is an important military position and dépôt, being within 27 kilometres, of Béni-Ounif de **Figuig** (the next station) adjoining the oases and territory of Figuig, containing 15,000 persons of the Amour tribe, and 250,000 date trees, now nominally subject to Morocco.

The *ksours* of Figuig, surrounded by verdure, are well kept, each with its mosque. The inhabitants are tall, clean, and hard working, active in exchanging their fire-arms, powder, jewellery, tissues, etc., for feathers, leather, and gold dust.

An excursion to some of these curious villages is a very interesting, if somewhat fatiguing, experience, but should not be undertaken without an escort, or without the sanction of the military authorities of Duveyrier. The line now (1908) extends 112 kilometres beyond Figuig to Colomb-Béchar (*see* p. 190).

In January, 1903, the Franco-Algerian Company proposed to the President of the Council in Paris to trace a plan for a railway from Duveyrier to Timbuctoo, or Gao, or Bourem, to be built within the space of three years, on certain conditions. To erect a telegraph along the route. To build seven " bordjs " or fortified villages. To establish a steamer service on the Niger, between Koulikovo and Say.

Since the above was written (April, 1903) the strategical importance of the Arzeu-Duveyrier railway has been abundantly proved.

[At the end of May, 1903, M. Jonnart, the newly-appointed Governor-General of Algeria, was making a tour through the provinces of Southern Oran, and arrived at Duveyrier. Accompanied by General O'Connor, a detachment of Spahis, and three companies of the Foreign Legion from Beni-Ounif, M. Jonnart started on an expedition towards Figuig. The Amel of Figuig, with thirty Moroccan horsemen, met the Governor-General to inform him that he could not be answerable for the maintenance of order among his people, but M. Jonnart decided to go on. When they had reached the plateau overlooking **Zenaga**, a body of 400 Moors armed with rifles rushed from their ambush and attacked the expedition. A fight lasting five hours ensued, and the French retired in good order, the odds being very much against them, to **Beni-Ounif**, where it was found that many of their men had been killed and wounded.

The French Government at once took vigorous measures to punish the revolt of the turbulent Moors; three columns were ordered to be formed at Oran to operate from three different sides. Three battalions of the Foreign Legion, three squadrons of cavalry, four new pattern

75-millimètre guns, two mountain guns, four 95-millimètre guns, and a force of 3,500 men arrived at Beni-Ounif on Monday, June 8th. Proceeding to within 1,300 yards of the defences of Zenaga, General O'Connor opened fire with melinite shells and destroyed the outer walls; then the fire was directed on the *ksar* or village at a range of 2,400 yards. The effect was astounding. The mud-brick houses were blown to atoms, and the minaret was cut in two.

At 11 a.m. firing ceased, and the French troops retired to Beni-Ounif, the artillery to Djeman-Eddar.

On the following day, Tuesday, the Djemmäa or delegates from the councils of chiefs from the seven *ksours* or communities of Figuig arrived in the French camp to tender their submission. General O'Connor told them the punishment was a warning, and would be continued if necessary. France did not desire the destruction of Figuig, but its prosperity. The railway that was being built would promote that prosperity if security reigned, and he must have guarantees for the future. He would inform them of the conditions to be imposed. and would not admit any discussion of the terms decided upon.

Next day the Djemmäa were informed of the following terms :—

1. The surrender of hostages.

2. The surrender of arms.

3. The payment of a war contribution.

The delegates accepted these conditions, and tendered their submission.

It will be seen that the French punitive expedition was a prompt and perfect success—less than a fortnight elapsing between the revolt and the submission of the Moors—and this brief record of the events may be of interest at some future time.]

DISTRICTS EAST OF ALGIERS.

ALGIERS TO TIZI-OUZOU, ETC. (UPPER KABYLIA).

There is a Kabyle proverb which says: "Who has not seen Kabylia, has not seen Algeria," and this is perfectly true, for no part of Algeria can compete with this magnificent country. The traveller is particularly struck with the picturesque aspect of the vegetation, which is totally different from that seen round Algiers. Indeed, in many parts of Kabylia the tropical vegetation has quite disappeared, and were it not for the huge fig trees and the olive trees of colossal dimensions, the traveller would fancy himself in a northern latitude. The land is well cultivated, and bears good testimony to the exceeding industry of the Kabyle race. These Kabyles, who are a hard-working, sober, and modest people, possess sometimes considerable property, and are in many respects superior to the Arabs of the present day. They give complete freedom to their wives, who are, in this one instance, happier than their Arab sisters. The Kabyle women do not hide their faces; they are allowed to attend to their duties outside the house without veils; but, apart from this particular liberty, they are considered by their husbands as much beasts of burden as the Arab women. The Kabyles are, however, very jealous of their wives, and for this, it is said, they have good reason.

Most of the Kabyle women and children are clad in very ordinary garments, consisting of white cotton *haicks*, fastened on the shoulders with silver or metal brooches. They all wear a great quantity of jewellery, bangles, bracelets, ankle bracelets, necklets, brooches, and hoop-earrings.

The Kabyle Women's Ceremonial Dress is almost uniform for all the wearers. It consists of two striped *foutas*, of dark-blue cotton material, striped with red and yellow, fastened on the shoulders with two brooches, and strapped round the loins with a leather belt. A black silk or cotton foulard is used as a head-dress; this foulard is sometimes red and yellow, but more generally black, framed with red. The costume is completed by an extensive stock of jewellery of every description, silver being the metal preferred. The women are all tattooed, chiefly with a cross between the eyes and on the chin. They are barefooted.

The Men's Costume consists of a gown or *gandoura*, of white or striped material, a leather belt, and one or two burnouses. The turban is the same as the one worn by the Arabs, white muslin, with a few yards of camel's-hair twisted round.

The Kabyle Houses are all built on the same model, but, contrary to the Arab custom, they have an inclined roof made of red tiles, instead of a flat terrace on the top. They are constructed with mud, stones, and branches. Some summer-houses are entirely made of branches. They generally stand in pairs, connected by a central yard surrounded by a wall. The natives sleep on the bare ground, and sometimes together with their cattle. They are filthy and dirty in the extreme. The children are very pretty-looking; the youngest of them are allowed to go almost naked. They all wear jewellery.

In each village there is a building called **Djeema**, used chiefly for the discussion of the village interests, and a mosque with its whitewashed minaret. These are the only features of a Kabyle village. The French inhabitants of Kabylia, who suffered the most treacherous and abominable treatment at the hands of the Kabyles during the insurrection of 1871, do not entertain any very tender feelings for the natives; but to the credit of the French Government it must be said that it does not share in the resentful feelings of its settlers, and that the greatest pains are taken to bestow on the natives the fruits of civilisation, and conciliate thereby to French interests this hitherto unmanageable and fanatical race.

Schools have been erected throughout Kabylia for the purpose of teaching the young Kabyles the elements of French education. There are also

Ecoles d'Arts et Métiers, or technical schools, where the Kabyles are taught the different manual and mechanical trades. The natives are remarkably quick and intelligent,

Village in Kabylia.

many of the industrious scholars having succeeded in securing substantial positions; others, who have passed through the superior schools, have acquired valuable berths in the Public Services or the Army.

Unhappily, the blind fanaticism, combined with the hatred of the foreigner, is so deeply rooted in the hearts of the Kabyles that the teachers experience the greatest difficulty in obtaining favourable results, which are, consequently, more the exception than the rule, and often the spirit of the scholars induces them not to attend the schools at all.

Table of Distances from Algiers to Tizi=Ouzou.

(The Capital of Upper Kabylia.)

Stations.	Distance in kilometres from Algiers.	Stations.	Distance in kilometres from Algiers.
Algiers	—	Belle-Fontaine ..	49
Agha	2	**Ménerville**	
Hussein Dey	6	(junction) ...	54
Maison Carrée ...	11	Blad Guitoun (Félix	
Oued Smar (halt) ...	16	Faure)	60
Maison Blanche ...	19	Isserville-les-Issers ...	64
Rouïba-Aïn Taya ...	26	Bordj Menaiel ..	69
Réghaïa ...	32	Haussonvillers ...	82
Alma	39	Camp du Maréchal ...	90
Corso	42	Mirabeau	97
Alléliguia (halt) ...	46	**Tizi=Ouzou...** ...	107

There are three trains a day from Algiers to Tizi-Ouzou—the Constantine train at 6.30 a.m., reaching Ménerville junction at 8.11 a.m., changing carriages and leaving there at 8.24 a.m., due at Tizi-Ouzou 10.21 a.m. The two other trains leave Algiers at 8.48 a.m. and 5.35 p.m., the journey occupying about 6¼ and 4¼ hours respectively—these are through trains, with no change of carriage. There is a buffet at Ménerville junction.

The carriages of the **East Algerian** Railway are comfortable and well aired; the roofs are protected against the rays of the sun by a wooden screen. From **Algiers** to **Ménerville** the average speed of the direct trains is about 30 kilometres an hour; from **Ménerville** to **Tizi=Ouzou** the train proceeds more slowly, on account of the differences of level in these wild regions.

The first station of importance is

Ménerville, 54 kilometres from Algiers, where passengers change carriages for **Tizi=Ouzou.**

From **Ménerville** the train proceeds slowly for many miles past a continuous line of well-kept fields and comfortable-looking farm-houses.

Haussonvillers, about half-way, is a thriving village, at the junction of the roads to Dellys and Tizi-Ouzou. The railway then traverses the valley and principal river of Kabylia— the **Sebaou.** But despite the vast extent of the rich valley, this is not yet the real Kabylia, which only commences at

Camp du Maréchal (where the steam tramway between Dellys and Boghni, 68 kilometres, crosses twice daily). There, a glorious line of snowy peaks rising straight from the plain and extending to the whole circle of the horizon, seemingly an impenetrable barrier, announce Upper Kabylia. As the train speeds on, peak rises behind peak, then dark bands of forest that reach up to the snowline come into view. The snow-fields and glaciers glisten in the sunlight, and over the rolling tops of the foot hills the passes are seen cleft deep into the hearts of the mountains. On past the grassy hills, on which horses, cattle, and sheep are fed, the train soon enters the actual mountain ranges, and then the route presents a never-ending, ever-changing scene of wild beauty and solemn grandeur. At **Tizi=Ouzou** the engine and cars are just 843 feet above the sea level.

Tizi=Ouzou, 107 kilometres from Algiers, the capital of Upper Kabylia, the seat of a sub-Prefecture, a Tribunal of First Instance, and garrisoned by a regiment of Tirailleurs, is a thriving village at the foot of Mount Belloua, with a population of 1,500 Europeans and, including the entire arrondissement, 30,000 Kabyles. **Hotels:** Grand Hotel, Hôtel des Postes. (Cook's Coupons, Series R, accepted at both.) At the **Grand Hotel,** a very comfortable and spacious house kept by M. Felix Lagarde, there is excellent accommodation for a large number of tourists, and a choice of carriages and horses for long and short excursions in Kabylia; and no one is better able to supply information, and to advise travellers on the subject of excursions, than M. Lagarde, who has resided in the country for more than thirty years.

The Grand Hotel is also the office and starting point for

the diligences and postal carriages to Fort National, Michelet, Azazga, and Azeffoun (Port Gueydon) which leave Tizi-Ouzou at 5 a.m. and 11 a.m. daily.

The French and the Kabyle villages are quite separate. The latter, situated on a plateau overlooking the plain of the **Sebaou,** on the road to Djebel Belloua, should be visited in order to obtain an idea of Kabyle villages in general, as described on p. 197.

The French village, planted with trees, is quite modern, and well supplied with shops and cafés. The Mairie, the Catholic Cathedral, and a new Mosque are the principal buildings. The **Bordj** or fort, to the north, overlooking the village originally built by the Turks, has been much enlarged and strengthened by the French since their occupation.

A considerable export trade is carried on in oil, olives, dried figs, and early grapes.

The native market, held on Saturday morning near the railway station, is worth noticing; the Kabyles come there in overwhelming numbers, bringing their sheep, cows, mules, honey, oil, leather, corn, and all sorts of wares. The Kabyle pottery is sold at reasonable prices, and is suitable for ornamenting brackets, etc. The **gandouras** and **foutas** vary in price from 1f. 50c. to 2f. each, and make very good souvenirs of the country. The Kabyle necklaces and earrings of white metal are very curious; they are sold for a few francs, but the largest assortment of these is to be found at the villages of the **Beni Yenni,** near **Fort National,** where they are manufactured (p. 203).

The white haicks and burnouses are woven by the natives on roughly constructed looms, and were one to see the unpromising looking workshops in which these garments are manufactured, it would seem incredible that they should be so clean in the dealers' tents.

Before leaving Tizi-Ouzou the excursion to

Mount Belloua (700 metres) is one which ought not to be missed. It can be made on mules or on horses, and part of the road is accessible to carriages. The ascent takes about two hours, and the return journey one hour. At the summit of the mount is a natural resting place, by the side of which stands the dwelling of a **marabout** or saint, Sidi-Belloua; it is a broad, level area, surrounded by mountain monarchs, all of them in the deadly embrace of glaciers.

Before reaching the resting-place, the tourist climbs along the mountain-side, through a marvellous and well-cultivated country, dotted with native villages. The view from the summit, in the midst of a wonderful group of peaks of fantastic shapes, is one never to be forgotten. Algiers is distinctly seen on clear days, and the beautiful peaks of the **Djurdjura** mountains unfurl themselves to the eye in all their capricious outlines. On the left is the village of **Dra el Mizan**, and in front, facing north, stand lofty hills overlooking Bougie and Dellys.

To accomplish the principal excursions in Kabylia, two routes, with good carriage roads, are available. By one the traveller can visit Fort National, Michelet, Col de Tirourda, and Tazmalt (the railway station for those persons going to Bougie), or to Maillot (the station for those returning to Algiers or Constantine). By the other route, with or without going to Fort National, Michelet, etc., from Tizi-Ouzou the drive includes Azazga, the forest of Yacounen, to El K'seur, where train can be taken for Bougie.

From Tizi-Ouzou the diligence starts for

Fort National at 11 a.m., the journey thither taking about four hours. The return journey takes a little less than three hours. The road is an excellent one; it was made in the extraordinarily short space of twenty days by Marshal Randon's soldiers in 1847. Of course it has been considerably improved since then, and in many parts shortened. For instance, the **Sebaou** is crossed now on two iron bridges, which reduces the distance from Tizi-Ouzou to **Fort National** from 23 miles, what it was before, to 17 miles, the actual distance. The road runs towards the north, winding through the hills first of all along the valley of the Sebaou, then ascending steadily some 2,300 feet between the two towns. At times it is tolerably open; at others it is cut in the massive rock rising perpendicularly on either side; sometimes again it passes for a considerable distance at the edge of a deep ravine, at the bottom of which runs a stream. The first village on the road is **Taza**, at the foot of the hill, about half-way to **Fort National**; next comes **Adni**, and then **Tamazirt**, where there is a French school for teaching the natives, and, branching off the main road a little lower down is a road which leads to the recently-built **School of Arts and Trades** for the Kabyles. **Azouza**, another Kabyle village, is passed, and then **Fort National** is reached.

Fort National is built on the territory of the warlike tribe of the **Beni Paten**. Its native name is **Souk-el-Arba**, which signifies Wednesday's Market. Situated 3,153 feet above the level of the sea, it is a unique village of about twelve acres, enclosed in a wall twelve feet high, flanked by seventeen bastions, to which there are two entrances, one by the Algiers, and the other by the Djurdjura gate. The road leads along a sort of terrace where the only good hotel is situated, the **Hôtel des Touristes**. Several cafés and shops are also on that side, overlooking the mountains opposite ; the edge of this terrace towers over a depth of about 2,000 feet.

The fortified town, or fort as it is called, was built by the French in 1857 as a protection against the neighbouring turbulent Kabyle tribes, and after the insurrection of 1871 the citadel commanding the fort was added. The barracks, arsenal, and other buildings, occupied by a battalion of Zouaves from 600 to 800 strong, are well worth visiting, and the view from the highest point over the Sebaou valley across to the mighty Djurdjura mountains is one of the most extensive in all Algeria.

Fort National is a good centre for several excursions. One of the most interesting, by mule or on foot, is to the Kabyle villages of

Benni Yenni (12 kilometres). These villages, four in number, are perched on steep places in the mountain, surrounded by precipices. The tribes, numbering 6,000, are very industrious, celebrated for the manufacture of pottery, moulded by hand by women ; also for the manufacture of pretty silver jewellery, either plain or enamelled, articles of furniture inlaid with tin, and arms of various kinds.

A still shorter excursion of the same description is that to the picturesque village of

Taourirt Amokrane, about 3 kilometres from Fort National. It is advisable to walk down the steep path to the right a short distance from outside the fort ; then take a mule (or walk) along the spur of the mountain to the end of the village overlooking the valley, visiting one or two of the Kabyle houses to see in what conditions of dirt and discomfort these sober and industrious tribes are contented to live.

Another easy excursion is that to

The **Obelisk of Icherriden,** but if the traveller is going on to Michelet he can visit the monument *en route* by turning off the main road a short distance when 7 kilometres from Fort National.

At Icherriden is the granite Obelisk, in the form of a pyramid, erected in 1895 to the memory of the French soldiers who fell in the expedition against Kabylia in June, 1857, and during the insurrection of 1871, when the French troops suffered heavily in dislodging the Kabyles from their entrenchments.

The view from the hill on which the monument is raised is strikingly bold, overlooking as it does the hills and valleys of the Sebaou, and embracing almost the whole range of the Djurdjura mountains.

If the tourist happens to visit Kabylia before the snow has fallen on the lower mountains, the grandest excursion is from

Fort National to **Michelet,** the **Col de Tirourda, Tazmalt** or **Maillot.** The route is as follows :—

From Fort National a charming drive to Michelet of twenty kilometres by either carriage or diligence requires only two hours, but it is desirable to sleep at Michelet (Hotel des Touristes. Cook's Coupons, Series R, accepted), and start very early in the morning for a long day's ride. Lunch must be taken from the hotel. Close to Michelet an important market of the Beni-Menguellet tribe is held every Friday.

After a ride of three hours the Col de Tirourda is reached, a magnificent pass 8 kilometres in length, through tunnels cut in the rock, and along almost perpendicular precipices. The ascent of the "monarch of Algerian mountains" can be made on foot in about an hour, and from an altitude of nearly 6,000 feet the panoramic view is magnificent.

Resuming the journey, the traveller arrives at Tazmalt (whence train may be taken to Bougie) or Maillot, as explained above.

The route from Fort National to **Azazga** and **El-K'seur** is of no great interest or beauty until Azazga is reached, and where the night is passed (Hotel Gebhard) or Hotel Vayssières. Both accept Cook's Coupons, Series R).

Making a very early start to accomplish the drive of

72 kilometres in time for the evening train at El-K'seur for Bougie, the road passes through miles of oak and cork oak forests. Lunch is taken at the

Chalet de Taourirt-Ighil, a small hostelry in the middle of the forest, with a few clean bedrooms suitable for sportsmen who may wish to spend some days in a district where both large and small game abound, including hyænas, panthers, wild boars, hares, and partridges.

After lunch the excursion is continued through the Forest of Yacounen, and passing numerous points of view of wild beauty, the drive ends at El-K'seur. Three-quarters of an hour by train to Bougie (p. 209).

For further information concerning this beautiful country an extract from Count Stackelberg's MS., a most accurate and concise description of the Kabyles, will be appreciated.

"The Berbers, or Kabyles, are the result of a fusion between the Aborigines, who were immigrants of Canaanitish origin, and the people who succeeded them in the domination of Algeria, and principally of the Vandals, who were all powerful in this country from 438 to 534. On the occasion of the great Arab invasion, the Kabyles retired into their mountain fastnesses; and although nominally embracing Islamism, contrived to maintain their independence, which was one of the causes of the hatred which has always existed between them and the Arabs. On no single occasion have they ever submitted to the Turks, who were, on the contrary, compelled to pay a kind of quit-money for passing through their territory when they went to raise taxes from the Arab tribes. It appears, however, that they must have more or less submitted to the Roman yoke, as even in their most distant and inaccessible valleys we find ruins which attest the presence of that great nation.

"The Kabyle language differs entirely from the Arabic; it is more guttural and wild. They are laborious, good agriculturists, and clever in manufactures, especially of linen and woollen materials. They live a sedentary life, have flourishing villages, and roofed and whitewashed houses. When they have no work at home, they go down to the towns to earn money, for their thirst for gold is equal to that of the Arabs. But their hatred of strangers soon drives them back to their mountain homes. No aristocracy is recognised by the Kabyles. Their form of Government is a Republican one, and even the chiefs have but little power. On the other hand, the influence of the **Marabouts** is supreme.

"The Kabyles are spread over the three provinces of Algeria. Those of the **Atlas** and in the neighbourhood of **Blidah** (like the **Beni Moussa**, the **Mouzaia**, etc.), who are subjected to the French, used in olden times, in consequence of their vicinity to Algiers, to consent occasionally to pay tribute to the Turks. Two of the most important branches of the Kabyle race inhabit the province of Algiers; to the West they occupy all the space between the **Cheliff** and the sea; to the East, what is called 'La Grande Kabylie,' which forms a triangle, the summit of which is at **Setif**, and the base on the seashore from **Dellys** to **Collo**. The first of these has been the scene of fierce struggles between the French and themselves. Here was the barbarous stifling in the grotto; and the natives, hunted, tracked, and impoverished, yielded from sheer exhaustion to their conquerors, but with undying hatred in their hearts, which subsequent events have developed.

"It is fair to add that as the Kabyles are in no way aggressive, and never fight, save when their own territory is invaded, they in no way interfere with the aggrandisement of French influence round them. Their position may be hostile, but it is the hostility of neutrals, unless directly attacked.

"All I have now said applies to the Kabyles properly so-called, who reside in the **Tell** of Algeria. In the south of the province of **Constantine** and on the confines of the **Desert**, is a tribe of these very people, who are nomads and shepherds, who live in tents like Arabs, and have all the external appearance of the latter. These are the tribe of the **Chaouyas**, who yet are of Kabyle or Berber origin, and speak the Kabyle language with very little variety; but, less happy than their brethren in the mountains, these Kabyles have remained in the plains, and have not been able to maintain their independence.

"But there is again another Kabyle tribe, the **Biskris**, living, as their name implies, at **Biskra**, and other parts of the Desert, under the shadow of the palms and in the oases which are scattered all along the edge of the Sahara. They are so transformed by their desert lives as to be almost impossible to distinguish from the Arabs, unless it be through their darker tint, which they owe to frequent mixture with the negroes of Central Africa. These **Biskris** may occasionally be met in the large towns, where they act as porters, water-carriers, and fortune-tellers, which is one of the characteristic trades of their race. Many of the Kabyle women fortune-tellers are met in the streets of Algiers, where they excite the curiosity of all foreigners ; but their home is the sandy desert, and their heart is thoroughly Kabyle."

Travellers to Kabylia coming from Tunis, Constantine, Bône, Biskra, or, in fact, from any part east of Setif, will enter Kabylia from Bougie, and finish at Tizi-Ouzou—the reverse routes to those described on pp. 202—205.

Excursions in Kabylia are arranged by THOS. COOK & SON, 3, Boulevard de la République, Algiers, *see* p. 46, 48.

FROM ALGIERS TO BOUGIE AND THE CHABET PASS.

Algiers (or Marseilles) to Bougie by sea.

Bougie can be reached by the Compagnie Générale Transatlantique steamer from Marseilles to Bougie every Tuesday at noon, but the best route is *via* Algiers, sailing from Marseilles every Thursday at 1 p.m. Also from Marseilles (Transports Maritimes à Vapeur) every Saturday 6 p.m., arriving at Bougie Tuesday 6 a.m., and from Algiers (Cie. Transatlantique) every Friday 8 p.m., arriving at Bougie at 6 a.m. next morning. (*Times subject to alterations*).

Algiers to Bougie by rail.

Stations.	Distance in kilometres from Algiers.	Stations.	Distance in kilometres from Algiers.
Algiers	—	Aomar dra el Mizan	99
Agha ...	2	**Bouïra** (buffet) ...	123
Hussein Dey ...	6	Aïn el Esnam ...	137
Maison Carrée...	11	El Adjiba	151
Oued Smar	16	Maillot	162
Maison Blanche ..	19	**Beni Mansour**(junc.)	172
Rouïba-Aïn-Taya ..	26	Tazmalt	180
Réghaïa ..	32	Allaghan	185
Alma	39	Akbou	196
Corso	42	Azib ben Ali Chériff	203
Belle Fontaine ...	49	Ighzer Amokran	207
Menerville (buffet and junc. for Tizi-Ouzou)	54	Takriets-Seddouck	213
Souk el Haâd	61	Sidi Aich	219
Beni Amran	65	El Maten	229
Palestro	77	El K'seur	237
Thiers	88	La Réunion	249
		Bougie	261

The best train from Algiers is at 6.30 a.m. (the Constantine train), arriving at Beni Mansour 12.2 p.m., where carriages are changed and time allowed for lunch. Leaving Beni Mansour at 12.30 p.m., Bougie is reached at 3.42 p.m. Seven miles from Algiers the line branches off on the left at

Maison Carrée, *see* p. 103. As far as Béni-Mansour, where the line to Bougie branches off to the left, the route is the same as that to Constantine (*see* pp. 216–220).

At Bouïra, 123 kilometres from Algiers, an hour and forty minutes before arriving at Beni Mansour, is a good buffet, and this train usually stops twenty-five minutes there.

Bougie, in Arabic **El Bedjaia,** a town of 14,400 inhabitants, the chief port of Eastern Kabylia, is built like an amphitheatre, very much the same as Algiers, surrounded by the mountains of **Babor** and **Tababort.**

Hotel: Hôtel de France, where visitors will find excellent accommodation, civility and good cuisine (Mr. Schacher, proprietor). Cook's Coupons, Series A, B, and C, accepted.

Bougie in the time of the Carthagenians was an important commercial depôt, and at the fall of Carthage it came into the hands of the Romans, who named it **Saldæ,** where they built fortifications, cisterns, palaces, baths and other large edifices. In the Algerian section of the Louvre Museum, in Paris, there is an inscription that runs thus: **Julia Augusta Saldantium.** Taken later by the Vandals it was occupied in the 11th century by the Berbers, who called it **Bedjaia,** and who raised the city to a great pitch of splendour and opulence, with a population of 100,000, many mosques, colleges, and manufactories of pottery and tiles. Even the heliograph was known.

In the 11th century, under the reign of Beni Hammad, Bougie contained 20,000 houses, and was called the little Mecca.

In 1512 Arondj, and later on, Kheir ed Din, endeavoured to occupy the city, but without success. In 1555 Salah Reis Pasha of Algiers besieged Bougie by land, and the town capitulated.

The Turks becoming masters in the 16th century, decay set in, piracy and constant wars during three hundred years completely ruined the city.

When Algiers was occupied by the French the forts of Bougie were held by the Mzaia Kabyles, and these were driven out in September, 1833, by General Trézel after a fight of three days.

Situated on the sea coast at the foot of the Gouraya, and surrounded by clusters of orange, pomegranate, and fig trees, the town of Bougie occupies a charming site, and the views from the forts are superb.

The old Municipality of Bougie has been superseded by a Local Board, which is working its hardest to improve its general sanitary condition. The town is now lighted throughout by electricity, and abundantly supplied with excellent spring water. The springs of Toudja have been brought to Bougie by a canal of 25 kilometres in length, at a cost of over 700,000 francs (£28,000). The Chambre de Commerce (Trade Board) and the Municipal Board are now busily engaged in building a new harbour, the scheme having been sanctioned by the Minister of Public Works and the necessary sums voted.

The town of Bougie was formerly surrounded by three rows of battlements and walls, testifying to the successive dominations that have ruled the country.

The Roman wall is still visible in many places.

The Arab or **Sarracene wall**, dating as far back as 1067, though in a very dilapidated state, presents several ruined remains in various parts round the town. **The Sar=racene arch,** or **Bab el Bahar**, as it was called, is still in a good state of preservation at the lower end of Bougie, opposite the harbour.

The present fortified wall was built by the French in 1842.

The **Casbah** is still a magnificent pile of buildings, built by Peter of Navarre in 1509, under the reign of Ferdinand IV. of Spain. It contains five cisterns, capable of holding 20,000 litres of water. The mosque within it was erected by the Turkish Pasha, **Mustapha Ben Ibrahim**, in 1797.

There is a beautiful forest behind the Casbah reaching to the summits of the mountains, where walks and drives are numerous.

The ancient forts are worth a visit. Near the jetty is the **Fort Abd-el-Kader,** partly destroyed by an earthquake in 1856 ; the **Fort Bordy el Ahmer,** near the Koubba of Sidi Fouati, was built in the 14th century. Roman remains may be seen in various directions—cisterns near the **Fort Barral,** traces of an amphitheatre near the Grand Ravin gate; also medals, mosaics and columns.

The great mountain of **Gouraya,** with a fort of the same name at the top, displays its grand profile over the town, rising 2,200 feet above the sea. It is an easy and pleasant excursion to the summit on foot, by mule, or by carriage — 3 or 4 hours.

Cape Carbon is about 7 kilometres to the north-west of Bougie; it is a great mass of red rocks, on which is the **Lighthouse** (the most powerful revolving light on the coast of Africa). One of these rocks, forming a natural arch through which the sea flows, serves as a shelter for fishermen in distress. From the lighthouse the panorama spread before the traveller is of exquisite beauty. Tradition says that Raymond Lulle, a Spanish philosopher (1235–1315), born at Palma, lived in some caves at the foot of the cliffs, accessible from the sea.

Toudja, 25 kilometres from Bougie, is a pretty little Kabyle village, situated in charming and picturesque scenery. The ruins of the celebrated Roman aqueduct are very interesting. The springs of Toudja (*see* p. 210) produce from 200 to 300 litres of water per second. Half a day's excursion.

From Toudja the ascent of the Arbalou (about five hours there and back) can be made.

Tiklat, 29 kilometres south-west of Bougie, on the **Oued Sahel,** possesses the ruins of the Roman city of **Tubusuptus.** These consist of large *Thermæ* and are well worth seeing.

Travellers from Bône or Constantine who intend to go through Kabylia will alight at Setif and proceed through the Chabet Pass to Bougie, the starting point for El K'seur, Azazga. Fort National, and Tizi-Ouzou.

✈ BOUGIE TO SETIF BY THE CHABET PASS.

Diligences start every day from Bougie at 3.30 a.m., but these conveyances are not very comfortable, and a portion of the journey is made in the dark. Price, 15f. in the coupé. Private carriages can be secured in advance by writing to M. Spitéri, at Bougie, or to Thos. Cook and Son, Algiers. In this way the journey is made comfortably in two days, passing one night at Kerrata.

The drive is not only the very finest in Algeria, but it would be difficult to mention any place in Europe to surpass the magnificent scenery of the mountains, rivers, and the stupendous gorge between Cape Okas and Kerrata.

For some miles after leaving Bougie, the almost level road lies between the well-wooded mountains and the sea, passing prosperous-looking farm-houses and rivers winding through. the fruitful plain, the commune of **Oued Marsa**, and the tomb of the venerated Saint Sidi bin Nasir, shut in by enormous olive trees, sacred and ancient; and soon after crossing the **Oued Djema**, where grand mountain scenery comes into view on the right, a road cut in the rocks leads to the top of the lofty promontory of **Cape Okas**, disclosing the most enchanting landscapes and sea views it is possible to imagine.

The road then descends to

Sidi Rehan, where, close by at a small inn and restaurant, the **Rendezvous de Chasse**, it is usual to stay an hour for *déjeuner* (ordered in advance).

Resuming the journey inland, the scenery changes, the Mediterranean is left behind, and, turning to the right, the route passes through a splendidly wooded district, bordered with several species of oak trees, olives, lentisques, and rose laurels, following the course of the winding **Oued Agrioun**, along a superb valley. *(The coast road to the left leads to the Stalactite Caves near Ziama on the way to Djidjelli, see p. 269.)* For miles the scenery is uninterruptedly charming, the nearest hills covered with forests of cedars, pines, ash, and oak, and behind these, mountains whose summits are clad in snow. The valleys and rivers, which in some places have been of considerable width, now contract, and the road ascends and descends until it reaches the Pass, or

Gorges du Chabet el Akhra or **Akra**; on a post to the right is an inscription, thus ·

Ponts et Chaussées
Setif
Chabet el Akra
Travaux executés
1863–70.

Here the gorge practically begins. It is an enormous defile, something like five miles in length, winding between two mountains from 5,000 to 6,000 feet high, at the bottom of which runs a deep and narrow stream. The rocks hang perpendicularly over the head of the traveller, and scarcely afford sufficient space for the sun's rays to clear their way through the ravine, rising in some places as high as 1,200 feet. The road sometimes follows one side of the torrent, sometimes the other, and more often is cut through the sides of the rocks, which in many places overhang the bed of the torrent and completely intercept the light. For about half its length the road passes along the left bank of the gorge, when it crosses to the right side on a bridge of seven arches, and continues on the same side during the remainder of its course.

Troops of monkeys are sometimes discovered, adding to the animation of this gigantic enclosure, and eagles may be seen hovering overhead for an attack on the numerous wild pigeons flying in and out of their hiding places in the rocks.

The road was designed by the military engineers, and completed by the departments of the Ponts et Chaussées. under the direction of M. de Launoy, chief engineer, in 1870.

Before reaching **Kerrata**, where this stupendous and magnificent gorge ends, a stone bearing this inscription is met ·

LES PREMIERS SOLDATS QUI
PASSERENT SUR CES RIVES
FURENT DES TIRAILLEURS
COMMANDÉS PAR M. LE
COMMANDANT DESMAISONS
7 AVRIL 1864.

The diligence changes horses at Kerrata, which allows about an hour's rest for refreshments.

Travellers by carriage will spend the night at either the Hôtel du Chabet (Cook's Coupons, Series A, B, and C, accepted) or the Hôtel de Kerrata (Cook's Coupons, Series R, accepted).

Continuing the journey to Setif next morning, an early start is necessary (for those who are not intending to stay at Setif) in order to arrive in time for the 4.30 p.m. train to El Guerrah or Constantine.

This is easily done by leaving Kerrata at 7 a.m. The journey takes about 8 hours and a-half, allowing 40 minutes at **Amoucha** for *déjeuner*, which should be ordered in advance.

For several miles beyond Kerrata the road ascends, crossing the **Oued Berd** and other streams, with nothing of importance to note. At the 20th kilometre a very short halt can be made at

Takitount to enjoy the view, and to taste some very agreeable aerated ferruginous water from a spring close by. On the summit of the hill is seen the Fort of Takitount, 3,500 feet above sea level, built on the site of a Roman settlement. *(Guides and mules can be obtained for the ascent of Mt. Babor 6,200 feet.)*

The next and last stay *en route* is for *déjeuner* at Amoucha.

Up to this village some of the points of view have been very enjoyable, but the scenery of the rest of the journey affords little to attract attention. Several farms and Kabyle villages are seen, and a long chain of hills is crossed, very tame and monotonous.

At **El-Ouricia** and beyond the valley is well cultivated by the Compagnie Genevoise.

Fermatou and the Bou Sellam are reached, then the large parade ground, and, entering by the Porte de Bougie, the traveller arrives at Setif.

Setif, 156 kilometres from Constantine, is a town of 6,500 inhabitants, or of 15,000 including its annexes of **Aïn Sfia, Lanasser,** and **Mesloug.** It is the ancient **Sitifis** of the Romans, and the capital of the province of Mauretania. Injured by an earthquake in the fifth century, it was later on destroyed by the Vandals and the Arabs, leaving the merest traces of a city that measured three miles in circumference.

Setif was taken by the French in 1839, and the present modern town is divided into two distinct quarters, the town quarter and the military quarter. The barracks in the military quarter are constructed to hold 3,000 troops. There are also other military buildings, such as the **Cercle des Officiers,** the **Manutention,** the **Hospital,** the **Direction du Génie,** and the **Hotel of the General Commanding the Subdivision.**

The town faces south of the military quarter; it is surrounded by a fortified wall with four gates, the gates of Bougie, Alger, Biskra, and Constantine.

The streets, bordered with trees, are well provided with shops, and the modern houses have a comfortable appearance.

The mosque, church, theatre, and other public buildings are of a very ordinary order. Outside the Porte d'Alger, on the Promenade d'Orléans, there is a small open-air museum or collection of Roman remains.

A very important market is held at Setif, and at certain times during the season it is not infrequently attended by 10,000 natives of various tribes.

Situated 3,500 feet above sea level, the climate of Setif is healthy, and the country around is very fertile; the vast plains to the east, occupied by Arabs, produce cattle and cereals in abundance. The mountainous districts to the north west are inhabited by Kabyles.

Hotels: the **Hôtel de France** and **Hôtel d'Orient.** Cook's Coupons, Series A, B, and C, accepted at both. Instead of going to Constantine direct, some people may prefer to stay at Setif (which is reached about 4 p.m.) dine and sleep there, and proceed to Constantine next morning. If Biskra be the object of the journey, then it is better to stop at **El=Guerrah**, dine and sleep comfortably there (*see* p. 217), and start next morning to Biskra. It saves time and distance, as well as affording more rest. The buffet at the Setif railway station is kept by the proprietor of the Hôtel de France, and the charges are very moderate.

ALGIERS TO CONSTANTINE, BISKRA, AND HAMMAM MESKOUTINE.

Stations.	Distance in kilometres from Algiers.	Stations.	Distance in kilometres from Algiers.
Algiers	—	**Setif** (buffet) ...	308
Agha	2	Chasseloup-Laubat...	322
Hussein Dey	6	Saint Arnaud ..	339
Maison Carrée (junc.)	11	Bir el Arch	354
Oued-Smar (halt) ...	16	St.-Donat	367
Maison Blanche ...	19	Mechta-Châteaudun	384
Rouïba-Aïn-Taya ...	26	Oued-Seguin	
Réghaïa ...	32	Télergma	403
Alma	39	**El-Guerrah** (junc.)	427
Corso	42	Ouled-Rahmoun	
Belle Fontaine ...	49	(buffet)	436
Menerville (junc.) ...	54	**Kroubs** (junc.) ...	448
Souk El Haâd...	61	Oued-Hamimim ...	453
Beni Amran ...	65	Hippodrome (halt) ...	460
Palestro ...	77	**Constantine** ...	464
Thiers	88		From Constantine
Aomar-dra-el-Mizan ...	99		
Bouïra (buffet) ...	123	**Constantine**	—
El-Esnam	137	**El-Guerrah**	37
El-Adjiba	151	Aïn Melila ...	50
Maillot ..	162	Les Lacs ...	68
Beni Mansour (junc.		Aïn Yagout	85
buffet)	172	Fontaine Chaude	
Les Portes-de-Fer ...	185	(halt) ..	93
Mzita	201	El-Mahader-Pasteur	101
Mansoura	209	Fesdis (halt) ..	107
El-Achir	226	**Batna** (buffet) ...	118
Bordj-bou-Arréridj ...	239	Aïn-Touta-MacMahon	151
El-Anasser ...	246	Les-Tamarins ...	159
Chenia	254	**El-Kantara** (buffet)	183
Aïn Tassera	264	Fontaine des Gazelles	201
Tixter	271	El Outaya	211
El Hammam ...	284	Ferme Dufour ...	222
Mesloug ...	297	**Biskra**	239

Stations.	Distance in kilometres from Constantine.	Distance in kilometres from Bône.	Stations.	Distance in kilometres from Constantine.	Distance in kilometres from Bône.
Constantine ...	—	—	Aïn Régada ...	57	162
Hippodrome ...	3	—	Oued Zenati ...	68	151
Oued-Hamimim	11		Bordj-Sabath...	84	135
Kroubs (junc.)	16	203	Taya	95	124
Bou-Nouara ...	30	189	**Hammam-**	111	108
Aïn-Abid ...	42	177	**Meskoutine** }		

There is only one through *day* train to Constantine, leaving Algiers 6.30 a.m., due at Constantine 8.40 p.m.

Passengers by this train who intend to visit Biskra before Constantine had better dine and sleep at El-Guerrah (due there 7.24 p.m.) at the hotel adjoining the station (Hotel El-Guerrah, Cook's Coupons, Series R, accepted), and leave by the 9.50 a.m. train for Biskra, due there 4.30 p.m. (Lunch at Batna.)

Those who prefer to go on to Constantine to sleep will leave Constantine for Biskra at 8.20 a.m., by the same train as the one from El-Guerrah alluded to above.

There is a *night* train from Algiers to Constantine every Sunday Tuesday, and Thursday, leaving Algiers at 7.41 p.m., due at Constantine 9.30 a.m. To the Sunday evening train in winter is attached the Oran-Tunis Express, with carriages of the Wagons-Lits Company, places for which can be booked at THOS. COOK & SON'S Offices, 3, Boulevard de la République, supplement Algiers to Constantine.

These night trains constitute a direct service to Biskra, changing carriages at El-Guerrah between 8 a.m. and 9 a.m., giving ample time for breakfast before leaving at 9.50 a.m. for Biskra. (Lunch at Batna.) There are buffets at Bordj-Bouïra, Beni-Mansour, Setif, El-Guerrah, and Kroubs.

Leaving the main station at Algiers the train stops at

Agha, for passengers from Mustapha, then at **Hussein Dey** and

Maison-Carrée, where the line turns to the right for Oran. The prison on the hill, formerly an old fort, can be visited from Algiers, and the Friday market also (*see* p. 103). At

Oued-Smar is a nursery of all kinds of Australian trees, many of which are being introduced with success into Algeria, more especially the eucalyptus.

Maison Blanche, Rouïba (Government School of Agriculture), and next

La Réghaïa, near a forest of the same name.

Alma, where in 1839 and 1871 the French troops successfully resisted much larger numbers of Arabs and Kabyles.

Corso.

Belle-Fontaine, a flourishing village inhabited by emigrants from Alsace and Lorraine.

Ménerville, also inhabited chiefly by families from Alsace and Lorraine. (Junction for Tizi-Ouzou, *see* p. 199.)

Souk-El-Haâd.

Beni-Amran. Between this station and

Palestro, the railway passes through the beautiful **Gorge of the Isser,** which in one part is only 275 feet wide, but owing to the numerous tunnels much of the rock and river scenery is lost. **Hotel :** Hotel du Commerce (Cook's Coupons, Series A, B, and C, accepted).

Palestro, situated on the banks of the Isser, inhabited in 1871 by French, Italian, and Swiss workmen who had been engaged on the railway, was the scene of a frightful tragedy enacted by Kabyles. The following account of what occurred is taken from Sir L. Playfair's description in Murray's Handbook for Algeria :—

The village contained about 112 inhabitants; its position was isolated, surrounded, and commanded on every side by mountains and on the border of two tribes, one Kabyle, the other Arab, both ripe for revolt. Still no serious fears were entertained till, on 18th April, 1871, it was suddenly surrounded by hostile tribes before any means could be adopted for defence. The village being entirely unfortified, it was determined to distribute the inhabitants in the three houses best suited to resist attack—the priest's house, the barrack of the gendarmerie, and the establishment of the *Ponts et Chaussées.* Captain Auger, of the Engineers, and the priest directed the defence of the first, the maire commanded the second, and the conductor of *Ponts et Chaussées* the third. In the last, which was the best of the three, the women and children were placed. Soon the attack began, the haystacks and buildings round about were set on fire. and such as could not get into the village in time were murdered.

The assailants now advanced in considerable numbers to attack the curé's house, led by the *Amin-el-Omina* of the *Beni-Khaefoun.* The door was soon driven in, but the defenders succeeded in escaping to the gendarmerie with a loss of four of their number. One woman remained behind; she was kept a prisoner for some time and then killed.

At this moment the conductor of the *Ponts et Chaussées* managed to escape to *Fonduk*, where he gave information of what was going on, leaving the house, however, in which he had been stationed, which contained all the women and children, without any one to direct the defence.

On the 22nd the maire, M. Bassetti, Captain Auger, and the brigadier of gendarmerie, entered into negotiations with the insurgents, who offered to conduct them safely to Alma, permitting them to retain their arms. Everything appeared settled, and the colonists in the gendarmerie were on the point of quitting, when one of their number made an offensive movement with his gun. This was the signal for a general massacre, in which only Captain Auger and the son of the maire were spared at the special intercession of the Amin.

In this horrible carnage forty-one Europeans were killed, and even their corpses were found to have been the object of the most brutal violence; some were thrown alive into the burning houses, and all were stripped of whatever valuables they had.

The house of the *Ponts et Chaussées* was next attacked. Its door, badly made, offered no resistance. The defenders retreated to the upper storey. Fire was applied to the ground floor, and they were again compelled to retreat higher to the terrace.

It was mid-day in April. In a space of 12 mètres, forty-five persons were crowded together behind the parapet of the terrace, 40 centimètres high. If they allowed their bodies to appear they were shot. The heat of the roof, brick vaults supported by iron girders, was intense; even their clothes caught fire. Stones and bricks were thrown upon them from below, which grievously wounded some of their number. A burning sirocco was blowing, and they had not a drop of water to quench their thirst. Several died, and one in a moment of madness committed suicide. The women uttered the most heartrending cries, but it was not till six o'clock in the evening, when the roof was on the point of falling, that those heroic men consented to treat with their assailants.

The Amin agreed to conduct all the men, women, and children to Alma, on condition that they consented to abandon their arms. This was agreed upon. Ladders were brought to permit them to descend. They were then taken to the residence of the Amin-el-Omina, where they found Captain Auger and the young Bassetti. Two days after Colonel Fourchault arrived on the spot with a column from Algiers, to find only corpses and blackened ruins. He had to fight his way there and back to Alma against those who had taken part in the massacre.

The prisoners, forty in number, amongst whom were thirty-two women and children, were kept in captivity for twenty-two days, and only released on the termination of the insurrection, when Mokrani was killed.

The remains of the victims repose under the shadow of the church, and a monument, in the worst style of art, has been erected to commemorate the event.

Now Palestro has been rebuilt, and considerably enlarged. Thirty families from Alsace and Lorraine have been located here, and additional concessions have been given to the families of the survivors with no sparing hand. A fort has been constructed, and considerable plantations of eucalyptus and other Australian trees have been made.

Market on Wednesdays.

Aomar-dra-el-Mizan, the station for two villages, Aomar and Dra-el-Mizan. The latter and larger village was destroyed by the Kabyles in 1871, but, thanks to a fort close by, the inhabitants were able to hold out until relieved. Omnibus to Dra-el-Mizan, 1f. Market day, Thursday. Roman remains at Ben Aroun.

Bouïra, or **Bordj Bouïra**, a prosperous locality, inhabited by rich proprietors; formerly a Turkish fort, in the valley of Oued Eddous. **Hotel:** Hôtel de la Colonie (Cook's Coupons, Series R, accepted). Numerous interesting excursions to Kabyle villages and the Djurdjura; Roman ruins at Aïn-Bessem; diligence to Aumale, 45 kilometres, in about 5 hours, 5f. (half an hour for lunch at Buffet). The line passes through the valley, and near several villages, to

Maillot (see p. 202), a healthy village, whence can be made the ascent, via Tala-Rahna, of the **Lella-Khadidja**, the highest point of the Djurdjura Mountains (7,570 feet) in appearance resembling a gigantic pyramid (see p. 202). There are two or three small inns in the village. Market on Tuesdays. Carriage road to Michelet, Fort National, and Tizi-Ouzou; another to Bougie.

Four miles beyond Maillot is the station of

Beni-Mansour, where passengers for Bougie change carriages, and where those who have not had lunch at Bouira have ample time for taking some before the train leaves for Bougie (see p. 209). There is nothing remarkable in the neighbourhood of Beni-Mansour, except the magnificent mountain view from the old fort.

Beyond Beni-Mansour the railway enters the province of Constantine, and quits the Oued Sahel for the Oued-Mahrir to arrive at the station called

Les Portes-de-Fer, about 2 miles from the two rocky passes, resembling perfectly constructed walls, called the **Bibans,** or **Portes de Fer.** There are two such portes or passes, the **Grande Porte** and the **Petite Porte.** The railway runs along the river Oued-el-Hammam through the Grande Porte, where, high above the river, the rocks resemble some luge old fortress or castle. The Petite Porte is the one through which the French army marched, under the Duke of Orleans, in 1839, a passage never before made even by Roman soldiers. In the neighbourhood are very hot springs used as baths by the natives. The water contains a large percentage of sulphate of sodium and sulphur, the temperature varying from 160° to 170° Fahr.

For some distance the mountain district is dreary and without vegetation as far as

Mansoura, a Kabyle village.

A long tunnel is passed, on emerging from which is seen a vast extent of plain of the Hauts Plateaux, and the journey, now rather monotonous, is continued to

Bordj-bou-Arréridj, an ancient Turkish fort, several times burnt by the Mokranis. The bordj was rebuilt by the French, and the town was destroyed by the Mokranis in the revolution of 1871, but the citadel resisted. The town has been rebuilt, and surrounded by a massive wall with four towers. The country round is now prosperous, and the mountain population of the Medjana have returned to the fertile plains.

Many charming excursions can be made from Bordj-bou-Arréridj, such as to

Bordj-Medjana (7 miles) within a mile of which, at Aïn Zourham, there are some Roman remains; to **Zamoura,** 15½ miles, a delightful ride by rivers and woods. Carriage road to Bou-Saäda.

But the grandest mountain excursion in all Algeria is from Bordj-bou-Arréridj to Fort National (see p. 202), through Bordj-Boni, Guelaa, Ighil-Ali, Akbou, over the Djurdjura range, etc., a long ride of 90 miles on mule or horseback. Tents, guides, and provisions must be taken, and only those who are able and willing to rough it should undertake the journey. At Guelaa or Kalaa, is the ancient fortress of the Mokrana, of whom the last representative was the leader of the 1871 revolt.

From Bordj-bou-Arréridj the line is flat and uninteresting for more than 40 miles, until the train arrives at

Setif. *See* p. 214.

On leaving Setif the railway crosses the **Oued-el-Hassi** to the station of

Chasseloup-Laubat, between which and the next station,

St.-Arnaud, may be seen on the right some peaks of the great Aurès mountains.

Next in succession come

Bir-el-Arch, St. Donat, Mechta=el=Arbi (station Mechta-Châteaudum), and

Telergma, near which, at **Oued-Atmenia,** on the estate of the Count Tourdonnet, large Roman buildings and stables have been excavated, the mosaic floorings of which were found in a perfect state of preservation.

The next station is

El-Guerrah, junction for Batna and Biskra. *See* note on pp. 215, 217.

Continuing the journey to Constantine by the valley of **Bou-Merzoug** we soon reach

Ouled Rahmoun, whence light railway to **Aïn-Beida** (white fountain), 93 kilometres, a pretty village containing a church, schools, synagogue, European and Jewish cemeteries, and two forts. The district inhabited by the Haracta tribe produces excellent cereals and fine cattle, and in several hills are remains of ancient lead and copper mines worked by the Romans. In many directions are numerous and important Roman and Byzantine ruins.

The next and last station at which the train stops is

Kroubs (Buffet) junction of the Bône-Guelma railway for Bône and Tunis. The Friday market here is one of the largest in Algeria. **Hotel:** Hotel d'Orient (Cook's Coupons, Series A, B, and C, accepted).

Passing stations **Oued Hamimim** and **Hippodrome,** the journey ends at

CONSTANTINE, 464 kilometres, or 288 miles, from Algiers (*see* p. **273**).

From **Constantine to Biskra,** a journey of 239 kilometres, or 148 miles, occupies about eight hours, leaving Constantine at 8.20 a.m., due at Biskra 4.30 p.m., and there is only one train a day. No change of carriages. (Lunch at Batna at noon.)

Between Constantine and El-Guerrah the only stop is at Kroubs, and leaving the junction of El-Guerrah at 9.50 a.m., the first station of importance on the road after the junction is **Aïn-Yagout,** the nearest point from which to visit the remarkable monument of the **Medrassen,** supposed to be the tomb of Masinissa, one of the Numidian kings, situated about six miles from the station, the charge for a conveyance being 6f. or 8f. As, however, one is not always sure of obtaining a conveyance at Aïn-Yagout, a better plan is to arrange for it to be sent from Batna to meet the train either at Fontaine-Chaude or El-Mahader Station. Distance 26 kilometres and 17 kilometres respectively from Batna by rail.

The **Medrassen** is smaller but similar to the Tombeau de la Chrétienne, between Tipaza and Marengo or Coléa (*see* page 121), with a cylindrical base 180 feet in diameter, on which is a truncated cone, the lower portion having sixty engaged columns with Greek capitals. The roof or upper part of the monument gradually diminishes by a series of steps; the apex is missing, and the total height to-day is 60 feet.

After many ineffectual attempts to open the building, it was entered in 1873 by Engineer Bauchetet; nothing was found in the central chamber, but traces of fire showed that, as in other instances, the tomb had been previously ransacked. The exterior is built of very large stones, but the chamber and galleries of the interior are less solid.

Continuing the journey, no places of note are passed until the train reaches **Batna,** where a stay is made for *déjeuner,* at a fairly good buffet.

Batna is a clean, well-built garrison town, a military subdivision of the province of Constantine. The barracks have room for 4,000 men. The town dates from the year 1844, and was formerly a camp to protect the route of the Tell to the Sahara.

Hotel : Hôtel des Etrangers et Continental (Cook's Coupons, Series R, accepted).

The modern town, with a population of 6,500, has broad streets, schools, churches, baths, and electric light. With the exception of the General's garden, which forms a delightful promenade, there is little in the way of verdure, the climate being very hot in summer and very cold in winter.

On one of the boulevards is a museum of some pretensions, with antiquities brought from Lambessa and Timgad. The nucleus of the present town was called New Lambessa until 1848, and became Batna in 1849.

From Batna charming excursions can be made on horseback to the **Cedar Forest of Mount Tougourt** if only for the splendid views; and to some of the interesting *Chawia* or Berber and Kabyle villages of the magnificent range of the

Aurès Mountains, where a guide, mules, provisions, and tents are required, and where of course there are no inns of any kind; but in the principal villages the Kaid has a guest-chamber that he is pleased to place at the disposal of travellers. The highest point of the range, and indeed in all Algeria, is the

Pic de Chellala, 7,611 feet above sea level, the ascent of which in the fine season can be easily made, almost to the very top on horseback. The descent is very enjoyable, through villages and cedar forests to

Khenchela, a considerable village, the flourishing centre of a commune containing 20,000 natives, connected by diligence with Batna. The ancient *Mascula* of the Romans, a great number of tombs and other Roman remains are met with in the neighbourhood of Khenchela.

From Khenchela train may be taken to **Aïn-Beïda**, (54 kilometres by rail in about two and a-half hours), and Constantine. **Aïn-Beïda** (the white spring), so called from its spring of pure water, yielding some 120 gallons a minute, is situated in the territory of the once formidable warlike tribe of the **Haracta**, now become quiet and successful agriculturists, with 100,000 acres of land in an excellent state of cultivation.

The principal buildings of the pleasant little town comprise a church, schools, market, synagogue, and two forts built in 1848 and 1850. On the outskirts are Negro villages, European and Jewish cemeteries.

The country for miles round is covered with pagan and Christian ruins, the most important of these being at **Fedj-Souïoud, Mrikeb-Talha** and **Ksar-Sbehi.**

Batna is the starting-place for excursions to the remarkable Roman ruins of Lambessa and Timgad. These ruins can be visited on the journey to Biskra, *or on the return*. If the traveller intends to visit them on going to Biskra he need not leave Constantine or El-Guerrah so early, as there is an evening train from Constantine at 5.45, due at Batna at 10.19 p.m. The next day can be devoted to the ruined cities, both of which can be visited by carriage, 37 kilometres, returning to Batna to dine and sleep. Lunch can be obtained at a small clean hotel, close to the museum at Timgad (*see* p. 228). If the above plan be adopted the journey to Biskra will be continued the following day by train leaving Batna at 12.48 p.m. reaching Biskra at 4.30 p.m.

With this idea in view, a concise description of the ruins of Lambessa and Timgad will be given here, which, of course, will be equally applicable if the visit be made on the return journey from Biskra. If the ruins of Timgad are visited on returning from Biskra a good plan is for travellers to wire or write to the proprietor of the Hotel Batna, for a carriage to meet them at Batna Station. A motor-car runs during the season between Batna and Timgad.

Lambessa (11 kilometres from Batna), the ancient Lambæsis, was built by the Romans A.D. 125, to form the headquarters of the famous Third Augustan Legion, and recent explorations show the form and size of the Roman camp. A large population soon occupied the city, which spread over some miles, and Lambæsis became rich and prosperous. The town was surrounded by ramparts, and entered by four gates, two of which can still be seen.

The most interesting and best-preserved ruins are the (so-called)

Prætorium, at the crossing of the streets that divided the city at right angles; and the recently cleared **Temple of Jupiter,** near the Forum. The **Prætorium** is a large building, measuring 92 feet long, 72 feet in breadth, and 46 feet high. The façade has a handsome peristyle with Corinthian columns. A museum, containing inscriptions, statutes, etc., has been installed in the village

Outside the camp is the

Arch of Commodus (176–192), in fairly good state of preservation; and near by are scanty remains of an **Amphitheatre,** said to have seated 10,000 people. Other ruins more or less possible to identify are the **Temple of Æsculapius,** the **Arch of Septimus Severus,** and the two **Forums.** Of the forty arches existing in the eighteenth century two only are now standing.

The **Temple of Æsculapius** dates from A.D. 162; the secondary chapels built during the reigns of Marcus Aurelius, Commodus, and Septimus Severus were finished in A.D. 211. The beautiful

Arch of Septimus Severus, with three openings, at the entrance of the city, was joined to the camp by a long route called " Voie Septimienne." Near this gate are the Thermæ and other ruins, among which have been found some fine mosaics. Of the two forums, one measured 185 feet by 170 feet, and the other adjoining, 230 feet by 108 feet. The first contained a temple, and was surrounded by a colonnade.

Amongst other miscellaneous ruins have been found a number of round stones, probably projectiles, in the neighbourhood of an arsenal.

The modern village and prison are close to the Roman ruins and in the neighbourhood are the noted vineyards of St. Eugène.

About two and a-half miles south of Lambessa, or Lambèse, are the ruins of

Markouna, a suburb of Lambèse, where are two Roman triumphal arches, but the traveller will probably prefer to push on to visit the most important ruins of Algeria (another Pompeii) namely those of

Timgad, the ancient **Thamugadi,** situated at the intersection of six Roman roads, which must have been a very large and important city, judging from the size, extent, and beauty of the monuments. Gradual and systematic excavations are being carried on, a very small Government subsidy of two thousand a year being allowed for the purpose. The ruins already unearthed rival those of Pompeii in interest, and in course of time we may hope to see the entire Roman city brought to light, and the visitor be able to walk from one end to the other on the streets of a city founded by Trajan.

The history of Thamugadi is the history of Numidia, and its end dates from the 7th century at the time of the Arab invasion, when it was a Christian city. Earthquakes, the dust and sand of the plains, the rain and soil from the mountains have all helped to complete the destruction.

A broad road or street, called by the Romans Cardo Maximus, separates the city into two unequal parts, divided at right angles by a smaller street, the Decumanus Maximus , and where these crossed was built the

Forum, which is now entirely unearthed. It had a splendid colonnade on the north side. Steps within a large gateway led to the interior of the Forum, paved and surrounded by a colonnade. Around the court on the east side are a

Basilica, or Court of Justice, and a number of small shops, while on the west side are various buildings identified as the **Curia** (Council Chamber), **Tribunes,** and **Temple of Victory.**

Close to the Forum is the

Theatre, a large building faced with stone, capable of seating 3,500 people, and about 800 in the galleries. The

THEATRE, TIMGAD.

auditorium and the colonnade of the portico are in good preservation. From the rising ground just behind the theatre there is a fine view of the ruins. In May, 1907, a performance of ancient tragedy took place here and will probably be repeated this year. A little of the south of the theatre are the

Thermæ, with inscriptions showing them to have been built in the reign of Septimus Severus, A.D. 179. The mosaic floors are in good condition. To the south-west of the forum is a very remarkable and beautiful

Triumphal Arch, or **Trajan's Arch,** built of sandstone, with marble columns. The arch has three openings, the central one 10 feet 2 inches wide, the side ones 6 feet 9 inches wide. The two fronts are alike, each decorated with Corinthian columns, 18 feet high (*see* p. 229). Near the Triumphal Arch is what must have been an exceedingly fine building,

The Market, erected in the 3rd century A.D. by a Roman lady, whose statue of white marble was found among the ruins. The bases of eight columns are seen, portions of a portico which lead to a court surrounded by galleries, and at the end of which were shops. Beyond the market to the south are the large and numerous ruins of a massive and handsome building, which is thought to be a

Temple to Jupiter Capitolinus. The walls in some places are 6 feet thick, with stones of 3 feet and 4 feet in length. The columns of the façade measure 4 feet 6 inches in diameter, and their Corinthian capitals are large in proportion. Sufficient material has been unearthed to enable the director to build up this important structure, but the means at his disposal are limited. However, the work is proceeding, and in time will doubtless be satisfactorily completed.

Further south overlooking the city are the remains of the famous

Byzantine Fort, the walls of which are in many places in a good state of preservation.

In various parts of the suburbs are ruins of bridges, of several basilicas, and of tombs that have not yet been explored.

At less than two miles south-west of Timgad, between two spurs of the **Aurès,** is a magnificent gorge (the Gorge of the Seven Sleepers) on the hills on either side of which are hundreds of circular tombs of unknown date.

The visitor arrives from Lambessa at the north side of the ruins, where, as already stated (p. 225) is a small clean hotel.

Close by is the

Museum, organised by M. Rottier, the director of the excavations. It is open to the public, and contains sculptures, inscriptions, vases, columns, capitals, lamps, coins, and a marble sarcophagus.

There are no guides to show visitors over the ruins, but in the museum, books, plans, and photographs can be purchased ; and when at liberty the energetic and obliging director is always willing to place his experience and knowledge at the disposal of inquirers.

All the above discoveries have been fully described (with photographs) by M. Ballu, the director and keeper of the historical monuments of Algiers (*see* list of books on p. 285).

An interesting native market is held on Thursday.

ARCH OF TRAJAN, TIMGAD.

Leaving Batna for Biskra the train passes over viaducts to the highest point of the line, 3,540 feet, to the station of **Lambiridi,** and on to **Aïn Touta-Mac-Mahon,** crossing several viaducts over the Oued-Ksour as far as **Les Tamarins,** amidst splendid mountain and valley scenery. Another station and the train stops at

El-Kantara, about half a mile north of the wonderful gorge of the same name. Beyond the station are some houses and the **Hôtel Bertrand** (Cook's Coupons, Series A, B, and C, accepted), about 200 yards from the commencement of the gorge, and travellers with a day to spare would do well to make a stay in this picturesque and charming corner, especially as much of the extraordinary effect of passing *suddenly* from the luxuriant vegetation of the valley to the oasis of the silent desert, which the Arabs call Foum-es-Sahara (the mouth of the Sahara), is lost from the railway carriage.

The gorge is only about 325 yards long, and never less than 120 yards wide, the rocks on either side are some 400 feet high, the river *when in flood* rushes below through a Roman bridge of one large arch modernised. Leaving the gorge the river widens and passes through thousands of date palms, a goodly number of orange, apple, and mulberry trees, losing itself in the immense desert, a sight the like of which is not to be seen in any other part of the world.

It is also an excellent centre for hunting or for exploring the Aurès Mountains.

Many enjoyable excursions can be made from El-Kantara. Carriages, horses, and mules are to be hired at moderate prices. Guides for the three interesting villages in the oasis 3f. a day ; for longer excursions, such as the ascent of **Djebel Metlili,** or the **Alabaster Mountain,** 5f. a day.

El-Kantara was a Roman fortress of great importance. The ground of this territory abounds with Roman ruins and fragments of the settlements of the Third Roman Legion. Its ancient name was **Calceus Herculis.**

The oasis of El-Kantara comprises three villages, or dacheras ; **Khrekar, Khbour el Abbas,** and **Dahraouïa,** containing more than 90,000 palm-trees. The population amounts to about 3,000 inhabitants.

The railway line, before reaching this oasis, passes successively under a tunnel of 160 metres, another of 20 metres and the third of 100 metres in length.

The passage through the wild and remarkable gorge of Kantara out into the mighty Sahara is thus described by a recent traveller: "I know not where so startling a contrast can be seen as during the few moments that carry you through the mighty gorge of El Kantara and over the bridge into the boundless Sahara. One minute you are in the dark shadow of towering mountains and cliffs, and passing over a rushing river, palms, oleanders, and green fruit-trees clothing either

EL KANTARA.

bank, in the next you are out in the blazing sun and endless desert. To the eye the rift in the mountain chain, that separates with giddy heights and cliffs the desert from the hills and valleys, the pastures and forests left behind, appears the only possible entrance. The moment the pass is cleared a desolate landscape lies before you, but amongst the burning red and orange rocks that are piled above, and the endless wilderness of sand and stones that stretches far away to the horizon, the eye rests on the belt of rich, green, close-packed palms that marks the exquisite oasis of El Kantara and its hidden villages, whose gardens hang over the steep banks of the river as it emerges from the gorge. Right and left of the chaos of crags and precipices, that guard each side of the cleft, the range strikes out east and west, and the steep sides are completely furrowed with ravines, as if a herculean plough had turned the mountains over into colossal ridge and furrow. After passing El Kantara the railway, an unfenced track of steel, winds along between the left bank of the river-bed and the foot of the mountains (Djebel Seltoum). The heights of the Djebel Seltoum are crowned by the ruins of an ancient fort, the Burgum Commodianum, built by the orders of Marcus Antonius Gordianus to protect travellers on the two roads that pass this way."

The railway then crosses the river-bed and continues on the right bank to

El Outaya (the Great Plain), now largely cultivated and irrigated throughout its eastern end with innumerable saggias. (Station for visiting the Djebel-el-Melah, a mountain of grey rock salt.) It then passes over the **Oued-Biskra,** and turns the corner of the last range of mountains through several deep rock cuttings, and the great oasis of Biskra, with the desert around and beyond, comes in sight.

Continuing the journey for 35 miles beyond El-Kantara the traveller arrives at Biskra.

BISKRA.

BISKRA AND THE DESERT FAR.

" Stretching away, that sea of sand to bar
The way, more than the ocean which we cross
Without much fear or pain, or care, or loss.
'Tis like an ocean, as we stand and view
The trackless sand in shades of grey and blue.
Oh! wondrous BISKRA! with your palm-tree groves.
Cooled by the rivulets the palm-tree loves,
And spreads her leafy foliage waving free,
As passing breezes kiss the stately tree.

Oh! silent BISKRA! when you tread the way
Where lofty palm-trees whispering seem to say
Rest from the care, the weariness, the strife,
And all the turmoil of this passing life;
Rest 'neath my graceful, waving branches tall:
It is a panacea true for all,
And I will sing a lullaby for thee
With my tall arms I cast about so free."

A. O. M., 1890.

Biskra, called by the Arabs the **Queen of the Desert,** the most charming town (population 7,600, of which only about 700 are French) of the Sahara, has deservedly gained of late years a considerable popularity. In addition to the railway from Algiers to Constantine briefly described above, the creation of a direct line of railway from Philippeville to Constantine putting Biskra within easy access of Marseilles and Paris and London, has chiefly contributed to the great success of this interesting place. Biskra is also easily accessible from Bône, *viâ* Kroubs and El-Guerrah.

Biskra thoroughly deserves the distinction of which visitors of all nationalities have made it the object. Its winter climate is in some respects assuredly without parallel. While London is deeply clad in January fogs, and Parisians are knee-deep in snow and ice, Biskra enjoys a clear blue sky, and is caressed by the rays of a glorious sun, developing from November to April an average heat of 60° Fahrenheit in the shade. The average maximum and mininum for December, January and February are 61° and 42° respectively. Indeed, the recent records of the Bureau Météorologique have greatly contributed to encourage tourists and delicate persons to repair to the **Desert Town**. When Nice, Mentone, and the chief winter resorts of Italy were experiencing frosts and inclement weather, Biskra was favoured with the most glorious temperature which any southern city can boast of in the winter months. While Rome, Pisa, Nice, Cadiz, and Malaga registered very low averages, Biskra never experienced a temperature lower than the one above mentioned. From November to April there are only eighteen or twenty days in which there is any rainfall. As a winter resort, Biskra is superior to any medical station, either in France, Italy, or in Spain. The season extends from November to April.

It must be noted, however, that north winds and dust storms sometimes prevail, and that the difficulties of transport are not favourable to patients suffering from phthisis or Bright's disease. The great virtue of the climate is the pure dryness of the air, plenty of sunshine, little or no humidity, qualities beneficial for catarrhal affections, gout and rheumatism, renal and pulmonary affections in their early stages.

Biskra, the capital of the Zab, comprises a wide district, and was formerly an important centre of commerce, but declined under the bad government of the Turks and the attacks of the Arabs.

On March 4th, 1844, Biskra was occupied by the Duc d'Aumale, who left there a company of native soldiers commanded by five French officers. They were all massacred by the fanatical tribes, and a large French force had to be organised to subdue the rebellion; in May, 1844, the French became permanent masters of the town and district.

The **Fort St.-Germain** is an important and extensive work, containing barracks, hospital, warehouses, and other buildings, capable of resisting any attack likely to be made against it by the Arabs. The importance of Biskra from a strategical point of view cannot be overlooked, and the French have effectually constituted it the guardian of the Algerian Sahara.

The military territory of Biskra covers an area of about $1\frac{1}{2}$ million hectares, and has a native population of about 55,000. It is called **Territoire de Commandement**—that is to say, it is one of the few territories in Algeria that remain under the rule of the military authorities. **Biskra** proper is under the command of a major, assisted by a captain, three lieutenants, and a military interpreter. The other six communes of the territory of Biskra, viz., **Ouled Djellel, Tekout, Tougourt, El Oued, El Amri** (oasis), and **Fougala** (oasis), are commanded by captains of infantry, with their lieutenants and interpreters, these being for the most part native interpreters belonging to the army.

The other military territories of the province of Constantine are: **Tébessa, Barika,** and **Khenchela. Biskra, Barika,** and **Khenchela** belong to the region of **Batna. Tébessa** belongs to the region of **Constantine.**

The oasis of Biskra contains 250,000 palm-trees, planted in groups bordering the road, or inclosing gardens of fruit and vegetables.

The centre is reached by a tramway 2 kilometres long, starting from the Casino (p. 238), ending at the old Turkish Fort on a mound commanding a fine view of the neighbourhood.

The following account, which appeared in the *Times*, gives an unexaggerated and correct description of the oasis of Biskra :—

" Some years ago the railway system in Eastern Algeria was extended south through the gorge of El Kantara to Biskra, the first, and perhaps the finest, of the oases in the Northern Sahara. It is now many years since a company of French gentlemen, the **Compagnie de l'Oued Rirh**, interested in the development of the country, conceived the idea of installing a series of artesian wells, and of increasing, by improved irrigation, the produce of some of the already existing oases, as well as forming new plantations for systematic cultivation. In spite of many obstacles, the project was steadily pursued. An evidence of the tenacity of purpose which has characterised the promoters is, that only recently has a return in the way of dividend been received. After travelling in the desert sometimes for days, with an unvarying

STREET IN BISKRA.

prospect of undulating plains of sand bounded by the horizon, the relief to the eye is even greater than that of the body when one of these little islands of green in the endless sea of sand is reached, and the sight of green trees, welcome shade, and running water is appreciated as it has been never before. The water from the wells is distributed in little canals, often only a few inches in depth and width, which wind through the gardens and round the roots of the palms, so as to ensure that condition under which alone, says the proverb, can the date flourish, 'its feet in the water and its head in the fires of heaven.' The artesian wells sunk by French engineers naturally require but little attention when once the flow of water is established; but with the Arabs' wells it is often quite another case. With a mouth at least a yard square, and sides shored up in a primitive fashion, it is natural that they should frequently become choked with *débris* and sand, and then it is that the Arab owning such a well sends for divers. These are Rouaras, and form a class apart, almost a religious sect, having special prayers and charms for use before descending a well. One of these men will remain between three and four minutes in a well, often over 100 feet deep, bringing up with him in his little basket a few handfuls of the sand or stones obstructing the flow of water. Date-growing brings in large profits in Algeria, where at the various properties of the company spoken of may be seen the results of years of patience and enterprise."

The town of Biskra, the **Ad Piscinum** of the Romans, called in the Arabic **Biskra el Nokkel** (or "Biskra the Palms"), is situated 35° 27' latitude N. by 3° 22' longitude E., at an altitude of 111 metres above the bed of the Oued Biskra. It is surrounded by a wall and a ditch. The suburbs are outside the ditch, and encircle the town on all sides, a vast garden covering an area of six miles. The inhabitants of Biskra follow the same Mohammedan rites as the inhabitants of the sacred city of Medina, in Arabia. One of the gates of Biskra is called **Bab el Mokhara** ("the gate of the cemetery"); another **Bab el Hammam** ("the gate of the baths"); the third, **Bab el Mouldoun** ("the gate of the negroes"). The town is divided into two distinct quarters, the European and the native.

The French town, which one enters when coming from the railway, consists of a large street, bordered on the one side only by brick houses, built on arcades somewhat resembling the Rue Bab Azoun at Algiers. The only difference is that the Biskra houses have but one storey, and sometimes only a ground floor.

The Native Quarter, called by the French *Village Nègre,* is the complement of the European quarter. Coming out of this quarter, a wide road of about 1,500 yards, bordered by a triple row of palm trees, takes you to the spot of the ancient villages of **El-Bekri** and **El-Aiachi,** which are marked by heaps of ruins.

The following villages are the groups of houses and tents,

which are spread out at a distance of 5 kilometres, and which constitute the modern native Biskra :—

Bab el Khroka, north of the Casbah.

Bab el Rhralek, west of same

M'Cid, south-west.

Kourah, south-east.

Bab el Darb, west part of **Oued Biskra.**

Gaddesha, north-west ; and

Filliash, south-east.

Hotels. There are several excellent first and second-class hotels, but none too many for a town that is constantly increasing its number of visitors.

The **Royal Hotel** is a large arcaded building in the Moorish style of architecture, in every respect a first-class establishment. Electric light, modern sanitary arrangements. The lounge, salons, and dining-rooms are very spacious ; many of the bedrooms open out on to a terrace, all are newly and comfortably furnished. The central court is laid out as a garden ; and from the upper terrace on the flat roof rises a graceful minaret, which commands a splendid view over the oases, the Sahara, the Aurès mountains, etc., and is a favourite resort of visitors for watching the glorious sunsets.

The **Hotel Victoria,** immediately opposite the railway station, is also a first-class hotel of long standing, with good public rooms and bedroom accommodation. The cuisine is well spoken of by the numerous English and American visitors who patronise the hotel. Electric light. Modern sanitary installation.

The **Palace** or **Dar Diaf** (or " House of the Hosts ") Hotel is a smart little hotel on a smaller scale than those already mentioned. It is built and tastefully furnished in the Mauresque and Oriental style, and forms a portion of the casino and theatre (*see* p. 238), surrounded by trees. All the above hotels accept Cook's Coupons, Series A, B, and C, and in the busy season it is advisable to write for rooms in advance.

The **Hotel de l'Oasis** is a very comfortable second-class house, and generally crowded from January to March. Cook's Coupons, Series R, accepted.

The **Amusements** found at Biskra are not very numerous, the majority of visitors being satisfied with the delightful climate, the interesting excursions, the Oriental atmosphere, and the luxury of idleness in the evening.

The **Casino and Theatre** is a modern building on the outskirts of the town, in the midst of gardens and palm trees; Mauresque in the style of its architecture, but European in its character. During the season plays and concerts are given in the theatre; a string band performs in the café and restaurant; the usual rooms are devoted to the cult of the "petits chevaux"; and in an adjoining wing baccarat or "rouge et noir" are in evidence.

The Almées, a particular class of women of the tribe of the **Ouled Naïl**, may be called one of the chief attractions of Biskra. Most of these Almées are dancing-girls.

Mr. George Gaskell describes them as follows, in his work "Algeria As It Is":—"Their complexions are darker than gipsies', for they daub their faces with tar and saffron, to deepen the colouring of the African sun. They are fond of gaily-coloured dresses, tattoo themselves like savages, and wear earrings as large as small hoops. Their hair, being mixed with wool and plastered with grease, forms a mass about the head which rivals the false locks of fashionable ladies, only the raven tresses of the Almées are worn differently, for they fall over the ears, and enclose the face as if it were framed in ebony. They literally cover their persons with gold and silver coins, coral and other ornaments, often carrying about them a small fortune in jewellery, which they display as proudly as if it had been virtuously acquired. These women, who live apart in one of the quarters of the town, frequent the **Cafés Maures** at night, where they dance a kind of bolero, but the performance of the Saharian girls is more unrestrained than that of the Spaniards. After a few years they return to their native oasis, and a marriage almost invariably follows this licentious escapade in their lives."

The Negro dances in the street should not be missed; they are extremely curious for a stranger. They take place generally at night, and are headed by a torchlight procession of white, ghostly Arabs dancing like maniacs, and followed by drummers and pipers, making curious cries and monotonous noises. Every now and then the torch-bearers halt and form a circle round some negro women in long, floating drapery, who dance furiously, with savage cries, till the procession moves on again into the thick blackness of the night, and the cries die away in the stillness.

The **Market,** near the Royal Hotel, is well worth a visit. Here every phrase of Arab and Biskrian business is carried on ; and during the date season, from November to February, the scene is especially animated. The variety of the food stuffs offered for sale is most interesting, but not more so than the open-air exhibition of the manner in which the food is cooked and consumed. Cattle market on Mondays.

Races take place some time in February (date uncertain), extending over three days, when Biskra is invaded by thousands of visitors, and those who have not secured rooms are unable to find accommodation. Valuable prizes are given for horse races, long distance camel races, where the camels are *supposed* to start from Tougourt, a distance of 210 kilometres. Fantasias, pigeon and quail shooting, add to the attractions, particulars of which are published a month in advance.

Church Service is held on Sunday at the Royal Hotel from the beginning of January to the end of April. A chaplain is supplied by the S.P.G.

Post and Telegraph Offices. Open from 7 a.m. to 9 p.m. There are four mails a week to and from the Continent. Time occupied to or from London five days. Postal rates, 10c. to France or Algeria ; 25c. to England and countries in the postal union (except Italy 20c.). Parcels must be sent from the *railway station ;* average time to or from England three weeks.

Bazaars. A great variety of Arab ware and curiosities can be purchased at Biskra, such as brass ware, leather goods for cushions, feathers, copper vases and bowls, skins, horns, Kabyle pottery and jewellery, etc. The principal bazaars are near the market, and swarms of itinerant dealers frequent the hotels.

There is no English-speaking doctor at Biskra, and the single French chemist does not know sufficient English or Latin to understand very thoroughly prescriptions written by an English physician.

The **Train from Biskra** leaves at 7.52 a.m. (Oct. to end of May), or 5.31 a.m. (June to September). Travellers who intend visiting Lambessa and Timgad from Batna must beware of the wind and cold, coming suddenly as it does after a warm residence at Biskra.

Trams run every hour from the Casino to Old Biskra, fare 10c., and four times daily (50c.) to the sulphur springs and baths of

Hammam-es-Salahin (or Fontaine Chaude), fare 50c., 6 kilometres to the west of Biskra. The baths and waters of this spring are not sufficiently known and employed by Europeans, but are largely used by the Arabs, who believe they will cure everything. The buildings for the Arabs, however, are quite separate from the general establishment.

The supply of water is 75,000 quarts an hour, at a temperature of 115° Fahr. The waters are recommended for rheumatism, tuberculosis, skin diseases, neuralgia, scrofula, renal affections, dysentery, bronchitis, wounds, partial paralysis, and diseases of women, but not for gout or heart disease.

Taken internally, the mineral water should be drunk in moderate doses in cases of arthritis, gravel, constipation, renal affections, scrofula, and diseases of the respiratory organs. It is useless for anæmia, neurasthenia, chlorosis, or brain diseases.

The establishment contains ordinary baths with dressing-rooms, shower baths, vapour baths, a large and a small piscine or common bath, electrical appliances, a gymnasium, offices and rooms for the employés.

It is, of course, a great drawback that visitors have to return so far by tramway or carriage after the treatment, and it has been suggested that the water should be conveyed in glazed earthenware pipes to **Beni-Mora,** close to Biskra, and a suitable establishment erected, a similar work having been successfully completed when the waters of Barzun (Hautes-Pyrénées) were brought to Luz, a distance of 7 kilometres.

This plan need not interfere with the use by the Arabs of their favourite " Fontaine." The baths now in existence could be left entirely for the Arabs, an arrangement to which they would offer no objection.

Excursions from Biskra.

It would require a stay of several days to exhaust all the interesting excursions for which Biskra is the centre. One of the earliest visits the traveller is likely to make is to

The **Jardin Landon** and **Old Biskra.** The former, created by a wealthy French nobleman, Comte Landon de Longeville, is a wonderful garden or park of several acres containing an endless variety of tropical and European trees

NATIVE GOURBI, BISKRA.

shrubs, and fruit trees. The enclosure is open from 8 a.m. until sunset, admission 2f. Some twenty gardeners are employed, and the property is kept in almost a painful state of order and neatness, never a leaf being allowed to remain an hour on any of the paths and walks. The Château consists of a number of detached buildings, the bedrooms and kitchens being separated from the living rooms

Q

A short drive from the Jardin Landon leads to

Old Biskra, on the Tougourt road, consisting of seven curious narrow villages, through which water runs and is distributed in turns over the gardens and oases by which they are surrounded.

Sidi Becker is a picturesque village about five miles from Biskra, where the grateful shade of palm trees and fig trees will be found. There is an unusually pretty mosque with a graceful minaret.

The **Col de Sfa,** situated about 8 kilometres to the north on the Constantine road, should be visited for the unsurpassed view over the immense desert and the Aurès mountains. The oasis, village, and mosque of

Sidi Okba are described on p. 244.

The oases of **Chetma** and the dunes of **Dumach** can be visited in one day, see p. 244. Excellent victorias can be hired from the hotels at the rate of 2f. 50c. per hour for the short excursions; 10f. or 12f. for half-days; and 20f. for the whole day, plus a fee for the coachman.

Those who wish to make a real desert expedition, prepared to put up with some discomfort and fatigue, should visit

Tougourt, an important military outpost, with a population of about 7,000, not including the native garrison, some 210 kilometres from Biskra in the Sahara. There is one hotel: Hôtel de l'Oasis.

This journey can only be accomplished between November and March, the heat during the other months being unbearable. A diligence runs three times a week, doing the distance in about twenty-six hours, but stopping at Mraïer, so that the journey occupies two days, fare, 40f. On horseback, or in a carriage with three horses, the journey can be made in five or six days there and back, the cost to be agreed on in advance—probably 350f. or 400f. for the carriage. There is only one place on the road where anyone can sleep with comfort (i.e. Mraïer), the caravanserais in the villages being of the most miserable description. Warm clothing should be taken, and in the case of a private conveyance, unless relays are arranged for, camping outfit, and provisions also. This journey affords an opportunity of becoming acquainted with the *real* desert, of which the neighbourhood of Biskra only gives a faint idea. Moreover, the Tougourt region abounds in magnificent oases.

At **Bordj-Saäda,** 30 kilometres from Biskra, there is a room for travellers, but no provisions, and the same *accommodation* at

Bordj-Chegga, 55 kilometres.

At **Mraïer,** about half-way to Tougourt (with an oasis of 125,000 date palms), bed and board can be obtained at an hotel under control of the military authorities.

Beyond **Tamerna,** a large village built of mud sun-dried bricks, and **Gamhra,** a large oasis, ascending the Kef-el-Dohr, the valley of the Oued Rirh is seen extending over 120 kilometres, with a population of 17,000, with 46 oases and 600,000 date palms. Here the Company of the Oued Rirh (*see* p. 234) have several oases and large numbers of palm trees.

Tougourt is a conspicuous object with its mosques and minarets, situated on a hill, and 170,000 palm trees forming the background. An important market is held on Fridays. Large quantities of carpets are manufactured here.

The streets are narrow, crowded with houses of one storey, built of mud bricks, and the town is divided into quarters, containing (1) the regular inhabitants, (2) the Jews who have been converted to Mohammedanism, (3) the negroes, and (4) the foreigners.

There are twenty mosques, few of which are of any importance, but one or two have some good plaster carving.

An opportunity should be taken to ascend the minaret of the large mosque, for an extensive view over the desert.

And when the traveller has seen what little there is to see he must retrace his steps over the same dreary road by which he came.

How to Spend Four Days at Biskra.

First Day.—After visiting the squares and the market Visit the oasis of Biskra, named the Queen of the Zibans, passing by the railroad at **Ras-el-Guerria,** and ascend the minaret of the mosque **Sidi-Youdi** for the finest panorama of the Sahara and the Aurès mountains. Resume the promenade to the village of Sidi Becker, visit the Zouayas (Arab schools), and observe some curious houses and interiors.

Q 2

Follow the road to the end of the oasis, then come back by the Tougourt road, which passes in front of the establishment of the Soldier monks or Frères du Sahara, an order created by the late Cardinal Lavigerie, having the aim of abolishing slavery. Gentlemen only are admitted to inspect the interior of the monastery. Visit the **Jardin Landon**, which will help you to form an idea of the fertility of Saharian vegetation in the hands of experienced capitalists.

In the evening go to the Ouled-Naïl quarter and visit the native cafés. The Ouled-Naïl dancers perform from 8 p.m. till 10 p.m. The entrance to the cafés is gratuitous. The drinks only are to be paid for. Charges 25 to 50 centimes.

Second Day.—Visit to **Sidi Okba**. This excursion requires a whole day. The drive, about 13 miles, (21 kilometres) occupies two hours, passing in view of the several oases at the foot of the Aurès mountains to the village of Sidi Okba, the religious capital of the Ziban. The chief object of interest in the village is the mosque, considered the oldest Mohammedan building in Africa. In it is the shrine of Sidi Okba, the warrior who at the bidding of the Khalifa Maouia went forth with a small number of Arab tribesmen and conquered Africa from Egypt to Tangier, A.D. 680.

The interior of the mosque of **Sidi Okba** is richly coloured, especially the *mimbar* and *mihrab*. On one of the pillars which support the chapel is an Arabian inscription recording the name and title of **Sidi Okba**, adding : " May God have mercy upon him." Fine view from the minaret. Sidi Okba is a great place of pilgrimage.

Third Day.—Morning. Visit to the oases of **Chetma**, the houses of which are on a larger scale than those at Sidi Okba. About an hour's drive (8 kilometres). In the afternoon excursion to the oasis of **Oumach** (28,000 palm trees)

Fourth Day.—Visit the sources of Hammam-es-Salahin, by carriage or tram (6 kilometres), and in the afternoon take a walk to the end of the Oued Biskra, opposite the Jardin Landon, and visit the Arab village **M'çid**.

Passengers landing at Philippeville from Marseilles (or from Algiers by sea) proceed by rail to Constantine (under four hours); thence train 8.20 a.m., arriving at Biskra 4.30 p.m. (All train hours subject to alteration.)

Biskra to Batna (for Lambessa and Timgad) and Constantine. *See* pp. 222-232 (reverse direction).

HAMMAM MESKOUTINE.

Access to Hammam Meskoutine.

Hammam Meskoutine can be reached :
From London in 3 days.
From Paris in 2½ days.
From Marseilles, *via* Philippeville, Bône or Tunis, by steamer
and rail. in 2 days.
From Genoa, Naples. Palermo, and Malta there is steamer
communication with Tunis, thence railway, about 11 hours, to (*via*
Duvivier) Hammàm Meskoutine.
From Algiers and Constantine (*see* pp. 216, 217) there is daily
communication by railway ; and by steamer *via* Bône weekly.
For dates of steamer sailings, passage fares, etc. (which are subject
to change), outward-bound travellers should apply for information
and tickets to THOMAS COOK & SON, London, Paris. Marseilles, or any
of their branch offices.

Hammam Meskoutine is situated on the line of railway
between Constantine and Bône, 111 kilometres from Constantine, 108 kilometres from Bône, 19 kilometres from
Guelma, 353 kilometres from Tunis. It is in the centre
of a triangle formed by the cities of Constantine, Philippeville, and Bône.

There are 3 trains a day from Constantine, at 8.20 a.m.
12.46 p.m., and 4.28 p.m. ; 2 trains a day from Bône, at
4.39 a.m., and 2.41 p.m. ; the journey from either town
occupying 3 to 4 hours. (*Time table subject to alteration.*)

Hotel : Établissement des Bains. (Cook's Coupons, Series
A, B, and C, accepted.)

The waters of Hammam Meskoutine were known and
employed at a very remote period of antiquity, but the oldest
monuments that have been discovered date from the Punic
period.

Of the Roman occupation, ample traces exist on every side
—ruins of baths, military works of defence, private dwellings,
agricultural buildings, etc.

After the destruction of the Roman and Byzantine monuments by the Arab invasion, barbarism succeeded to civilisation, the Arabs built nothing, added nothing, and although

they used the waters of Hammam Meskoutine, they built no baths ; the ruins of the old Roman baths or the river sufficed for them.

Soon after the French occupation of Algeria the French army were quick in discovering the virtues of the climate and waters of Hammam Meskoutine.

In 1837 the troops detached for the siege of Constantine were encamped at Medjèz-Amar, three miles from the hot springs. Medical men and chemists were appointed to report on the nature of the waters, and on the climatic conditions of the district, with the result that a

Military Hospital and Piscines (Baths)

were built for invalid and wounded officers, soldiers, and members of different administrations on the left bank of the **Chedakra**, opposite the Cascade.

In 1872 a more solid set of buildings were erected on the right bank of the Chedakra.

In 1892, the necessity for such an establishment having ceased, for various reasons, the use of the hospital was discontinued, and the building was then occupied by the manager and farm servants of the proprietor of the estate, M. P. Rouyer, of Paris.

The present establishment was built by Dr. Moreau, a retired army surgeon, who proposed to create an important bathing station—second to none in Europe—but he passed away before his large ideas were realised.

The hotel was afterwards carried on by managers in the employ of M. P. Rouyer, but no improvements were made, very little was done to attract visitors, and the establishment gradually fell into disrepute until 1902.

In November, 1902, M. Mercier, the well-known caterer and proprietor of the Hôtel d'Orient, of Bône, sold his property at Bône, and obtained a long lease of the hotel and baths and 100 acres of gardens and grounds at Hammam Meskoutine, and has since devoted his experience and capital to effecting alterations and additions in order to r̃nder his property on a small scale one of the most complete of its kind.

The hotel and hot springs are placed on a plateau in the valley of **Bou-Hamdam**, on an estate of 3,250 acres, surrounded on the south-west by the hills of **Beni-Braham**, on the north by the imposing mass of **Djebel-Debar**, rising

3,700 feet above sea-level, on the north-east by the wooded hills of **Beni-Addi**, on the south-east by the fertile slopes of the **Mahouna**, and on the west by the rugged peaks of the **Gorge of Taya**.

The hotel and baths are 960 feet above the valley, in the midst of luxuriant vegetation, of rivers bordered by creepers, wild vines, rose-laurels, smilax, and myrtles; also of olive, poplar, palm, and ancient terebinth trees of stately growth, affording grateful shade in every direction.

In the grounds and gardens will be found various kinds of fruit trees and plants, including orange, lemon, peach, vines, gooseberry, and strawberry; and of the many flowers flourishing in winter, may be mentioned bulbs, roses, stocks, geraniums, wallflowers, mignonette, and honeysuckle. Vegetables of almost every description abound from November to May; and in the plantations or fields, ferns, orchids, creepers, and wild asparagus can be had for the seeking. Game of various kinds is plentiful, the largest animal being the wild boar, very numerous in the mountain woods, affording good sport. Hares, partridges, and wild pigeons are the principal fur and feather game, and of these the partridge is everywhere in evidence. The only fish of any value in the Chedakra and the Bou-Hamdam are the barbel and the eel.

The hotel is constructed on a novel plan, so as to prevent the crowding of visitors in one building, and consists of four detached pavilions or bungalows of one storey, forming a huge square, in the centre of which are gardens, and out-of-door museum of Roman antiquities, and a croquet lawn, the whole surrounded by alleys planted with plane, terebinth, olive, mimosa, and orange trees.

The north pavilion contains fourteen bedrooms and lavatories, the doors opening to a covered gallery.

The south pavilion, in the form of a cross, comprises the dining-rooms, salon, billiard-room, offices, and a few bedrooms. On one side is a flower garden, and on the other a large terrace shaded by an enormous terebinth tree, several hundred years old, where luncheon is generally served, even in winter.

The east pavilion is sometimes reserved for the use of M. Rouyer, the superior landlord (eight rooms).

The west pavilion consists of three separate sets of rooms, with lavatories, a convenient arrangement for large families or parties, in all eight chambers.

Behind the south pavilion are the kitchens, store rooms, poultry houses, stables, and other buildings.

Everything connected with the establishment is carried on in a pleasant, comfortable style; great care is displayed in the preparation of the meals, and life in the hotel partakes of the character of a family gathering. The cost of living is about 14f. a day for short periods, and this includes bus fare to and from the station, and all extras. There is no village or town within 12 kilometres, so that everything that is not grown on the estate has to be sent from long distances, and this naturally increases the price. Arrangements can be made for reduced terms when a long stay is intended, or in the case of large families.

In addition to the splendid air, and to the wonderful natural phenomena of the place (described below), many delightful and interesting excursions are to be made; wild boar can be successfully hunted, and in the season hare, partridge, pigeon, and small bird shooting is available.

Beyond these advantages, there are none of the gaieties of the large European watering-places; no balls, theatres, concerts, rouge et noir or baccarat; and those who cannot live without such distractions would probably vote Hammam Meskoutine a dull place.

Climate.

The climate is intensely hot in summer, from the end of June to the middle of September, when of course the establishment is closed.

The autumn is generally very lovely, with occasional storms and rain; and from the month of November the ground is covered with verdure.

Winter does not exist, snow is unknown except on the distant mountains. The thermometer seldom falls below 50° Fahr.

December and January are very enjoyable, but in March there may be a few rough days. April and May are pleasantly warm. Rain may be expected from the middle of May to the end of June.

The establishment is open from November 15th to May 15th, and during that time the climate as a rule is soft, with blue sky, no snow, and little rain.

Hot Springs and Baths.

. Hammam Meskoutine, or the "Accursed Baths," were known to the Romans under the name Aquæ Tibilitinæ, so called from the neighbouring town of Tibilis, afterwards Announa.

The sources from which rise the waters of Hammam Meskoutine are numerous, at least twenty, all of them hot, but varying in temperature according to their position, and the outflow of water. The greater the quantity the higher the temperature. The nine principal sources on the right bank of the Chedakra are named as follows :—

1. Aïn-Srouna.
2. Grande Cascade du Nord.
3. Grande Cascade.
4. Source of the Baths.
5. Source of the Bridge.
6. Source of the East
7. Source of the Ruin, or Cascade du Chemin de Fer.
8. Source of Bou-Hamdam.
9. Various sources.

The source of the Grande Cascade has always a temperature of about 96° Cent., equal to 205° Fahr., or nearly boiling heat, being higher than any mineral waters in Europe, or Africa, and only equalled by the Geysers in Iceland, New Zealand, and the Philippine Islands. Dense clouds of steam rise from the falls and the surrounding earth. Clear and limpid, the water has a strong odour of sulphuretted hydrogen, which is lost as the water cools. It then becomes quite drinkable.

One other source need only be mentioned. The **Source du Pont**, at the foot of the bridge on the Guelma road, which is ferruginous, and has a different chemical composition, and is not so hot as the water of the "Grande Cascade," being only 81° Centigrade, or 178° Fahr., and is used for drinking purposes when cold.

The composition of the waters for bathing is allied to those of Uriage, Aix, and Dax ; and taken as drink the water is like that at Contrexéville.

From statistics extending over 60 years carefully kept by the

military authorities, it is found that the waters of Hammam Meskoutine are suitable for, and have proved highly advantageous in, cases of rheumatism, affections of the joints, and strains, sciatic neuralgia, fevers, partial paralysis, chronic bronchitis, and emphysema, localised tubercles, and some skin diseases.

They are unsuitable and even injurious in cases of congestion, especially in pulmonary tuberculosis, heart disease, and gout.

When the waters overflow from the sources or from fissures in the rock, being strongly impregnated with carbonate of lime, they produce, when cold, a white mass in the form of **Cascades**, presenting the appearance of petrified rapids, as seen in the accompanying illustration.

In other places the water rising above the rock has deposited a circle of sediment, then a second circle, and so on, until the spring had not sufficient force to mount higher, when the water had to find an issue elsewhere. The masses of carbonate of lime thus formed are called **Cones**, varying in size and height from a few feet to forty feet. On some of these cones, a quantity of earth having collected, self-sown shrubs and plants have sprung up, and added greatly to their picturesque appearance.

In connection with the cones in the illustration (*see* next page) called **The Arab Marriage**, there is a celebrated Arab legend which runs as follows :—

The Legend of the Cones.

A rich Arab, who had a most handsome sister, finding her too beautiful to be married to any save himself, determined to espouse her, in spite of the prohibition of Mohammedan law and the supplications of the elders of his tribe, whose heads he cut off in front of his tent. The usual marriage festivities commenced, and a magnificent feast was given on that occasion. But just before the completion of the wedding ceremony, when the accursed couple were about to retire, a tremendous earthquake supervened, the demons were let loose, the elements set in motion, fire came out of the earth, the water left its bed, and the thunder pealed forth in a fearful manner. When tranquillity was restored, all the unfortunate bridal party were found turned into stone, including the Arab,

CONES—THE ARAB MARRIAGE.

his sister, the father and mother of the bride, and the cadi who had presided at the ceremony ! The Arabs of the present day point out the petrified cones representing the actors of this terrible drama, and even point out the granulated fragments of sulphur below as being " petrified couscous," the remains of the marriage feast.

The two colossal stones which mark the spot where Ourida and Ali—these are the names of the heroes of this incestuous marriage—were struck by Divine chastisement are a vivid testimony in the minds of the inhabitants of those countries, and reminds them of the punishment of the culprits. Near these, a more elevated cone of granite personifies the cadi, who performed the marriage, and who is easily recognised by his turban.

Behind Ourida can be seen the camel who bore the bridal presents, and farther off, the unfortunate father and mother of the bride, who acceded to their marriage. The other cones represent the minor lookers-on, the musicians, and the servants. The tents are also detected in the shape of petrified cones of different sizes : and, in order that men shall ever bear in their minds the memory of this infernal deed and the solemn punishment that followed it, God allows that the fires of the feast may be kept burning eternally, a dense smoke arising from the boiling waters clouding for ever the site of this lamentable region.

Is there a more scientific explanation that could surpass this very pathetic narrative ? What on earth are the alkaline salts, the thermal springs, the petrified cones of Hammam-Meskoutine compared to the touching remembrance of Ali and Ourida, the accursed couple !

In her narrative, " A Search after Sunshine." Lady Herbert writes as follows :—

" One curious effect of the exhausted cones is that the earth having accumulated above, and the birds having dropped seeds on it, they appear like a species of gigantic flower-pots, from which graceful ferns and grasses fall on the sides of the cones. The crust of earth, or rather sulphur, on which you walk, is so thin, that it is even difficult to escape being scalded, without proper precautions, by the little streams which perpetually cross your path ; and hence the Arabs have invented a multitude of stories connected with the wedding legend, and no power on earth would induce them to go near this, which they consider ' accursed ' spot, after dark."

The Baths.

The bathing portion of the establishment comprises baths, shower-baths, and vapour baths, with retiring rooms.

The installation at present is on a small scale, and somewhat primitive, owing to the difficulty in fixing modern arrangements because of the enormous deposits of carbonate of lime. Metal pipes and appliances would be choked in a very short time, and only stone conduits with wooden taps are possible.

M. Mercier, however, is studying the question of alterations and additions, and having entered on a lease of the premises for 20 years he will spare no pains to provide for the requirements of the increasing number of bathers and visitors.

Excursions.

Many delightful and attractive excursions are within easy reach of Hammam Meskoutine. The valleys and rivers of **Oued-Bou-Hamdam**, and **Oued Cherf**, which meet at Medjez-Amar and form the Seybouse, afford charming walks. In the **Oued Chakra** it is curious to notice the fishes and crabs in the lower and cooler regions of the hot water of the river, on the banks of which pink laurels grow.

One of the most interesting and easily accessible curiosities of the neighbourhood is the **Subterranean Lake,** about three kilometres south of the hotel :—

In the month of July, 1878, after a very stormy day, the soil suddenly gave way, on a surface extending over 30 metres in diameter, causing a tremendous noise, which attracted the attention of the neighbouring shepherds. On close examination, a large crevice was discovered creeping downwards, towards the centre of the earth, conducting the explorers to a large mass of water forming a lake of about 50 metres long by 30 wide. On the right side of the cavern a stream, three metres wide, carried with terrific crash an enormous quantity of water to this subterranean lake. During six weeks this stream continued to pour water into the lake, in the same capacious quantity, and ceased suddenly one day. This phenomenon has been very clearly explained by the scientific men who were entrusted with the analysis of the springs of Hammam Meskoutine. The reasons which are given are briefly outlined in this way : One of the cavities, like many that are hidden in the territory of Hammam Meskoutine, was concealed at the depth of two or three metres under the ground. Higher up, at a supposed distance, was situated a large natural tank of water, which, breaking its barriers, engaged itself by way of numerous rivulets, more or less voluminous, in the direction of the underground cavity or grotto, and filled it with water, until the level of this underground lake was equal to the other recipient. The stream continued for some days, until the equilibrium was perfect, and the cataclysm is thus very clearly demonstrated by the deduction that the waters, in penetrating with great violence into the underground grotto, caused the falling-in of the upper ground, which led to the discovery of the lake.

It is advisable to make use of torchlights when visiting the interior of the grotto; but this precaution is not altogether indispensable, for at the end of about ten minutes or a quarter of an hour the eye gets sufficiently accustomed to the obscurity which reigns in the interior to distinguish the remote corners of this interesting labyrinth. The most favourable time for the visit is between 2 and 4 o'clock in the afternoon, when the rays of the sun strike directly on the entrance of this immense grotto.

Another favourite excursion is to the ruined city of

Announa (ancient Tibilis). This can be made by carriage or mule ; if by mule the journey is shortened by being able to follow the bridle path over the hills. Passing the tomb of Dr. Moreau, the road lies through fields gay with flowers, bordered by olive trees, one of which, a sacred tree, is some eight hundred years old, then leaving Dar Othman and the lake on the left, the ascent of the valley of Bou Hamdam discloses superb views, to be followed by an equally charming descent to the villages or hamlets of St. Charles and Aïn-Amara. Beyond, after traversing the steep ravine of the Oued Announa, a path leads to the plateau, on which stand the ruins of the ancient Tibilis.

Judging by the splendid situation and the extent of the ruins, Announa must have been a prosperous Roman settlement. The antiquities that have been excavated, principally by M. René Bernelle, the administrator of the district, are

A Christian Basilica,

Two Triumphal Arches,

A fine Roman paved road,

Several important houses,

Statues, fragments of columns, funereal and other inscriptions.

Although of less importance, an agreeable excursion can be made to the ruined Roman fort,

La Guelaat Serdouk, a steep ride of an hour, passing a canal which supplies three primitive flour mills, thence to a plateau, on which a marabout and a few Arabs dwell. Higher up is the fort, and a cistern, from which the extensive and diversified views will repay the visit. Beyond, on a still loftier peak of the mountain, is

Fedj-Abdallah, another Roman fort.

The excursion to the immense prehistoric cemetery at

Roknia can be accomplished by mule in two hours. The cemetery is about 12 kilometres from Hammam Meskoutine, situated between the **Djebel Debar** and the **Djebel R'rara.** Spreading over a surface of several kilometres a thousand dolmens are to be seen more or less intact. They are generally composed of four upright stones, and one horizontal stone. Four or five of these monuments very close together are often grouped in the same enclosure.

A longer and more exciting, not to say dangerous, excursion than any of the above is a visit to the stalactite

Grottoes of Taya, 6 kilometres from the station of the same name, half an hour from Hammam Meskoutine, but it is not to be recommended to ordinary travellers, and must never be attempted without Arab guides, or an ample supply of magnesium, blue lights, candles, matches, etc.

The entrance passage is spacious, with Roman inscriptions of the third century on the sides. Beyond the passage the grotto descends very steeply, the rough, treacherous ground and deep holes leading to narrow muddy passages before arriving at the vast halls and vaulted chambers, from which hang or spring huge masses of stalactites and stalagmites of every shape and form. On the left-hand side of the steep slope is an abyss of great depth, not yet explored. Care should, therefore, be taken to keep to the right. The halls or galleries are called after the earliest or most important explorers of the caves, such as the galleries Challamet, the hall of **Flogmy**, of Djermâa, of Faidherbe; the boudoir Gabrielle, in honour of the Princess de Croix, the first woman who had the courage to make the excursion.

The cave or grottoes are 1,850 feet in length, and the largest chamber measures 900 feet.

From Hammam Meskoutine to Bône, two trains daily, at 12.4 p.m. and 4.42 p.m. For description of Bône *see* pp. 280–284.

From Bône to Souk-Ahras, 107 kilometres, four trains daily, at 4.39 a.m., 12.16 p.m., 2.41 p.m., and 4.37 p.m.

ALGIERS TO TUNIS. (By Rail.)

Stations.	Distance in kilomtrs. from Algiers.	Stations.	Distance in kilomtrs from Kroubs.
Algiers	—	**Kroubs**	—
Agha	2	Bou Nouara	14
Hussein Dey	6	Aïn Abid	26
Maison Carrée (junction)	11	Aïu Regada	41
Oued Smar	16	Oued Zénati	52
Maison Blanche...	19	Bordj Sabath	69
Rouïba-Aïn-Taya	26	Taya ...	80
Réghaïa	32	Hammam Meskoutine	96
Alma	39	Medjez Amar ...	101
Corso	42	**Guelma** (buffet)	114
Belle-Fontaine ...	49	Millésimo (halt)	118
Menerville (junct., bufft)	54	Petit	123
Souk-el-Haàd ...	61	Nador	135
Beni-Amran	65	**Duvivier** (junction for	
Palestro ...	77	Bône; buffet)	148
Thiers ...	88		From
Aomar-dra-el-Mizan	99	**Duvivier**	Duvivier.
Bouïra (buffet) ..	123	Medjez-Sfa ...	10
El-Esnam	137	Aïn-Tahamimine	19
El-Adjiba	151	Aïn-Affra ...	24
Maillot ...	162	Laverdure ...	36
Beni-Mansour (junct. bft)	172	Ain-Sennour	42
Les Portes-de-Fer	185	**Souk-Ahras** (buffet)	
M'zita	201	(Br. to Tébessa) ...	52
Mansoura... ...	209	Tarja	61
El-Achir	223	Sidi-Bader	69
Bordj bou-Arreridj	239	Oued-Mougras	85
El-Anasser	246	Sidi el Hemessi... ...	101
Chénia	254	**Ghrardimaou** (Customs	
Aïn-Tassera	264	Exam.) (buffet)	111
Tixter ...	271	Oued Méliz	121
El-Hammam	284	Sidi Meskine	132
Mesloug ...	297	**Souk-el-Arba**...	144
Setif (buffet) ...	308	Ben Bachir	155
Chasseloup-Laubat	322	Souk-el-Khemis	167
St. Arnaud	339	Sidi Zéhili	180
Bir-el-Arch	351	Pont de Trajan (buffet)	
St. Donat ...	367	(Branch to Béja) ...	193
Mechta-Châteaudun	384	Oued Zargua	214
Oued-Seguin-Telergma...	403	Medjez el Bab	234
El - Guerrah (junct.		Bordj Toum	249
bft.)	427	Tebourba	266
Ouled Rahmoun (junct.)	437	Djédéida (Br. for Bizerte)	275
Kroubs (junction for		Manouba ...	290
Phillippeville; buffet)	448	**Tunis**	300

For description of route from Algiers to Kroubs, 448 kilometres (278 miles), *see* pp. 217–222.

From Kroubs to Tunis, 448 kilometres (278 miles), (total 896 kilo metres, 556 miles) as follows :

There is only one through train a day (Restaurant Car) from Kroubs (or Constantine) to Tunis, leaving Kroubs at 9.14 a.m., due at Tunis 10.39 p.m.

There are buffets at Guelma, Duvivier, Souk-Ahras, Ghrardimaou, Souk-el-Arba, and Pont de Trajan (Buvette). *Gharardimaou is the frontier station, where the examination of baggage takes place, at which passengers must be present to facilitate the work of the Customs' officials.*

At Kroubs the traveller leaves the East Algerian Line for the Bône-Guelma Railway to Tunis

There is nothing very noteworthy during the first 70 kilometres of the journey. The villages and land near the stations of **Bou-Nouara, Aïn-Abid, Aïn-Regada**, and **Bordj-Sabath** are mostly the property of the *Compagnie Générale Algérienne*, to whom the Government in 1878 granted hundreds of thousands of acres for industrial and agricultural development at a mere nominal rent

Four miles from the station of

Taya, on the side of a mountain, is a remarkable **Cave** or **Stalagmite Cavern,** the exploration of which is so difficult as to be almost dangerous. The entrance passages, on which are Roman inscriptions, are accessible enough, but to penetrate and to *descend* into the various vaults, chambers, and passages, from which hang the extraordinary stalagmites, requires qualities of nerve, caution, and endurance to which few ordinary travellers can lay claim (*see* pp. 256–257).

A much more pleasant and profitable time can be spent a few miles further on, at the hotel and thermal baths of **Hammam Meskoutine,** for description of which *see* pp. 245–257.

A short but charming ride to

Medjez=Amar, a thriving farm, formerly a camp ; and a stay of twenty minutes for lunch is made at the more important station **Guelma,** a pretty, well-built town of 7,000 inhabitants, picturesquely placed near the river Seybouse. **Hotel :** Hôtel d'Orient. (Cook's coupons, Series A, B, and C, accepted.) The ample streets are shaded by trees, and in the principal square are a mosque and a church. Monday is market day. The town is fortified and surrounded by walls. (Buffet close to the station.)

Ruins of Roman baths and of a theatre, some portions of which are in a fair state of preservation, may be seen, and near the church is a small museum of statues, tombs, and inscriptions in the public garden.

On the banks of the **Oued Berda** are the remains of Roman baths near a spring ; and at **Djebel Mahouna** are Roman quarries of rose-coloured marble, now worked by the French.

Beyond Guelma, the railway passes through delightful country, along the Seybouse valley to **Millésimo, Petit,** and

Nador, then enters the narrow gorge of the Nador, whose almost perpendicular rocks are covered with wild myrtle, and continuing along the valley of **El-Ahmar** reaches

Duvivier (junction for Bône), a village noted only for its Sunday market.

Beyond Duvivier the views from the railway are still very enjoyable ; the line penetrates the valley of the **Oued Melah** to the junction of the Oueds Sfa and Melah at

Medjez-Sfa, then arrives at the wooded district of

Aïn=Tahamimime and **Aïn=Affra,** between which station and

Laverdure is a remarkable almost circular tunnel, emerging from which is seen the cork oak forest of **Fedj-Makta.** Beyond the Colimaçon ravine the line boldly runs above river and valleys to the springs of **Aïn Sennour,** and through forests to

Souk=Ahras (buffet), a prosperous and improving town of 6,000 inhabitants. **Hotel:** Grand Hotel d'Orient. (Cook's Coupons, Series A, B, and C, accepted.) An important station of the Bône-Guelma railway, junction of the line to Tébessa, 128 kilometres, two trains a day. *See* p. 261.

Souk-Ahras is the ancient Thagaste, where St. Augustine was born in November, A.D. 354. He made his first studies at Madaura, and completed them at Carthage, returning to Thagaste as a teacher, being converted and ordained as a priest some years later, at Hippone, or Hippo, *see* p. 282.

In 1852 and in 1871, Souk-Ahras was more or less destroyed by the Arabs. The modern town is well laid out, the large streets planted with trees, converging on the "Place de Thagaste." At one end of the town is a fine square, and at the other a shaded promenade. The town is surrounded by flourishing vineyards, beyond which are magnificent forests.

Roman antiquities are found in many of the immediate

suburbs, and in several directions are sulphur and other baths, some of which are used by the natives.

The most important excursion within a *short* (7 kilometres) distance of Souk-Ahras is to

Khamisa, the ruined **Thubursicum Numidarum,** a very extensive city of the second century. Some of ruins are in a very dilapidated and imperfect state, but are sufficient to show that the public buildings must have been of a splendid size. Mention may be made of the **Theatre,** in good preservation ; the **Basilica,** in bad condition, evidently a very large edifice ; **Baths, Triumphal Arch,** and **Tombs** in a fair state of preservation.

On the hills outside Khamisa the great river of Tunisia, the **Medjerda,** takes its rise.

Souk-Ahras (junction) is 107 kilometres from Bône and 248 from Tunis, and is the station from which starts the branch line for visiting the Ruins of Theveste, now called **Tébessa.** There are two trains a day, at 5.15 a.m. and 4.10 p.m., doing the journey (128 kilometres) in 6 and 5½ hours respectively.

The return train from Tebessa at 12.33 p.m. only arrives at Souk-Ahras at 7.5 p.m., too late for the evening train to Tunis. Thus passengers must spend nearly twenty hours at Souk-Ahras, where, fortunately, they will find good accommodation at the **Grand Hotel d'Orient.**

Tébessa (Theveste), founded in the first century during the reign of Vespasian, was the first headquarters of the Third Augustan Legion.

Tébessa was the junction of nine roads, and the Roman rampart against the attacks of the Berbers. In the second half of the second century it was the richest city of Africa next to Carthage, then raised from its ruins, to which city it was joined by a road 190 miles long. A Roman road also connected Tébessa with Timgad (p. 226). Under Septimus Severus (193-211), Tébessa attained its greatest state of prosperity, and became the central dépôt of the country. Market Tuesday and Wednesday.

There are not many monuments of this period, but there is one magnificent and almost unique monument : the triumphal

Arch of Caracalla, dating from A.D. 212, of the style called *quadrifons,* that is, of four faces of equal dimensions, each face a single arch.

This splendid monument is almost intact, thanks to the eunuch Solomon, the successor of Belisarius, who, after Tébessa had been destroyed by the Numidians in the fifth century, restored the city in the sixth century, and made the arch of Caracalla the principal entrance gate.

The entire arch is built of stone, each arch has two disengaged columns on either side, with Corinthian capitals, behind which are pilasters. The central ceiling is elaborately decorated ; above the entablature is a cornice, above this a frieze and another cornice. The arch is dedicated to Septimus Severus, to his wife Julia Domna, and to their son Caracalla, the inscription of the fourth arch is missing.

With the exception of the Arch of Janus at Rome, and the great arch at Tripoli, the Arch of Caracalla is the only example known of an ancient quadrifons, or four equal-sided arch. The height from the ground to the cornice is 34 feet, and the space separating the two opposite faces is the same, so that the monument is a perfect cube.

Not far from the Arch of Caracalla, in the interior of Solomon's citadel at present limiting Tébessa, is the

Temple of Minerva, the date of which is not known for certain, but is probably of the third century. The portico has. six Corinthian columns, four in front and one on each side, approached by a flight of stone steps. The sides of the temple are supported by four pilasters, over these and the columns are sculptured panels.

The temple is 45 feet in length, 28 feet broad, and 27 feet high without the basement. This interesting and beautiful monument has been converted into a museum by the Curé of Tébessa, M. Delapart, a devoted collector of antiquities, whose death took place unexpectedly at the close of 1902, to the deep regret of everyone who had been privileged to know the worthy, learned, and unselfish curate.

We come now to the

Citadel of Solomon, as it was built in haste after the destruction of the city in 535, with all kinds of material the Byzantine soldiers found at their disposal.

The walls, which extend 1,300 yards, are 22 feet high and 6 feet 6 inches thick, flanked by fourteen towers. Three gates gave access to the citadel, the one to the cast, called Solomon's gate, being defended by two square towers two storeys high. The south gate is called the Cirins gate, being near the unearthed remains of an amphitheatre to contain 7,000 spectators. The north gate is the one described above as the Arch of Caracalla. About two-thirds of a mile from this gate is an hexagonal building surmounted by a cupola, supposed to be an ancient **Mausoleum,** that the Arabs covered with a koubba for one of their holy men.

A third of a mile from the modern town are the splendid ruins of the **Basilica** of a vast monastery dating from the first centuries of Christianity, namely, the end of the fourth or the beginning of the fifth.

The monastery, surrounded by a wall, was approached by a massive gate, and contained a cathedral, a residence of the bishop, cells for the clergy, a forum, and extensive, massively built stables. Between these and the basilica was a covered way for the use of the clergy in bad weather.

The basilica was approached by a flight of steps leading to a court surrounded by stone and marble cloisters, with a font in the centre. Beyond the court was the main building, consisting of a nave and two aisles.

The basilica, measuring 142 feet in length and 68 feet in width, was magnificently decorated. Splendid marble mosaics have been found, also marble columns, highly sculptured capitals and cornices, marble tablets and mosaics that adorned the walls, the foundations of an altar, many tombs with inscriptions, and a sarcophagus.

The ruins of the entire monastery have been unearthed and excavated by the Service des Beaux Arts, under the direction of M. Sarazin, details of which have been published by M. Albert Ballu in a pamphlet with photographs, issued by MM. Berthand Frères, 9, Rue Cadet, Paris, from which the condensed description of the monuments given above has been taken, after an interesting visit to Tébessa.

The modern town is within the walls of the ancient citadel, and is supplied with water from a spring by an aqueduct half a mile in length, and in the town is a large Roman house, part of which is now used as a dwelling. With the exception of the French Casbah, a Catholic church, and a few European houses, the town is entirely Arab.

Beyond the town to the west are a number of megalithic tombs, and the remains of a Byzantine tower.

Leaving Souk-Ahras, from which there is only one departure daily for Tunis, the train runs along the left bank of the Medjerda, a charming ride through vineyards and superb pasture lands to the stations of **Tarja** and **Sidi Bader,** then for several miles traverses deep cuttings and many tunnels, crossing and recrossing the river over bridges and viaducts to

Oued-Mougras and **Sidi el Hemessi** to the frontier station of

Ghrardimaou (buffet), where luggage is examined (by the Algerian or Tunisian customs officers, as the case may be) during a stay of twenty minutes. Passengers should take care to be present at the examination, to avoid delay. This is much more strict on entering Tunisia than Algeria, owing to the tobacco monopoly.

Judging from the number of ruins within a short distance of the station and of the Medjerda, this district must have been a flourishing one in the Roman period of occupation.

Two and a-half miles from the next station,

Oued-Meliz, the ground is covered with the remains of the Roman city **Simittu,** the most remarkable of which (in very imperfect condition) are the **Bridge** over the Medjerda, the immense **Aqueduct,** the **Baths,** a **Theatre,** and various ruins too dilapidated for identification.

On the surrounding hills are vast quarries of rose-colour and other marble, having evidently been worked by the Romans. The marble was shipped from Tabarca (*see* p. 383). The quarries of **Shemtou** are now being worked by a company.

Ten kilometres beyond the station of

Sidi Meskine, is an important market and French camp at

Souk-el-Arba, a commercial centre at the junction of several roads. (Buffet and small inn at the station, where as a rule ample time is allowed for dinner.) Arab market on Wednesday.

Many interesting excursions can be made from Souk-el-Arba, one of two or three days being by carriage to **Aïn Draham** (silver spring) (p. 383) and to **Tabarca,** *see* p. 383. Moderately good accommodation at both places.

Between four and five miles from the station are the ruins of the once important Numidian city of

Bulla Regia (Hammam Derradji of the Arabs). Most of

the buildings destroyed by an earthquake are buried in the soil, but when the work of excavation is carried out many and valuable archæological results will be obtained. The spring of sweet water, near which a large nursery garden has been created, is utilised to supply the camp and town of Souk-el-Arba, the source having been enclosed by the military (*see* p. 384).

The ruined buildings scattered over a considerable area comprise **Baths, Cisterns, Amphitheatre,** remains of **Temples,** and a **Theatre.**

Continuing the journey, no particular features are noticeable at **Ben-Bachir, Souk-el-Khemis,** or **Sidi-Zéhili** (numerous ruins), until arriving at

Pont-de-Trajan (buffet), whence a branch line (three trains a day), of eight and a-half miles leads to

Béja, the Vacca of the Romans, at one time a rich and prosperous city surrounded by walls with twenty square towers. It was then the granary of North Africa, situated in a rich and fertile plain producing immense harvests of cereals. The Arab town has been built from the stones of some of the Byzantine walls, the barracks are in the old Casbah, and few traces of the old city remain. Market Tuesday.

The next station beyond the Pont-de-Trajan is

Oued-Zargua, where in 1881 the stationmaster and the railway staff were massacred and burnt by the Arabs. A commemorative monument has been erected at Pont-de-Trajan (*see* above).

Between **Oued-Zargua** and

Medjez-el-Bab the line crosses several bridges and tunnels and the main road from Carthage to Tébessa.

The little town (population 1,200) is of Spanish origin, and the district around is crowded with ancient remains, cisterns, triumphal arches, baths, and mausoleums. At least half a dozen interesting short excursions may be made.

A longer excursion to the magnificent ruins of

Dougga (*see* p. 380) requiring two days, can be made partly by carriage and partly on mule back, travelling to **Testour** (a village of Spanish origin) and **Teboursouk.** The ruins of Dongga (or Djongar), the ancient Thugga, are of the most interesting kind, affording an endless field of research for archæologists. The principal buildings already recognised are the beautiful **Temple of Jupiter,** the **Temple of Saturn,** the **Triumphal Arch,** the **Mausoleum** (a stone taken from it, bearing an inscription, is now in the British Museum, London), the **Theatre,** the **Circus,** and the splendid stone **Aqueduct.**

The next stations, of no importance, are **Bordj-Toum, Tebourba** (another Spanish town originally), and

Djédéida, junction of the line to Bizerta; but travellers will doubtless prefer to visit Bizerta after reaching Tunis, a pleasant one day's excursion by train (*see* p. 374).

Beyond Djédéida the line passes between a portion of the magnificent aqueduct constructed by Hadrian, in the second century, to supply Carthage with water from Zeugitanus, now called Zaghouan. Through a very pretty district studded with gardens and villas, the train arrives at

Manouba, at one time the country palace of Kheir ed-Din Pasha, Prime Minister of Tunis, now the property of a French company. The train soon passes in front of the **Bardo** (*see* p. 314), the salt lake of El-Sejoumi, the Mussulman cemetery, and enters the terminus at

TUNIS, p. 308.

ALGIERS TO TUNIS BY SEA, viâ PHILIPPE=VILLE, AND BÔNE.

From Algiers to Tunis by *sea* the distance is about 385 miles (by *rail viâ* Setif, Constantine, Tunis, about 576 miles)

Steamers from Algiers for Tunis, and *vice versâ*, perform the voyage once a week as follows:—

		Arrive.			Depart.		
Algiers...	...	—			Saturday	8 0	p.m.
Bougie	...	Sunday	6	30 a.m.	Sunday	12 30	p.m.
Djidjelli	...	Sunday	3	30 p.m.	Sunday	10 0	p.m.
Collo ...	..	Monday	2 30	a.m.	Monday	8 0	a.m.
Philippeville...	...	Monday	10 0	a.m.	Monday	10 0	p.m.
Bône ...	...	Tuesday	3 30	a.m.	Tuesday	noon.	
La Calle	...	Tuesday	3	0 p.m.	Tuesday	7 0	p.m.
Tabarca	...	Tuesday	8 30	p.m.	Tuesday	midnight.	
Bizerta		Wednes.	6	30 a.m.	Wednes.	10 0 a.m.	
Tunis ...	... ...	Wednes.	3	0 p.m.			

		Arrive.			Depart.		
Tunis ...	...				Thursday	10 0	a.m.
Bizerta	..	Thursday	3	0 p.m.	Thursday	8 30	p.m.
Tabarca	..	Friday	3	0 a.m.	Friday	5 30	a.m.
La Calle	..	Friday	7	0 a.m.	Friday	10 30	a.m.
Bône ...	...	Friday	1	30 p.m.	Friday	10 0	p.m.
Philippeville...	...	Saturday	3 30	a.m.	Saturday	noon.	
Collo ...	... ...	Saturday	2	0 p.m.	Saturday	10 0	p.m.
Djidjelli	...	Sunday	2 30	a.m.	Sunday	9 0	a.m.
Bougie		Sunday	noon.		Sunday	7 30	p.m.
Algiers ..	... ...	Monday	6	0 a.m.	—		

Time table subject to alteration.

Taking an easterly course across the bay, with Algiers and Mustapha in the background, the steamer passes Cape Matifou, and in about four hours is opposite

Dellys, a small seaport in the Kabylia of Djurdjura, where it is not always possible to land in rough weather. The modern town, containing 4,000 inhabitants, has several good streets, a church, hospital, a school of arts, and large barrack accommodation.

A corniche road is being constructed to connect with Port Gueydon (formerly Azeffoun), 60 kilometres.

Light railway from Dellys to Boghni (68 kilometres; fare, 1st class, 5f. 10c.; second class, 3f. 75c., in about five hours).

After passing Cape Tedles, Cape Corbelin (near Port Gueydon), and Cape Carbon, the steamer calls at

Bougie, the seaport of Eastern Kabylia, early in the morning and remains until about noon, thus giving sufficient time to visit the ancient forts, and slight traces of Roman and Saracenic occupation, or to drive round the fertile plain and gardens (*see* p. 209).

From Bougie there is railway communication with Algiers or Constantine, changing carriages at Beni-Mansour. Daily diligence and carriage services to Setif through the Chabet-el-Akhra Pass. (*See* p. 211.)

Crossing the Gulf of Bougie, the ruins of a Roman town are seen before arriving at Cape Cavallo, beyond which is a small island of a red hue, then the lighthouse of

Djidjelli, a small seaport on the site of the Roman Colony of **Ingilgitis.** The town, formerly built on the west point of the bay, was destroyed by tremendous shocks of earthquake on the 21st and 22nd August, 1856. A new town has been built on the east shore of the bay. Djidjelli is the port to which comes the rich produce of the district between it, Mila, and Constantine, abounding in mineral and vegetable products awaiting development. A light railway is projected from here to Constantine.

Djidjelli was the scene of a terrible disaster and defeat inflicted on the French troops and a battalion of the knights of Malta in 1664. The town had been taken possession of by an army under the command of the Duc de Beaufort by order of Louis XIV. for the purpose of keeping the Kabyles and the pirates in check. But a large force of Turkish troops with artillery arrived from Algiers, and dissensions arising between the French and Maltese commanders the troops became demoralised, and the Comte de Gadagne in command of the Maltese ordered them to embark. The French army was overcome with a loss of 1,500 men, and 90 guns and mortars.

Djidjelli continued to be the head-quarters of a nest of pirates, who frequently captured French fishing boats, and in 1839, after the Kabyles had made prisoners of a shipwrecked crew, the town was captured by the French under Colonel de Salles

When the snow has left the mountains, the ascent of

Babor and **Tababort** can be made on horseback (or mules) in a little less than three days (or Babor alone in one day) with the assistance of guides. Several rivers are crossed, and the scenery along the route is very beautiful. Forests of cedar and African pine crown the summit of the mountains.

From Djidjelli (or Bougie) some interesting **Stalactite Grottoes** can be visited (small charge for admission). They are situated about 6 miles from **Ziama,** where at one of the two or three small inns visitors may sleep, and after inspecting the caves proceed through the Gorge du Chabet, or to Bougie, as may be preferred.

Continuing the voyage from Djidjelli, in about four hours the steamer passes the most northerly point of Algeria, at **Cape Bougiarone,** lighthouse visible twenty miles, rounding which into the bay of Collo is reached the cultivated district of

Collo, a well-protected little harbour with a considerable coasting trade. It was a city of importance during the Roman empire. Occupied by General Baraguay d'Hilliers in 1843, it is now a small French village in a fertile cultivated plain, in the streams of which are the only waters where trout are found in Algeria. Market on Friday.

Leaving Collo, and passing the island of **Srigina,** then **Stora** (page 271), the steamer arrives at

Philippeville, thirty-eight hours' steaming from Algiers. The steamer comes alongside the quays at Philippeville the same as at Bône and Algiers, thus saving the annoyance of small boats, and as a rule remains several hours, enabling passengers to visit the town.

Hotel: Grand Hotel. (Cook's Coupons, Series A, B, and C, accepted.)

Philippeville (population, about 20,000) may be called the gate of the province of Constantine and the harbour of the city of Constantine. It is altogether a European town. During the great storm of January, 1878, the harbour works were destroyed, and every vessel in the harbour was wrecked. The damage has been solidly made good, and the outer and inner basins and dock are protected by a long, broad breakwater. The present excellent harbour of Philippeville was practically completed in 1892, but is still undergoing extensive alterations, and it is calculated that when the additional works are carried out it will be the largest and safest harbour in the colony, not excepting the harbours of Bône and Algiers.

. **British Vice-Consul,** J. O. Watson.

The modern town differs in nothing from the usual French style of Algerian cities. The inhabitants are chiefly Maltese and Italians, with a tolerable amount of French and other European nationalities. The Arab element is there in a very small minority. A railway connects the town of Philippeville with Constantine, a distance of only 87 kilometres (*see* p. 273).

Philippeville, the old **Rusicane** of the Romans, which was destroyed in the fifth century, has very little history, either Roman or modern. General Negrier came to Rusicane, the actual site of Philippeville, which was then but a desolate spot, marked by heaps of Roman ruins, in 1838, after the storming of Constantine, and established his headquarters, with 4,000 men, there. The ground was purchased from the Kabyle tribe, who claimed to be the owners of the land, for the sum of 150f.

Nearly all the Roman antiquities have disappeared; the few that were spared are preserved in the ancient theatre.

Philippeville is in direct communication with Marseilles by

Steamers of the Compagnie Transatlantique, leaving Marseilles for Philippeville direct Saturday noon; and *viâ* Bône Tuesday 5 p.m.; leaving Philippeville for Marseilles direct Friday noon, and *viâ* Bône Monday midnight.

Steamers of the Compagnie de Navigation Mixte (Touache) leave Marseilles for Philippeville Thursday noon, due Friday, 9 p.m.; leave for Bône Saturday 10 a.m., due Saturday, 3 p.m.; leave Bône Sunday noon, arrive Philippeville Sunday 5 p.m.; leave Monday noon, due Marseilles Tuesday 9 p.m. (*Dates subject to alteration*).

There are five squares or **Places,** called: The **Place de la Douane,** the **Place de la Marine,** the **Place Corneille,** the **Place de l'Eglise,** and the **Place Bélisaire.** The streets are wide and regular. Many of them are very steep, like those of the Arab quarters of Algiers, owing to the amphitheatre position of the town. The **Rue Nationale** is the most important thoroughfare, and the centre of the trade of the city.

The fountains are well supplied with water ; and there are very important Roman cisterns, in thorough repair, especially those of the **Fort d'Orleans,** which hold an enormous quantity of pure water.

The **Cathedral** was built between 1847 and 1858. It contains a fine work of Van Dyck—Christ at the Tomb.

Most of the monuments and houses of modern Philippeville are built on old Roman ruins and cisterns. The **Theatre,** for instance, a stately edifice, capable of holding 600 to 700 people, is built on two large Roman cisterns.

The principal industries are its distilleries, tanneries, breweries, conserves, wool, skins, fruit, fish, and cattle. Iron mines and marble quarries are worked in the neighbourhood.

The excursion from **Philippeville** to **Stora** (5 kilometres) is interesting, affording a charming promenade through the most beautiful scenery. The road borders the sea at a great elevation, passing through gardens and villas of the prettiest effect. The lovely gardens inaugurated by Count Landon at Saf-Saf are on this road, and are open to public view by the courtesy of the present owner (see p. 241). They extend from the road to the sea.

Stora is built on a steep rock above the sea. Its curious detached little church being the only building visible from the distance.

The bay is magnificent, and was the principal harbour of the province of Constantine before the creation of Philippeville, which has entirely ruined its prosperity.

The only commerce of any importance remaining to Stora is the sardine trade, still very considerable.

PHILIPPEVILLE TO CONSTANTINE BY RAILWAY.

Table of Distances.

Stations.	Distance in kilometres from Philippeville.	Stations.	Distance in kilometres from Philippeville.
Philippeville ...	—	Bougrina	37
Damrémont ...	6	Col des Oliviers ...	46
Saf-Saf	11	Condé Smendou ...	60
Saint Charles ...	19	Bizot	74
Robertville-el-Arrouch ...	30	Hamma	80
		Constantine ...	87

From Philippeville to **Constantine** the journey occupies from three and a-half to four hours. There are four trains a day in each direction, the times from Philippeville being at 4.55 a.m., 8.19 a.m., 12.5 p.m., and 4.5 p.m. *Time table subject to alteration.*

The railway belongs to the P.-L.-M. Company, and cost an immense sum of money before it was completed, owing to the engineering difficulties. It must be borne in mind that the line has to cross a chain of mountains and to accomplish a difference of level of 2,500 feet between the two termini at Philippeville and Constantine. The views on the road are very captivating; but on arrival one misses, unfortunately, the grand scene of the site of Constantine and its approaches, which is one of marvellous beauty. For the requirements of the service the line has necessarily been carried along the rocks above Constantine, and therefore the splendid *coup d'œil* above referred to is entirely lost.

A few words will be sufficient to describe the route between Philippeville and Constantine.

Leaving the station the train passes through a tunnel under **Djebel Addouna**, then travels along the valley of the **Oued Saf-Saf** to the stations of **Damrémont** and **Saf-Saf**, the stations and villages of **Saint Charles** and **Robertville** amidst fertile corn lands. Five kilometres from **Robertville-El-Arrouch** station is an important weekly market (El-Arrouch), where the Kabyles bring considerable quantities of oil, cereals, skins, wool, and tissues.

Beyond **Bougrina** the train ascends to **Col des Oliviers** (buffet), situated between two valleys overlooked by **Djebel Toumiel** (2,950 feet), whence the zig-zag ascent of **El-Kantour** is made, affording beautiful views over the Valley of **El-Arrouch.** The train next descends to

Condé-Smendou, a pretty well-shaded village of 2,200 inhabitants, and the valley of **Oued Smendou** to the station and village of **Bizot,** fertile in fruit trees and vines. Soon the hot springs of **El-Hamma** are seen forcing their way out of the limestone rocks, and irrigating the district, which in consequence produces excellent corn, figs, and other fruit. When the station of

Hamma is reached the journey quickly ends at

CONSTANTINE.

Post and Telegraph Office, Rue d'Orléans, near the Place du Palais.

Carriages. The course, 1f. 25c.; per hour, 1st hour, 2f. 50c., 2f. after; per half-day, 10f.; per day, 20f.

Tramways. Horse tramways from the Place de la Brèche, through the Rue Nationale, to the railway station, etc., 10c.

There are three good hotels, the **Grand Hotel,** the **Hôtel d'Orient-St. Georges,** and the **Hôtel de Paris.**

The **Grand Hotel** is fitted with new furniture, clean, comfortable, and well appointed. The cuisine is excellent and attendance good. Telephone, large smoking and conversational rooms, baths, etc.

The **Hôtel d'Orient-St. Georges** is very comfortable, furnished in accordance with modern requirements, good and punctual service. Moderate charges.

The **Hôtel de Paris,** opposite the Grand Hotel, has good public rooms and bedrooms; moderate charges. (All three hotels accept Cook's Coupons, A, B, and C.)

This, the chief city (population 49,700), of the Department of Constantine, stands 600 metres above the level of the sea. It is a fortress of the first order ; and by reason also of its exceptional natural position, the city may be said to be practically impregnable. The town of Constantine is situated on an isolated block of rocks, rising perpendicularly

s

nearly 1,000 feet, encircled on the north and east by a deep ravine, from 60 to 70 metres wide, through which runs the river Rummel. It resembles Monaco in its principal outlines, minus the sea.

Divided by its natural dyke, through which flows the **Rummel** (River of Sands) the city is united to the suburbs of El-Kantara and Mansourah by an iron bridge (El-Kantar) of only one arch, high above the ravine. Beneath the bridge the river disappears below a vault of rocks, emerging further on in the form of rapid torrents and waterfalls.

CONSTANTINE.

This imposing fortification of rocks enabled Constantine to withstand 80 sieges. Taken by the Romans in the fourth century, it assumed the name of the Roman Emperor Constantine, by which it is known to this day.

Falling later into the hands of the Arabs, it became a centre of literary and religious life, like Tlemçen and Bougie. In 1535 Constantine fell into the power of the Turks, and formed part of the province of Algiers.

In 1836 Constantine repulsed an attack by a French

army under Marshal Clauzel, who was compelled to retreat to Bône, where he was recalled to Paris; but another expedition under General Damrémont and the Duc de Nemours was successful, and Constantine became French in 1837. General Damrémont was killed on this occasion, and great were the losses on both sides; hundreds of the inhabitants who attempted to escape by means of cords into the ravines below were dashed to pieces.

Constantine is now a well-built and prosperous city, with wide, open streets, large squares, such as the **Place de la Brèche,** the two **Squares** laid out as gardens, the **Place du Palais** and the **Place Négrier.** The principal buildings are the **Casbah,** the **Mosques, Cathedral, Prefecture, Theatre, Palais de Justice, Civil Hospital, Markets, etc.** Constantine is rapidly extending towards the southwest. The new Faubourg of St. Antoine is becoming a populous suburb, and the eminence between this faubourg and the corn market, called Koudiat Aty, is being metamorphosed for the construction of houses and streets on a great scale by a company whose headquarters are at Lyons. The chief commerce of Constantine is in leather, wool, and cereals; the corn market near the Place Valée being the most important in Algeria. The manufacture of woollen garments, such as haïcks and bournouses, is a very flourishing industry; also of those called gandouras, which are a mixture of silk and wool. There is a large consumption of dates and oil, and in the Arab quarters the manufacture on a small scale of native jewellery, of articles in wood, leather, and metal, will attract the notice of visitors.

Constantine, like Algiers, is divided into an Arab and a French town, the Arab town being the most interesting to visitors, with its native cafés, shops, and Oriental customs. The streets in the latter are extremely narrow, the houses almost meeting overhead. The different trades have each a special quarter assigned to them, as at Cairo or Tunis.

The **Cathedral,** which was formerly the old Mosque of **Souk el Rézel** ("Gazelle's market"), situated between the Rue de France and the Place du Palais, contains beautiful marble columns, coloured tiles, arabesques, and a richly-carved cedar **mimbar.**

The **Place du Palais** is one of the chief popular resorts containing some shops and cafés, also

The **Palace of Ahmed Bey** and the **Military Club.**
A military band plays in the square on Sunday and Wednesday. There are also musical and dramatical societies, fencing and shooting clubs.

The **Place Négrier,** at the north end of the Rue de France, is planted with trees, and bounded on one side by the **Mosque of Salah Bey,** or the **Mosque el Kattani.**

The **Djama el Kebir,** or Great Mosque, situated in the Rue Nationale, is built on the ruins of a Roman temple, but contains nothing to attract the attention of visitors.

The **Djama El-Kattani** (on the western side of the Place Négrier), as mentioned above, is the most beautiful of all the mosques of Constantine. Beyond the door (where it is necessary to wait for permission and slippers to enter), a flight of marble steps leads to a court from which the mosque is visited. White marble columns divide and subdivide the naves, above which the painted ceiling is surmounted by cupolas. The walls are covered with coloured tiles, the " Mihrab," supported by four columns, is a lovely specimen of plaster carvings, and the " Mimbar " is of white Italian marble, onyx, and agate.

The **Djama El-Akhdar,** in the Rue Combe, is in some respects a poor imitation of the previous mosque, but the octagonal minaret, 78 feet in height, with a projecting gallery, is very handsome.

The **Synagogue,** in the Jewish quarter, at the bottom of the Rue Thiers, is a spacious building without any architectural pretensions. The services of the Temple are held in a large apartment on the first floor. A Jewish wedding ceremony (open to everyone) is a very interesting sight.

There are several other mosques in the city of Constantine, but they are of less interest than those described.

The **Palace of the Bey el Hadj-Ahmed** is an excellent type of Arab architecture. The gardens, four in number, enclosed in the quadrangles of which the palace is composed, are surrounded by handsome galleries, where a fine view of the orange and citron trees and flowers below is enjoyed. The frescoes on the walls are original, but weak in conception and execution.

The palace is not old, having been built by El-Haj Ahmed, the last bey, between 1836 and 1830, but it contains thousands of old tiles, and works of art taken from palaces and mansions of Constantine; marble columns innumerable, brought from Italy and other places; and in the upper rooms, now occupied by the French general, are numerous specimens of carved oak and cedar. The bey's pavilion is now the private office of the general. In the corridor is a statue of the mother of Caracalla, the only *perfect* one ever found in Algeria.

The premises adjoining the palace are occupied by the various military offices, in one of which permits to visit the Casbah can be obtained on presentation of an address card. No permission is necessary for admission to the palace, the custodian on the left of the entrance door will show the various rooms and objects of interest, for which a small fee will not be refused.

The **Mairie**, or Town Hall, a handsome, newly-erected building, is situated at the corner of the Rue de la Tour and the Rue Sauzai, where all the municipal business of the city is transacted. The façade is very handsome, and the interior corresponds with the exterior, the fittings and decorations in marble from Aïn-Smara being especially worthy of notice. In the same building are lodged an important **Library**, and

The **Museum**, containing a very good and interesting col lection of ancient pottery and earthenware ornaments, arms, jewellery, and medals (open daily 1 to 4, except Tuesday). There is a handsome and celebrated statue of " Winged Victory," twenty-three inches high, discovered in the old Casbah in 1858.

The **Prefecture**, another recently-constructed edifice of bold proportions and design, is hidden between the old houses of the Rue Leblanc and the Boulevard du Nord, the entrance to the council chambers being in the Boulevard.

The apartments of the Prefect are splendidly furnished, the reception rooms and the Mauresque salon being admirable.

The **Casbah**, which from the time of the Romans has been the stronghold of the possessors of Constantine, is placed on the highest point south of the town, and above the deep ravine of the Rummel. The view from its ramparts or from the arsenal gardens is glorious, looking over the fertile plains extending from the town to the range of mountains in the horizon. Many Roman inscriptions have been discovered here. In the Casbah are barracks for

3,000 troops, a large military hospital, immense Roman cisterns, and a Roman store for corn.

From the Casbah, or from the Place de la Brèche, descending the Philippeville road, a most enjoyable if rather fatiguing walk can be made to the baths of the **Sidi-Meçid**, returning by the Corniche road.

After passing some Arab *gourbis* a steep road leads to the **Lavie Flour Mills,** beyond which are the cascades or falls in the ravine of the Rummel, more or less voluminous according to the season, but the surroundings always magnificent. Overhead towers the tremendous rock from which criminals and unfaithful wives were precipitated—the Tarpeian Rock of Constantine.

Crossing by a wooden bridge a path winds under the cliff to the baths of

Sidi-Meçid, situated in lovely gardens, a favourite resort of the Constantinois, being cool in summer and milder than Constantine in winter. The bathing accommodation consists of one very large bath, two smaller ones, and three private baths enclosed. The water, which is quite clear, has a temperature of 104° Fahr., and can be used at all seasons. A restaurant for light refreshments is attached to the establishment.

From Sidi-Meçid a path leads to the Corniche road, along which, with superb views of the ravine and rocks, the return walk is made to the famous bridge of El-Kantara and Constantine.

If so disposed after the above excursion the visitor can explore the

Chemin des Touristes cut through the ravine, one entrance to which is close to the town end of the bridge. Or he may prefer to postpone his visit to another day, from the opposite direction, starting from the Place de la Brèche down by the Arab market and the abattoir (slaughter-house) to the **Pont du Diable** (Devil's bridge), and there enter the Chemin des Touristes. In either case a fee of 2f. is charged for each person.

The visit is one the like of which cannot be experienced elsewhere, and should be made by the majority of travellers— but it is certainly exciting and fatiguing, and should not be undertaken by delicate or nervous ladies.

Until some years ago portions of the route were inaccessible owing to the accumulation of vegetation and filth, but such places have been cleared and converted into cultivated slopes and paths, and on the right bank of the river a road has been cut in the face of the rock, accessible by staircases. This enables tourists to see to perfection the bed of the river with its stupendous rocks overhead, to examine the remains of ancient bridges, the bas-relief of the lady and the elephants on a portion of one of the arches of the old bridge, over which the present iron structure of El-Kantara was built in 1863. Wild pigeons, storks, eagles, and other birds fly in and out this strangely charming spot, one of the most impressive and bizarre it is possible to meet with.

Numerous walks, drives, and distant excursions may be undertaken in and around Constantine, but unless the traveller stays several days he will be unable to visit many of them, and after all the great attraction of Constantine is its exceptional site and immediate surroundings, the gorge of the Rummel, the Corniche road, and the Chemin des Touristes, which can easily be visited in a day. A three or four hours' carriage drive to the town suburbs will suffice for visiting the El-Kantara bridge, built on the ruins of one of the five bridges which formerly at various points united the two sides of the ravine ; the plateau of Mansourah, the Pépinière, the pretty village of Sidi-Mabrouk, the racecourse, the remains of the Roman aqueduct, etc., returning by the new quarter called Coudiat-Aty to the Place de la Brèche, and the hotel.

For those who wish to make longer excursions the following list is given :—

To **Bou Merzoug Spring** (about 35 kilometres south of Constantine).

Es-Soumah and Mahadjiba.

El Kheneg (Ravine similar to that at Constantine, and ruins, 34 kilometres).

Sidi Mabrouk.

The **Hamma** (a pretty village, with hot springs, 7 kilometres by rail).

Salah Bey.

Oudel and **Aïn el Bey** (about 7 kilometres, fine view of Constantine).

Resuming the voyage from Philippeville to Tunis, *viâ* Bône, the steamer proceeds past the **Ras el Hadid,** or Iron Cape, thence before the **Cap de Garde,** the **Fort Génois,** and Bône is reached almost immediately.

BÔNE.

Bône, or Bona, population of the commune 43,000, was founded by the Arabs after the destruction of Hippo or Hippone by the Vandal King Genseric in 431 A.D. It is called Annaba (jubube trees) by the Arabs, and has constantly changed rulers, until it became permanently occupied by the French in 1832.

Bône is a bright, clean, healthy town, one of the prettiest in Algeria, situated in the middle of a superb bay. It is abundantly supplied with water from Mount Edough, is well drained, well lighted, and many of the streets are broad, handsome thoroughfares; but some of them, owing to the nature of the ground, are steep and narrow.

The **Casbah,** the oldest portion of the town, was erected by the Bey of Tunis in 1300.

British Vice-Consul. H. Scratchley, M.V.O.

United States Consular Agent. G. S. Burgess.

Belgian Consul. Abel de la Croix.

Italian Consul. D. Geralamo.

Hôtel d'Orient. Cook's Coupons, Series A, B, and C, accepted.

Hôtel du Commerce. Cook's coupons, Series R, accepted.

The **Harbour,** which rivals and even surpasses that of Algiers, is the most protected, and consequently the safest, of the Algerian harbours. The cost of the enlargements and works now nearly finished, will amount to about 22 million francs. The new quays have a length of 1,200 metres, and a communication is being made from the harbour to the northern end of the Cours Jérôme-Bertagna by a tunnel, which will be prolonged as far as the "pépinière" (or nursery), outside the town.

The **Cours Jérôme-Bertagna** (formerly Cours National a favourite promenade between the cathedral and the harbour, is planted with trees and flowers, on each side of which are the finest shops and public buildings, the theatre, hotels, banks, etc. The bronze statue of **Thiers** by A. Mercié is at the southern extremity, and at the opposite end is the modern **Cathedral of St. Augustine,** a conspicuous monument in the Byzantine style of architecture with an imposing façade.

The mosques are none of them of any considerable importance. The Great Mosque occupies one side of the Place d'Armes. The Mosque Djama-El-Bey with an elegant exterior was built with materials taken from the ruins at Hippone. The Arab town has been entirely destroyed.

There are barracks for 3,000 men, a military hospital with 600 beds, and a civil hospital for 320 patients.

From Bône there is a railway line in communication with Constantine, the journey occupying seven hours. Steam Tramway to La Calle (*see* p. 284).

Bône is in constant steamer communication with Marseilles, Algiers, Tunis, Oran. etc.

MOSQUE IN BÔNE.

From Marseilles by the Compagnie Générale Transatlantique, Tuesday, 5 p.m., direct ; Saturday, noon, *via* Philippeville.

By the Compagnie de Navigation Mixte (Touache). Thursday. noon. *via* Philippeville. By the Société de Transports Maritimes à Vapeur, Monday or Tuesday, 6 p.m., direct.

To Marseilles, Thursday, 6 p.m., *via* Philippeville. Cie. Transatlantique.

Tuesday, 11 p.m., direct. Cie. Transatlantique.

Sunday, noon, *via* Philippeville. Cie. de Navigation Mixte (Touache).

Thursday, noon, direct. Soc. de Transports Maritimes.

Passengers land and embark on the quay.

Quite a number of charming excursions can be made from Bône, but the nearest and most interesting is to the site of the ruined city of **Hippone** (about 2 kilometres, south) where St. Augustine lived and died.

In the third and fourth centuries Hippone vied with Carthage in being the most prosperous city of Roman Africa. The town was ruthlessly destroyed by the Vandals in 431, with the exception of the cathedral and St. Augustine's Library. It was afterwards occupied by Belisarius in 534 ; but in 697 it fell into the power of the Arabs, who completed the work of destruction ; and all that can now be seen of its ancient splendour are the ruins of its immense aqueduct and cisterns recently repaired to supply Bône.

St. Augustine was ordained priest at Hippone A.D. 390, remaining there as priest and bishop about forty years, dying in 430, a year before the city was destroyed. St. Augustine was buried in the Basilica of Hippone, but later his remains were taken to Cagliari, religiously kept there for 200 years, and then removed to Pavia, where they now are in the cathedral.

A bronze statue was erected by the Church to his memory in 1840 amid the ruins of Hippone, the spot chosen being, it is believed, the site of the monastery where St. Augustine lived and wrote his " Confessions " and his " City of God." The statue was consecrated and enclosed with rails, and a religious service is always celebrated on the anniversary of his death. On the crest of the hill overlooking Hippone a spacious and ornate **Basilica**, dedicated to the Saint, has been recently erected—a replica of the cathedral at Carthage. The nave has a double row of rose-coloured marble columns, and the high-altar is composed of specimens of marble from various African quarries. Underneath the basilica is a handsome crypt where low mass is said on Sundays, at which the aged people of the hospice close by are present.

An unusual feature of the basilica is that the entrance door faces the east, and the chancel faces the west.

In the midst of the fertile plain below the church, where formerly stood Hippone, some valuable archæological discoveries have been lately made. At the dwelling-house on a farm that had been occupied by M. Chevillot and his family for many years, the proprietor had occasion to make a cellar underneath the villa, and in doing so came unexpectedly in the presence of a well-preserved mosaic of considerable dimensions. This led him to extend his excavations in other parts of the grounds, and in every direction (so far as his means have allowed) magnificent mosaics and portions of large edifices have been exposed to view.

The mosaics are still undisturbed, and visitors are freely admitted to inspect them. Photographs can be purchased at the villa. Some of the mosaics, such as the Triumph of Boccus I., the Muses, Fish and Fruit, the Enlèvement de Ganymede, are of the finest possible work, equal to anything found in Tunisia or Pompeii. A coarser black and white mosaic, some sixty feet long, is thought to have been the floor of a passage to some public baths, but the extent of the great buildings at present disclosed is insufficient to signify the nature of such constructions.

On every account it is devoutly to be wished that excavations on a serious and systematic scale should be continued on ground which is second only in interest to that of Carthage.

A new road along the shore, called the **Corniche Road,** affords an agreeable drive of about six miles to

Fort Génois, and two miles beyond to

Cap de Garde. Leaving Bône by the western end, the road skirts the shore to the pretty bathing station of **La Grenouillère,** and passing the Batterie du Lion, continues through the **plage Luquin** and the **plage Chapuis,** with their villas and bathing establishments, as far as the **Oued Koubba.** A continuation of the Corniche amidst striking land and sea views leads to the important **Fort Génois,** 350 feet above sea level, beyond which is the lighthouse (the light visible thirty-three miles), some few hundred yards from **Cap de Garde,** where can be visited the quarries from which Hippone was built, and some curious grottoes.

Time permitting, an interesting excursion can be made by railway to the iron mines of

Mokta el-Hadid, 34 kilometres, or 21 miles (three trains a day to Aïn-Mokra in one and a-quarter to one and a-half hours). This has been a wonderful property ; at one time all above ground was almost pure iron, but the rich veins have been exhausted, and the work now carried on in galleries is not so profitable. The mines belong to the same company as the mines at Béni-Saf, near the River Tafna, which are still very prosperous, shipping large quantities of hematite iron ore containing 60 per cent. of iron, see p. 186. Half-way between Bône and Mokta el-Hadid, near the station of **Oued Zied,** is the so-called

Lake Fetzara, a swampy plain, some 35,000 acres in extent which in winter is covered with wild fowl.

Another delightful excursion from Bône is to ride or drive through the

Forest of Edough, and make the ascent of **Djebel Edough**, 12 kilometres. Passing through the suburb of the Colonne Randon and the small plain of Bône, the road leads to the south side of the mountain to penetrate a forest of oaks and cork oaks to the Alpine village of **Bugeaud**, 3,000 feet above the sea, with an uninterrupted view over land and ocean.

A mile beyond the village of **Edough** are the works connected with the large cork business of the Company who own thousands of acres of cork oaks in the forest. From here a path leads to the old Roman aqueduct, near the **Fontaine des Princes**, in a delicious valley thick with creepers, ferns, neaths, myrtle and other flowers in luxuriant wildness, watered by the same stream as supplied Hippone 2,000 years ago, and supplies Bône to-day.

Beyond Bône the coast becomes more hilly and wooded, **Cape Rosa**, with lighthouse and fixed light visible 12 miles, is next passed; then, weather permitting, the steamer stops at

La Calle, a little town of 5,500 inhabitants, also reached by steam tramway from Bône (*see* p. 281). This was the old French factory known by the name of **Bastion de France**. La Calle has always been famous for its coral fisheries, which are still carried on, but on a reduced scale. The Island of **Tabarca**, once a Roman colony (*see* p. 383), then **Cap Negro**, and **Bizerta** (*see* p. 376), are passed on the road to Tunis.

Travellers to Tunis are recommended to land at Bizerta, and proceed to Tunis by railway, 98 kilometres, or 61 miles, if they wish to visit the remarkable harbour formed by Lake Tindja or Bizerta, the value of which as a military Mediterranean station was doubtless one of the reasons which decided the French to occupy Tunis. The lake, completely landlocked, is about 8 miles long by 4½ miles wide, with an average depth of 36 feet, affording perfect anchorage of about 35 square miles for the very largest vessels. A wide and deep canal, provided with quays for vessels and cargoes, connects the lake with a spacious commercial harbour, where large numbers of ships can anchor, but no merchant vessels are allowed to enter the lake. In a few years Lake Bizerta will be converted into a first-class military and naval arsenal, and rendered impregnable, thus becoming a splendid strategical harbour between Gibraltar and the Suez Canal (*see* also p. 376).

The steamer proceeds past the tunny fisheries at Ras Sidi El-Mekki, near the lake of Porto Farina, into which the river Medjerda flows, Ras Es-Zebib, and doubling Cape Carthage, in view of the site and ruins of mighty Carthage, soon arrives at

Goletta (or La Goulette), which until quite recently was the port of Tunis, and Tunis could only be reached by railway, 17 kilometres. Now a canal has been cut through the lake with large basins at both the Goletta and Tunis ends *(see* p. 337).

LIST OF MODERN BOOKS RELATING TO ALGERIA.

Atterbury (A. P.), Islam in Africa. New York, 1899.

Auclert (H.), Les Femmes Arabes en Algérie. Paris, 1900.

Ballu (A), Guide illustré de Timgad. Paris, 1903.

Barail (General du), Mes Souvenirs. Paris, 1895.

Barclay (E.), Mountain Life in Algeria. London, 1882.

Bourmand (F.), Le Maréchal Bugeaud. Paris, 1895.

Bridgman (F. A.), Winters in Algeria. in-8. New York, 1890.

Castéran (A.), L'Algérie Française. Paris, 1900.

Charveriat (F.), A travers la Kabylie et les Questions Kabyles. Paris, 1900.

Dessoliers (F.), Organisation politique de l'Algérie. in-8. Paris, 1894.

Estoublon (R.), Collection complète de la Jurisprudence Algérienne depuis la conquête jusqu'à 1895. 24 vols. in-8. Alger.

Estournelles de Constant (Baron P. de), Les Congrégations religieuses chez les Arabes et la Conquête de l'Afrique du Nord. in-12. Paris, 1887.

Fage (R.), Vers les Steppes et le Oasis (Algérie-Tunisie). Paris, 1906.

Fillias (A.), L'Algérie ancienne et moderne. in-12. Alger, 1875.

Giffarel (P.), L'Algérie : histoire, conquête, colonisation. Paris, 1888.

Graudin (L.), Le dernier Maréchal de France (Canrobert). Paris, 1895.

Guillaumet (G.), Tableaux Algériens. Paris, 1888.

Haufort (F.), Au Pays des Palmes. Biskra. Paris, 1897.

Hilton-Simpson (M. W.), Algiers and Beyond. London, 1906.

Knox (Alex. A.), Algeria, or the New Play Ground. London, 1881.

Lallemand (C.), De Paris au Désert. Paris, 1895.

Laveleye (Emile de), L'Algérie et Tunisie. Paris, 1887.

Lebon (A.), La Politique de la France en Afrique, 1896-98. Paris, 1901.

Leroy-Beaulieu (P.), L'Algérie et la Tunisie, 2nd ed. Paris, 1897.

Masquéray (E.), Souvenirs et Visions d'Afrique. Paris, 1894.

Nugent (E. G.). A Land of Mosques and Marabouts. London, 1894.

Pease (A. E.), Biskra and the Oases and Desert of the Zibans. London, 1893.

Playfair (Sir R. L.), The Scourge of Christendom. London, 1884. Ditto. Supplement to the Bibliography of Algeria, from the earliest times to 1895. London.

Pommerol (Madame J.), Among the Women of the Sahara. Translated by Mrs. A. Bell, London, 1900.

Prax (V.), Étude sur la Question Algérienne. in-8. Bône, 1892.

Revue Africaine. Alger. Yearly since 1856.

Rinn (L.), Histoire de l'Insurrection de 1871 en Algérie. Alger, 1891. Marabouts.

Robert (G.), Voyage à travers l'Algérie. Paris, 1891.

Sauvaigo (E.), Les cultures sur le littoral de la Mediterranée. Paris, 1894.

Sabatier (C.). Touat, Sahara et Soudan. Paris, 1891.

Shaw (Thomas, D.D., etc.), Travels or Observations relating to several Parts of Barbary and the Levant. Oxford, 1838-46.

Sommerville (M.), Sands of Sahara. London, 1901.

Tchihatcheff (M.), L'Algérie et Tunis. Paris, 1880.

Tripp (C. Howard), Beautiful Biskra. London, 1903.

Vignon (L.), La France en Algerie. in-8. Paris, 1893.

Villot (Capitaine), Mœurs, coutumes et institutions des indigènes d'Algérie. .in.12. Paris, 1872.

Wahl, L'Algérie. 3rd ed. Paris, 1904.

Wilkins (A.), Among the Berbers of Algeria. London, 1900.

(*See* also pp. 119, 140, 167, and 402).

WORKS OF FICTION.

W. Le Queux. Zoraida.

G. Flaubert. Salambô (Translation).

A. Daudet. Tartarin of Tarascon (Translation).

Grant Allen. Tents of Shem. Dumaresq's Daughter.

W. E. Norris. Mdlle. de Mersac. Billy Bellew.

TUNISIA.

PART I.

TUNISIA.

FROM ALGIERS TO TUNIS,
By Rail.

Stations.	Distance in kilometres.	Stations.	Distance in kilometres.
	From Algiers.		From Bône.
		Duvivier ...	55
Algiers	—	Medjez Sfa	65
Kroubs (*see* p. 216)	448	Aïn Tahamimine	74
		Aïn Afra ...	79
		Laverdure ...	91
		Aïn Sennour	97
		Souk=Ahras	107
		Tarja ...	116
	From Kroubs.	Sidi Bader ...	124
		Oued Mougras	140
Kroubs	—	Sidi el Hémessi ...	156
Bou Nouara	14	**Ghrardimaou**(bft.)	166
Aïn Abid ...	26	Oued Méliz	176
Aïn Regada...	41	Sidi Meskine ...	187
Oued Zenati	52	**Souk el Arba** (bft.)	199
Bordj Sabath	69	Ben Bachir	210
Taya	80	Souk el Khemis	222
Hammam Meskou-		Sidi Zehili .	235
tine	96	Pont de Trajan B.	248
Modjez Amar ...	101	Oued Zargua	269
Guelma (buffet) ...	111	Medjez el Bab	289
Millésimo (halt) ...	118	Bordj Toum	304
Petit...	123	Tebourba	321
Nador	135	Djédéida	330
Duvivier (buffet)		Manouba	345
(Branch for Bôna)	148	Bardo	349
		Tunis	355

HISTORY OF TUNISIA.

TUNISIA, originally called Lybia, was already in a fairly civilised state when the Phœnicians landed on its shores about twelve hundred years B.C. They founded new cities, such as **Outih** (Utica), **Hadrumetum** (Susa or Sousse), **Hippo Zarytus** (Bizerta), and **Thines** or Tounès (Tunis).

The most famous historical city of Africa, the ancient Carthage, was built 800 years later by Phœnician emigrants, accompanied, as the fable by Virgil relates, by the unfortunate Princess Elissa, daughter of Belus, King of Tyre, or Dido, flying from her brother Pygmalion, by whom her husband had been assassinated. The fable describes how Dido purchased from the natives as much land as could be covered by a bull's hide, then cunningly cut the hide into the narrowest possible strips, and thus enclosed sufficient space on which to build her city, at first called **Byrsa** (meaning bull's hide), and afterwards Carthage.

The new colony flourished, and soon became eager for colonial extension. Under Malkus, Carthage acquired the Balearic Islands and Corsica. Hamon the Great and his sons Hasdrubel and Hamilcar added to its prosperity.

Later, the city under Hamilcar (B.C. 481) allied itself with Xerxes against the Greeks, and made war on Sicily. Beaten by the Prince of Syracuse, under the command of the celebrated Timoleon Carthage was compelled to accept peace.

In 406 B.C., under the command of Hannibal, son of Gisco, Carthage sent a large army to invade Sicily, which was partially successful; and Hannibal returned to Carthage with the spoils of war, and to prepare for the complete conquest of Sicily. On arrival a second time in Sicily the army was destroyed by plague and famine, and a treaty disastrous to Carthage was concluded with Rome.

Invaded by Agathocles, B.C. 310, and by the famous Pyrrhus, King of Epirus, Carthage was reduced to one possession.

The Carthaginians refused to evacuate Sicily, and augmenting their troops, succeeded in compelling Pyrrhus to embark for Tarentum.

Then commenced the struggle between Rome and Carthage for the possession of Sicily, Spain, and of Africa, which lasted 120 years.

Soon began the tragic events known as the three Punic

T

Wars, which terminated B.C. 146 with the capture of Carthage by Scipio, who destroyed the forts and fortifications. The city was given over to the flames, and, under the eyes of her defeated husband, the wife of the commander threw herself and children into the burning temple of Æsculapius.

The **First Punic War** was a struggle between Rome and Carthage for Sicily during twenty years, which ended in the loss of that island to Carthage and other possessions, also of her prowess on the sea, B.C. 242 ; and thus began her fatal decline.

From 240 to 237 B.C. occurred the war of the mercenaries, which ended in favour of the Carthaginians, but she lost Sardinia, which was attacked and captured by the Romans.

The **Second Punic War** saw Carthage deprived of her fleet and her colonial possessions. Under Roman protection, Masinissa, King of the Massylians (one of the great Numidian tribes to the west of Carthage), defeated Syphax, king of another Numidian tribe of Masæssylians, in B.C. 212 ; but during the absence of Masinissa in Spain civil troubles ensued, Syphax conquered the country, and reigned at Cirta (Constantine).

In B.C. 204, Scipio, with the help of Masinissa, defeated Syphax, and Masinissa was given Cirta, with royal titles.

All this time the famous Hannibal, son of Hamilcar, had been absent from Africa.

When the Carthaginians had somewhat recovered from their losses in the First Punic War they sought to make fresh conquests in Spain.

Hamilcar, after subduing the rebellious tribes all along the African coast, passed over into Spain, taking with him his son Hannibal, then nine years of age, who swore implacable hatred to the Romans.

Hamilcar gained many victories, founded Carthagena, which became the emporium of Carthage in Spain, and, after various successes during several years, fell fighting. He was succeeded by his son-in-law, Hasdrubal, who remained governor of Spain for nine years, and was murdered by a Gallic slave. At his request the Senate of Carthage elected Hannibal as his successor, then only twenty-four years of age, but who had already given proofs of great generalship and courage.

After strengthening his army in Spain and in Africa, Hannibal resolved to march upon Italy, and in the spring of 218 B.C. quitted Spain, and entered on his tremendous task with 90,000 infantry, 12,000 cavalry, and forty elephants. Crossing the Pyrenees, the Rhone, and the Alps, he encountered enormous difficulties, and, on reaching .Italy, his army was reduced to 30,000 infantry and 6,000 cavalry, to oppose an army of 200,000 Roman soldiers.

He took Turin, and owing to superior generalship gained several victories, which caused Cis-Alpine Gaul and Liguria to revolt from Rome and become his allies; in this way his army was increased to 90,000 men.

Other victories followed at **Cannæ** and at **Allia;** but Hannibal, requiring reinforcements from Spain and from Carthage, which never arrived, hesitated to march on Rome. Full of resources and spirit, the Romans formed new legions Hannibal was kept in check, but maintained his position for years with varied successes and reverses.

His brother, coming from Spain with 50,000 men, was defeated at **Placentia**—a crushing blow for Hannibal. By this time, Scipio, who had gone with an expedition to Spain, conquered all the Carthaginian fortresses and possessions there; the last Punic troops were driven from Cadiz, and Scipio crossed over to Africa, where he besieged **Utica,** and afterwards annihilated the armies of Hasdrubal and Syphax near **Testour.**

Then it was that Hannibal, who had been sixteen years in Italy, was recalled by the Senate to oppose Scipio. Hannibal returned to Africa B.C. 203, landed at **Hadrumetum** (Sousse), was joined by Masinissa, and took command of 50,000 men and eighty elephants at **Zanna,** where Scipio gave them battle; and notwithstanding his great generalship and prestige, Hannibal was entirely routed, compelled to sue for peace, and practically to abandon Carthage to his rival.

Hannibal retired to Hadrumetum, but was invited by the Senate to come to Carthage. Scipio remained at Tunis. The terms of peace were indeed hard, but Hannibal advised the Senate to accept them. Carthage was to give up Spain, Sicily, all islands in the Western Mediterranean, her fleet, elephants, and prisoners, to pay 10,000 talents (two million pounds sterling) in fifty years, and to make no war without the consent of Rome.

Peace was concluded, Carthage in reality becoming the subject of Rome; and thus ended the Second Punic War.

Hannibal then devoted himself to the regeneration and resurrection of his country. He adopted measures for the repression of abuses and robberies, for the reform of the finances, and for the revival of agriculture. He planned steps to secure allies abroad; but spies from Rome denounced him, and, the Roman Senate demanding his surrender, he left Carthage, and sailed from **Zella** (now Mahdia) for Armenia, B.C. 195. He visited King Antiochus of Ephesus, and King Prusias of Bithynia; and the Roman Senate again and again demanding his surrender, he swallowed poison and died 183 B.C., at the age of sixty-five years.

The **Third Punic War.** Rome and Carthage remained at peace for some fifty years, when, at the constant instigation of Cato the elder, hostilities were commenced against Carthage. Scipio Emilianus (the second Africanus) laid regular siege to the city, which, by degrees, fell; and, as already stated, the fortifications and public buildings were burned.

A **Roman Colony** was established, B.C. 116, by Caius Gracchus, and, under various consuls, little progress was made. War was declared against Micipsa, King of Numidia, who was eventually taken, and died in prison.

Numidia was given to Juba, son of Hiempsal, and Africa was ruled by the sons and relatives of Pompey, from Rome. But Julius Cæsar, wishing to destroy this government, came to Africa with a small force, landed at Hadrumetum (Sousse) B.C. 46, was joined by native tribes, and defeated the Pompeian army at **Thapsus,** where Cato, Scipio, Varus, Afranius, Juba, and others were killed or killed themselves. In less than six months Cæsar exterminated the party of Pompey in Africa; he then crushed that party in Spain, and returned to Rome as dictator.

Numidia and Cirta, the capital, were placed under the rule of Sallust and P. Sittius. In B.C. 26 Juba II., who had been educated at Rome, was married to Selene, daughter of Anthony and Cleopatra; and Augustus Cæsar, thinking it politic to win the goodwill of the Numidians, made Juba II. king of his father's dominions. The capital was removed to Jol and called Cæsarea (*see* p. 115).

After the death of Juba II., a learned and good king, the Mauretanians revolted under the rule of his son, and troubles ensued. The inhabitants were badly governed by the consuls and pro-consuls, but order was restored from Rome, the retention of the riches of N. Africa being essential to the empire; and, although insurrections were frequent in the next 300 years, it was during that time when prosperous cities were founded, the ruins of which we now see in Tunisia and Algeria.

Christianity was introduced at the end of the second century, the natives supporting the various sects with passion, causing much disturbance. In the fourth century as many as 580 Christian sees are mentioned by historians.

The Roman emperors wished to extirpate Christianity in Africa, and their persecution extended all over the province. Noble women, like Perpétué and Felicité, perished in the amphitheatre at Carthage; Cyprian, Bishop of Carthage, was beheaded; at Cirta, Lambessa, and Utica hundreds of Christians were burnt in furnaces.

About 311 A.D. the Bishops of Numidia and Carthage quarrelled over the election of a Bishop of Carthage, and the schism of the Donatists took place owing to the violence of Bishop Donatus, and in many cities there were two bishops. An enquiry instituted by the Emperor Constantine decided against the Donatists, who were deprived of their churches, and their bishops banished. They retired to the Atlas mountains, and were guilty of constant ravages and disturbances.

At this time arose the man who, from being a teacher, then a priest, became Bishop of Hippo (*see* p. 282), and, as St. Augustine, was the greatest figure of the Catholic Church in Christian Africa for thirty-five years. He strongly opposed the Donatists, who gradually lost ground.

Africa continued under various civil and military governors appointed from Rome, and was more or less in a condition of bad government and anarchy from A.D. 326 to A.D. 429, whence dates the

Vandal Period.—Boniface, Governor of Africa, treasonably invited Genseric, King of the Vandals in Spain, to invade the country, and, on being joined by native Moors and the fanatical Donatists, he conquered the provinces, destroyed the cities and monuments, and in A.D. 439 occupied Carthage, which had again become a prosperous city.

Genseric died A.D. 477, and his successors, after fifty years of the same oppressive rule and extortions as their predecessors, gave occasion to the advent of the

Byzantine Period, when Belisarius, from Constantinople, with a large fleet and army, landed and took possession of Carthage, completely routing the Vandals, A.D. 533. Belisarius was succeeded by his celebrated general, the eunuch Solomon, who was killed before Theveste (Tébessa), *see* p. 262. The Berbers, oppressed as before, revolted, but were compelled to submit ; and when, a century later, the Khalifa Othman, with an army of 20,000, reinforced by 20,000 Egyptians, invaded the country, the Berbers made common cause with them as they had previously done with Genseric.

Gregorius, then Governor of Africa, met the invaders with an army of more than 100,000 men, but was defeated by the Mohammedan general. Thus commenced the

Arab Period, when the country was ruled by Emirs, appointed by the Khalifas, with their capital at **Kairouan.**

In the year 662, Okba-ben-Nafy invaded Byzacium, and gained possession of the Island of Djerba, Sousse, and Bizerta, and in the year 670 founded the city of Kairouan (p. 368), which became the holy city of Africa, and the capital of the Mussulman possessions in the Magreb.

The African church was swept away, the Berbers and Moors adopted the religion of the Arabs, a swarm of Arabs from Upper Egypt spread over the country to the Atlantic, and for nearly twelve centuries Tunisia (and Algeria) lived under the Mussulman rule, until the French occupation of Tunisia in 1881.

The history of the Mussulman rule can be divided into five periods :—

1. The **Arab Period,** from the conquest to A.D. 1041, when various dynasties succeeded each other, the Fatimites, the Aglabites, etc., and the Khalifa Aroun er-Rashid sent presents to Charlemagne.

2. The **Berber Period,** when the Zirites (followers of Ziri, who built Algiers), always at war, and during whose reign the Normands from Sicily occupied Sfax and Tripoli, were succeeded by the Almohades until 1270, with their capital at **Tlemçen.** At this date also Louis XI. occupied Tunisian soil with a French army, but being carried off by the plague hostilities ceased. To the Almohades succeeded the Hafsides, when Mulai Hassan fled to Spain, and then ensued the

3. **Spanish Period.** Charles V. sailed from Barcelona with a large army, seized Goletta, and marched on the capital,

in spite of the vigorous defence of Barbarossa, and placed Mulai Hassan on the throne as his regent, but no sooner had Charles V. left than his vassal was dethroned, and the Spanish occupation weakened until it was replaced by the

4. **Turkish Period,** under Smane Pasha, during whose sway piracy and slavery became rampant. In May, 1577, Henry III. of France established a consulate at Tunis, and owing to the cruel treatment of Christians (when, amongst others, St. Vincent de Paul was kept a slave for two years), the French fleet was sent into Tunisian waters to suppress piracy and slavery.

In April, 1655, the entire piratical fleet of the Bey of Tunis was destroyed by Admiral Blake in the port and arsenal of Porto Farina, one of the boldest and most splendid naval actions in English history. During the following

5. **Husseinist Period** piracy was arrested, reforms were inaugurated, public works carried out, and debts were contracted. A financial commission was established, and owing to the various French interests involved, and to disputes between the Beys and the French companies, it was evident that sooner or later a French protectorate would be proclaimed, and Tunisia practically become as much a part of French territory as the colony of Algeria.

It was not long before this state of affairs became realised, and, without enquiring too closely into the various excuses more or less serious, it is sufficient to state that in April, 1881, a French expedition was sent to punish the **Khroumirs**, said to be an uncivilised, troublesome, and independent tribe occupying some miles of sea coast and the mountains between Tabarca and Fernana on the borders of Tunisia and Algeria (*see* p. 381).

This proved to be a short and easy task. Tabarca, Bizerta, and other places were occupied ; the French general advanced on Tunis, and at very brief notice the Bey was required to sign a treaty officially announcing the protectorate of France.

The anger of the Mohammedans was naturally greatly aroused, and the population, disgusted with the Bey, refused to acknowledge his authority, so much so that when the French soldiers were withdrawn a general revolt ensued, and the French Government were obliged to send a large army to subdue the various tribes, to occupy the cities from one end of the Regency to the other, and thus to the present day, every important point is garrisoned by French troops.

REGENCY OF TUNISIA.

Until 1881 the rulers of Tunisia were hereditary Beys, who acknowledged the suzerainty of the Porte.

The Regency of Tunisia may now be considered an informally annexed dependency of France, nominally under the dominion of the Bey, but in reality under the control of a French Resident. By treaty, May 12, 1881, "the occupation is to cease when the French and Tunisian authorities recognise by common accord that the local government is capable of maintaining order." By a convention signed 10th July, 1882, France administers the country and collects the taxes in the name of the Bey, who is granted a civil list of £37,500, and the princes a sum of £30,000.

The Bey of Tunis, **H. Sidi Ali Bey,** was born in 1817, and died June 11, 1902. His heir, **S. A. Sidi Mohammed Hadj Pasha,** residing at the Marsa, succeeded to the Beylick the same day, but died May 11, 1906. The present ruler (succeeded May 12, 1906) is **S. A. Sidi Mohammed=en= Naçer Bey,** a cousin of Sidi Ali Bey.

The French protectorate in Tunisia has been most successful, and the country is better governed and more contented than any other of the French possessions. The reason of this is that the French have wisely left the natives to govern themselves, at least in appearance, and have not insisted on that excessive centralisation which governs distant provinces directly from Paris, without any reference to local conditions. The consequence is that Tunisia has prospered steadily since France assumed the protectorate, and is in a far better state than Algeria or any other of the colonies. In Tunisia the Bey nominally makes all the laws, but he does it on the advice of a Resident and six French administrators, who, with the help of the Bey's Ministers and certain representatives of the French colonists, really decide what measures are to be taken. Even if the Bey has but little power, his presence on the throne is a guarantee to the Mussulman population that their prejudices are being respected. The French Resident-General is **M. C. Alapetite. M. le Général Herson** commands the French division of occupation.

In his very interesting work, *Carthage and Tunis, Past and Present*, published in 1869, Amos Perry, twice United States'

Consul for the City and Regency of Tunis, thus sums up in the last chapter of his book the prospects of the political future of the country :—

"I am, then, persuaded that the country will at length come under the acknowledged protection and control of France, if not with the consent and approbation of other nations, probably without violent opposition. Such, at least, is the manifest tendency of affairs at the present time, notwithstanding a species of state-craft employed to produce a counter result.

"The malady is too deeply seated to be overcome by empirics in the name of diplomacy.

"The Gallic Eagle, already scenting the prey, prepares to clutch it, despite the lion's growl, and all the shrieks and howls that may be raised as he enjoys his repast."

A singularly far-sighted prophecy.

GENERAL DESCRIPTION OF TUNISIA.

Tunisia, in the north of Africa, is situated between latitude 32° 20′ and 37° 25′ N., and longitude 7° 40′ and 11° 15′ E.

Bounded on the north and east by the Mediterranean, and on the south by the Sahara, it is physically a continuation of Algeria, the frontier station being at **Ghrardimaou,** 189 kilometres, or 118 miles, from Tunis. It comprises an area of 44,920 square miles, and has about 1,800,000 inhabitants.

Tunisia is divided by the Atlas mountains running from north-east to south-west, and four distinct regions exist between the extreme north-east of Africa and the Sahara.

The principal river is the **Medjerda** (ancient Bagradas), 300 miles in length, which rises in the beautiful valley of **Khamisa,** in Algeria, between Tébessa and Souk-Ahras, amongst the ruins of the ancient city of **Thubursicum Numidarum**, enters Tunisia by the wild gorges of **Rebka,** continuing its sinuous course through the fertile plains of **Djendouba**, on to **Tebourba** and **Djédéida**, then, running north-east between Bizerta and Tunis, falls into the sea through the salt lake at Porto Farina. It thus traverses some of the richest districts of Tunisia associated with many of the most important historical events of the Roman occupation.

The railway very frequently travels along the left bank of the Medjerda, winding around valleys and gorges of great beauty, or crossing it to penetrate the hills by tunnels to enter some vast plain.

The next most important rivers are the **Miliane,** the ancient **Catada;** the Oued el-Kebir or Ez-Zan (River of Oak Trees), and the Oued Kerma (River of the Fig Tree), both of which fall into the sea near the frontier at Tabarca. Other rivers may be mentioned, such as the Oueds Sfa, Melah, Méllègue, Tefkhasid, Tessäa, Zargua (Gray River), Rezla, Endoum, Zeroud, Djilma, Hatob, Gabès, Sbeitla, Sbita, El Hammam, etc., but many of these are dry for more than half the year, and others are lost in the arid desert soon after leaving their source.

North of the Medjerda is a narrow slip of cultivated land, a well-watered mountain region, with oak and cork oak trees. South of the Medjerda are the mountains and hauts plateaux of the **Tell.** Between the Tell and the Sahara are large plains, called the **Sahel,** with forests of olive trees, not very fertile, but growing crops of cereals after abundant rain ; and south of all is the **Sahara Desert,** composed of sand dunes, oases, and *chotts.*

CLIMATE.

The climate of Tunisia is one of the healthiest and best on the south shores of the Mediterranean. The average temperature at Tunis and generally on the coast is 64° Fahr., and in winter the thermometer seldom falls below 48° Fahr. in the daytime. The summer months are very hot, especially in the interior, where the thermometer often marks 120° Fahr. in the shade.

The seasons succeed each other at regular periods. Winter, with intermittent rains, commences in December, and ends in March. Spring begins in March, and gives way in May to summer, which ends in September, to be succeeded by autumn until November, a delightful season. March, April, and May are very pleasant months, when vegetation shows itself in all its magnificence. June is the harvest month. The two most fatiguing months are August and September, when storms and south winds prevail, and the country is dried up by the sun.

January and February are generally the most rainy months, but if the winter has been exceptionally dry and warm, then rain falls freely in spring on the thirsty earth. The winds are variable and frequent. Those of the north-west and of the east prevail in winter, those of the south and east in summer.

At the period of the Equinoxes violent winds set in from the south-west.

The water supplied to Tunis is perfectly pure, and can be drunk with impunity—being brought from the springs at the foot of Mount Zaghouan in closed aqueducts and pipes (see p. 361).

The drainage of Tunis has been remodelled, and is now perfect. Pumping stations exist at intervals, and there is plenty of water for flushing.

INHABITANTS.

The great majority of the population are either **Arabs** or **Berbers.** To these must be added the **Moors,** the **Negroes** from the Soudan, and the **Jews,** who are very numerous in Tunisia. French, Maltese, Italians, and other Europeans swell the total in ever-increasing numbers.

In the absence of a census it is difficult to be certain, but the entire population of Tunisia in 1905 was estimated to be about 1,800,000, composed as follows :—

Mohammedans (Natives)	1,680,000
French	30,000
Italians	90,000
Jews	60,000
Maltese	12,000
Other Nationalities	4,000
	1,876,000

The **Arabs** are descended from the Arab immigration which overran the country in the 7th and 8th centuries. They are a nomad race, living in tents and moving from place to place, their only occupation being agriculture and raising sheep.

The Arabs, with some splendid exceptions, are generally of medium stature—face long and firm, complexion pale.

The **Berbers** live in baked mud or stone houses, roofed with tiles, in the mountain districts, as do the Kabyles in Algeria, who are descended from the Berbers (see p. 205).

The Berbers and the Kabyles are usually tall and well built ; high neck and broad shoulders ; complexion dark and forehead square ; occupation, farmer or mechanic.

The **Moors** have sprung from various races, and are Arabs

who live in towns following some occupation other than agriculture, such as shopkeepers, artisans, embroidery, and perfume distilling. They are conspicuous for their showy dress and indolent habits.

The Moors are called Hadras by the natives, Moors by Europeans. They are generally above the medium height and size, with sallow complexion black eyes, straight nose, and black beard.

The **Jews** in Tunisia are divided into two classes—the Leghorn Jews, engaged principally in exchange and banking transactions, professions, and business. The others are native Jews, often poor, working as tailors, shoemakers, embroiderers, butchers, and small shopkeepers.

The great immigration of the Jews into North Africa took place from Spain, Portugal, and Genoa in the 15th and 16th centuries. But their own writers say they found on arrival in Tunisia and Tripoli numbers of their brethren originally from Judæa.

Jews are now met with in every city and town, also in the mountain districts, and in the oases of the Sahara.

In Tunis, the wealthy Jews, and families in easy circumstances, live in luxurious or comfortable houses in the higher parts of the city, and only the poorer classes live in the *harra*. European Jews dress like other Europeans ; native Jews much like Mussulmans.

Tunisian Jewesses of the ordinary type have a costume very similar to that of the Mussulman women, only more full and flowing, and of better material. Married women wear pointed head-dresses to conceal their hair, but their faces are exposed. In full or visiting dress the eyes and eyebrows are powdered, face rouged, necklaces and finger rings worn, clothes embroidered.

After marriage the ladies mostly acquire formidable not to say ungainly proportions.

The **Negroes** in Tunisia number about 25,000, and of these 3,000 inhabit Tunis, engaged as servants, pedlars, bakers, and small shopkeepers. They are generally clad in white costumes, adorned on holiday occasions with very bright colours. Originally the offspring of slaves from the Soudan, they are Mohammedans with superstitions of their own, and given to frantic dancing and wild music at certain seasons.

Of the Europeans the **Italians** are the most numerous. The majority (60 per cent.) are engaged as workmen of various kinds, and next in order come tradesmen and small shop-keepers, agricultural labourers, merchants, bankers and agents, clerks and assistants, sailors and fishermen. About 75,000 are from Sicily and Southern Italy, and 10,000 from Sardinia and other districts.

The **Maltese,** although bigoted and superstitious, are industrious and peaceful. They are very frugal, with a view of saving enough to enable them to return to Malta.

The **French,** rapidly increasing in numbers, are contributing more than any other European nation to the prosperity and expansion of the country. In 1881 there were under 1,000 French in Tunisia; to-day (1908) there are over 30,000, not including 18,200 men and officers of the army. Large sums have been invested in commerce and in bringing hundreds of thousands of acres of land into cultivation.

Under the French Protectorate roads have been opened up in every province; ports have been created or enlarged at Bizerta, Tunis, Sousse, and Sfax; the postal and telegraph services have been extended in all directions; a hundred schools have been opened; a lycée for boys, and a secondary school for girls have been established in Tunis; the natives have been treated with consideration; and everywhere life and property are safe.

AGRICULTURE, HORTICULTURE, Etc.

Tunisia is essentially an agricultural country, and the cultivation of cereals is very great and important. Hard wheat, almost the only quality known, is grown on 440,000 hectares (1,100,000 acres). Barley, which ripens quicker and is more profitable than wheat, is cultivated to the same extent. Oats and maize are grown on only a few thousand acres. The soil, rich in potash, and the warm climate account for the excellent crops secured. Both wheat and barley are exported in large quantities to Marseilles, the former for the manu-facture of semolina, vermicelli, or macaroni: the latter for malting purposes. The **Olive Tree** is cultivated on some 200,000 hectares (500,000 acres) in the districts of Bizerta, Tunis, Cape Bon, Zaghouan, Sousse, Sfax, Djerba, etc. The trees, numbering 15,000,000, in good years produce 35,000,000 litres of olive oil.

Other plants rich in oil are the flax, castor, and colza.

The cultivation of the **Vine** is a profitable industry rapidly increasing in extent. French colonists have planted vineyards over more than 40,000 acres, from which some 320,000 hectolitres of wine are produced annually.

Fruit trees of various kinds flourish in all the littoral, such as the fig, orange, lemon, almond, tangerine, apricot, cherry, plum, banana, apple, pear, peach, medlar, carob, chestnut, and mulberry. The natives eat freely of the prickly pear (Barbary fig), and cattle are fed on the raquettes.

In the south 2,000,000 date palms produce dates to the value of 8,000,000f. per annum, the fruit being of excellent quality, and exported all over the world. The trees come into flower in April, and the fruit is ripe in October.

Alfa or esparto grass grows wild on the **Hauts Plateaux,** especially to the south of the forest of Tersana, much of which is exported to Europe for the manufacture of paper.

Forest trees extend over 5,000 square kilometres, of which 1,200 kilometres are covered with valuable oak and cork-oak trees in the Khroumir district, between La Calle, Tabarca, and Souk el-Arba. The oak timber is used principally for railway and building purposes; the cork-oak is stripped of its bark every ten years, and after the age of thirty-five or forty years, a single tree when stripped will yield several hundred pounds weight of cork.

Another valuable tree is the acorn oak, of which the fruit is roasted and ground into flour, or eaten whole.

The Aleppo pine, poplar, cedar, thuya, pomegranate, shumac, tamarisk, and myrtle are all utilised for some industry.

As in Algeria, so in Tunisia, the forests have been greatly· damaged by fires caused by the Arabs, partly to obtain more land for their sheep, and partly from ill feeling against the French; but all this has been put an end to, the forests are now protected, and young trees have been extensively planted by the Forest Department. (*See* also p. 135).

FLORA AND FAUNA.

Flora. In addition to some indigenous plants most of the flowers that are grown in Europe are to be seen in the gardens and country districts of Tunisia, such as roses, geraniums, wallflowers, lilies, stocks, carnations, violets, mignonette, anemones, poppies, marguerites, lupins, auriculas, honeysuckle, asters, narcissi, daffodils, hyacinths, and other bulbs, etc., many of which are in flower during autumn, winter, and spring. In the fields and hedges various kinds of iris, ferns, cyclamen, wild arum, the familiar daisy (marguerite), and buttercup ; the stately agave and the prickly pear are always in evidence ; and in the spring the fields are covered with wild flowers, yellow, white, and blue, an unusual proportion being blue.

The climate of Tunisia is particularly favourable to the culture of plants from which perfumes are extracted, including the rose, geranium, jessamine, clematis, and violet. The natives cultivate also the poppy, saffron, and henna for industrial purposes.

Vegetables of all kinds are grown in profusion, especially in the neighbourhood of large towns, where potatoes, beans, green peas, tomatoes, and artichokes are ready in winter and early spring for exportation to Europe. Other vegetables which are abundant are onions, leeks, beetroot, cucumbers, lettuces, lentils, cauliflowers, carrots, asparagus, parsnips, turnips, mushrooms, cardons, and celery, some of these yielding crops all the year round.

Fauna. The panther, tiger-cat, and lynx are sometimes found in the district of Aïn-Draham, Béja, El-Fedja, and the Khroumir forests. The hyena and jackal are found more or less frequently all over the country. The fox, genet, mongoose are mostly in evidence in the mountain districts, but sometimes frequent the suburbs of Tunis. The loutre (otter) is met with at Tabarca and along the river Medjerda. Wild pig and wild goat are found everywhere, especially in the forests near Mateur, Aïn-Draham, and in the south at Djebel Seltoum. Gazelles of several kinds inhabit the plains and hills of the centre of Tunisia ; antelopes are numerous on the frontier of Tripoli. The pine forests of Ghrardimaou, Tébessa, and Fériana give shelter to Barbary deer. Falcons are snared and trained in the neighbourhood of Kef, and a " Chasse au Faucon " is highly esteemed in the plains of Le Sers.

The **Domestic animals** of Tunisia comprise the dromedary, employed as carriers and in the fields, the horse, the donkey, cattle of Guelma and Mateur, sheep, and goats.

Game of every kind is plentiful in Tunisia, and shooting is permitted to those provided with a gun licence, to be obtained from the Direction of Public Safety. The season lasts from August 15 to the beginning of February and from March 15 to April 15 for birds of passage.

Guns, firearms, and gunpowder or filled cartridges may not be imported. Empty cartridges with percussion cap may be brought, and can be filled in Tunis. For shooting birds on Lake Bahira (Lake of Tunis) it is necessary to obtain permission from the fishing concessionnaires, the Société des pêcheurs réunis (*see* also p. 338).

In addition to the big game alluded to above, the smaller game, affording good sport in various districts of both North and South Tunisia, includes hares and partridges in abundance ; bustards (poule de Carthage), herons, pelicans, cormorants, eagles, and other birds of prey ; plovers, wild duck, woodcock, snipe, grèbes, flamingoes, quail (in April and May), wild pigeon, ortolan, sand grouse, and numerous small birds according to the season.

The **Fish** of Tunisia belong to the Mediterranean system, and at every point of its 1,300 kilometres of coast the variety and quality of the fish add considerably to the riches of the country. From Cape Rosa to Cape Bon the sea yields large quantities of tunny, dories, red and grey mullet, conger, anchovies, soles, and sardines; with turbot, whiting, and mackerel less abundantly ; and of shell-fish, excellent lobsters, prawns, oursins, mussels, crawfish, and oysters.

The largest catches of fish are made at Tabarca, Bizerta, Tunis, Sidi-Daoud, Sousse, Monastir, and Sfax.

In the warm springs of Djerid small fish live in a temperature of 130° Fahr. ; these have no bones, muscles, or eyes, and die in the air or in cold water.

From Cape Bon, along the south coast of Tunisia, the sponge, pulp, and coral fisheries yield a revenue of several million francs.

HOT SPRINGS.

From time immemorial the mountains of Tunisia have provided hot springs of mineral waters, and in every direction one sees ruins of ancient baths and hot springs of the Romans. Amongst the best known and most important thermal sources may be mentioned :—

Hammam-Lif (Hammam-el-Enf, bath of the nose), 17 kilometres from Tunis (*see* p. 357).

Hammam-Korbous, or **Kourbès** (Carpi), Roman baths

near Cape Bon. There are three sources, the principal one with a temperature of about 133° Fahr. (*see* p. 362) being in the middle of the village.

Hammam=Djedidi, between Zaghouan and Hammamet, two sources, 149° Fahr.

Hammam M'siada, near Béja, a small establishment with two piscines, the property of the municipality.

Hammam=Ouled=Zeid, at **Djebel=Meid,** near Souk-Ahras. Sulphur waters. Temperature 90° Fahr

Hammam=Tassa, 10 kilometres south-east of Souk-Ahras. Baths frequented by the Arabs, efficacious in skin diseases. Temperature, 110° Fahr.

Hammam=Ouled=Messaoud, between Souk-Ahras and La Calle. Temperature, 117° Fahr.

Hammam=Soussa, 6 kilometres north of Sousse.

El=Hamma de Gabès, 26 kilometres to the west of Gabès. Roman baths recently restored, situated near the charming oasis of **El=Hamma** (*aquæ Tacapitanæ*).

El=Hamma de Tozeur, between Gafza and Tozeur, in the Sahara, a few miles only from the latter, a large town and oasis containing 9,000 inhabitants and half a million palm trees, on the north-west of the **Chott-el-Djerid.**

El-Hamma is a small oasis with 900 inhabitants and 50,000 palm trees. The waters from the source, **Aïn Choua,** have a great reputation among the natives for diseases of the blood and skin (*see* p. 273).

Hammam Zeriba. Old Roman baths, situated 9 kilometres from Zaghouan in a wild and picturesque gorge of the **Djebel bou-Hamida.** The baths have been restored by the Arabs, and in a large building surmounted by a koubba are two piscines, constantly supplied with water at a temperature of 122° Fahr., much used by the natives for various forms of skin disease (*see* p. 361).

In most cases the waters mentioned above contain sulphate of lime, chloride of sodium, sulphate of magnesia, and secondary mineral substances, differing to some extent in the respective proportions and in the degrees of heat.

With the exception of those at Hammam Lif the baths at present are little used; but in view of the pure air, abundance of sunshine, and the general therapeutic advantages to be obtained from the warm baths and genial winter climate,

U

many of the districts named are suitable for the establishment of sanatoria.

At **Aïn-Garci,** near Enfidaville, between Tunis and Sousse (*see* p. 363), is an excellent cold spring of effervescing mineral water, the property of a Tunis company, by whom the water is delivered in bottles in all the chief towns of the Regency.

INDUSTRIES.

Although essentially an agricultural country there is no reason to doubt that in course of time many important industries will flourish. It is true that so far no coal has been found, but in other minerals the country is rich; iron, copper, tin, lead, marble, and phosphates abound, and are only waiting the opening up of communications, and the investment of capital to become sources of revenue. For centuries the natives have been engaged in the manufacture of carpets, burnous, of red caps or chechias (the fez in Turkey and the tarboosh in Egypt), of blankets, tiles and perfumes. They are also proficient in the tanning and dyeing of skins, in the making of mats, baskets, and harness.

European capitalists are principally engaged in producing cereals, oil and wine, or in extracting phosphates, in working mines and salt lakes, or in the coral, sponge, and other profitable fishing industries already mentioned. Europeans of smaller means find profitable occupations in building operations, in the manufacture of various pâtes (pastes), bread, soap, and in retail business generally.

COMMERCE.

The exports and imports of the Regency are steadily improving, and the exports to France are increasing yearly, thanks to the Customs' regulation of 1890, which allows the importation of cereals, oils, and cattle into French ports free of duty.

Of fifty-eight million francs of exports in 1905, twenty-four were received by France; Italy, England, and Algeria coming next in order, with nine, eight and six millions respectively.

Of ninety-one million francs of imports in the same year, forty-eight came from France, eight from Algeria, seven from England and Malta and five from Italy.

The chief articles of export are olive oil, wine, cereals,

fruits, vegetables, alfa, cork, cattle, horses, mules, wool, skins, woollen tissues, carpets, wax, salt fish, pulps, sponges, coral, minerals, and soap.

The imports consist of animals, butter, cheese, lard, skins, flour, dried fruits, tea, sugar, coffee, beer, spirits, petroleum, coal, steel, iron, cement, marble, bricks, wood for building, tiles, tissues, thread, silk, clothing, furniture, matches, paper, books, machinery, jewellery, and hardware.

The following artiles of *French* or *Algerian* orgin are admitted free of duty, viz.:—Wool, silk, sugar, pure olive oil, linseed oil, butter, wheat, corn, malt, spirits, liqueurs, metals, thread, tissues, carriages, and animals.

The following articles are *rigidly prohibited*, viz.:—Arms and munitions of war, tobacco, hashish, salt, vine stock, fruit, vegetables of every kind, playing cards, uncurrent gold and silver coin, filled cartridges, gunpowder.

MONEY.

Notes of the Bank of France circulate in Tunisia (as well as in Algeria, *see* p. 33), also those of the Bank of Algeria, issued for amounts of 1,000, 500, 100, 50 and 20f. There are local coins (gold) of the value of the value of 20 and 10f.; 5f. pieces of the Latin Union take the place of local coins; local coins are also in circulation as follows: 2f., 1f., ½f. (silver) and 10 and 5c. (bronze).

HOTELS.

Those hotels at which THOS. COOK & SON's coupons are accepted are indicated in the text referring to the respective places (*see* also p. 24).

PART II.

TUNIS.

More ancient than Carthage, Tunis (Thines or Tounès) was gradually supplanted in importance and population by its powerful Phœnician rival. When, however, at the end of the seventh century. Carthage was overthrown, Tunis became the capital. Once during twelve centuries did Tunis fall into the power of the Christians, and of Charles V. in 1535, and then only for a few years, for in 1574 the Turks retook Tunis from the Spaniards, and retained possession until the arrival of the French.

During the Turkish period diplomatic relations were established with France. On May 27, 1577, Henry III. appointed a consul at Tunis. The governing Beys encouraged piracy and slavery to such an extent that France and other countries decided to interfere, and, notwithstanding the friendly relations of Louis XIV. and the Dey Hadj Mohamed Laz, a French fleet, and later on an English fleet, were sent to the Tunisian coast to suppress the ravages of the pirates and to put an end to Christian slavery (*see* p. 295).

During the Husseinist period the new rulers saw the necessity of instituting reforms, and under Ahmed Bey and his successors improvements were effected—a Constitution was published, a plan of the country was made by French engineers, the Carthage aqueduct was repaired to convey water to Tunis. But all this cost money, the finances of the Regency became hopelessly involved, disputes with French subjects and contractors constantly occurred, and on April 4, 1881, it was decided that France should enter Tunis; on April 24 troops crossed the frontier, and on May 12 the so-called treaty of Bardo (*see* pp. 316, 317), was signed in the palace of Kasr es-Said (or K'sar Said).

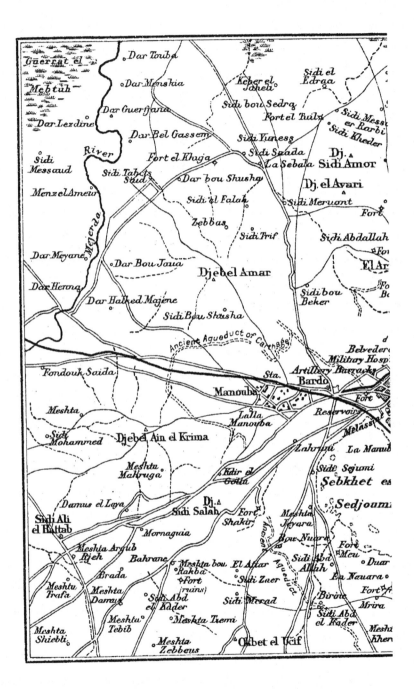

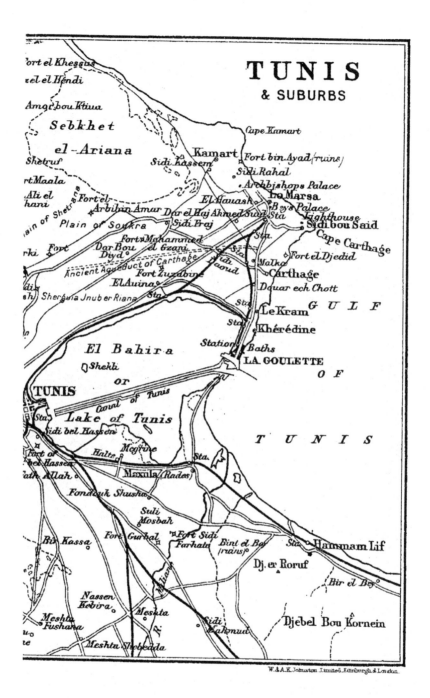

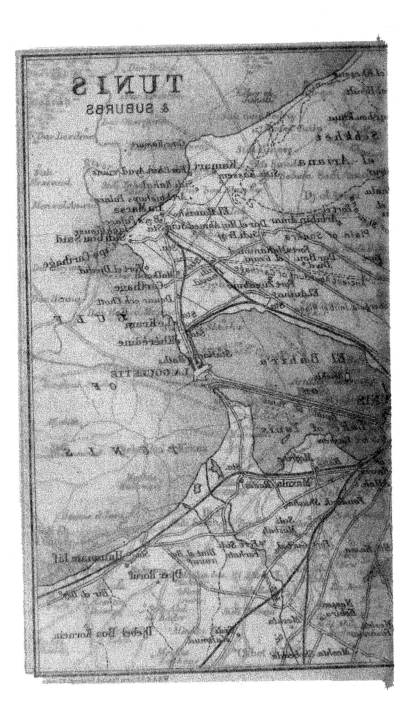

BAB-SIDI-ABDALLAH (GATE).

In June began the repatriation of the French army, leaving only 15,000 men behind, barely sufficient to keep order in the north of Tunisia. As might have been expected, this premature departure was the signal for a native revolt, which started in the south and extended as far as Sfax, Kairouan, the holy city, being the centre of operations. It, therefore, became necessary to re-conquer Southern Tunisia. Sfax was first bombarded by sea and, after reinforcements had been sent from France, Tunis was occupied by the troops on October 10. From Tunis the army marched on Kairouan, which surrendered at discretion on 26th of the same month, one of the principal Arab chiefs having been killed in an engagement a few days before. With the taking of Kairouan the insurrection was practically at an end, and since that time Tunisia has been as safe and peaceful as Algeria.

Tunis was formerly surrounded by a wall and ramparts. Some of these have been demolished to make room for fine streets and boulevards. The city is entered by five gates—

Bab Souika on the north ;

Bab Cartagena on the east ;

Bab el-Djedid on the south ;

Bab al-Djazira on the south ;

Bab el-Bahar, or **Porte de France** on the south-east.

Tunis is divided into two distinct quarters, the old and the new, the French authorities having wisely decided to preserve the native quarter intact. The city and suburbs, however, form four districts, known as—

The Medina, the city in the centre.

The Faubourg of Bab-Souïka to the north.

The Faubourg of Bab-al-Djazira to the south.

The Marine, or European quarter.

The gates by which the native town is enclosed are—

Bab-el-Kadra, towards the Bardo.

Bab-Abd es-Salem, towards the Bardo.

Bab-es-Sajen, towards the Bardo.

Bab-Sidi Abdallah, near the Citadel.

Bab-Sidi Alewa, towards Zaghouan.

Bab-Saâdoun, towards the north-west.

Bab-Fellah, towards the south.

Bab-Benat, below the Citadel.

The three forts that overlook the native town, Bordj-Felfel,

Bordj-el-Andalous, and Bordj er-Rebta, are dismantled, and of no importance or interest.

The French and other Europeans inhabit the new quarter, the Mussulmans the old or higher part of the city, in which, below the Casbah and the Dar-el-Bey (Bey's Palace), are situated the labyrinths of souks or bazaars, each street tenanted by persons of the same occupation, such as jewellers, perfumers, saddlers, woollen dealers, silk merchants, shoemakers, embroiderers, etc. Here may be seen workmen of different trades at their work, cafés, mosques, and a motley crowd of nationalities and races — Tunisians, Algerians, Moroccans, Negroes, Bedouins, Moors, and Jews.

Tunis, "La Blanche," "L'Odorante" was considered by the Mussulmans before the Turkish domination as a city without equal—more beautiful and powerful than all Eastern cities; and to-day, for the Mussulmans of North Africa, Tunis, with the exception of Egypt and Morocco, is still without a rival.

ROUTES TO TUNIS.

The direct route from England to Tunis is *viâ* Calais, Paris, and Marseilles, the journey to Marseilles by the Rapide trains, which only carry first-class passengers, occupying about twenty-two hours.

From **Marseilles to Tunis** the voyage is effected by the steamers of various Companies as under, and occupies about thirty-six to forty hours.

The **Compagnie Générale Transatlantique**, two services weekly.

The **Compagnie de Navigation Mixte** (Touache), two services weekly.

The **Société de Transports Maritimes à Vapeur,** about every ten days.

From **Genoa, Leghorn, Naples, Palermo, Castellamare, Trapani, Marsala, Tripoli,** and **Malta,** Tunis can be reached by steamers of

The **Compagnie de Navigation Générale Italienne.**

From **Palermo** by

The **Compagnie de Navigation Mixte,** weekly.

From **Algiers, Bougie, Philippeville, Bône, Bizerta,** by
The **Compagnie Générale Transatlantique.** Also from
Malta.

Services liable to alteration. Consult Official Time Tables.

Tunis may be reached from England by sea by the North
German Lloyd Steamers from Southampton (fortnightly),
which call at Algiers; thence train or other steamers.
Steamers of the **Prince Line,** from Manchester or London,
call at Tunis every ten days or fortnightly.

From **Oran, Algiers, Biskra, Constantine, Bône,** etc.,
there is a daily service of through trains of the P.-L.-M., East
Algerian, and Bône-Guelma Railways, passengers arriving at
the Tunis terminus, Place de la Gare du Sud, in the centre of
the European quarter.

TUNIS, the Capital of the Regency, has now (1908) an
estimated population of about 177,000 inhabitants, composed,
including the suburbs, of—

French	10,000
Italians and Maltese	17,000
Jews...	50,000
Mussulmans	100,000
	177,000

The principal objects of interest are—

The **Native town** and **bazaars** (Souks), *see* below.

The **Casbah** and **Dar-el-Bey,** *see* p. 313.

The **Bardo** and **Musée Alaoui,** *see* p. 314.

Carthage, *see* pp. 317–334.

The **Belvedere** and **Jardin d'Essai** *see* p. 340.

The **Mosques** (exterior only), *see* pp. 343–345.

The **Municipal Theatre, Casino, and Winter Garden,**
Restaurant, Club, *see* pp. 339, 340.

The **Port** (and canal), *see* p. 335.

Hammam Lif, and various **Excursions,** *see* pp. 356–401.

One of the first visits of the traveller whose stay is limited
will probably be to the

Native town and **bazaars.** To accomplish this comfortably and without loss of time, the stranger should be accom-

panied by a friend who knows the tortuous passages well, or by a guide from the hotel. Afterwards, if opportunity offers, nothing is more enjoyable than to saunter about alone in these quaint, picturesque streets and shops, passing mosques (which no Christian or Jew may enter) and curious old vaulted labyrinths.

It is unnecessary to mention all the bazaars (souks) worthy of being visited; the perfume of jessamine, geranium, or attar of roses will tell the traveller when he is in the neighbourhood of the Perfumers' Bazaar (Souk-el-Attarin); then the crowd and noise caused by the native auctioneer will indicate the Bazaar of the Tailors (Souk-el-Trouk), full of velvet, silk, woollen, and cloth fabrics, gandouras, vests, etc., in all the colours of the rainbow, some of which in the morning are sold by auction. Near the ancient mosque of Sidi-ben-Ahrous, with its beautiful octagonal minaret, in the Rue Ben-Ziad, under its colonnades embroiderers will be seen at work in their diminutive shops, and not far off is the interesting Bazaar of the Saddlers (Souk-el-Serajin), where leather and velvet of every colour take the form of shoes, slippers, saddles, harness, bags, purses, and other fancy articles, either plain or embroidered.

If the visitor proposes to postpone until another day his promenade to the Carpet Bazaar (Souk-el-Farashin), to the Bazaar of Arms (Souk-et-Turc), rich in guns, pistols, daggers, etc., and to the Bazaar of Dyers, most ancient of all, he can, before returning to the hotel, being in the neighbourhood, visit the Casbah and the Dar-el-Bey.

The **Casbah** formerly contained the palace of the Beys, barracks for troops, and the *bagnios* or prisons for Christian slaves. All these buildings have disappeared, and the enclosure is now a fortress, and a caserne for the French garrison. Of the ancient Casbah only the exterior wall remains.

It was here that 10,000 Christian slaves, confined by Kheir-ed-Din, escaped from their prison and opened the gates of Tunis to Charles V. in 1535.

The panoramic view of Tunis and suburbs from the heights of the Casbah is as remarkable as it is extensive.

Descending the Place de la Casbah some 300 yards on the right is the

Dar-el-Bey, or town palace of the Bey, but seldom used

as a residence, except during the month of Ramadan. The palace, built by Hamouda Pasha about 115 years ago, has a very plain exterior, but some of the older rooms, reserved for the Bey and for distinguished visitors, are decorated in the very highest form of Moorish art.

Permission to visit can be obtained from the officer at the palace. The ground floor is occupied as public offices. The upper reception-rooms and private apartments of the Bey are decorated with the delicate Arabesque plaster work, called *Nuksh hadida*, specimens of which we have seen in the mosques at Tlemçen, Constantine, Kairouan, and elsewhere.

Some of the rooms are rich in coloured marble and tiles, and the Hall of Judgment has a splendid dome of most artistic lace-like plaster carving. The modern state rooms are in painful contrast to the others, being furnished and painted in a showy display of red and gold. The late Sidi Mohammed El-Hadj resided at his La Marsa palace in summer, or at K'sar Said (near the Bardo) in winter (*see* p. 316).

Queen Caroline, wife of George IV., resided at Dar-el-Bey in 1816. Other visitors include the Prince de Joinville, the Duke d'Aumale, the brother of William I. Emperor of Germany, and some of England's royal princes.

The large buildings opposite the Dar-el-Bey, formerly souks, belonging to the Tunisian General Khérredine, are now occupied by the Ministry of Finance and the Ministry of Public Works.

One of the most interesting and agreeable ways of spending a short afternoon is by a visit to the

Bardo and the **Musée Alaoui,** distant about two miles from the centre of the town.

This can be made by train from the Nord station, Rue de Rome; by electric tram to the **Bab-Saâdoun,** thence by another electric car to the Bardo; or by carriage, a pleasant drive, passing through the ruins of the aqueduct constructed by the Romans, and destroyed by the Spaniards in the sixteenth century.

The **Bardo** was formerly a vast palace, the winter residence of the Beys, around which other palaces were grouped without much regard to order. The whole was surrounded by a wall with fortifications; now, however, most of these constructions have been destroyed, and the stones thereof form part of the ground reclaimed from the lake to make the new port (*see* p. 335). A battery of six small rifled guns (the gift of Napoleon III. to Mohammed Sadok) and a small caserne for soldiers have been allowed to remain.

Of the Bey's palace some portions have been spared, and in the main building, approached by a flight of steps flanked by eight lions in white marble from Venice, are a number of halls, spacious reception-rooms, and galleries. Permission to visit by card can be obtained from the officials at the Dar-el-Bey.

Amongst the handsome and well-proportioned apartments, the most conspicuous is the vast **Hall of Justice,** the walls covered with portraits of Beys, Victor Emmanuel, Louis Philippe, and Napoleon III. In this hall former Beys came to confirm or alter the sentences of death passed by the Tunisian tribunals, and if confirmed the culprits were executed within the precincts of the Bardo. Executions now take place at La Marsa.

Adjoining the apartments alluded to, in the ancient harem of Mohammed Bey, has been installed an important collection of antiquities and Mauresque and Arabesque decorative carving, under the name of the

Musée Alaoui, which is open free every day except Monday, from 9 a.m. to 11 a.m., and from 1 p.m. to 4 p.m. in winter (October to April); and from 2 p.m. to 5 p.m. during the rest of the year, but the Arab section is not open every day (*see* p. 316).

The museum was opened to the public on April 9, 1891, under the direction of M. de la Blanchère, and the present conservator is M. B. Pradère.

The museum in question, as well as the museum at Carthage (under the devoted care of the Rev. Père Delattre, *see* p. 320), and all the historical monuments or ruins of Tunisia are now subject to an administration of **Antiquities and Fine Arts,** Rue des Selliers, 66, Tunis, of which M. d. Merlin is the Director.

The Museum is entered through a vaulted vestibule on the ground floor, containing some sarcophagi, inscriptions, and other antiquities.

The first floor is composed of three principal apartments, the patio in the middle, with one hall to the right, and another to the left.

The patio, decorated in bad taste, and with the usual marble fountain, has nothing to detain the visitor save some inscriptions and statues. The room to the right, called the

Hall of the Women of the Harem, is indeed a gem of an apartment, in the form of a cross, with a cupola in the centre, and from the four sides or arms of the cross lead four square rooms with cupolas, all covered with lovely Arabesque plaster carvings of every conceivable design. The rooms contain antique sculptures, faiences, old tiles framed, busts, terracotta, glass, arms, and in a separate room a complete collection of cooking utensils. In the opinion of M. de la Blanchère the decorative art displayed in these rooms is worth all that the palace has or will cost.

The **Hall** to the left is one spacious apartment, measuring 60 feet by 37 feet, in which may be seen some of the finest mosaics of the world. The floor is covered with one large important mosaic, measuring 170 yards square, the **Triumph of Neptune,** found at Sousse. The walls are occupied with mosaics from various districts — pagan mosaics from Zaghouan, mosaic of Neptune and the Winds from Sousse, representations of a circus from Gafsa, mosaics depicting a Roman farm found at Tabarca, and from the same place Christian mosaics from the Necropolis, together with figures of birds, fishes, wild boar, varying in size and execution. Here also are collected numerous statues, bronzes, glass, terra-cotta, pottery of every kind and age, the result of excavations in various parts of the Regency.

There is no catalogue for visitors, but a complete illustrated catalogue is being prepared by the " Direction of Antiquities," entitled " Collections du Musée Alaoui."

A **Musée Arabe** was established in 1900 in a small modern building, a good example of local architecture. Entrance to it is gained from the top of the staircase leading to the Antiquities section. Open Thursday and Sunday mornings and Friday evenings.

K'sar Said.—Three hundred yards beyond the Bardo is the former palace of the ladies of the harem, now a winter residence of the present Bey. The palace is surrounded by extensive gardens and orangeries, and although the palace is no longer open to the public, permission to visit the famous orangeries can be obtained.

It was at K'sar Said that the famous treaty of occupation

was signed on May 12, 1881, by the Bey Mohammed Es-Sadok and General Bréard.

Beyond K'sar Said, near the station at **Manouba**, is situated the **Hippodrome**, where horse races take place in the spring. Here also are cavalry barracks, ruins of the great aqueduct, villas, gardens, and the ancient Palace of Hamouda Pasha.

Environs of Tunis.

Every one, however short may be his stay in Tunis, will be anxious to visit the site of ancient Carthage. He may go by rail from the Nord station, Rue de Rome; there are six trains daily, but there is no direct train to Carthage (La Malga) between 11 a.m. and 2 p.m. The visitor is sometimes advised to go also to **La Marsa** the same day, but he will find this very fatiguing after doing justice to Carthage, and there is nothing of any moment to see at La Marsa beyond the villas and views of a pleasant seaside resort.

If the excursion is to last all day it might be desirable to hire a carriage with two horses, fare 15f. or 20f., with or without La Marsa, but this involves a journey of from 30 to 40 kilometres (there and back) over a dreary and uninteresting route. There are two hotels at Carthage, close by the entrance to the museum grounds, where lunch can be served, but it is well to give notice as to requirements.

A half-day's visit for those whose time is limited, or for those who contemplate making more than one visit, can be recommended, leaving Tunis by the 2 p.m. train, and hiring a carriage at Carthage station to drive to the cathedral, museum, and principal places of interest (*see* below), fare 5f., and 1f. for the driver, returning to Tunis by train at 4.54 p.m.

Supposing the visitor to arrive at Carthage (La Malga) Station by train, the following itinerary (or a portion of it) will be found useful:—

(1) On the hill (Byrsa) visit the Cathedral, Chapel of St. Louis, Palace of the Proconsul, museum, underground temple, wall of Amphoræ, Punic cemetery, Roman ruins, Byzantine house.

(2) Odeon.—Punic cemetery, ruins of baths (Dermèche), cisterns, remains of supposed bath of Dido, basilica of Thrasa mund (Damous-el-Kareta).

(3) Malga.—Village and cisterns, amphitheatre (close to the station), cemetery of the officials (Ber-ed-Djebbana), Villa Scorpianus.

CARTHAGE.

The history of the rise and fall of Carthage having been related with the history of Tunisia (*see* pp. 289-295) very few additional words are necessary here.

No country in the world, with the exception of Italy, is more remarkable for its memorable events and monuments than Tunisia, and of all the periods of Tunisian history the Roman occupation was the one that has left its greatest mark in the country, where the name of Carthage stands pre-eminent.

Carthage is generally said to have been founded by a Phœnician colony, B.C. 850, but long before that date a small colony was established by Phœnicians near the sea, called Kombé or Kambi, a kind of market or depôt, later on known as the **Agora.** The high ground behind was reserved for the burial of their dead, and thus Byrsa was a cemetery before it became the citadel and acropolis of Dido.

But the Carthage we are visiting was founded, as already mentioned, about B.C. 850 on the hill called Byrsa (fortress), around which sprang up houses and suburbs in all directions, extending along the seashore from the harbours to beyond Sidi-Bou-Said. In a few centuries Karthad-Hadtha, or Carthago in Latin, had a circumference of nearly 20 kilometres, or 12 miles.

For more than 700 years the power and prosperity remained undisturbed, until, at the end of her long conflict with Rome, the city was taken by Emilianus Scipio, and given over to the flames, B.C. 146.

A Roman colony was established by Caius Gracchus, B.C. 116, and Carthage, restored by the Cæsars Julius and Augustus, soon gained much of its former importance.

In the second century Carthage became the chief seat of Christianity in Africa.

In 439 the city fell into the hands of the Vandals, and was retaken by Belisarius under Justinian in 533.

In 698 it was captured and overrun by the Arab invasion, and ruined by them for ever.

Of all the splendour and glory of Carthage there now remain but a few traces. From time to time the Genoese, the Pisans, and the Tunisians have carried off valuable marbles, statues, columns, capitals, vases, inscriptions; others have been secured for the museums of St. Louis, the Bardo, Sousse, and Paris.

Carthage, splendidly situated on the shores of a large well-protected bay, was composed of three distinct districts—

(1) The **Byrsa,** or citadel, which led by three broad streets, bordered by lofty houses, to the

(2) **Cothon,** the mercantile quarter and harbours, and

(3) **Megara,** extending to behind the hill of Sidi-Bou-Said, the whole surrounded by a wall.

On the side of the lake of Tunis the walls served to fortify the city. According to Diodorus these walls were built of hewn stone, 60 feet high and 33 feet thick; they were hollow, and divided into storeys. On the ground floor were stables for 300 elephants, with necessary provisions for their support. Above them were stalls for 4,000 horses, with corn and straw for a long siege. In addition 20,000 foot soldiers and 4,000 horsemen were lodged in these magnificent walls, which the Consul Censorinus compared to an encampment.

The panoramic view from the Byrsa to-day is one of extreme variety, interest, and beauty, embracing the Gulf of Tunis with its distant islands, Zimbra and Zimbretta, to the east; on the opposite side of the gulf, Radès and Hammam-Lif at the foot of Djebel-bou-Korneïn, and La Goulette to the south; on the north, La Marsa and Kamart; the hills and slopes of Ariana and Soukra to the west; and behind Tunis "La Blanche," far in the distance, Djebel Zaghouan, whose springs joined to those of Dougga supply the water for Tunis, La Goulette, Le Kram, Khéreddine, and Carthage by an aqueduct 130 kilometres in length.

Before the French occupation the antiquities and ruins all over Tunisia were abandoned to their fate by the authorities, and no steps were ever taken to put a stop to the vandalism of amateur collectors, or of dealers in antiquities. But, after the establishment of the French Protectorate in 1881, measures were concerted between the Beylical and the Resident Minister which ended in the formation of a department for the preservation of antiquities, for the creation of museums, and for the exploration and classification of ruins, under the direction of M. P. Gauckler.

By decree of August 17, 1896, this service was definitely

sanctioned, and its powers set forth, the execution thereof being left in the hands of the Bey's government, without any pecuniary contribution from the French.

For several years this newly-created Direction of Antiquities and Arts, the missionaries at Carthage, and officers of the army, have been busily engaged in the search for antiquities; and among their principal *finds* at Carthage, assisted by the energetic explorer and archæologist, the Rev. Père Delattre, chaplain of St. Louis, are the following :—

A **Wall**, 150 feet in length, 14 feet in depth, and 18 feet high, of the time of Augustus, composed of **amphoræ** in layers, without stones of any kind, the interstices only being filled in with earth ; the amphoræ that are intact, bearing the maker's mark, and the name of the consuls at the time they were filled with wine, so as to be able to verify its age. The dates inscribed on the amphoræ in question run from 43 to 15 B.C.

A **subterranean chapel**, the ruins of which show a corridor, mosaic pavement, and the image of a saint ; traces of other statues were discovered in April, 1895.

A **Wall** of 250 feet, built during the reign of Theodosius II., A.D. 428.

Punic and **Roman cemeteries.**

Roman cisterns.

Roman road, ruins of one leading from the Byrsa to the harbour and quays.

Byzantine house, with cisterns, fragments of mosaics, columns, lamps, head of Minerva, bronze and iron keys, etc.

Mussulman cemetery ; the tombs of unusual form, and the richest of them, in white marble, have been transferred to the museum garden.

Punic cemetery, in the chambers, tombs, and common burial places of which some hundreds of skeletons, funeral furniture, and coins, have been found. One of the skeletons, as well as the lamps, vases, small glass bottles, etc., will be seen in the museum.

At the office on the left hand, just inside the entrance to the museum garden, from a small collection of Punic and Roman antiquities, purchases can be made at reasonable prices. There is no official catalogue, but photographs and illustrated guide books to Carthage are on sale. A concise little work, entitled " Carthage autrefois, Carthage aujourd'hui," by two of the " White Fathers," can be recommended, price 2f.

The **Cathedral of St. Louis,** erected by Cardinal Lavigerie, Archbishop of Carthage and Primate of N. Africa, was commenced in May, 1884, and consecrated by the Cardinal on May 15, 1890, in the presence of prelates and other dignitaries of the church from France, Italy, and Africa, as well as of the French resident officials, and officers from Tunis.

The cathedral is open every day from 5.15 a.m. to 11.15 a.m., and from 12.30 to 5.30 p.m. in winter, and to 6.45 p.m. in summer.

The usual entrance is by the small door which faces La Goulette.

This conspicuous and important monument in the Byzantine-Mauresque style of architecture is built on the site of a Temple of Concord in the form of a Latin cross, measuring 200 feet by 93 feet. The façade is flanked by two square towers containing the carillons. The large dome on which rises the primate's cross is surrounded by eight turrets.

In the interior, the three naves are separated by arcades resting on columns of Carrara marble, with gilt capitals. Above the side naves is a gallery running round the entire building. The ceilings are ornamented with sculptured Arabesque divisions, which, as also the side walls, are gilded or painted in various bright colours. The choir has only a temporary altar. In a splendid reliquary of gilded bronze, representing the Ste. Chapelle in Paris, the work of Armand Cailliat, of Lyons, are portions of the remains of St. Louis, brought from the church of Monreale, near Palermo.

Cardinal Lavigerie died at Algiers in November, 1892, and, after a state funeral there, his body was brought to Carthage and placed in a tomb selected by himself beneath the altar, on December 8, 1892. The following inscription was composed by the Cardinal, and engraved on his tomb (except the date) during his lifetime :—

†

HIC

IN SPEM INFINITAE MISERICORDIAE REQUIESCIT

KAROLUS MARTIALIS ALLEMAND–LAVIGERIE

OLIM

S. R. E. PRESBYTER CARDINALIS

ARCHIEPISCOPUS CARTHAGINIENSIS ET ADGERIENSIS

AFRICAE PRIMAS

NUNC CINIS

ORATE PRO EO

NATUS EST BAYONAE DIE TRIGESIMA PRIMA OCTOBRIS 1825

DEFUNCTUS EST DIE VIGESIMA SEXTA NOVEMBRIS 1892

In February, 1894, Monseigneur Combes appealed to the clergy and faithful for funds to erect a mausoleum in memory and admiration of the devoted Cardinal Lavigerie. The appeal was warmly responded to, and the work was entrusted to the skilful hands of M. Crauk, the sculptor, of Paris.

The Cardinal is represented in a semi-recumbent position. Erect, on one side of the statue, is an adult negro in chains, and a younger one carrying a palm ; on the other side is a negress with an infant in arms; below, in different attitudes, are Pères Blancs (White Fathers) kneeling. The mausoleum was inaugurated and consecrated January 29, 1899, by Archbishop Combes, in the presence of six bishops and the authorities, civil and military, of the Regency.

Chapel of St. Louis. After the capture of Algiers in 1830, Charles X. obtained from Hussein, Bey of Tunis, through Consul-General Mathieu de Lesseps, the grant of a site on the plateau of Byrsa on which to erect a monument in honour of St. Louis. A chapel and house were erected by Louis Philippe on the ruins of the temple of Æsculapius (the God Eschmoun of the Phœnicians), which were consecrated in 1845.

The chapel is unworthy of the monarch to whom it is dedicated, being little better than an Arab koubba. Above the door is the following inscription :—

LOUIS PHILIPPE PREMIER, ROI DES FRANÇAIS,
A ÉRIGÉ CE MONUMENT,
EN L'AN 1841,
SUR LA PLACE OÙ EXPIRA LE ROI SAINT LOUIS, SON AÏEUL.

Over the altar is a white marble statue of Saint Louis.

The remains of Consul-General de Lesseps, father of Ferdinand de Lesseps, of Suez Canal fame, are interred within the chapel. High mass was regularly celebrated on the fête day of St. Louis until May, 1890, since which date the service is carried out more worthily in the new cathedral.

Immediately behind the chapel is the

Grand Seminaire, a spacious building with two wings, built in 1879, and inaugurated in 1881 by Cardinal Lavigerie as a college for the "White Fathers," who are intended to be missionaries in Africa, and wear the Arab bournous.

On the ground floor, to the left, beneath the arcades, are three apartments, one being the

Salle de la Croisade, on the walls and ceiling of which are frescoes representing the principal events in the life of St. Louis at Carthage. In the fourth painting, depicting the death of St. Louis, are the portraits of Cardinal Lavigerie and many ecclesiastics then attached to his person. The other rooms constitute the interesting

Museum Lavigerie, or St. Louis, approached also from an entrance (opposite the hotels) through a garden, in the alleys of which are exposed a number of fragments of columns, statues, torsos, sarcophagi, mosaics, amphoræ, numerous stellæ and bas-reliefs fixed into the walls, illustrative of the Punic, Roman, Christian, and Crusade periods of Carthage.

The museum is open on Mondays, Thursdays, Fridays and Saturdays, from 2 p.m. to 5.30 p.m. On application by letter or telegram, however, to the Director, permission to visit it at other times (at any given hour) will be granted. On Sundays and fête days the museum is closed during the hours of service, and during the four last days of Holy Week it is entirely closed.

The museum has been formed with the results of the explorations of the missionaries, under the zealous and intelligent guidance of the Rev. Père Delattre, and, with a few exceptions, contains only the objects found among the ruins of Carthage; visitors are thus enabled to examine the remains of a civilisation spreading over nearly three thousand years.

The contents of the museum are divided into four sections.

The **First,** and most attractive to the antiquarian and archæologist, displays the objects dating from the time of Dido, Hannon, Hamilcar, and Hannibal. Most of the antiquities of this period have been found in the Punic cemeteries. They consist of lamps, vases, tear-bottles from the tombs, also rings, necklaces, and different articles for which the dead had shown a partiality during their life. Outside the cemeteries, however, other pottery, rings, statuettes, amulets, etc., have been found, also vases, amulets, and searabees bearing the name of Thotmes III. of Egypt, B.C. 1600, and of Mycerinus, who built the third large pyramid at Gizeh. Vases imported from Greece in the sixth and fifth centuries B.C., jewellery, mirrors, masques, vases in bronze and terra cotta, are all there for inspection.

The **Second,** or Roman section, contains a large collection of statues, reliefs, mosaics, more or less mutilated, found near the amphitheatre and the Villa Scorpianus; a perfect statue, 4 feet 6 inches in height, of the goddess Ceres; a statue of

Æsculapius, portions of which were found at various intervals; imperfect torsos of Diana, Bacchus, and Pluto; two heads of Jupiter Serapis, one in marble, the other in onyx, and so on. Bas-reliefs of elegant workmanship dated 200 A.D. Terra cotta figures of the second century, one representing an organist and his organ, showing the construction of the instrument; lamps of several epochs, the earliest being round and of fine pottery, representing animals, birds, flowers, warriors, bacchantes. Other lamps of a coarser material, some of them bearing the name of the potter; some with two or three burners; amphoræ for wine (*see* p. 320).

In the collection of coins the earliest specimens are of the time of Julius Cæsar, 46 B.C., and the latest are of Jean I. Zimisces, 969—976 A.D. Mention also must be made of some beautiful cameos, precious stones, cut and engraved stones. Unique specimens of iridescent glass vases and tear-bottles are also on view.

The funereal inscriptions, of which there are a great number, generally relate short details of the life of the deceased. It would be interesting to reproduce some of these, but fuller descriptions than we can afford will be found in the Rev. P. Delattre's "Epigraphie Païenne de Carthage," 1891.

The **Third** section comprises a valuable souvenir of precious monuments of the Christian period, which followed after the pagan epoch. Amongst these may be briefly mentioned two bas-reliefs from the basilica of Damous-el-Karita, one representing the *Angel of the Lord* announcing to the shepherds the birth of the Messiah, the other the *Adoration of the Magi*.

The funereal inscriptions give the names of a number of, Christians of the Carthage Church, including bishops, priests, deacons, sub-deacons, acolytes, and readers.

The collection of lamps of this period is the largest and most varied in the world, numbering more than a thousand. The subjects represented on these lamps are taken from the Old and New Testament, some from heathen mythology. Abel offering up the lamb, the sacrifice of Abraham, Jonah cast up by the whale, Daniel in the den of lions, the two Hebrews before the statue of Nebuchadnezzar—such are the subjects from the Old Testament. Those from the New Testament refer directly or indirectly to the Saviour, such as Christ carrying the Cross, the lamb bearing a disc with a monogram of Christ, or Christ driving out devils.

The **Fourth** and last section contains antiquities belonging to divers epochs, including the crusade of St. Louis in 1270. Of these the most numerous are Arab, Cufic, Venetian, Spanish, Sicilian, and French coins, with some bronzes, buckles, rings, and clasps.

The Forum was situated between Byrsa and the sea, not far from Cothon, the military harbour. It was one of the most important public buildings of Carthage, the resort of orators, bankers, and merchants. On one side was the temple of Apollo, and on another the splendid Baths of Theodora, erected in 540 by the Emperor Justinian. In the Forum Christian martyrs were tortured, and from the Forum commenced the large routes of communication with the interior.

What is meant when speaking of the Forum to-day is in the district between the military port, **Douar=ech=Chott,** and **Dermèche,** which the Arabs call Kheraïb (the ruins), where, at **Feddan-el-Behim,** M. de Sainte Marie unearthed 2,000 votive stelæ in honour of the goddess Tanit and of the god Baal Hammon. The Rev. P. Delattre has found more than a thousand stelæ, two hundred impressions of seals of Egyptian and Grecian style, portions of seats and tables of red stone, and a large number of amphoræ handles bearing Punic or Greek marks.

The only important modern building in this quarter is the Palace of Mustapha ben Ismaïl, ex-prime minister of the Regency, built on the ruins of an ancient monument. It was the usual residence of H.H. Mohammed-en-Nacer Bey, the present ruler, when heir presumptive.

Harbours and Quays. Carthage had two harbours contiguous to each other : the mercantile harbour and the military harbour. These are represented to-day by two quite small lakes to the south of Douar-ech-Chott.

The southern or mercantile port was rectangular, 2,000 feet long and 800 feet wide, covering a surface of about 50 acres, and was surrounded by a quay 14 feet wide. It communicated with the sea by a channel (discovered by M. Beulé), which has a width of only 14 feet, and cannot have been the original entrance, which is spoken of as being 70 feet wide.

A channel, 60 feet long and 70 feet wide, connected the mercantile with the military harbour, which was circular, surrounded by large quays, and covering a surface of about 21 acres. Along the quays were numerous " slips " for sheltering vessels, and all round rose colonnades of Ionic columns. In the centre of the harbour, on an island, was the palace of the admiral.

The total superficies of the two harbours, as ascertained by M. Beulé and M. Caillat, corresponds almost exactly with that of the "Vieux Port" of Marseille, another Phœnician colony.

The harbours of Carthage were filled in by the Arabs by order of Hassan in 698, and the two basins or lakes spoken of above were made some years ago in order to represent on a small scale the position and form of the old harbours. All around are vines and fig trees, and a caserne, formerly the harem of the Bey of Tunis.

Damous-el-Karita and the Great Basilica. The discovery of one of the oldest monuments of Christian art is thus related by the "White Fathers" in their book already referred to :—

"One day the Père Delattre was on his way to visit a sick friend at **Sidi-bou-Said,** when, in the district of Damous-el-Karita outside the ramparts, near some land known as Bir-er-Roumi (pits of the Christians), his attention was attracted by some fragments of inscriptions lying scattered about. Arab boys were employed, and a large number of fragments were brought in, from which the Père Delattre found they were Christian inscriptions.

"Funds were provided, and explorations commenced; and after many years 25,000 cubic metres of earth were removed, the outline of a large Christian basilica revealed, and 14,000 inscriptions recovered, most of them incomplete, of which however a description was published by the Père Delattre in 1891."

The ruins disclose the basilica divided into three distinct parts; to the left the semi-circular Atrium, with its trichorum and nymphæum; in the middle the basilica itself; and to the right a second basilica with a baptistery.

(1) The **Atrium,** or semi-circular court open to the sky, was generally surrounded by a gallery formed by columns. The trichorum, the walls of which were covered with marble, it is thought, was reserved for the burial of martyrs.

(2) The **Basilica,** which was 65 metres long and 45 metres wide, was divided into nine naves by eight rows of pillars, the capitals of some of which have been found.

The principal centre nave was nearly 13 metres wide, and at the transept, that is to say in the centre of the basilica, were found four bases of large pillars, the basis and capitals of white marble, the columns of green marble.

(3) **Basilica of the Baptistery.** Smaller than the principal basilica, this second basilica was chiefly used for the administration of the sacrament of baptism. In the centre is the font, with three stairs on two sides, the interior lined with green marble.

The cemetery occupies a portion of the ancient cemetery where they buried the faithful whose rank at Carthage, or the want of room, did not allow of their being buried in the basilica.

The floor of the basilica was covered with tombs, in which were found skeletons. The entire pavement was a mass of epitaphs.

Two hundred bas-reliefs were taken principally from sarcophagi, two of which of great beauty are now in the museum, *see* p. 323. There yet remain to be explored the ruins that surround the basilica, where in all probability will be brought to light the buildings wherein dwelt the bishop and his clergy.

Sidi-bou-Saïd. On the summit of the hills above the ancient Cape Carthage and all along their slopes is the picturesque village of **Sidi-bou-Saïd**, so called after a marabout of **Béja**, *see* p. 384, who is held in such veneration by the Mussulmans that a pilgrimage to his tomb can in some circumstances replace a pilgrimage to Mecca.

The houses of the village rise in terraces, ascending the hill like a staircase, and are conspicuous from a long distance, being all whitewashed.

The lighthouse built on Roman ruins 440 feet above the sea commands the Gulf of Tunis, Cape Bizerta, and Cape Blanc, and naturally there is a magnificent view from the lantern.

There is a military post near the lighthouse, and a koubba built over a tomb of a dervish.

Few antiquities have been as yet recovered from Sidi-bou-Saïd, but the native village is extremely interesting.

Cisterns near the Sea. Among the most important monuments of Carthage must be reckoned the cisterns of **La Malga,** and those near the sea close to the fort of **Bordj-el-Djedid.**

Those of La Malga were larger than the others, but are now in a ruinous condition. Those by the sea were repaired in 1887, and are now, after fifteen hundred years, supplying water to Carthage, to La Goulette, and the intermediate villages. The water, as elsewhere stated, comes from Zaghouan and Dougga, 130 kilometres to Tunis, where, at the Château d'Eau (see p. 329), it is diverted in sufficient quantity by pipes to the cisterns at Carthage. The length of the cisterns is 135 metres, and their breadth 37 metres; they are divided into eighteen vaulted compartments, containing 25,000 to 30,000 metres cube of water. Before being repaired the cisterns or reservoirs were carefully cleared of rubbish, the vaults and walls were covered with cement, and everything is now in perfect working order.

Permission to visit the establishment can be obtained from the Director of the Company at Tunis, Rue es Sadikia, or from the foreman at the cisterns.

La Malga. Within easy distance of the present village of La Malga many interesting curiosities of Carthage may be visited, such as the ruined cisterns, in which some of the villagers live; the amphitheatre, the Villa Scorpianus, the cemetery of the officials, and the circus, all of which lie between the station of La Malga and the village of **Sidi Daoud.**

The **Cisterns at La Malga** (ruins) were 24 in number in a single line, all of the same vast dimensions—130 metres long and 26 metres broad. They were surmounted by cupolas, and between each cistern were pipes for distributing the water.

Many conjectures have been made as to whether these cisterns were Punic or Roman, but the balance of opinion seems to rest with M. Victor Guérin, who, in his " Voyage dans la Régence de Tunis," says, " they were Punic in their origin, but Roman in their definite construction."

In the early history of Carthage the city was supplied with water by numerous basins or pits, in which rain water was preserved, but later on it became necessary to construct large public cisterns or reservoirs, such as those described above.

Aqueduct. The water to supply Carthage was brought from **Zaghouan** (and later from Dougga), 130 kilometres, by a superb aqueduct constructed by order of the Emperor

Hadrian at a time when a severe drought desolated the country. This gigantic work delivered some 6,000,000 gallons of water a day, carried part of the way by underground canals, and along the **Oued Miliane** or other valleys, over thousands of magnificent arches, hundreds of which may be seen at the present time. The aqueduct was destroyed by the Vandals, restored by the Byzantines, and finally destroyed by the Spaniards.

In 1859, the then reigning Bey, Mohamed-es-Sadok, under·took to restore the aqueduct in order to supply Tunis, as well as Carthage and the suburbs, with pure water. A sum of nearly 8,000,000f. was set apart for this purpose, the carrying out of which was entrusted to M. Colin, a French engineer. The Roman route was followed, iron pipes were used instead of arches, but the old masonry channels were utilised wherever possible, and in less than three years the work was completed. This involved the employment of 43,000 metres of iron pipes, 88,000 metres of masonry, together 131,000 metres, including 40 bridges, 79 culverts, 162 underground channels, 7 build-ings necessary for the water syphons, and 6 waste overfalls. The daily supply averages 28,000 cubic metres. The reservoir at Tunis, called the **Château d'Eau**, is in the highest part of the city to the west of the Casbah. From this point Tunis receives an ample service of water, and a branch aqueduct is continued in pipes to the cisterns at Carthage, *see* p. 327. The Château d'Eau is open to the inspection of visitors.

The cost of this enormous work is said to have exceeded the estimate by several million francs.

The **Amphitheatre**, situated to the west of the Byrsa, a short distance from the village of La Malga, was in a good state of preservation as late as the 14th century, but is now a mere elliptical space, showing its original form and size. An Arab historian of the 12th century, Edrisi, says the amphitheatre was composed of 50 arches of 23 feet each, or a circumference of 1,150 feet, and that five tiers of such arches of similar form and dimensions one above the other in finely wrought stone completed the most beautiful building of its kind ever known.

By the influence of Cardinal Lavigerie, explorations were commenced at the expense of M. H. Morel, of Paris, and later on by subscriptions of other wealthy people. A good deal of work has been done, and some fragments of columns and capitals, a statuette of Diana, Pagan, Jewish, Christian and

Arab lamps have been found. A vault enclosing money, rings, pottery, glass, etc., was discovered, and this has been converted into a chapel paved with marble, the altar of yellow marble from the temple of Æsculapius, dedicated to the memory of those holy women, Sainte Félicité and Sainte Perpétué, and other Christian martyrs.

These devoted women fought and died for their faith in the amphitheatre, March 7, 202, and on March 7, 1895, the anniversary day of their martyrdom, Monseigneur Combes, Archbishop of Carthage and Primate of Africa, celebrated high mass in the amphitheatre chapel for the first time. The major part of the numerous Roman tombs, etc., discovered in the immediate vicinity have been preserved in the Musée Lavigerie (*see* p. 323).

Cemeteries of the Officials. The Roman law allowed all citizens and slaves the right to form associations in which members by an annual payment were assured of receiving decent burial at their death. In 1888, Père Delattre published the description of two cemeteries not far from the amphitheatre in which were buried the officials of the Imperial household. These cemeteries occupy a space of about 1,000 square metres outside the ancient ramparts, known by the Arabs as **Bir-el-Djebbana** (the pits of the cemetery).

The tombs were placed close together, made of masonry, nearly square, and on the outside figures, flowers, garlands, birds, etc., were moulded in stucco.

Inside, the tombs were furnished with urns to receive the ashes of the deceased, figures and lamps, tear-bottles, pins of copper and ivory. More than eight hundred epitaphs with their names gave an insight into the various functions of Roman officials, including librarians, notaries, schoolmasters, curators, doctors, soldiers, philosophers, nurses, dancers, and slaves. Of 289 epitaphs found in the first cemetery, 187 were of men, 100 of women; and of slaves 103 were men, 27 women. In the second cemetery of 295 epitaphs are the names of 160 men and 135 women, of which 110 are slaves and 19 freed.

During the excavations of 1895 and 1896, several series of tombs were found built over one another. These date before the Christian era. About two hundred yards from the cemeteries on the road to Tunis are the ruins of

The **Villa Scorpianus.** Very little remains in a state

of preservation of what, no doubt, was a very elegant villa, inhabited by Scorpianus, an *aurige* of the Circus of Carthage. During some excavations a beautiful Corinthian capital was unearthed close to the bases of ten columns that surrounded the bath, near which was a stove made of tiles, blackened by the smoke. A narrow passage led to a large room paved with mosaic, and the walls decorated. In a smaller room was an extremely beautiful mosaic representing the seasons, portions of which are now in the museum.

Whilst excavating in the neighbourhood of the Villa Scorpianus some Christian tombs were discovered, near which were lamps, both Pagan and Christian, also a number of ivory pins, and a few coins.

About a third of a mile from the amphitheatre was

The **Circus,** of which only the outline remains. It was a large, solid building, measuring 700 metres in length and 100 metres wide. A little beyond the circus are the ruins of another building, which are supposed to have been the stables and the dwelling of the director of the races

To the north-east of these ruins is the hill generally called the **Hill of Juno,** it having been thought that one of the most beautiful temples of Carthage was erected here, and dedicated to Tanit or Astarte, the Juno Celeste of the Romans. Below this hill, towards the sea, are

The **Theatre** and the **Odéon.**

The **Theatre** was no doubt a very magnificent place of entertainment; and in one of his orations to the people of Carthage, Apuleius dwells on its grandeur, the columns of red and black marble, the beauty of its decorations, and boasts of the talent of the various actors and artists. Nothing remains to-day but the bare site. A colossal statue of Apollo was found here, and is now to be seen in the Musée Alaoui, Bardo (*see* p. 314).

The Institute of Carthage arranged for performances of plays of a purely Roman or Carthaginian character by Parisian artists in May, 1906. These were so successful that they were repeated in April, 1907, and will no doubt become an annual institution.

The **Odéon,** where the Pythian games took place, was an immense building, erected 204 A.D. on the plateau below the theatre. In the ruins, which cover a space of about two acres, many fragments of coloured marble, of statues and statuettes, have been found; and the excavations of the enclosure have succeeded in disclosing the semi-circular form of the building, the stage, the orchestra, the doorways, and passages.

In the neighbourhood of the Odéon explorations undertaken by the Direction of Antiquities have brought to light tombs of a

Punic Cemetery, from which numerous articles of funereal furniture have been secured, including lamps, figures, coins, tear-bottles, and pottery. From these it has been possible to decipher the date as being of the last years of Punic Carthage.

Due south of the Hill of Juno was discovered, in 1895, another

Punic Cemetery of Douïmes, where, at a great depth, a number of tombs of the first Carthage were excavated, some of these containing vases, the like of which had never been met with before.

Beautiful articles in gold, silver, bronze, and faience were secured by M. P. Gauckler, including earrings, and an inscription bearing the name of Pygmalion in gold; scrolls and leaves in silver, discs, beads, pins, buckles, rings, clasps, razors, and figures in bronze; cornelian, coral, agate, ivory, glass, and white clay in the shape of small animals and figures; scarabees, on which are represented heads of dogs, of monsters, of Isis, of Osiris, Phtah, with hieroglyphics, some in praise of Râ, one giving the name of the king who built the third Pyramid of Gizeh. All these have rewarded the perseverance of the excavators, and contributed largely to the value of the various collections.

Above this cemetery the Department of Antiquities and Arts were able, in 1899, to unearth a

Roman House, supposed to date from the fourth century, and the ruins of a **Christian Basilica** close by, which has not been identified, but is thought to have been built in the reign of Justin'an

The **House** contained two mosaics, one representing a hunt of wild animals, the other a seascape. Underneath were rooms stuccoed and painted, containing mutilated statues in terra-cotta and marble; and in a place of concealment were four beautiful statues of women, not quite perfect, but in a good state of preservation. These and other objects found have been transferred to the Bardo (*see* p. 314).

The **Christian Basilica** is described by M. S. Gerl, in 1900, as originally having five naves, the apside surrounded by a gallery. On the left the oratory and baptismal fonts, the basin lined with marble.

Bordj-el-Djedid. On the sea-shore, north-east of the Byrsa, there was until lately a Turkish fort, called Bordj-el-Djedid (new fort). After having had the battery changed in 1895, it was condemned and disarmed by the French authorities in 1901.

During the construction of the new battery in 1895, a large number of bas-reliefs, capitals, and cornices were found in the ruins; and among the excavations of adjoining Roman cisterns were unearthed bronzes, Christian lamps, and an immense block of marble more than five feet in circumference, a portion of the arm of a colossal statue, possibly the statue of Hercules spoken of by St. Augustine.

Some 50 to 60 feet below the battery platform **Punic Tombs** of the fourth and third centuries B.C. were disclosed.

Thermes.—At the foot of Bordj-el-Djedid will be seen a mass of ruins of extensive Thermæ (warm baths), to which it has not been able to assign their name. M. Vernaz, however, in his excavations discovered an inscription enabling him to gather that the **baths** were erected by permission of the Emperor Hadrian about the year 145, at the time of the construction of the great aqueduct from Zaghouan.

The baths were supplied with water from the neighbouring cisterns by a large underground leaden pipe, laid in a passage some 10 feet high and 830 feet in length. Along this passage, at a depth of from four to six metres, more than twenty Phœnician tombs were excavated by M. Vernaz from the rock, and in them were vases, Phœnician lamps, and Corinthian pottery.

The district of **Dermèche,** wherein these baths and tombs lie scattered, is rich in ruins. The Arabs remember the excavations of Sir Thomas Reade, H.B.M. Consul-General in Tunis, seventy-four years ago, who, according to M. Beulé, in his " Fouilles à Carthage," p. 18, discovered a basilica built by Thrasamund, a Vandal king, and carried away to England some beautiful marble columns.

Virgil's account in the Ænid of the foundation of Carthage, as rendered by Dryden, will here be read with interest. The beautiful Venus is represented as standing on a hill (Sidi-bou-Said), and enlightening the pious Æneas with the following narrative, which has come to be a part of the poetry of the country :—

"The rising city, which from far you see.
Is Carthage, and a Tyrian colony.
Phœnician Dido rules the growing state,
Who fled from Tyre, to shun her brother's hate :
Great were her wrongs, her story full of fate ;
Which I will sum in short. Sichæus, known
For wealth, and brother to the Punic throne,
Possessed fair Dido's bed ; and either heart
At once was wounded with an equal dart.
Her father gave her, yet a spotless maid,
Pygmalion, then the Tyrian sceptre swayed,
One who contemn'd divine and human laws.
Then strife ensued, and cursèd gold the cause,
The monarch, blinded with desire of wealth,
With steel invades his brother's life by stealth ;
Before the sacred altar made him bleed,
And long from her concealed the cruel deed.
Some tale, some new pretence, he daily coined
To soothe his sister, and delude her mind.
At length in dead of night the ghost appears
Of her unhappy lord ; the spectre stares,
And with erected eyes his bloody bosom bares,
The cruel altars and his fate he tells,
And the dire secret of his house reveals ;
Then warns the widow and her household gods
To seek a refuge in remote abodes.
Last, to support her in so long a way,
He shows her where his hidden treasure lay.
Admonished thus, and seized with mortal fright
The Queen provides companions of her flight :
They meet and all combine to leave the state.
Who hate the tyrant, or who fear his hate.
They seize a fleet, which ready rigged they find,
Nor is Pygmalion's treasure left behind.
The vessels, heavy laden, put to sea
With prosperous winds : a woman leads the way.
I know not if by stress of weather driv'n,
Or was their fatal course dispos'd by Heav'n ;
At last they landed, where from far your eyes
May view the turrets of New Carthage rise ;
There bought a space of ground which (Byrsa called
From the bull's hide) they first enclosed and walled."

(see p. 289.)

Having given some account of the principal monuments in the suburbs, for the benefit of travellers in a hurry, attention can now be directed to some of the features of

MODERN TUNIS

Between the " Porte de France " and the " Lac Bahira " the land now covered by a large European city with broad avenues, boulevards, and public buildings, was twenty-five years ago a mere swamp, the resort of snipe and wildfowl.

The principal thoroughfare, the Avenue de France, commences at the Porte de France, and is continued by the Avenue de la Marine to the new port. In the Avenue de France, always busy and animated, are situated many of the most important banks, shops, cafés, and the Grand Hotel. In the Avenue de la Marine (or Jules-Ferry) are the Palace of the Resident, the new Municipal Theatre, Casino, and Winter Garden, the new theatre or Politeama Rossini, cafés, and shops, on the right; the Roman Catholic Cathedral, shops, cafés, and restaurants on the left. The avenue is intersected at right angles by two spacious thoroughfares, on one side the Avenue de Carthage leading to the Mosque and Fort of Sidi-bel-Hassan, and on the other, the Avenue de Paris, extending as far as the Belvedere.

The broad Avenue de la Marine (or Jules-Ferry) is bordered by double rows of trees, under the shade of which a military band performs every Sunday and Thursday afternoon: on Wednesdays opposite the Cercle Militaire, Avenue de France. A frequent service of electric trams runs from the Porte de France to the port; fare, 10c. At the port end of the Avenue de la Marine (or Jules-Ferry) is a statue of Jules-Ferry (by A. Mercié).

The creation of a

Port

at the very doors of Tunis was first entertained by the late Bey, who gave a concession for the purpose to the Bône-Guelma Company in August, 1880; but with the reorganisation of Tunisia, after the French Occupation, the contract was cancelled in 1885.

In May, 1887, the Société des Batignolles was invited to present plans and offers, which were approved and accepted by

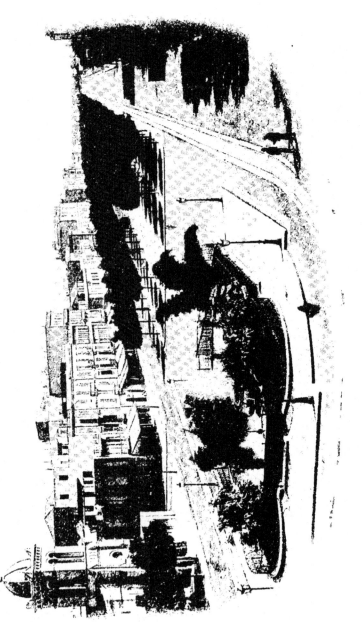

AVENUE DE LA MARINE, TUNI

the Council General of Ponts et Chaussées in July, 1888, and the **port** was made in 1892.

There, however, remained much to be done to complete the work, quays had to be formed, land reclaimed, warehouses and sheds to be built, appliances for loading and unloading to be erected, railway lines and sewers to be constructed, gas and water to be provided. To effect all this, a decree was passed in April, 1894, with MM. Duparchy and Préault for com-

ARAB INTERPRETER AND FAMILY.

pleting the port of Tunis, and for the construction of new ports or harbours at Sousse and Sfax.

By another decree of July, 1894, the firm of Duparchy & Préault was converted into a joint-stock company, under the title of the " Compagnie des Ports de Tunis, Sousse, and Sfax." The port of Tunis was completed in 1897, and all three ports are now managed by the company alluded to.

The port of Tunis is in direct communication with the sea at

La Goulette, by a canal 11 kilometres, or nearly 7 miles, in length, 93 feet wide, and 21 feet deep, through the shallow lake of El-Bahira (the little sea). (*See* also p. 304.) In the centre, the canal is widened to 140 feet for a distance of 1,625 feet, enabling vessels to cross each other *en route*. The Goulette entrance to the canal is 325 feet wide, and about a mile in length ; and the exit at Tunis is 1,300 feet long, with a breadth of 975 feet. Since the cutting of the canal and the completion of the port,

La Goulette has lost its former importance. The town, which has been constructed with the stones of ancient Carthage, is divided by an artificial passage between the sea and the lake into two parts. It contains a population of 5,000, which is considerably increased in the summer by visitors from Tunis for the sea bathing and breezes. The fortress in the northern half of the town is celebrated in history as having been besieged and carried by assault in July, 1535, by the fleet and army of Charles V., when thousands of Christian slaves were released from the citadel. Kheir-ed-Din (Barbarossa) and the garrison retreated to Tunis, but were followed by Charles and completely defeated.

In the southern part of the town are a former Bey's summer palace, prison, arsenal, and Custom-house. The canal may be crossed by a steam-ferry.

About a mile from La Goulette, in the direction of Carthage, are the favourite seaside resorts of

Khéreddine and Le Kram. In the former is a spacious Casino with the usual attractions, and facilities for bathing, but few houses, and no shops of any kind. At Le Kram are a number of villas, some of them being owned by families in Tunis, others are let for the season to persons unable to leave for Europe during the hot summer.

La Goulette can be reached by railway from Tunis in half an hour by some trains, fifty minutes by others. There are nine trains a day between 6 a.m. and 7.15 p.m.—three of these go direct, and six *viâ* Carthage and La Marsa ; all start from the Nord station in the Rue de Rome. By the electric tramway in course of construction La Goulette will be within 20 minutes of Tunis.

Hotels.

For a large city Tunis cannot be said to be over well supplied with hotels. The largest and those most frequented by winter visitors are :—

(1) The **Grand Hôtel de Paris**, centrally placed in the

Rue Al-Djazira (23), with tramways passing the door   The hotel has been conducted for a great number of years by M. Audemard and members of his family, from whom visitors receive every possible attention.   The rooms are some of them spacious, the sanitary arrangements ample, and the cuisine excellent.   Electric light throughout.

(2) The **Grand Hôtel de France**, 8, Rue Léon Roches, conveniently situated in a quiet street, has been recently erected for the present obliging proprietor, M. Ferrier, and consequently the rooms are newly and suitably furnished.   The sanitary installation is modern, and the cuisine is both liberal and good.   Lighted throughout by electricity

(3) The **Grand Hotel**, 13, Avenue de France, an old-established house, is situated in the busiest and most important thoroughfare of Tunis.   The bedrooms are sufficiently comfortable, but the public rooms are small.   The cuisine is excellent.

(4) The **Tunisia Palace Hotel,** Avenue de Carthage, adjoining the Casino, belongs to the Cie. des Stations Hivernales Africaines.   Closed June to October.   Restaurant and American bar, table d'hote at separate tables, 150 rooms.

All the above hotels accept Cook's Coupons, Series A, B, and C.

(5) Imperial Hotel, rue Al-Djazira (M. Audemard, proprietor).   Cook's Coupons, Series R, accepted.

There are a number of smaller hotels in various parts of the city, and a few hotel-pensions (*see* p. 355).

Restaurants.

With the exception of the restaurant attached to the Casino, where the tariff is sufficiently high, there is no first-class restaurant in Tunis.

The next best is the Restaurant Chianti, 11, Avenue de France, where the cuisine is good and the charges moderate.

Other restaurants and *pensions bourgeoises* at very reasonable figures will be found in various parts of the town, especially in the Avenue de la Marine, the Rue d'Allemagne, etc., see p. 355.

Municipal Theatre, Casino, and Winter Garden.

By far the most attractive place of amusement and resort for visitors is the handsome and extensive block of buildings adjoining the Palace of the French Resident, on the Avenue de la Marine, the **Municipal Theatre, Casino, and Winter Garden**.

This establishment was built by the " Société d'Hivernage," which obtained a concession of the ground and the sole right to the use of gaming tables from the Municipality of Tunis. The premises were afterwards sub-let at a rental of 200,000f. a year to the *Compagnie Fermière des Théâtre et Casino Municipaux de Tunis*. The official opening took place on November 20, 1902, since which date entertainments to suit every taste, and within the means of the most slender purse, have been provided during the winter months. The theatrical season lasts from November 15 to May 15.

In the Theatre, operas and plays are performed several nights in the week, and first-class classical or symphony concerts are given every Friday night. Promenade concerts take place three times a week in the Winter Garden, which is also used as a *foyer* between the acts of the theatrical performances. Leading out of the Winter Garden are *salons de jeu*, reading rooms, and a café. The Salle des Fêtes provides space for a thousand dancers.

On the ground floor, facing the Avenue, is a spacious café, over which is a private club, and behind the café is a first-class dining and grill room.

The premises are elegantly decorated and furnished throughout, the accommodation is everywhere comfortable, and the entire building is supplied with the electric light.

In the Avenue de Carthage, at the back of the Winter Garden and communicating with it is the " Tunisia Palace Hotel." (*see* p. 339).

The Belvedere, Jardin d'Essai.

The Municipal Park of the Belvedere, within an easy walk or drive of the centre of Tunis, along the Avenue de Paris, should certainly be visited. The park, planted with various species of shrubs and trees, to which additions are being constantly made, is surrounded and intersected by broad, well-kept paths and carriage roads, leading to the summit of the hill overlooking the streets, terraces, mosques, and minarets of Tunis. The view, extending to the Mediterranean and to the distant mountains behind the Gulf of Tunis, is probably the most extensive and interesting to be obtained in the district. The grounds of the park are gradually being ornamented with elegant pavilions, always open to visitors. Mention may be made of the transfer from the ancient palace of Khéreddine at **Manouba** of a Mauresque pavilion with five cupolas, decorated with plaster carving of the finest description of work, called *nuksh hadida*—a charming example of Arab architecture.

In 1901, a large and elegant public pavilion was erected on an eminence not far from the entrance, under the same management as that of the Municipal Theatre and Casino in town, where, in summer, an excellent restaurant, and open-air theatre, or café-concert and *salons de jeu* are provided. This is a favourite resort of the Tunisians in summer evenings when the Municipal Theatre and Casino are closed (*see* p. 354).

Electric trams run every 10 minutes from the Rue de Rome to the Belvedere, through the Place de la Residence, Avenue de la Marine, Avenue de Paris. Fare 10c. Another line runs from the Porte de France (cars every 7 minutes. Fare 15c.) to the south-east entrance *via* the Rue des Maltais and passing the European Cemetery.

Near the entrance to the Belvedere Park is the

Jardin d'Essai, founded in 1892 with the object of studying in a scientific manner the different varieties of plants shrubs, and trees, with a view to determine the best species for cultivation in Tunisia. Fruit trees, ornamental trees, and forest trees from countries of different climates; flowers and vegetables of every description are made the subject of careful cultivation and observation. Hundreds of thousands of plants or trees are sold yearly to colonists at nominal prices.

Adjoining the Jardin d'Essai is a

Model Farm, with cowhouses, sheep-folds, and piggeries, where experiments in breeding are carried on. Some fields are devoted to the culture of various kinds of fodder; in others, a special study is made of the growth of vines and tobacco.

Close to the Belvedere Park is the newly-built (1904) *Institut Pasteur*.

On the road to **Ariana**, a charming village surrounded by gardens and orchards, is a

Colonial School of Agriculture (opened 1898), where pupils in easy circumstances who wish to become agricultural colonists may acquire a theoretical and practical knowledge of the science necessary to produce the most successful results. The course of study is spread over a period of two years. Many other interesting visits can be made in the different faubourgs of Tunis by tramway or on foot by those who are making a prolonged stay.   Such, for instance, as to the

Jewish quarter or harra (ghetto), between the Rue de la Casbah, the Rue Carthagena, and the Rue Sidi Mardoum—where the corpulence and the costumes of the married ladies will excite considerable curiosity.

In the Faubourg of **Bab Souïka,** to the north of the city, the native quarter of **Halfaouine** conveys a vivid impression of

JEWESS AND DAUGHTER.

the every-day out-of-door Arab life.   Although lacking the real Oriental character of the souks or bazaars (p. 312), it is well worth while to watch the motley crowd of itinerant pedlars, vendors of clothes, fruit, vegetables, cooked meat (principally liver), syrups, sweets, cakes, and fritters ; and to peep into the Cafés Maures, where groups of listless Arabs are playing draughts, sipping excellent coffee at the ruinous price of a half-penny a cup, or inhaling opium from diminutive pipes, regardless of the noise and crowd without.

Close by, in the **Rue des Potiers**, may be seen the manufacture of native pottery, and in the **Souk Djedia,** the native weaving of silk goods.

During the month of Ramadan, the Halfaouine quarter is turned into a fair, when plays, performances, dances of the most riotous and licentious kind produce a perfect pandemonium.

It will be noticed that very little mention has been made of mosques, but as in Tunis and throughout the Regency, except in the holy city of Kairouan, Christians are excluded from entering them, it is impossible to describe the interiors. A list of the principal mosques will be found on pp. 344, 345.

PUBLIC BUILDINGS.

Churches

English Church. The English Church, recently built, is a substantial stone edifice, situated in the disused English cemetery of St. George, close to the **Bab Carthagena,** a few minutes' walk or tram ride from the Avenue de France. Services on Sundays at 10.15 a.m.

The British population in Tunis is very small, and the church has therefore been built with a view of providing service and sitting accommodation for travellers and visitors. Having no grant from any society the church is entirely dependent on self-support, and it is hoped that friends in England will help to finish and maintain the only British establishment that exists in Tunis.

The **St. George's Cemetery**, which has belonged to the British community since 1635, is a spot of great historical interest, as in it are interred the remains of several consuls, both British and American. John Howard Payne, the author of "Home, Sweet Home," died at Tunis in 1852, and the United States Government has erected a monument to his memory in the St. George's Cemetery. There is also a memorial window in the English Church.

St. George's Cemetery, being within the town, is now closed to all interments. A Protestant municipal cemetery has been established about a mile out of town.

Mosques. As already mentioned, Christians are never allowed to enter any of the mosques in Tunisia except at the holy city of Kairouan (*see* p. 368). There are fifty mosques in Tunis, nine of which have schools attached to them. The principal mosques are the

CAFÉ MAURE.

Grande Mosquée Ez-Zitouna, "mosque of the Olive Tree," founded in A.D. 698. In it a number of youths receive ι religious education. The mosque is reached by a flight of steps, leading to seven open courts, with porticoes sustained by marble columns. The exterior and central court can be seen when visiting the bazaars near the **Souk des Parfums.**

Djama El Casbah (the mosque of the Casbah), built 1230–1240. It was formerly inside the walls of the Casbah, but since the French occupation the entrance is now in the road outside.

Djama Sidi Mahrez, in the **Bab es-Souika** quarter, built in the seventeenth century by a French architect, a prisoner of the corsairs. The large central dome is surrounded by several smaller cupolas, presenting a faint resemblance to the mosque of Ste. Sophia, at Constantinople.

Djama-Sahab-Taba (mosque of the master of the prison), **Place Halfaouine**, one of the richest and most highly decorated mosques of Tunis.

The **Djama-el-K'sar**, the **Minaret Sidi ben-Arous**, the **Tombs of the Beys**, near the **Souk el-Belad**, and a multitude of minor mosques and zaouias are met with all over Tunis.

The **Roman Catholic Cathedral**, a conspicuous building of no particular style of architecture, is situated opposite the French Residency, at the end of the Avenue de France and the commencement of the Avenue de la Marine. The Archbishop, who is also Primate of all Africa, and who succeeded the celebrated Cardinal Lavigerie, is Monseigneur Combes. Other Roman Catholic churches will be found in the convents, notably **Trinity Church**, much frequented by Italians and Maltese, in the Zankat Mordjani or Rue de l'Eglise, just inside the Porte de France, adjoining the Capuchin Convent. Another in the home of the Christian Doctrine Brothers, which was formerly the parish church.

The **Greek Church** is close to the Marsa-Goulette railway station, Rue de Rome.

Colleges and Schools.

The **College Alaoui**, Place aux Chevaux, founded by Ali Pasha Bey, is a spacious building, in which primary, superior, professional and commercial education is given.

There are large class-rooms for drawing, photography, natural history, chemistry, agriculture, and a *jardin d'essai.*

Boarders pay 450f. a year, including foreign languages ; day boarders 225f.

Day scholars 54f. a year.   Cantine (hot) on the premises.

College Sadiki, Boulevard Bab-Benat, established by Mohammed Es-Sadik Bey in 1876, and reorganised after the French occupation.

Primary and secondary education is given in Arabic and French.   Admission is obtained by competition from public schools of the Regency.

Day scholars, half-boarders, and boarders are received. Mathematics, physics, history, geography, French and Arabic literature are included in the curriculum.

Lycée Carnot, originally founded by the Cardinal Lavigerie as the College of St. Louis at Carthage in 1880, was removed to Tunis in 1881 as the College of St. Charles. In 1889 it was ceded to the Tunisian Government and became a lay college.

Reorganised in September, 1893, it was, on the death of President Carnot, called the Lycée Carnot.

About 300 scholars receive superior education in classics, modern languages, and commercial subjects.   There are classes for French, Arabic, Italian, and English languages, for history, geography, mathematics, chemistry, writing, and bookkeeping.

There are also primary classes for young scholars conducted for two years by lady teachers, the children then enter the elementary school for boys as boarders, demi-boarders, and day scholars.   In all about 850 pupils receive instruction.

The educational charges vary according to the category.

The **Ecole Jules-Ferry,** a secondary school for young girls, Rue de Russie.   After being insufficiently lodged for some time, a suitable building was erected by the architect of the Public Works Department, and opened in 1891.

Excellent accommodation has been provided, including spacious class-rooms, chemical laboratory, work-room, library, refectory, infirmary, yard, and rooms for the professors.

Day scholars, demi-boarders, and boarders are received at various charges.

Instruction is given in ancient literature, foreign languages and literature, Arabic, geography, history, mathematics, physics, chemistry, natural history, domestic economy, needlework, drawing, music, and religious instruction according to the wishes of the parents.

In 1894 an annexe was added for infantile and primary and secondary classes. There are about 720 girls in the school.

École Émile-Loubet, a technical school for boys, Porte Bab-el-Allouch.

Public Schools. Eleven secular schools for boys and five for girls.

Private Schools. Four French religious communities have schools, viz. :

The Sisters of St. Joseph, two.

The Dames de Sion, one for girls and boys under seven years of age.

The Dames de Sainte Marie, one.

The Frères des Ecoles Chrétiennes, three.

The Alliance Israelite has three schools.

The London Jews' Society, (established in 1830), has now three schools of 250 pupils, Arabic and primary, with one evening a week for English and book-keeping. Rev. C. F. W. Flad, chief of the mission.

There are eleven Italian schools for primary and commercial instruction.

Libraries.

Bibliothèque Française, Rue de Russie. Open daily (Sunday and fête days excepted), from 9 a.m. to 11 a.m., and 2 p.m. to 4 p.m. in winter, from 8 a.m. to 11 a.m. in summer. Closed August and September.

The library contains a large number of works on history, geology, archæology and agriculture ; also the African library of the late Charles Tissot.

The **Popular Library,** 31, Rue Al Djazira. Open Sundays from 9 a.m. to 11 a.m., Tuesdays and Thursdays from 8 p.m. to 9 p.m. from October 1 to June 30. On Sundays from 8.30 a.m. to 10.30 a.m. from July 1 to September 30.

This library, under the patronage of the Alliance Française, contains about 7,000 volumes consisting of French and general literature, novels, and scientific works.

There is also a small circulating library at 17, Rue de Russie for school-teachers, etc.

Hospitals.

Tunis is well provided with civil hospitals, belonging to four communities, French, Israelite, Italian, and Mussulman.

The **French Hospital,** outside the gate of Bab el-Allouch, built in 1898, stands on 12 hectares of ground. It contains 230 beds (to be increased to 400). Twenty-four beds are reserved for inmates who pay 5f. to 10f. a day.

The **Jewish Hospital,** Place Halfaouine, was opened in 1895. It is governed by a superior council and an administrative council. Five doctors are in charge of 40 beds. Consultations free Monday and Thursday, from 2 p.m. to 5 p.m.

Italian Hospital, formerly the Infirmary Ste. Marguerite, Rue Ben Abdallah, was opened by the Italian Colony in 1890 as a hospital for poor Italians, free. Others in a common room pay 2f. a day, and those wishing a private room pay 5f. to 10f. a day. Consultations gratis Monday and Thursday.

Arab Hospital, Rue des Béchamkia, formerly a caserne, was opened as a hospital in 1880. It has accommodation for 210 beds, of which 37 are for women (separate). Patients must all be natives of Tunis, but not necessarily Mussulmans. The building is very well kept, the institution having an income of several thousand pounds a year arising from the rents and produce of land.

Institut Pasteur, *see* p. 341. Town office, Rue du Contrôle-civil.

Prisons.

There are two principal prisons, viz. :—

The Zendarla at the Bardo.

The Karaka at La Goulette.

Prisoners are employed in making routes and roads, clearing land, and in laying out public squares, parks, and gardens. In various parts of the Regency fifteen French penitentiaries are established, of which five are in Tunis, and one each at the Bardo, La Goulette, Porto-Farina, Sousse, Kairouan, Sfax, Gafsa, Gabès, Le Kef, and Tabarca.

Palais de Justice.

This important and commodious building, covering 5,500 square metres of ground, in the Boulevard Bab-Benat, near the Casbah, was opened in October, 1901.

In addition to the several Courts of Justice provision has been made for the anthropometrical and topographical services, and eventually for the Court of Appeal.

The **Hôtel de Ville**, not yet completed, is situated in the Avenue de Carthage.

Post and Telegraph Office.

This, the finest and best arranged public building in Tunis, commenced in 1889 and finished in 1892, is situated in the Rue d'Angleterre, near the Bône-Guelma railway station.

The ample ground floor includes a spacious postal office for the public, the telegraph, telephone, and parcel post departments, and the savings bank office.

On the first floor are the director's rooms, a library, and the residences of the postmaster and principal receiver. The entire building, including stables and coach-houses, is lighted by electricity.

The Residency.

The French Resident-General, M. C. Alapetite, lives in an unpretentious but comfortable house, facing the Place de la Residence, between the Avenue de France and the Avenue de la Marine, with a large garden in the rear.

The house was erected in 1860, enlarged and restored in 1890, and wings added in 1892. Official receptions are held at the Residency on Tuesday and Saturday.

The Resident-General has a summer villa at La Marsa, to which a pavilion was added in 1887, and further improvements made in 1892.

Casino, Theatre, Winter Garden, &c., see pp. 339, 340.

Abattoirs.

The abattoirs or slaughter-houses of Tunis, occupying some thirty thousand square metres of land on the outside of the town, are arranged on a magnificent scale with modern appliances. There are three spacious slaughter-houses, one each for the Mussulmans, Jews, and Christians, but all animals are killed in the Jewish fashion.

Markets.

Tunis is well supplied with markets. Provisions of all kinds are good and moderate in price, but becoming dearer with the increase of visitors. Fish from the Tunis lakes, and from Bizerta, *see* p. 378, is plentiful, and delicious prawns five and six inches in length are commonly served at hotel tables. The large central market, near the Hôtel de France, with its excellent assortment of fish, flesh, poultry, fruit, vegetables and flowers, is worth a visit in the early morning.

English Enterprise.

The only English companies or businesses of any kind are in the hands of the Baron de Kusel. They are:—

The **Soukhra Salt Works**, situated close to La Marsa, about 16 kilometres from Tunis, which are well worth visiting.

This is a French concession worked with English capital. The salt obtained from the salt lake of **La Soukhra** is considered one of the best salts in the Mediterranean for *fish curing*, and large quantities are exported annually to Norway and Sweden, Finland, Holland, Belgium, Newfoundland, and Halifax, Nova Scotia. The company own a private railway, running on the public road for a distance of five miles, connecting the salt works with the **Sidi-Dood** railway station on the Tunis-Marsa railway. The salt is collected during the months of July, August, September, and October, and is shipped from the port of Tunis all the year through.

The **English Stores**, 11, Rue de Constantine, opposite the **Compagnie Algérienne Bank,** and within a few yards of the Avenue de France.

This dépôt has been established lately under British management for the sale of *bonâ fide* British manufactures exclusively. Tourists and residents are now able to obtain a variety of English articles, such as saddlery, harness, guns, cartridges, cutlery, chemicals, bedsteads, preserves, teas, etc., mineral waters, beer, stout, whiskey, and wines.

Miscellaneous Information.

Strangers in Tunis intending to enter into any profession or business must inform the authorities within five days of their arrival, producing proofs of identity.

Employés of residents must be registered as soon as possible. A short delay is allowed, and if the registration is not then effected, a fine of 50f. to 200f. is imposed.

A false declaration incurs a fine of 100f. to 300f., and from six days to one month in prison.

Improper persons may be expelled.

Dangerous arms or weapons are prohibited without a licence. Any person found infringing this law may be imprisoned for from six days to six months, and fined 16f. to 200f.

Mails leave Tunis.—Monday, 2 p.m., due Marseilles Wednesday, 5.15 a.m.

Wednesday, 12.30 p.m., due Bizerta Wednesday, 4.30 p.m. Marseilles Friday, 7 a.m.

Friday, 9 p.m., due Marseilles Sunday, 4.30 a.m.

Mails leave France.—Monday, noon, Marseilles, due Tunis Tuesday, 7.30 p.m.

Wednesday, 1 p.m., Marseilles, due Tunis Friday, 4.15 a.m.

Friday, noon, Marseilles, due Bizerta Saturday, 7.30 p.m. ; Tunis Sunday, 5 a.m. ; Sfax Monday, 10 a.m.

Post, Telegraph, and Telephone Office, Rue d'Angleterre.

Postal Rates.—Letters. For the Regency of Tunis, Algeria and France, 10c. per 15 grammes, or fraction. For England and all countries in the postal union, 25c. for the first 15 grammes. 15c. for every 15 grammes, or fractions, afterwards. (Italy 20c.)

Post Cards.—Local, 5c. For France and Algeria, 5c., if containing not more than five words of text. Abroad 10c. Local stamps are used, not ordinary French ones as in Algeria.

Registered Letters.—25c. tax in addition to the postage weight on letters. Other documents, 10c.

Printed Matter.—5c. per 50 grammes, up to 3 kilos. weight.

Postal Orders.—10f., tax 10c.; 20f., 20c.; 20f. to 50f., 25c.; 50f. to 100f., 50c.

Parcel Post.—All packages must be prepaid, and the weight must not exceed 5 kilos. or 11 lbs. Parcels up to 3 kilos. (6½ lbs.) pay to Algeria and France, 1f. 25c.; to England, 3f. 25c. Parcels between 3 and 5 kilos. pay to Algeria and France, 1f. 45c.; to England, 3f. 75c. Average time required for parcels from Tunis to London, or *vice versa*, is about two weeks.

Telegrams.—The charge for messages to the interior of the Regency, to Algeria and to France, 5c. per word, minimum tax 50c. To Great Britain, 25c. per word; Alexandria, 1f. 60c.; Malta, 40½c.; Italy, 30c.; To New York, 1f. 40½c. per word.

Telephone.—Tunis is in telephonic communication with Carthage, La Marsa, La Goulette, Sidi-bou-Said, Crétéville, etc., the charge for conversation per three minutes being 25c.; also with Kairouan, Sousse, Mahdia, Moknine, Monastir, Souk-el-Arba, Le Kef, Tabarca, etc., the charge per three minutes being 50c. Sfax, 1f. Tunis (local) 10c. per three minutes.

Public Carriages.

	2 horses (4 places)	1 horse (4 places)	1 horse (2 or 3 places)	2 horses (4 places)	From Livery Stables.
	francs	francs	francs	francs	
The day of 12 hours	15·00	12·00	12·00	25·00	
By the hour in the town	1·80	1·50	1·30	2·40	
The course in the town	1·00	0·90	0·80	1·60	
By the hour outside the town	2·40	2·00	1·80	3·20	
The course outside the town	3·00	2·70	2·50	4·50	

Electric Tramway Routes.

1. Porte de France to the Casbah, by the Rue des Maltais, Rue Bab-Carthagena, Rue Bab-Souika, Place Bab-Souika, 5c.; Rue Bab-Souika, Boulevard Bab-Benat, Casbah (every four minutes); whole distance, 10c.

2. Porte de France to the Casbah, by the Rue Al-Djazira Carrefour Bab-Dzira, 5c.; Avenue Bab-Djedid, Boulevard Bab-Menara, 5c. (every four minutes); whole distance, 10c.

3. Porte de France to Bab-el-Khadra and Avenue Carnot, by the Rue des Maltais, Rue Bab-Carthagena, Rue Bab-el-Khadra, Station Avenue de Londres, 5c. ; Rue Bab-el-Khadra, Porte Bab-el-Khadra, 5c. ; Avenue Carnot, 5c. (every seven or eight minutes) ; whole distance, 15c.

4. Avenue de France to the Port, by the Place de la Résidence, Avenue de la Marine, Square Jules-Ferry, 5c. ; Avenue du Port, 5c. (every six minutes) ; whole distance, 10c.

5. Porte de France to the Abattoirs, *via* Hôtel de Ville, 5c., and Bab-Aleoua, 10c. ; whole distance, 15c.

6. Rue de Rome to the Belvédère, by the Place de la Résidence, Avenue de la Marine, Avenue de Paris, Passage à Niveau, 5c. ; Station Rue la Fayette, 5c. ; Avenue de Paris, rond-point du Belvédère, 5c. (every ten or fifteen minutes) ; whole distance, 10c., after 8 p.m. and Sundays, 15c.

7. Rue de Rome to the Abattoirs, by the Place de la Résidence, Avenue de la Marine, Avenue de Carthage, Station à l'Hôtel de Ville, 5c. ; Avenue de Carthage, Route d'Hammam-Lif, Bab-Aleoua, 5c. ; Route de Zaghouan, Abattoirs, 5c. ; whole distance, 15c.

8. Al-Djazira to Bab-Saàdoun, by the Rue d'Algerie, Rue Es-Sadikia, Place de la Residence 5c. ; Avenue de la Marine, Avenue de Paris, Passage à Niveau, 5c. ; Avenue de Londres, Rue de Alfa, Rue et Place Bab-Souika, 5c. ; Rue Bab-bou-Saàdoun to Porte Bab-Saàdoun, 5c. (every nine minutes) ; whole distance, 15c.

9. Bab-Saàdoun to the Bardo, 15c. ; return fare, 25c. Bab-Saàdoun to Manouba, 25c. ; return ticket, 50c. Bab-Saàdoun to Kasnadar, 15c. Bardo à Kasnadar, 10c. Kasnadar to Manouba, 10c. Bardo to Manouba, 15c. ; return ticket, 25c.

10. Rue de Rome to Ariana, 30c.

Tunis Directory.

Banks.—Banque de Tunisie et Transatlantique, 5, Rue Es-Sadikia. Compagnie Algérienne, Rue de Bône. Comptoir National d'Escompte, 12, Avenue de France. Co-operative Italiana di Credito, 7, Rue Es-Sadika. Credit Foncier et Agricole d'Algérie, 8, Rue Es-Sadikia. Banque d'Algérie, 18, Rue de Rome. Banque Commerciale Tunisienne, 7, Rue d'Alger.

Baths.—European, 17, Rue d'Allemagne and Rue de Suisse. Arab, Rue des Libraries.

z

Brasseries.—Des Deux Charentes, 68, Avenue Jules-Ferry, Taverne Maxéville, 63, Avenue Jules-Ferry. Du Phénix, Rues Annibal and Amilcar. Tantonville, Rue Amilcar. Du Casino, 64, Avenue, Jules-Ferry.

Cafés.—De France, 9, Avenue de France. De Tunis, 2, Avenue de France. De Paris, 16, Avenue de France. Du Commerce, 9, Avenue de France. Du Casino, 64, Avenue Jules-Ferry. Belle Vue, Avenue du Port.

Carriages.—Public—*see* p. 352.

Churches.—**English**, Bab Carthagena, 10.15 a.m., Sunday and Holy days. **French Protestant**, 36, Rue d'Italie, 10.15 a.m., Sunday, winter; 8.15 a.m., summer. **German**, in the house of Rev. C. F. W. Flad, 20, Rue de la Montagne. **Greek.**—Rue de Rome, 8–10, Sundays and fête days.—**Jews' Synagogues,** three times a day.

Clubs.—Military, 1, Avenue de France. Du Casino, Avenue de Carthage. De Tunis, 2, Rue du Lycée. D'Escrime, 4, Avenue de France. De l'Union, 11, Avenue de France. European, 1, Rue Hannon. Des Etrangers, at the Belvedere (*see* p. 340). De Tir, Brasserie du Phénix, Rue Amilcar.

Colleges and Schools.—*See* p. 345.

Comité d'Hivernage de Tunis et de la Tunisie.—8, Avenue de Carthage (open 9–12 and 2–5).

Concerts.—Casino, Avenue de la Marine; des Variétés, Avenue de France; Café-Concert (in summer) at the Pavillon du Belvédère (*see* p. 341).

Consulates.—**Austro-Hungary,** 23, Rue de la Commission. **Belgium,** 60, Rue des Selliers. **British,** Place de la Bourse (Consul-General E. J. L. Berkeley, C.B., Vice-Consul, R. Schembri). **Denmark,** 19, Rue de la Commission. **France,** Place de la Goulette. **German,** 12, Rue Zarkoun. **Greece,** 2, Rue d'Alger. **Holland,** 17, Rue du Maroc. **Italy,** 5, Rue Zarkoun. **Monaco,** 19, Rue de la Commission. **Norway,** Quartier St.-Georges. **Portugal,** Place de la Bourse. **Russia,** 23, Rue d'Angleterre. **Spain,** 2, Rue Sidi-el-Bouni. **Sweden,** Rue de Monastiri. **Switzerland,** Place de la Goulette. **United States** Consular-Agent, A. J. Proux, 28, Rue Es-Sadikia.

Doctors.—Dr. Domela, L.R.C.P. London, and M.R.C.S. England, 72, Avenue Jules-Ferry. Dr. Lemanski, 6, Rue d'Algérie. Dr. Schoull, 19, Rue d'Italie. Dr. Bruch, 17, Avenue de France.

Hotels.—Grand Hotel de Paris, 23, Rue Al-Djazira. Grand Hotel de France, 8, Rue Léon Roches. Grand Hotel, 13, Avenue de France. Tunisia Palace Hotel, Avenue de Carthage. All these hotels accept Cook's coupons, Series A, B, and C. Imperial Hotel. Cook's Coupons, Series R, accepted.

Hotel Pensions.—Veuve Capellano, 15, Rue d'Allemagne. Marion, 8, Avenue de Paris. Mme. Salles, 12, Rue d'Italie.

Hospitals.—*See* p. 348.

Post, Telegraph, and Telephone Office, Rue d'Angleterre. Post, 7 a.m. to 9 p.m.; telegraph, 7 a.m. to midnight. (For tariffs, etc., *see* pp. 351, 352).

Public Buildings.—*See* pp. 343–350.

Railways.—(1) From the Nord Station, Rue de Rome, to the Bardo, La Marsa, Carthage, La Goulette, Le Kram, etc. (2) From the French or Sud Station to Hammam Lif, Sousse, Kairouan, to Oudna, Zaghouan, to Bizerta, to Algeria.

Restaurants.—Restaurant du Casino. Salvarelli, 11, Avenue de France. Diner Français, Avenue de la Marine. Déjener Français, Avenue de la Marine. Brasserie Tantonville, Rue Amilcar. Brasserie du Phénix, Avenue de France.

Steamer Companies.—Transatlantique, 5, Rue Es-Sadikia. Navigation Mixte (Touache) 4, Rue d'Alger. Navigatione Générale Italiana, 5, Rue de Hollande. Adria, 12, Rue Es-Sadikia. Prince Line, 6, Avenue de Paris. Deutsch-Levante Line, 5, bis Rue d'Italie. Franco-Tunisienne, 6, Rue d'Alger. Compagnie Méditerranéenne, 5, Rue St. Charles.

Theatres.—Municipal, Avenue de la Marine. Belvédère Pavilion, Belvédère. Politeama Rossini, Avenue de la Marine. Concert des Variétés, Avenue de France.

Tramways.—Electric tramways run in every direction. (For routes and fares, *see* p. 352.)

PART III.

EXCURSIONS FROM TUNIS.

The following excursions will be described more or less in detail, so as to enable visitors whose time is limited to select those in which they may feel most interested :—

1. Hammam-Lif (one day, or even half a day).

2. Hammamet and Nabeul (one day).

3. Oudna and Zaghouan (two days).

4. Sousse, El-Djem, and Kairouan (two and a half days). (Sbeitla.)

5. Bizerta (one day). (Utica-Bou-Chater.)

6. Dougga (two days).

7. La Khroumire (three or four days). (Tabarca.)

8. El Kef, Kaalât-es-Sénan and Kalaa-Djerda (three days). (Moktar.)

9. Along the coast to the Island of Djerba. Eight days there and back, one and a half days in Djerba.

10. Rail to Sousse, automobile to El-Djem, Sfax, and Gabès ; steamer, Gabès to Djerba, three hours. Five—six days there and back.

11. Tripoli (Barbary). By steamer.

(1) Tunis to Hammam-Lif.

From 6 a.m. to 7.15 p.m. there are nine trains daily to and from Hammam-Lif (or Hammam-el-Lif), and for the return to Tunis extra trains during the season. Distance 17 kilometres. Time occupied about half an hour.

Ten kilometres from Tunis the line passes **Radès**, the ancient **Maxula,** a small picturesque village between the Lake and the Gulf of Tunis.

The station **Maxula-Radès** divides the village into Maxula, the native quarter, to the right, **and** Radés, the French quarter, to the left, to which a tramway conducts visitors.

On a small scale during the hot season Radès is bright and gay with the usual casino, sea bathing, pretty villas, and an excellent climate, which form its principal attractions.

Two stations beyond Radès, the charming bathing resort of

Hammam-Lif, on the shores of the Gulf of Tunis, is a deservedly popular resort of the residents of Tunis in summer, and of visitors in winter. The sea bathing in summer is on a beach of fine sand, and the well-arranged establishment of the warm mineral baths is available at all seasons of the year.

The spacious and handsome **Casino** overlooking the blue Mediterranean, and surrounded by gardens, contains, in addition to the usual musical, dining, and gambling attractions, several elegantly furnished bedrooms, some of these open to the delicious sea views and breezes, others to the perfumed mountain air from the fir-clad slopes of the **Djebel-bou-Korneïn.** (*Cf.* Flaubert's *Salammbô*.)

The **Thermal Establishment,** situated in the centre of the village, a few minutes' walk from the railway station, is fitted with large and small baths, shower baths, and rooms for massage, the tariff being very moderate. The temperature of the water at its source in the mountain is about 49° Centigrade or 110° Fahr., which is reduced, unless otherwise ordered, to 38° Centigrade or 93° Fahr. in the baths.

The waters are efficacious in cases of scrofulous, nervous, and allied diseases; also for rheumatism, wounds, fistula, diseases of the bone and skin. Taken internally the water is purgative, and when warm is clear and tasteless, but becomes nauseous when cold.

The waters of Hammam-Lif very nearly approach those of Bourbonne-les-Bains in their chemical composition.

Visitors to Hammam-Lif should not fail to make the delightful and easy excursion to the summit (about two hours on foot) of Djebel-bou-Korneïn (Father with two horns), both for the walk through the forests and for the lovely panoramic view.

Another interesting and easy excursion is to visit the model farm and colony of

Potinville, consisting of 7,000 acres of cultivated land, 1,250 acres being planted with vines. M. Gauvry, the representative of M. Potin, is always pleased to receive visitors interested in agricultural development.

The casino at Hammam-Lif is only open from May to October, but at the **Café Hotel de Paris** and **the Rosbif** there is fairly good accommodation for déjeuner or dinner at all times.

(2) Tunis to Hammamet and Nabeul.

There are only three trains a day to Hammamet and Nabeul, so that both places cannot be visited in one day. If only Nabeul be visited. the traveller will leave Tunis at 6.53 a.m., due Nabeul 9.48 a.m.; leave Nabeul 3.27 p.m., arrive Tunis 6.28 p.m.

Except Hamman-Lif, already described (p. 357), which is on the same line of railway as that to Nabeul, there is no place of interest until arriving at

Hammamet (64 kilometres), a bright little village situated on the gulf of the same name, a quiet and inexpensive health resort, becoming increasingly popular with Tunisian families. Furnished villas are available, and two small hotels near the seashore provide for a limited number of guests. The town, surrounded by a wall, is protected by a Casbah or citadel, which is worth visiting for the sake of the view. The productive gardens and the fertile lands of the district yield large harvests of oranges, lemons, tangerines, and early vegetables.

Bathing, boating, fishing, and shooting are the only distinctive features for the amusement of visitors.

At **Siagu, Puppu,** and **Ksar-er-Ghoula,** some three or four kilometres to the west, Roman ruins may be visited; and at Siagu excavations undertaken by the Direction of Antiquities and Arts have disclosed the remains of a Byzantine basilica, of a fortress, and of baths paved with mosaics, dating from the fourth and fifth centuries.

Thirteen kilometres beyond Hammamet is the terminus of the line at

Nabeul (close to the site of the ancient **Neapolis**) a very pleasantly-situated town near the sea, noted for its exceedingly mild and equable climate, and for its manufactory of quaint and bright pottery. At the Hotel de France and the Nabeul Hotel board and lodging (for a few) can be obtained for 6f. a day, carriages 10f. to 12f., and mules 2f. a day.

Nabeul is surrounded by splendid gardens, from which the essences of rose, geranium, and orange flowers are distilled;

and many agreeable walks or drives may be taken by invalids who may be recuperating in this genial health-giving climate. Good shooting in the neighbourhood.

There is a splendid view to be obtained from the top of **Ras-Tefel** (about two kilometres to the north-west of Nabeul), the mountain from which the potters procure their particular earth.

Dar-Chabane, a large inland Arab village of 4,000 inhabitants, and **Beni-Khirar,** a smart little Arab village by the sea, with a fine sandy beach, will repay a visit.

· The country between Nabeul and Cape Bon to the northeast, passing **Kourba** (colony Lulio), **Menzel,** and **Kelibia** (ancient Clypea), is covered with Roman ruins, which, however, can only be explored on foot or on mules

(3) Tunis to Oudna and Zaghouan.

There are only three trains a day from Tunis to Oudna and two to Zaghouan, viz., at 6.30 a.m., 12.55 p.m. and 5.35 p.m. and 6.30 a.m. and 5.35 p.m. respectively; it is therefore impossible to visit both places in one day.

Leaving Tunis by the early train, ample time can be taken for the ruins of Oudna, afterwards continuing by the evening train (6.48 p.m.) for Zaghouan (Hôtel de France), changing carriages at Smindja. (*Time tables subject to alteration.*)

Oudna alone can be comfortably visited in the day, returning to Tunis in the evening by train (or carriage, 20f.).

The route by road passes through the deserted village of

La Mohammédia (ancient Adherculanum), where Ahmed Bey caused to be erected a spacious palace designed in bad taste, but containing numerous apartments luxuriously furnished, in which resided with him the Ministers of State and their officers. Room was provided for 15,000 soldiers, and in the courtyards of the palace various shops and souks were established for the supply of necessaries and luxuries. At the death of Ahmed, the contents of this vast building were plundered, and nothing now remains.

Beyond Mohammédia, at the **Oued Miliane,** are seen portions of the ruins of the great aqueduct of Carthage, built by Adrian, 130 A.D. (*see* p. 328).

In three-quarters of an hour from the bridge of the Oued Miliane are reached the ruins of

Oudna (the ancient **Utina**), extending over several kilo-metres of ground, proving it to have been a place of consider-able importance. The principal ruins more or less capable of identification are

The **Citadel,** on the highest part of the city, containing a well-preserved hall in the centre, and several chambers with vaulted roofs.

The **Amphitheatre,** of vast proportions, with some of the entrances and seats still existing.

Thermes, or baths, the cisterns of which can be traced.

The remains of a **Theatre.**

Triumphal Arch, small portions only.

East of the citadel are the ruins of an immense structure, underneath which are enormous reservoirs, all so destroyed and scattered it is impossible to imagine the original nature of the building.

By far the most interesting and authentic discoveries at Oudna are the excavations effected by M. Gauckler, Director of the Service of Antiquities, of

Three Villas entirely paved with splendid mosaics, some depicting mythological scenes, such as the rape of Europa, Orpheus charming the wild beasts, Venus, Diana, Mercury, Neptune, etc., etc., others portraying the daily life of the people, or charming pictures in natural history, sport, etc., all of the greatest artistic value. Some of these may now be seen in the Musée Alaoui at Tunis (p. 315).

Taking the evening train at Oudna station, the excursion is continued *viâ* Smindja to Zaghouan, where the night is spent (Hôtel de France). The little town of

Zaghouan, situated on the northern slopes of the mountain of the same name, is a quiet, pleasant spot surrounded by gardens of fruit trees and flowers, the air being laden with the perfume of roses, lilies, violets, myrtle, and orange. The town itself exhales perfumes of a different quality, being dirty, un-paved, and ill-kept. The population, numbering about 2,000, finds employment in the manufacture of *chechias*, mats, and charcoal, and in the calamine mines of the Compagnie Lyon-naise. Chechias are the red caps called fez in Turkey and tarboosh in Egypt, the manufacturing and dyeing of these being a monopoly confined to **Zaghouan.**

No Roman ruins are to be seen with the exception of a triumphal arch, which forms the principal entrance to the town. But two and a half kilometres distant, towards the mountain, are the remains of a temple in the centre of a semi-circular colonnade, the **Nymphea**, built over the famous spring that supplied water to Carthage eighteen hundred years ago, as it now does to Tunis.

The spring flowed into an area about 90 feet square paved with stones, and passed into a basin where the conduits in connection with the great aqueduct commenced.

The excursion to the Nymphea can be extended to the

Ras-el-Kasa, the highest peak of the **Djebel Zaghouan** (4,248 feet). The ascent requires about five hours, but for those fond of mountain-climbing this excursion will prove very interesting and not too fatiguing. The view from the summit embraces a half of the whole territory of Tunisia. A heliographic station can be visited. Nine kilometres from Zaghouan, in a wild and picturesque gorge of the **Djebel bou-Hamida,** are the old Roman baths of

Hammam Zeriba. These have been restored by the Arabs, and in a large building surmounted by a koubba are two baths supplied with water 122° Fahr. at the spring, very efficacious in various forms of skin disease. The overflow falls between banks of laurel-roses into the Oued el-Hammam.

(4) Tunis to Sousse, El–Djem, and Kairouan.

For this excursion, one of the most important and interesting that can be made from Tunis, two and a half or three days are required (without extensions).

Leave Tunis by the early morning or afternoon train, in either case sleeping at Sousse (Grand Hotel), visit casbah, souks, museum, etc. Leave at 11.54 next morning for Kairouan, arrive 2.10, obtain *permit*, from the Civil-Controller (*see* p. 368) and visit mosques (by carriage) same afternoon ; sleep Hôtel Splendide, or Grand Hotel. Next morning visit bazaars, leave by train 11.47, due Tunis 6.28.

Tunis to Sousse.

STATIONS.	Dis. in kil. from Tunis.
Tunis (*B*).	
Hammam-el-Lif	17
Fondouk-Djedid	29
Bir-bou-Rekba (*B*)	60
Bou-Ficha	79
Aïn-Hallouf	87
Enfidaville (*B*)	100
Menzel-dar-bel-Ouar	114
Sidi-bou-Ali	123
Kalaa-Kebira	137
Kalaa-Srira (*B*)	143
Sousse	150

Sousse to Kairouan.

STATIONS.	Dis. in kil. from Sousse.
Sousse (*B*).	
Kalaa-Srira (*B*)	8
Reservoir	13
Oued-Laya	16
Krouss-Sahali	28
Sidi-el-Hani	37
Aïn-Ghrasesia	49
Kairouan	58

At Fondouk-Djedid-Mesratya a branch line running almost due east serves Soliman (6 kilometres from Fondouk), a small native town of about 2,500 inhabitants, and Menzel-bou-Zalfa (14 kilometres from Fondouk), and at a distance of about 21 kilometres from Soliman, on the Gulf of Tunis, facing Carthage, is **Hammam-Korbous,** a thermal station dating from Roman times and still much frequented by natives. A new establishment (opened in 1907) has been inaugurated here by a Company, and the waters are suitable for rheumatism, diabetes, skin and nervous diseases.

The most important place between Tunis and Sousse is the famous domain of

Enfidaville, 100 kilometres from Tunis. (**Hotel :** Grand Hotel. Cook's Coupons, Series A, B, and C, accepted.) This immense property, extending over 300,000 acres, was the subject of an historical dispute in 1880, and was one of the causes which brought about the French protectorate.

The property, in itself a small kingdom, in the richest district of the **Byzacène,** had been granted by the Bey to Kheir-ed-Din Pasha, then Prime Minister of Tunis, in consideration of his having obtained from the Sultan the right of succession to the Beylick by members of his (the Bey's) family. Wishing to leave Tunis in 1879, Kheir-ed-Din Pasha endeavoured to dispose of his estates to his own countrymen, but failing to find purchasers, he sold it to a French company, the *Société Franco-Africaine.*

The Tunisians then sought to invalidate the sale by exercising the Arab right of pre-emption (Chefäa). Litigation ensued, and after considerable diplomatic action the sale was confirmed, and the vast domain remained the property of the original purchasers.

Enfidaville is now a magnificent colony, numbering 1,400 Europeans, some thousands of natives, with a railway station, post and telegraph offices, and an hotel—the Grand. Branches have been created at **Reyville** and **Bou Ficha.** An excellent mineral water, ferruginous and gaseous, rises close to the estate, at the foot of **Djebel Garci** (*see* p. 306). This water finds a ready sale throughout Tunisia, and is exported to Europe.

In addition to its agricultural and commercial value, the property in various directions is rich in historical ruins, of fortresses, bridges, cisterns, tombs, temples, theatres, and baths. The site of ancient **Aphrodisium** (the city of Venus) is 15 kilometres distant. Interesting ruins of a triumphal arch, temple, amphitheatre, etc.

From Enfidaville the journey to Sousse occupies rather less than two hours.

Sousse (or **Susa**), the capital of the **Sahel,** is a charming little town and seaport of 25,000 inhabitants, including 1,200 French and 5,000 Europeans of other nationalities, built on an amphitheatre, and from the sea bearing some resemblance to Algiers.

Hotel.—Grand Hotel. (Cook's Coupons, Series A, B, and C, accepted.)

British Vice-Consul: W. Galea.

Sousse is the ancient **Hadrumetum,** founded by the Phœnicians in the ninth century B.C., and, therefore, before Carthage. It became a Roman colony under Trajan, and remained an imperial city until the second century of the empire. In 430 it was taken and destroyed by the Vandals, and under Justinian it opened its gates to the army of Belisarius.

It was invaded by the Arabs in 663 A.D., and definitely taken in 689, after the defeat of the Byzantine army at **Thysdrus** (El-Djem), and governed by the Khalifat of Bagdad. In the eighth century it took the name of Sousse, was fortified in 827. Mosques and citadel were built, and, holding a very strong position, it became the haunt of corsairs and pirates.

In 1537 Sousse was bombarded by a Spanish fleet under the command of the Marquis of Terra Nova, but successfully resisted the attack. Later on another assault by Andrea Dorea was more successful; but when he returned to Spain the town revolted and piracy flourished again under Dragut.

In 1881 Sousse was occupied by the French without difficulty.

The old town is surrounded by a crenelated wall, with bastions and square towers, the walls serving for shops and stores, somewhat after the manner of the *souks* at Tunis, but no manufactory of native work is seen. Several gates give access to the old town, on the summit of which is the

Casbah, a spacious building in part occupied by the colonel commanding the troops. A large room contains some armour, guns, antique vases, and mosaics, and from the tower there is a unique view over land and sea. Permission to visit it is readily granted on application at the guard-house.

The modern town is increasing daily in prosperity, and is already the second most important town of the Regency. Old walls have been removed, boulevards and new streets have been created, in which are found banks, consulates of all nations, first and second-class hotels, churches and synagogues, post and te egraph offices. Various public buildings have been erected, including a Palais de Justice. The French military station is outside the town.

SOUSSE.

The new port, constructed at the same time as the ports of Tunis and Sfax, between 1894 and 1899, is managed by a joint stock company under the title of " Compagnie des Ports de Tunis, Sousse, and Sfax." The remains of the ancient harbour and Roman breakwater may still be seen between **Ras el-Bordj** and the Quarantine Fort.

The new port affords facilities for shipping and exporting the rich products of the fertile plains of the central region of Tunisia, growing vast quantities of cereals, olives, and fruit, including almonds, apricots, pomegranates, and oranges. The animals of the Sahel are another source of wealth, numbering, as they do, 16,000 cattle, 19,000 camels, 20,000 goats, 120,000 sheep, and a fair proportion of horses, mules and donkeys.

Extensive factories for the manufacture of oil and soap are established near the harbour, as well as an *entrepôt* for all kinds of merchandise, called *Les Magasins Généraux du Centre Tunisien.*

The **Museum**, in the Place du Musée—open daily, 8–11 and 2–4, except Sunday and Thursday afternoons—contains numerous antiquities and some superb mosaics found in the neighbourhood of Sousse.

Beautiful mosaics from **Sorothus** may also be seen (7–10 and 1–4) in the Salle d'honneur of the Tirailleurs regiment. The Archæological Society of Sousse, under the presidency of M. le Dr. Carton, with the assistance of Captain Ordioni, have disclosed extensive cemeteries, Punic and Roman, and are now engaged in excavating other ruins of ancient Hadrumetum.

The **Great Mosque**, dating from the ninth century, during the reign of Abou-ben Mohammed El-Aghlab, is built with the columns going up to the ceiling without any arches, in the same way that some of the mosques at Tlemçen and Oran are constructed.

The **Kahwat-el-Koubba**, or Café of the Dome, is a curious little building, square from the ground, then cylindrical with arched niches, the whole surmounted by a fluted dome. It is now used as a native café.

The **Ksar-er-Ribat**, a large, square edifice, formerly a Byzantine fortress, then a monastery, now a medersa (college), occupied by a few students in some cells on the first floor. The Ksar is flanked by bastions and towers, the principal tower, of elegant proportions, being some 60 feet higher than the others. When used as a convent, it was inhabited by volunteers, who combined military service with their devotions, and took the name of *Morabet*, from which is derived the word Marabout.

The remains of seven large cisterns, each 330 feet long by 24 feet wide, and of the ancient Roman necropolis outside the town, may be visited if time permits. Some extensive Christian catacombs have been found here.

Sousse is surrounded by villages of considerable importance, and is the centre for visiting the following towns and seaports :—

Sousse to **Monastir** (ancient Ruspina), 21 kilometres by carriage, diligence, or bicycle. A pleasant seaport, celebrated for its tunny fisheries and olive groves (*see* p. 390).

Sousse to **Moknine,** Arab town of 7,000 inhabitants, 37 kilometres by railway, two trains a day.

Sousse to **El-Djem,** 64 kilometres, by diligence or by automobile, leaving Sousse daily at 1 p.m., after the arrival of the mid-day train from Tunis, fare 5f. and 12f. 50c. respectively. (The automobile continues to Sfax, 64 kilometres further, performing the whole journey in 6½ hours. Fare 25f., return 40f. Leave Sfax at 5.30 a.m., calling at El-Djem 9 a.m., due Sousse 12.30 p.m.)

The following short account will give some idea of the magnificent

Amphitheatre of El=Djem.

Twenty miles from the sea, in the miserable Arab village of El-Djem, the ancient city of Thysdrus, stands the grandest Roman monument of all Tunisia and perhaps the best preserved amphitheatre in the world—the amphitheatre of El-Djem —surpassed only in size by the Coliseum at Rome or the amphitheatre at Pozzuoli, near Naples.

The construction of the amphitheatre is attributed to the Emperor Gordian the Elder, who reigned in 236 A.D. After the Arab invasion the building was turned into a fortress, where, in the year 689 A.D., the Berber heroine El-Kahenna sustained a long siege, and from this time dates the partial destruction of the fabric when the staircases were demolished, and the arches of the lower storeys were walled up. Of late years the interior of the building has been used as a quarry by the Arabs, by whom the stones and columns have been carried off, arches and passages broken down.

This splendid monument, running from east to west, forms a long ellipsis, of which its greater axis is 489 feet, and its smaller 407 feet ; its circumference is 1,200 feet. The arena is 213 feet long and 172 feet wide ; the wall is 66 feet thick, leaving galleries 60 feet wide. Above the ground were four storeys, each storey supported by 64 arches, separated from each other on the exterior by beautiful Corinthian capitals, but the upper storey was probably never finished, and has now disappeared. The long and high galleries with broad staircases, which served as seats for the spectators, have nearly all been destroyed. To witness the feats of gladiators, or to see Christian martyrs given over as food for the wild beasts, the amphitheatre was capable of holding 60,000 spectators.

The outside gallery on the ground floor, where it is possible to do so, has been converted by the Arabs into stores for their corn, and some of the arches are turned into shops.

In the village many inscriptions have been found ; and in 1902, as the result of excavations by the Direction of Antiquities, extensive **Thermes** have been unearthed in a good state of preservation, the floors covered in mosaics. Near the baths two large cisterns have been discovered, also a wide street supposed to lead to the amphitheatre.

Comfortable board and lodging can be obtained at the schoolhouse, or at a restaurant kept by a Jew.

Continuing the journey from Sousse to Kairouan by train, at 11·54 a.m., the holy city is reached at 2.10 p.m., giving time for visiting the mosques. Kairouan is the only city in the Regency where Christians are permitted to enter the sacred buildings ; but an order (gratis) is necessary, obtained at the offices of the Contrôle civil, opposite the Hôtel Splendide.

Hotels.—Hôtel Splendide (Cook's Coupons, Series A, B, and C, accepted). Grand Hotel (Cook's Coupons, Series R, accepted).

British Vice-Consul.—W. Galea.

Kairouan (caravan, or resting place) was founded by General Okba-ben-Napy, generally known as Sidi Okba, in the 50th year of the Hejira (670 A.D.), to serve as a camp, and a centre for Islamism for ever. It is said that seven pilgrimages to Kairouan are equal to one to Mecca itself. The place selected is said by historians to

EL-DJEM AMPHITHEATRE

have been a forest infested with wild beasts and serpents, and that these were removed by miracles, and that the direction of Mecca for the true position of the Grand Mosque was revealed by God.

The holy city, however, soon became involved in wars, and was more or less destroyed by the Mohammedans themselves in 703 and 724, and was rebuilt by Ziadet Allah,· second prince of the Aghlabite dynasty in 821, and from this epoch the present Grand Mosque actually dates.

Kairouan is a large Arab city of 23,000 inhabitants, of whom only 300 are French. It is surrounded by a crenelated brick wall nearly 20 feet high, with towers and bastions, and pierced by five gates. It contains 23 mosques, 90 zaouias, 3 large cisterns, bazaars, and baths.

The principal mosques to be visited (with an order from the civil controller, *see* p. 368) are the Grand Mosque, the Mosque of the Three Gates, the Mosque of the Swords, and the Mosque of the Barber. Slippers should be taken by visitors.

The **Great Mosque** (Djama-Kebir) is near the ramparts in the north east corner of the city. It is of rectangular form, with a vast court which covers a cistern, surrounded by a double arcade of marble columns. From the north-west side of the court is a lofty minaret, of three storeys, from the summit of which the Muezzin calls the faithful to prayer, and whence there is an uninterrupted view over the city and plain of Kairouan.

On the side of the court opposite the entrance to the minaret is the mosque itself, the prayer chamber or **Maksoura**. This large rectangular interior consists of 17 naves of 8 arches each, resting· on 296 marble and porphyry columns, with capitals of various kinds of architecture. At the end of the central nave is the Mihrab, or sacred niche, facing the direction to Mecca, flanked with columns of red porphyry brought from Cæsarea in Algeria, the walls being covered with fine plaster work, or decorated with mosaics of marble and lapis-lazuli; and to the right of this is the mimbar or pulpit, 18 feet high, said to have been constructed by Abou-ben Mohammed El-Aghlab, who obtained the wood from Bagdad. All the panels are beautifully carved with extracts from the Koran, or inscriptions relating to the sacred building.

The dome is supported by porphyry columns, each nearly 40 feet in height, and the dim religious light from the coloured glass adds to the solemn and simple character of the prayer chamber.

The **Mosque of the Three Gates** (Djama Tleta Biban) dates from the third century of the Hegira, and is one of the oldest in Kairouan. The interior is a plain single chamber supported by sixteen columns. The façade records in Cufic inscriptions the date of its construction, and of its restoration in 844 of the Hegira.

The **Mosque of the Swords** is dedicated to **Sidi Amor Abada**, a marabout, who, to impress the people with his power and importance, employed himself in the manufacture of huge swords, anchors, pipes, etc. These he covered with Arabic inscriptions, and one of them, strangely enough, predicted the French occupation.

The mosque, of modern construction, is in the form of a cross, and is remarkable only for its six fluted domes, the interiors of these being decorated with inscriptions from the Koran.

The **Mosque of the Barber** (Djama Sidi-Sahab) situated outside the town near the cisterns of the Aglabites, is the most beautiful and important edifice of Kairouan, wherein is buried **Abou-Zemaa el-Beloui**, said to have been one of the prophet's barbers, and with him three hairs of the prophet's beard, which he carried about him when living.—one under his tongue, one next his heart, and one on his right arm.

The entrance to the mosque is through a beautiful vestibule lined with tiles and lace-like Arabesque plaster work. Next comes a cloister similarly decorated, and the arches supported by marble columns. Another vestibule, also decorated in the same style as the others, with the addition of stained glass, leads to a broad court surrounded by arcades of white marble columns and splendidly adorned with glazed faïence and plaster work. From this court the small shrine of the Barber or Companion is entered, or perhaps only caught a glimpse of, being generally occupied by pilgrims worshipping at the shrine. It is furnished with a large chandelier, flags, ostrich eggs, small lamps, carpets, etc., the tomb covered in black velvet and brocaded palls. Persian tiles and plaster arabesques cover the walls of the chamber. At the entrance of the mosque is a minaret faced with tiles.

The **Zaouia** of **Sidi Abid el Ghariani**, from whom the hereditary Governor of Kairouan is descended, is an excellent

2 A 2

MOSQUE OF THE SWORDS, KAIROUAN.

example of Moorish architecture, with arcades of black and white marble, a court of two storeys, the upper storey containing cells for thirty dervishes. The **Zaouia** of **Sidi Abd-el-Kadir el-Djilani**, with numerous cloisters and cells, the sacred well, **El-Barota**, in the centre of the town, the **Mosque of Olives** outside the city, the **Zaouia** of the **Aïssaouia**, whose members practise the same revolting rites of self-torture as at Algiers, are all interesting buildings, but the traveller must not omit to visit the **Souks**, which, although less important than those of Tunis, are equally busy and characteristic. The principal industries that will attract the stranger in these bazaars are those connected with the working of leather in the shape of harness, saddlery, etc., or of bright yellow slippers, in the manufacture of Arab jewellery, and of carpets, for which Kairouan has a certain reputation.

There are absolutely no drives or visits to be made in the immediate suburbs of Kairouan, but interesting excursions extending over three or four days may be pointed out as follows :—

If the traveller has journeyed straight from Tunis to Kairouan without visiting Sousse and El-Djem, he can go by carriage from **Kairouan** to **El-Djem**, 97 kilometres ; **El-Djem** to **Mahdia**, 45 kilometres ; **Mahdia** to **Sousse** by road, 61 kilometres ; or to Moknine, thence rail to Sousse, 64 kilometres. Time necessary, three days. Only a modest hotel at Mahdia. From Sousse to Tunis by train.

Kairouan to **Sbeitla** (114 kilometres, two days by carriage), where are to be seen some of the best-preserved ruins in North Africa. The scenery along the route is dreary and unlovely, there is no accommodation at Sbeitla beyond a miserable dirty **fondouk**, or country inn, so that bedding and provisions must be carried. For the first stage, 64 kilometres, at

Hadjeb-el-Aïoun, where a strong French camp is established, a sleeping tent may be procured if the traveller be provided with an introduction to the officer in command of the camp.

From Hadjeb-el-Aïoun, 20 kilometres, to **Oued Djilma** (where lunch can be taken), ruins of villages and towns are passed, and between Oued Djilma and Sbeitla beds of watercourses are crossed no less than seven times, which means that the journey should only be made in the dry season, there being no bridges. The entire district is strewn with Roman remains until the traveller arrives at **Sbeitla,** the Roman city of **Sufetula,** a beautiful and prosperous district in the fifth century, situated where the great highway from Carthage intersected the main road from Théveste.

The most important and best-preserved ruins of Sbeitla are in the enclosure, containing **Three Temples,** placed side by side and partly attached. The enclosure, paved with large stones, is about 500 feet in length and 230 feet in breadth, access to which was obtained through a triumphal archway. The central temple was larger than the others, and connected with them by archways, which led from a street behind the three temples. Judging from the mass of sculptured fragments, the broken shafts, monoliths 30 feet long, and cornices covering the ground, the temples must have been very beautiful. The central and larger temple was of the Ionic and Corinthian order mixed, the side temples entirely Corinthian. They are attributed to the time of Antoninus Pius, 138–161 A.D.

To the south of the town is the

Triumphal Arch of Constantine, 305 A.D., forming the principal entrance to the city An inscription records the dedication of the arch to both Maximian and Constantine, so that it was probably built at the end of Maximian's reign and at the beginning of the reign of Constantine. The arch has a single opening, and the four Corinthian columns of the façade are scattered on the ground.

The city of Sufetula can be traced for nearly a mile in each direction, and ruins of important buildings of various descriptions open out a large field for intelligent and systematic exploration on the part of the Direction of Antiquities and Arts at Tunis.

(5) Tunis to Bizerta.

Bizerta can be visited and the return journey made in a day.

Leave Tunis 6.34 a.m. from the Gare du Sud, arrive Bizerta 9.6 a.m. Visit the Arab town, the Casbah, harbour, the " Pont Transbordeur," etc., and, after lunch at the Grand Hotel, drive through the new European quarter to the lake and the fisheries, taking train at La Pêcherie (the first station from Bizerta) at 4.47 p.m. for Tunis, due 7.11 p.m.

Bizerta can also be visited from Tunis by steamers of the Compagnie Générale Transatlantique, sailing Thursday evenings *(subject to alteration).*

Tunis to Bizerta.

STATIONS.	Dis. kil. from Tunis.
Tunis (*B*).	
Djédéida	25
Chaouat (halt)	30
Sidi-Athman	38
Aïn-Rhelal	50
Mateur	65
Oued-Tindja-Ferryville	80
Sidi-Ahmed	89
La Pêcherie (halt)	95
Bizerta (*B*)	98

Time Table subject to alteration.

The first station of any importance beyond the suburbs of Tunis is

Djédéida, a junction where sometimes carriages are changed. Situated on the right bank of the Medjerda, the river affords facilities for milling operations, and the country round is fertile and well cultivated. Thirteen kilometres beyond, passing large farms and **Djebel Ahmar** in the distance, is **Sidi Athman,** called after a saint of that name, where the line runs in a north-westerly direction to

Mateur, the great market of the Mogods, an important agricultural centre, rich in cereals and cattle. At the Hôtel de France the proprietor, M. Thébault, provides guides and interpreters for excursions, also carriages, horses, or mules. The town, situated a mile from the station, is built from the materials of the ancient **Matarense.** The district, containing a population of 10,000, including the **Béjaoua** and **Hedil** tribes, comprises forests, mines, and cultivated lands, growing maize and tobacco. In the mountains of the Mogods there is abundance of game, including wild boar, jackal, and hyænas, hares and partridges. The **Sedjenane Lake** affords good wild-fowl, woodcock, and ibis shooting.

Charming excursions, offering few difficulties, can be made in the neighbourhood, and at some 15 kilometres, in the direction of Sidi-Ahmed, is the enormous spur of the **Djebel Ischkeul,** on the lake of the same name, where thousands of wild buffaloes, the property of the Bey of Tunis, hold undisputed possession.

The traveller is now in a district of many lakes, winding through olive plantations, between Ischkeul and Tindja, and skirting the vast lake of Bizerta, passes by the side of fields and gardens to the terminus of the line at

BIZERTA,

The ancient **Hippo Zarytus,** and a Tyrian colony in the fourth century B.C. After becoming a Roman colony it was conquered in A.D. 661 by Moaouia-ibn-el-Hodaij; then the Moors driven from Spain came to Bizerta in large numbers, and built an Andalusian quarter (**Houmt-Andless**). When Barbarossa took possession of Tunis the inhabitants of Bizerta were the first to acknowledge his sway; but when he was expelled they received a Turkish garrison, and Charles V. sent Andrea Doria to subdue and punish them, which he did by taking the city and massacring many of the inhabitants.

On May 3, 1881, the French fleet occupied Bizerta without resistance, and on May 11, 1890, under the French Protectorate, the Beylical Government granted a concession for the construction of a new harbour and canal. These were completed in 1895, and in May, 1896, two French ironclads, the "Brennus" and the "Redoutable," entered the harbour and the Lake of Bizerta, followed in July by the French Mediterranean fleet, the lake containing fifty square miles of anchorage for the largest vessels. It was found that the outer harbour and the canal giving access to the lake were not sufficiently large and protected from the weather, and on December 27, 1899, a further concession was granted to MM. Hersent and Couvreux, administrators of the "Compagnie du Port de Bizerte." In February, 1900, the works, which are estimated to cost £344,000, were commenced, and have been proceeding slowly ever since. The widening of the canal has necessitated the removal of the "Pont Transbordeur," a remarkable contrivance for the passage of the traffic from one bank to the other. This massive bridge, under which the largest vessels could pass, will be replaced by a steam ferryboat with submerged chains. Another steam ferry is in a line with the Rue de Naples.

These important alterations are made to facilitate the establishment of a strong naval and military base in the narrowest part of the Mediterranean between Gibraltar and Malta. Already a large arsenal has been created at **Sidi-Abdallah,** at the south-east extremity of the great lake, **fifteen kilometres from the sea,** where docks, sheds, quays, warehouses, workshops have sprung up as if by magic. Close by are separate buildings for ammunition and provisions; and at **Ferryville,** where nine years ago no house existed, a well-built town now provides comfortable quarters for the men employed in the dockyard, who, together with their families, make up a colony of 6,000 inhabitants.

On both sides of the town, and of the entrance to the harbour, old fortifications are being replaced with new forts of the most modern type, some facing the Mediterranean, others protecting the town, the harbour, and the lake. Barracks are being built for the reception of several thousand troops, and in every way it is clear, as French writers themselves avow, that Bizerta is intended to be one of the strongest fortresses in the world.

At the present moment (1908) the work is not being carried on with the same degree of energy as previously, arising probably from the fact that the original estimate of 40,000,000 francs will be largely exceeded.

The modern town of Bizerta is in a transition state; land has been reclaimed, houses, squares, and hotels have been built, banks have been opened in anticipation of the good times coming.

Hotels.—Grand Hôtel (Cook's Coupons, Series A, B, and C, accepted); Hôtel Métropole (Cook's Coupons, Series R, accepted).

British Vice-Consul.—Hon. T. Bourke.

Post and Telegraph Offices in the modern part of the town.

Railway Station.—Trains for Tunis and (*viâ* Djédéida) for Bône, Guelma, Constantine, Algiers, etc.

The town and district contains about 30,000 inhabitants, of which 4,000 are French; other Europeans, 9,000; natives, 12,000; and military, 4,000. The military governor is a general of brigade, and there are colonels of engineers, artillery and infantry in his command. The naval division is under the charge of the commandant of "La Tempête."

On the Mateur road, a new suburb of villas with gardens extends almost to the borders of the **Baie de Sabra,** at the entrance to the great lake. The visitor should drive through this suburb of Bijouville to the **Fisheries,** carried on by the Port Company under a concession expiring December 26, 1965. From one point of the lake to the opposite side, a barrage of strong wire netting has been erected with a moveable opening for the passing of boats or steamers, serving also for the annual immigration of innumerable fish from the sea to the lake.

Later on, when the fish seek to return to the sea, they are caught in a series of cages about 20 ft. square, into which they enter but cannot escape, and thus thousands of fish are taken daily. The annual production of the fisheries amounts to between 500,000 and 600,000 kilogrammes, consisting principally of mullets, dorys, and loups. More than half the quantity is exported in refrigerator boxes to France, the ice for which is manufactured by the company, and the rest of the fish supplies Tunis or other towns.

The value of this enterprise may be judged from the fact that the French Government, anxious to cancel the concession, have offered the Port Company a sum of fourteen million francs.

An interesting excursion can be easily made from Bizerta to Utica (Bou Chater) and Porto Farina, returning to Tunis by road.

Bou Chater is the site of the ancient **Utica,** a famous city before Carthage was founded. It continued to exist until the Arab invasion, and is now a miserable village, and a large farm, the property of the Count de la Palice, 8 kilometres from the sea. The scanty ruins of the ancient city are those of the theatre, amphitheatre, the quays on the river Medjerda, and the remains of a Carthaginian palace. From Utica the tourist can visit

Porto Farina (20 kilometres), called by the natives **Ghar-el-Melah,** or salt lake, into which flows the river Medjerda, and on which fisheries are established.

Porto Farina was at one time the great winter port of the Tunisian fleet, but is now a place of no importance. Here it was that Admiral Blake destroyed the piratical fleet of the Bey of Tunis in 1655. The climate is mild in winter, and in

the surrounding fields, poppies and potatoes are largely cultivated. Sleeping accommodation can be obtained at two
village restaurants.

(6) Tunis to Dougga.

This excursion requires two long days. Leave Tunis by the Bône-
Guelma line (Gare du Sud) 7.25 a.m., arrive **Medjez-el-Bab** 9.7 a.m.
Leave Medjez-el-Bab by diligence 10 a.m., arrive **Testour** at noon
(lunch at the restaurant); leave by diligence 1 p.m., arrive **Teboursouk**
3 p.m., sleep at hotel. Proceed early next morning on mule to Dougga,
6 kilometres. After visiting ruins, return to Teboursouk before noon,
lunch, and leave by diligence for Testour and Medjez-el-Bab, where
train at 9.2 p.m., due Tunis 10.39 p.m.

Carriages may be hired at Medjez-el-Bab for 20f. a day (four
persons).

From Tunis, the train first passes the **Bardo**, the former
winter residence of the Beys (see p. 314), then stops at the
garden village **Manouba**, studded with handsome Arab
palaces and villas (see p. 317).

Djédéida. Junction for the line to Bizerta (see p. 375.)

At **Tebourba**, 34 kilometres, mules or carriages are to be
obtained for visiting many important Roman ruins in the
neighbourhood, such as an amphitheatre, cisterns, the bridge
over the Medjerda at El-Bathan. The land around Tebourba
is admirably cultivated by French colonists, and two manufactories of oil and one of cement are obtaining excellent
results.

Passing two small stations, the train arrives at

Medjez-el-Bab (see pp. 258 and 265), a district filled with
Roman remains, where diligence or carriage is taken for

Testour, 20 kilometres, a charming drive by the course of
the Medjerda, between two chains of mountains. The
village (population about 5,000), has a European appearance,
accounted for by the fact of the majority of the inhabitants
being descended from Moors driven out of Andalusia. There
is a fine view from the minaret of the principal mosque.
Roman works are traceable by the side of and in the bed of the
river. Market on Fridays.

Lunch having been procured, the excursion is continued by
diligence or carriage to

Teboursouk, about 25 kilometres, passing about half way the
extensive ruins of **Aïn-Tunga** (ancient Thignica), comprising

a citadel constructed by Justinian, arches, a small semi-circular building, Temple of Mercury, 169 A.D., cisterns, and numerous fragments of columns.

From Aïn-Tunga to Teboursouk (ancient Thubursicum), the road passes farms and ruins of **Henchir Goléa,** surrounded by gardens and verdure ; and at **Bir-Tersas** the remains of a Byzantine fortress.

The village of Teboursouk, with the exception of its main street, which is fairly well paved and kept, has a deserted and dirty appearance. It is situated on high ground, enclosed by a wall of defence with square towers at intervals, constructed by the Byzantines, and has no other architectural monuments.

Dining and sleeping at Teboursouk (Hotel International), an early start should be made by mule in the morning for

Dougga, about 6 kilometres (**Thugga,** as it was called by the Romans), standing on a hill overlooking a fertile plain. From a distance, with its numerous ruins spread over an area of several kilometres, Dougga is even now a most attractive spot, but on reaching the miserable Arab dwellings of the modern village it is painful to see the extent of dirt and squalor extending even to the ruins of the temple.

The most important of the historical remains, all of which the ordinary traveller will not have time to visit, are the temple, theatre, triumphal arch, mausoleum, columbarium, circus, fortress, and aqueduct.

The **Temple of Jupiter and Minerva** is the most beautiful and most prominent of all the antiquities of Dougga. The elegant portico, still in fairly good order, is composed of six white marble columns, monoliths, each measuring 33 feet in height, including the capitals and the base. An inscription on the frieze records the fact that the sanctuary dedicated to Jupiter, Juno, and Minerva, was built during the reign of Marcus-Aurelius (161–180 A.D.) at the expense of two inhabitants of Thugga.

The **Mausoleum** was a handsome and solid construction, commemorative of a Numidian who died before the Christian era. Sixty or seventy years ago the mausoleum was in a good state of preservation, but only a few steps forming the base now remain. And the reason of its destruction is not creditable to England. The structure bore on two stones a remarkable bi-lingual inscription in the Libyan and Punic tongues, the only known example in North Africa. In 1842, Sir T.

Reade, then H.B.M. Consul-General at Tunis, obtained permission from the Bey to remove these stones, which he did, but instead of looking after their careful removal himself he entrusted the work to ignorant and clumsy Arabs, who, in getting out the two stones and their valuable inscription, practically demolished the entire mausoleum. The stones are now in the British Museum, having been bought by the Government at Sir T. Reade's death.

The **Theatre,** and the remains of the only **Triumphal Arch** still standing, preserve a few traces of their original construction, excavations undertaken by **Dr.** Carton in 1893 having disclosed the stage and most of the seats of the theatre.

The **Aqueduct,** traversing valleys a distance of 8 kilometres, sometimes by a double series of arches, and sometimes underground, gives proof of solid and careful construction.

Recent excavations have discovered a gallery surrounding a temple in the basement of the grand semi-circular monument, similar to but larger than the semi-circular building at Teboursouk. A fine mosaic, discovered in the *thermes*, is now in the Musée Alaoui, Tunis (*see* p. 315).

A ruined temple of Saturn, the remains of three triumphal arches, of cisterns, of two fountains formerly embellished with colonnades like those of Zaghouan, of the columbarium, and the fortress, may be included in the visit, with or without a guide, time permitting.

Thanks to a recent credit placed at the disposal of the "Service of Antiquities," the excavations and researches in the neighbourhood have lately been carried on with increased activity. M. Merlin, member of the École de Rome, is the Director in charge of the works, several Arab houses covering ruins have been bought, and a wooden building has been erected for the service and as a dépôt.

From Dougga it is a day's excursion on mules (provisions should be taken) to the Djebel Gorra mountains (highest point Kef Gorra, nearly 3,300 feet), the most interesting of which is Djebba where deposits of galena (worked by the Romans) and calamine are found. These are now exploited by the Société de la Vieille Montagne.

(7) Tunis to La Khroumirie.

This excursion requires four or five days if the journey there and back be made entirely by land, but a full day may be saved by returning to Tunis by steamer from Tabarca (Tuesday evening).

Leave Tunis by the Bône-Guelma line (Gare du Sud) 7.25 a.m., arrive Souk-el-Arba 11.35 p.m. Lunch at the buffet, continue by diligence. horse, or carriage to **Fernana**, 23 kilometres, and **Ain-Draham**, 18 kilometres, sleep at the latter. Hôtel de France, or Hôtel Serrière. Visit neighbourhood of Aïn-Draham. proceed to **Tabarca**, 26 kilometres. Return same route, or if the Tuesday evening boat can be caught, by steamer from Tabarca to Tunis; but embarking or landing at Tabarca or La Calle (30 kilometres west of Tabarca) is not always practicable.

La Khroumirie, or the country inhabited by the Khroumirs (perhaps more correctly written Khoumair and Khomiri) is one of the most attractive districts of Tunisia, covered with beautiful forests of cork-trees. It extends from Tabarca on the sea coast some 50 kilometres in a southerly direction to Fernana. Situated on the borders of Algeria and Tunisia, surrounded by forests and mountains, little was known of the inhabitants until the French occupation of Tunisia, except that they led an independent life, resisting all attempts at subjection, and plundering with equal impartiality the districts on either side of them.

The subjection of this turbulent people was one of the excuses for the French occupation of Tunisia, and the end seems to have fully justified the means, for now this once inaccessible region is covered with good roads, is perfectly safe for travellers, and the women, as well as the men, are occupied with the cultivation of the soil.

The route to Souk-el-Arba by railway is the same as that described in the excursion to Dougga as far as Medjez-el-Bab (*see* p. 379).

Five other stations are passed before arriving at

Souk-el-Arba, whence the excursion is commenced to Aïn-Draham and Tabarca, *viâ* Fernana, the southern boundary of La Khroumirie. At a few kilometres distance a path branches off to the right to the Roman ruins of **Bulla Regia** (*see* p. 384). Near Fernana two military columns of Trajan's road are seen.

At **Fernana**, refreshments may be obtained at a café-restaurant, but except the ruins of a Christian basilica (5 kilometres) there is nothing to detain the traveller, who will continue his journey by an excellent road which soon enters the splendid oak forests of La Khroumirie.

On a hill overlooking the valley of **Ben-Metyr** is the **Camp de la Santé,** formerly occupied by French troops, and near by is a sanatorium, recently built as a health resort for Tunisian families. From the hill referred to there is an extensive view of Algeria and Tunisia, but a still grander panorama of sea and landscape is obtained from the **Djebel-Bir,** easy of access from the village of

Aïn-Draham, where the night must be spent at one of the hotels mentioned above. There is nothing to be seen in this quiet village but the view towards the sea ; but it is the centre of delightful excursions, such as to the **Col des Ruines,** the warm source of **Bordj-el-Hammam** on the Algerian frontier, once used by the Romans, the sulphur baths of **Hammam des Gouadia,** at the end of a picturesque gorge.

After the French expedition Aïn-Draham was occupied by a force of 3,000 men, now reduced to a detachment.

The climate of Aïn-Draham is very enjoyable during spring and autumn, but often cold and wet in mid-winter. Wild boar, hares, and partridges afford good sport in the forest.

Leaving Aïn-Draham for Tabarca there is nothing remarkable to note during the drive of 26 kilometres except the beauty of the landscape. The road gradually descends, passing through forests of cork-oak trees, carpeted with ferns, myrtles, and creepers, sweet to the smell; and passing the Tunisian Custom-house near the **Col-de-Babouch,** the scenery becomes wilder, hill and dale succeed each other, the country being covered with brushwood and other luxuriant vegetation, intersected by deep ravines. Approaching the coast, beautiful views open out, and the drive ends at

Tabarca, the ancient **Thabraca,** now a small town of 900 inhabitants, chiefly Europeans, divided into two parts, consisting of the village and small harbour, and the island crowned by a Genoese fort in ruins. Remains of jetties can still be distinguished between the coast and the island.

Tabarca is a great fishing centre, and between February and September a large fleet of Sicilian boats obtain an abundance of sardines and anchovies along the coast. Coral boats also take shelter in the small harbour when the weather is rough at sea. With a larger and safer port the commerce of Tabarca could be developed by shipments of wood of various kinds, minerals, tannin, and cork from the adjacent forests and mountains.

The history of Tabarca is very interesting. It was a Roman colony in the third century, and remains of Roman buildings

may still be seen.   It was an important city of the African
church, and mosaics of the Christian period were found in
1884.   Some of these are in the Musée Alaoui (*see* p. 315).
At one time it was a strong seaport, and from it three or four
important roads led to the rich districts of the interior.   It was
occupied by Spain, then by the Genoese, and taken by Tunis
in 1741, when hundreds of the inhabitants were sold as slaves.

Returning by the land route already described, when the tourist
arrives at Souk el-Arba, he is within five miles (about 7 kilometres) of
the ruined city of **Bulla Regia,** now called by the Arabs **Hammam
Derradji,** from its copious spring of fresh water enclosed by them for
the supply of water to Souk-el-Arba.   The overflow from the reservoir
forms a marshy lake, in which are barbel and eel.

Bulla Regia, situated on the Roman road from Carthage to Théveste,
once the residence of Numidian kings. was a large and prosperous city
under the Romans.   It was destroyed by an earthquake, and the ruins.
which extend over many acres, are more or less buried in the soil.
The principal remains are those of a theatre, the thermæ, a nymphæum, an amphitheatre, large cisterns for the collection of rain
water. a Byzantine fortress and a fine Roman house, the latter
recently unearthed (*see* p. 264).

Should the traveller wish to extend his journey before
returning to Tunis, he can do so to advantage by taking train
from Souk-el-Arba to Pont-de-Trajan (four stations), thence
by branch line, 14 kilometres, to

Béja, an Arab town of 12,000 inhabitants, built on the
ruins of the ancient **Vacca,** a prosperous and wealthy Roman
town, once the granary of North Africa.

The Casbah, or Byzantine citadel, which commanded the
eastern district of **La Khroumirie,** has been dismantled and
replaced by large French barracks.   The principal mosque
was originally a Christian basilica.   Remains may be seen of
the Byzantine wall, towers, and gates, which enclosed the
ancient city.   In the neighbourhood are the ruins of the
basilica of **K'sar Riria,** of the fortress of **K'sar Zaga,** and
of funereal chambers cut in the rocks.

Mule route from Béja to Aïn-Draham (p. 383), *via* **Souk-el-
Tnin,** 50 kilometres.

Mule route from Béja to Tabarca (p. 383), over the Khroumir
mountains by the magnificent gorges of the **Khanguet,**
72 kilometres.

Mule route to Tabarca through the splendid forest of
Nefzas, and by the **Djebel-Abiod,** where the traveller will
find a capital hotel, called the **Rendezvous de Chasse de**

Nefzas, kept by the Dames Genin. Plenty of game, including wild boars, in the neighbourhood. Post and telegraph office in the hotel.

(8) Tunis to Le Kef (El Kef), Kalaât-ès-Sénam and Kalaa-Djerda.

Tunis to Kalaa-Djerda.

STATIONS.	Dis. from Tunis in kil.
Tunis (Buffet).	
Djebel-Djellou	6
Bir-Kassa (halt)	8
Les Nassen	13
Khledia (halt)	20
Oudna	24
Bou-er-Rebia (halt)	28
Cheylus (Djebel Oust)	36
Smindja	49
El-Aouja	55
Pont-du-Fahs	64
Tarf-ech-Chena	78
Bou-Arada	89
El-Aroussa	105
Sidi-Ayed (halt)	113
Gaffour (Buffet)	121
Le Krib	139
Sidi-bou-Rouis	150
Le Sers	166
Les-Salines (junction for **Le Kef,** 31 kilometres from Les Salines).	
Les Zouarines (halt)	180
Ebba-Ksour	191
Aïn-Mesria	201
Oued-Sarrat (junction for **Kalaât-ès-Sénam,** 32 kilometres from Oued-Sarrath)	223
Kalaa-Djerda	235

The following excursion to Le Kef and return to Tunis can be done in two days. Leave Tunis, Bône-Guelma line, at 6.30 a.m., arrive at Le Kef 3.21 p.m. (only one through train per day each way between Tunis and Le Kef). There is time for lunch at Gaffour station, reached at 11.28 a.m. Next day, the return journey, if preferred, may be made by diligence from Le Kef to Souk-el-Arba (48 kilometres in 6 to 7 hours); thence train, 6.35 p.m., to Tunis, arriving there 10.39 p.m. For the route between Souk-el-Arba and Tunis, see p. 381.

Time Table subject to alteration.

From Tunis to Oudna, *see* pp. 359, 360. Passing Bou-er-Rebia (halt) at 28 kilometres and Cheylus (Djebel-Oust) (36 kilometres), **Smindja** (49 kilometres, junction for Zaghouan, p. 360) is reached. Then comes Pont-du-Fahs (important market on Saturday) at 64 kilometres. Near here (3 kilometres) are the ruins of Henchir Kasbat, consisting of two temples, three gates, thermes, cisterns, basilica, mausoleums and a Byzantine fortress. Other stations are Bou-Arada (89 kilometres), El-Aroussa (105 kilometres) and **Gaffour** (121 kilometres), lunch.

At **Les Salines** (171 kilometres), the line branches off to the right for Le Kef, continuing to Oued-Sarrath, where the line to the left goes to Kalaa-Djerda and that to the right to Kalaât-ès-Sénam.

Le Kef, or **El-Kef** (the rock), is a town of 6,000 inhabitants, perched on a rock at the western extremity of Djebel-Dir, surrounded by rocky ramparts of all shapes and forms. The town, built of Roman ruins, has six gates and six mosques, is badly paved and dirty, the population Arab, with the exception of 200 Maltese and Italians.

Hotels.—De France, du Commerce, d'Europe.

Le Kef, the ancient city of **Sicca Veneria**, was founded by a colony of Phœnicians, who introduced there the worship of the Asiatic Venus adored in Assyria, and in the Temple dedicated to Venus were practised the disgraceful mysteries that gave the place its evil repute.

After the Roman conquest, **Sicca** became a prosperous city, and because of its resemblance to Constantine in being built on a rock it was called **Colonia Julia Cirta Nova**. The Carthaginians sent the mercenaries who revolted to this city, a vivid description of their exile being given by Flaubert in *Salammbô*. (*Cf.* also Cardinal Newman's *Callista*.)

The principal remains that can be traced in the city are the ruins of a temple dedicated to Hercules, and of a Christian basilica. There are also vestiges of a palace, and large blocks and walls of the thermæ. A monumental fountain supplied from a subterranean source still provides the town with water in abundance.

Outside the city are the old Roman cisterns, eleven in number, in a good state of preservation, vaulted chambers 84 feet long, 21 feet wide, and 20 feet deep. They were supplied from a spring, and were connected by a tunnel with the fountain mentioned above. Now they are used by the French soldiers as billiard rooms and gymnastic saloons. Higher up than the cisterns is the site of an ancient basilica, called by the natives **Kasr-er-Roula** (the castle of the throat of the magician), and evidently from the large, well-worked stones, and from the fragments of marble columns and capitals among the ruins, it must have been a handsome and spacious building.

The Casbah, occupied by the French, of Roman construction, or built from the blocks of ancient Roman buildings, is on the highest point of the city, but overlooked by a rocky platform at the top of the mountain ; and on the high ground close to the Casbah are the barracks for the soldiers.

To the west of El Kef, opposite **Bab-Cherfin**, are traces of an amphitheatre, and in the opposite direction of a theatre.

The distance from Le Kef to Souk-el-Arba is about 48 kilometres. Diligence daily.

Turning eastward the road ascends to the heliographic station (3,110 feet above sea level) at Djebel Dir. From this point a descent is made, passing ruins of koubbas, to the Oued-Mellègue. About half way is seen on an eminence about a mile from the road the considerable village of Nebeur, built with materials from the Roman city of Castellum. Souk-el-Arba is reached through the valley of the Medjerda. From Souk-el-Arba train to Tunis (see p. 382).

To visit **Ellez, Ksour** and **Medeïne** from Le Kef instead of from Tunis, the Kalaât-Djerda line is joined at **Les Salines** (see p. 386). There are two trains a day in both directions, but only one through train a day between Tunis and Kalaât-ès-Sénam.

Resuming the journey at Les Salines, close to the next station, Ebba-Ksour, are the ancient ruins of Ebba, and Ksour is about 9 kilometres to the south-east. At Ellez, about 10 kilometres to the east of Ebba-Ksour are numerous megalithic monuments, a Byzantine fortress and Roman remains.

Aïn-Mesria (30 kilometres beyond Les Salines) is the station for Medeïne, the site of ancient Althiburos, where are important ruins on both banks of the Oued-Medeïna, including a

2 B 2

temple, a theatre and a monumental gateway.   At Oued-Sarrath (52 kilometres from Les Salines) the line forks continuing (*right*) to Kalaât-ès-Sénam (32 kilometres from Oued-Sarrath) and (*left*) to Kalaa-Djerda (12 kilometres from Oued-Sarrath).

The Kalaât-ès-Sénam, close to the Algerian frontier, is a formidable rock perched on the summit of a pyramid about 660 feet high, perpendicular on both sides, and which can only be scaled by a flight of steps cut in the rock.   About half-way up the stairway is a doorway dating from Byzantine times. The fortress was formerly impregnable, but is now a mass of ruins.

A junction between Tébessa and Kalaât-ès-Sénam will no doubt shortly be made, thereby much facilitating access to this part of the country by rail, including the Djebel-Kouif, Huïdra (Tunisian Customs) on the Algerian frontier, the site of the ruined Ammœdara, a large area, comprising a triumphal arch, a Byzantine citadel of imposing aspect, mausoleum, etc.

Travellers who have not visited **Kairouan** from Tunis (*see* p. 368) may do so from El Kef, stopping at Maktar, La Kessera (wild boars abound in the forest), and El-Ala.

A carriage may be hired at Le Kef at from 20–25f. per day, or possibly at Le Sers, the nearest point on the railway (*see* p. 385).   Whole distance about 170 kilometres.

Maktar, the ancient **Mactaris,** 72 kilometres from El Kef, is a veritable mine of riches for the archæologist.

Some excavations have been made by the Director of Antiquities, but no extensive and systematic explorations have as yet been undertaken.   MM. Bordier and Delherbe have made some interesting discoveries, including portions of statues of emperors of the 4th century, sarcophagi, funereal altars, cornices, neopunic and Christian inscriptions, some of which have been forwarded to the Alaoui Museum (*see* p. 315).

The principal ruins are as under :—

The mausoleum of the Julia family, in the form of a square tower.

The Byzantine basilica of Rutilius, built of material from Pagan and Christian monuments.

A small amphitheatre (traces).

A Roman paved street, which probably led from one arch (Bab-el-Aïn) to the triumphal arch of Trajan.

A large building, the original nature of which cannot be fixed for certain. It may at one time have formed part of a Byzantine citadel, and it bears considerable resemblance in design to the Pretorium of Lambessa, or it may have been the Thermes.

A pyramidal mausoleum, an elegant funereal monument, 45 feet in height.

The mausoleum of Verrius, a square tower.

The aqueduct, several arches still standing.

A temple of Diana and Apollo.

Outside the ruins are numerous megalithic monuments dating from a period anterior to the Roman town of Mactaris. In fact, the whole district abounds in ruins and must have been densely populated in ancient times.

Travellers can also visit Kairouan from Le Kef by way of Sbeitla.

The following information as to the route has been courteously supplied by the Civil Controller of El Kef :—

"The journey can only be made in four long stages, averaging 80 kilometres a day.

     1st day, sleep at **Henchir Rohia.**
     2nd ,,   ,,   Sbeitla.
     3rd .,   ,,   Hadjeb el-Aïoun. } *See* also p. 373.
     4th ,,   ,,   Kairouan.

"A good interpreter guide can be engaged at El Kef at the rate of 5f. a day, or 120f. a month, food and means of transport at the expense of the traveller.

"In all the localities accommodation can be obtained in native houses, or in clean Arab tents, according to the number of tourists, on application to the Civil Controller of Maktar for Henchir-Rohia, to the Civil Controller of Thala for Sbeitla, and to the Civil Controller of Kairouan for Hajeb el-Aïoun. Bedding as required must be carried by the traveller."

(9) Tunis to the Island of Djerba, along the Coast.

This most interesting and enjoyable excursion can be conveniently accomplished in eight days, including the return to Tunis, by steamer.

The steamer accommodation from Tunis is very good, and by consulting the time-tables of the Compagnie Générale Transatlantique (as far as Sfax) the Compagnie de Navigation Mixte, or of the Cie de Navigation Générale Italienne, the traveller will be able to arrange his voyage according to the time at his disposal.

Supposing the traveller to secure his passage by the steamer of the Compagnie de Navigation Mixte, his itinerary at the present date (1908) would be as under:

Leave Tunis, Friday, 7 p.m.
Arrive Sousse, Saturday, 7.30 a.m.
Leave Sousse,   ,,   1 p.m.
Arrive Monastir   ,,   2.15 p.m.
Leave Monastir   ,,   4 p.m.
Arrive Mahdia   ,   7 p.m.
Leave Mahdia   ,,   9 p.m.
Arrive Sfax, Sunday, 8.30 a.m.
Leave Sfax   ,,   midnight.
Arrive Gabès, Monday, 5.45 a.m.
Leave Gabès   ,,   noon.
Arrive Djerba ,,   3.45 p.m.
Leave Djerba, Wednesday, 9 a.m. (calling at the same ports on the return voyage as mentioned above).
Arrive Tunis, Saturday, 9.30 p.m.

Starting from the port of Tunis, through the canal to La Goulette, the steamer continues in a north-easterly direction, and doubles **Cape Bon** (Ras Addar), on which is a powerful red intermittent light visible at a distance of about thirty miles. Then, steering south, is seen the town of **Kelibia**, one of the earliest cities occupied by the Romans, and the last in the possession of the Christians after the Arab occupation ; ruins of a Roman acropolis and of a Spanish fortress

Beyond **Cape Mustapha** and **Menzel Temine** is **Nabeul,** the ancient **Neapolis,** see p. 358, then **Hammamet,** see p. 358.

Crossing the Gulf of Hammamet the steamer reaches

Sousse, or **Susa,** remaining sufficiently long for a run on shore, the landing-place in the harbour being close to the town, see p. 363.

About 20 kilometres, or 12½ miles, from Sousse, the steamer calls at

Monastir, the ancient **Ruspina,** a pretty little town, surrounded by ramparts built by the Spanish. **(British**

Consular Agent : S. Diacono.) Close to the shore on a small island is the tunny fishery establishment of **El-Rhedemsi,** and on the **Islands of Kuriat,** about 12½ miles from the coast, is a similar tunnery; also ruins of cisterns cut in the rocks.

The **Château el-Kahlia,** a former residence of the Bey's férik (general), splendidly situated on sea-girt rocks, repays a visit. The valuable olive groves of the district give occupation in winter from November to March to several oil presses, and Monastir is the last place in the north of the Regency where the fruit of the date tree ripens. Monastir has a population of 7,000, two hotels, Custom-house, post and telegraph office.

Important ruins can be visited 7 kilometres to the south at **Lamta,** the ancient **Leptis Parva** of the Romans, notably traces of an amphitheatre, cemetery, aqueduct, and remains of the harbour and quays.

Leaving Monastir, and rounding **Ras Dimas,** are the ruins of **Thapsus,** celebrated for the great victory gained by Cæsar over Scipio and King Juba. Remains of a fort, a large amphitheatre, a vast reservoir, consisting of twenty-five cisterns, each 250 feet long by 14 wide, also many smaller cisterns in a good state of preservation, used probably for Roman villas.

The next calling station is at

Mahdia (or **Mehdia**), the site of ancient **Zella,** where Hannibal embarked after his flight from Carthage; formerly a powerful Phœnician city and an important seat of commerce under the Romans. After the battle of Thapsus the city was deserted, then rebuilt in 912 by Obeid Allah el Mahadi, from whom it derived its name. It was fortified in the tenth century, and became for a time the seaport of Kairouan. Taken by Roger, the Sicilian, in 1147, it was retaken by the Arabs in 1160.

In 1390 the Duc de Bourbon, with a French, Genoese, and English fleet and army, laid siege to Mahdia, and was obliged to retire after sixty days. This is the first time that an English expedition was sent to North Africa.

In 1551 Mahdia was captured by the Spanish, but Charles V., being unable to retain possession, destroyed the fortifications, which have never been rebuilt.

Since the French occupation Mahdia has become a charming little town, old houses and ramparts have been removed, a small harbour has been made, villas surrounded by palm trees have sprung up, barracks for French troops, and other important buildings complete the many recent improvements.

British Consular Agent.—G. Violante.

In the old Arab quarter little or no change has taken place. The great mosque very much resembles the one at Kairouan and would be worth a visit if permission could be obtained.

The old Spanish citadel on the eastern promontory has been restored, and under its walls is a small harbour or **Cothon,** opening to the sea by a canal, some 60 feet broad, probably of Phœnician construction.

Outside the town are Roman cisterns and an Arab cemetery, and at 3 kilometres to the west a Punic cemetery has been discovered similar to those at Carthage.

Mahdia contains nearly 10,000 inhabitants, and a fairly comfortable hotel.   Carriages for visiting **El-Djem** (two days) can be hired at the rate of 15f. a day (*see* p. 367).

From Mahdia the steamer passes **Ras Capoudia,** and in about ten hours arrives at

Sfax, a city of Phœnician origin, and the Roman **Taparura** until the eighth century.   The Arab historians El Bekri and Edrisi speak of Sfax as a flourishing and important city, with monumental buildings, manufactories, wealthy inhabitants, fertile gardens, souks, fisheries, etc.   The town sustained five bombardments at different periods, the last being in July, 1881, when a landing was effected by the French.   Sfax was the only place on the coast that offered any resistance to the French occupation, but a French squadron of nine ironclads and four gunboats soon silenced the guns of the Casbah, and the town quietly submitted. The Europeans who had taken refuge on board English or French men-of war during the bombardment returned to the town, as did also the Arabs who had retired to the country, but the Bedouins fled to Tripoli.

Since 1881 the trade and commerce of Sfax have made rapid strides, and the present population is estimated at about 66,000 inhabitants, of whom 5,000 are Europeans, including 1,500 French.

The modern name is said to have been given from the Arabic word *fakous* (cucumber) on account of the abundance of this vegetable in the neighbourhood.   Sfax, however, has riches of greater value than cucumbers in its harbour, commerce, and countless olive trees.

The European quarter is situated near the new port and along the seashore, where the great development and improvements are going on. Here are installed the public offices, schools, market, churches, theatre, and many handsome private houses.

The first-class port constructed by and under the management of a joint-stock company, the "Compagnie des Ports de Tunis, Sousse, et Sfax," is well sheltered by the **Kerkenna Islands**, and is accessible by vessels of very large tonnage. During the necessary excavations and building operations in 1897, several Roman ruins were unearthed, mosaics of the Christian period, large basilica, and baptistery

The Arab town, into which no Europeans were allowed to enter before 1832, is surrounded by a crenelated wall flanked by round and square towers. Here there is no change or improvement. The streets are as narrow and dirty as ever, the souks noisy, animated, and in some respects picturesque. The principal mosque dates from the year 200 of the Hegira, and its lofty minaret is seen from all directions.

Outside both the European and native quarters are delightful suburbs, occupied by residents preferring to return to their houses and gardens after the business is over in town.

Sfax has two fairly large hotels, the Hotel de France and the Hotel Moderne, oil presses, daily markets for the sale of cattle, oil, alfa, sponge, wool or provisions.

British Vice-Consul.—S. Leonardi.

There are also Consuls or Consular Agents at Sfax for Austro-Hungary, Belgium, Denmark, Spain, Greece, Italy, Holland, Sweden and Norway.

Time permitting, a drive in the suburbs will be found interesting (*carriages* 12f. *to* 15f. *per day*). Start from the vegetable market by the Gates road to the village of **Picville**, and on to the **Public Garden**, laid out with considerable taste, partly as park and shrubbery intermingled with flower beds, and partly as a pépinière or nursery garden. It is planted round two enormous reservoirs or **Fesquias**, the water from these, with the additional supply brought in pipes from the wells of **Sidi-Salah** (16 kilometres beyond Sfax), being sufficient for the consumption of seventy or eighty thousand people.

Some distance beyond the garden, and opposite the camp of the Spahis, within a walled enclosure of several acres, are five or six hundred bottle-shaped reservoirs called **Nasrias**, gifts to the town by wealthy Arabs. The cisterns are maintained in good order by the municipality, and the water is supplied to those who prefer it to that from Sidi-Salah.

A longer excursion can be recommended to the plateau of **Bokaât-el-Beida** to obtain an idea of the immense olive forests, covering a district of 70 or 80 kilometres around Sfax, the property of the state. *Carriage for the drive, 30 kilometres, 12f.*

Since 1871, the Beylical Government have by liberal concessions greatly encouraged the cultivation of olive trees on this land (originally called " Les Terres Sialines," the property having once belonged to a family named Siala), and in 1881 there were 18,000 hectares planted with 380,000 trees, but at the present time all the available land is under cultivation, with the estimated number of 1,400,000 trees.

Boats can be hired for an excursion to the **Kerkenna Islands,** the *Circinæ Insulæ* of the Romans, where Hannibal and Marius took refuge, and where Sempronius Gracchus, the lover of Julia, daughter of Augustus, was banished, and put to death by Tiberius. From 4 to 5 hours must be allowed to reach the nearer of the two principal islands (Gharbi).

The two islands, **Cherka** and **Gharbi**, now separated by a considerable channel, were formerly joined by a bridge, traces of some of the masonry being still visible. Gharbi is about 18 kilometres, or 11 miles, from the coast, and both islands are chiefly noted for their valuable sponge fisheries. The inhabitants, some 9,000 in number, a mixture of many nationalities, are very industrious, engaged principally in sponge and other fishing, in the manufacture of alfa mats and baskets, and in making wine from dates of inferior quality.

The several villages of the islands can b visited by boat or mule, guides can be obtained, but there are no hotels or inns of any kind.

The most notable antiquities on the islands consist of cisterns and towers, but a very elegant white marble ossuary of the first century has been recently discovered, and removed to the museum at Sfax.

Sfax to Gafsa and Metlaoui.

STATIONS.	Dis. in kil. from Sfax.
Sfax	—
Oued-Chaffar	29
Maharès	36
Oued-Chahal	50
Graïba (buffet)	63
Mezzouna	98
Maknassy	123
Sened	158
Aïn-Zannouch	178
Gafsa	205
Metlaoui	243

This light railway, the property of the "Compagnie des Phosphates et du Chemin de fer de Gafsa," but open to the public, runs almost parallel with the sea as far as Maharès, a native village surrounded with olive plantations, and then turns inland, afterwards running almost due west to Gafsa and and Metlaoui. At Graïba there is a buffet, and arrangements may be made with the Railway Company for excursions by automobile to Gabès, either from Sfax or Graïba. Fares from Sfax to Gafsa (two trains a day) 12f. 30c., 17f. 45c., and 22f. 95c.; return, 17f. 20c., 24f. 40c., and 32f. 15c.

Gafsa, the capital of the **Djerid**, once the powerful city of **Capsa**, destroyed by Marius, and afterwards restored by the Byzantines, is a curious old town pop. about 5,000) surrounded by one of the most beautiful oases of date and other fruit trees in the Sahara. Market on Wednesday.

The only building of interest is the Casbah, a native structure of the Middle Ages, probably erected on still more ancient foundations. There are several thermal springs, a source of supply for several ancient piscinas. But the chief attractions of Gafsa are its lovely walks and environs. There is a beautiful view from the heliographic station on the Djebel-Orbata (a day's excursion with mules; provisions should be taken) at an altitude of 3,838 feet. The ascent and descent occupy about 4 or 5 hours, and El Guettar, the starting point, is about 2 hours' journey from Gafsa.

The same railway extends to **Metlaoui**, 38 kilometres further inland than, and almost due west of, Gafsa. Fares from Sfax 14f. 60c., 20f. 65c., and 27f. 20c.; return, 20f. 40c., 28f. 90c., and 38f. 10c. The whole line was built in 18 months.

In the near neighbourhood are the phosphate quarries worked by the Company owning the railway, and the concession extends from Gafsa as far as the Algerian frontier. The quantity of phosphate seems almost inexhaustible. In 1905, 520,000 tons were exported, representing a value of about 10½ million francs. (To inspect the works apply to the engineer in charge at Metlaoui.)

From Metlaoui the grand gorge of the Seldja may be visited in from 4 to 5 hours (distance from the station to the entrance of the gorge 7 kilometres) on mules. The lower part of the defile is comparable to that at El Kantara (*see* p. 230).

Gafsa to Tozeur, 86 kilometres. Train to Metlaoui, 38 kilometres, thence carriage or mules, the conveyance or animals being sent forward the previous day.

Gafsa to Tébessa, 184 kilometres.

Within a radius of 15 or 20 kilometres of Sfax are sites of several Roman towns, in some of which remains of considerable interest may be examined.

At **Thyna**, the ancient **Thæna**, 12 kilometres on the Gabès road, are ruins of a large fortress, of an amphitheatre, and many Roman inscriptions have been discovered by the "Direction of Antiquities."

Ruspœ, Usilla, Taparura, Oungha, and **Oleastrum** are all places of interest to antiquarians.

Leaving Sfax, and passing Maharès, coasting along the Gulf of Gabès, the steamer calls at

Gabès, the ancient **Tacape**, a small town (pop. about 1 200) and military station, created since the French occupation. There is absolutely nothing to attract the notice of visitors. The little town is mainly occupied by Greeks and Jews, surrounded by the beautiful oasis and several Arab villages, the largest of these being **Menzel, Djara**, and **Chenini**. The barracks and camp are to the south of the town.

British Consular Agent.—F. Calleja. There are also Consular Agents for Belgium and Italy.

Starting from close to Gabès are a series of large **Chotts,** or salt lakes below the level of the sea, extending nearly 400 kilometres, to within eighty kilometres of Biskra. Some thirty years ago a French officer proposed to make an enormous inland sea by cutting through the narrow isthmuses between the lakes, then to cut a canal from the Mediterranean, north of Gabès, through which the sea would flow into the chotts.

A company was formed in 1882, and concessions granted by the Tunisian Government for the formation of a harbour at **Oued-el-Milah.** Artesian wells were sunk, large quantities of fresh water were obtained, and a certain acreage of land brought into cultivation, but the originator of the work (the Commandant Roudaire) passed away, and the great scheme of an inland sea has been abandoned.

Gabès is the starting point for visiting the district of the **Troglodytes,** or dwellers in caves. Among the several categories of these curious people those of the **Matmatas** mountains are best known, and their villages of **Hadèje** and **Toujane** can be reached by carriage in two days. (Provisions must be carried for the journey.)

Another excursion, involving some fatigue, can be made in a carriage to

Médénine. 80 kilometres, a large Troglodyte village (the most curious in Tunisia) and the site of an important military camp. The houses consist of vaults of several floors, sometimes as many as five, a succession of vaults without doors or windows; in some cases there is an outside staircase, but generally the occupiers of the upper floors have to climb from vault to vault by the aid of projecting stones. Many of the natives sleep in tents, others in the lower floors of the houses, the upper vaults being used as stores for various kinds of merchandise.

From Médénine an excursion occupying about six days may be made to several troglodyte villages, Foum-Tatahouine, Douirat, Chenini and Guermessa, but before undertaking this journey, notice should be given to the civil and military authorities.

If the traveller does not wish to return to Gabès he can proceed to the Island of Djerba from Médénine by going to **Djorf bou-Grara,** 30 kilometres, on horseback, thence boat (one and a-half hours) across to **Ajim**, and from Ajim by diligence or carriage to **Houm-Souk**. At Bou-Grara, the ancient **Gigthi**, are many important historical and archæological ruins. Assisted by the military, M. Gauckler and M. Sadoux, director and inspector of antiquities, have recently unearthed the beautiful **Forum** and adjoining temple, rich in marble inscriptions, sanctuaries and other monuments of the second century.

Continuing by the steamer from Gabès, in a little over three hours the voyage ends at Houm-Souk, the administrative capital of

Djerba, the " Island of the Lotophagi," where the landing is effected in boats, the steamer being unable to anchor nearer than four miles from the shore.

British Consular Agent.—G. Pariente.

The island, which is about 30 kilometres square, has a population of 60,000, of Berber origin, the villages of **Harat-el-Kebira** and **Harat-es-Srhira** being inhabited by Jews.

The Mohammedans belong to the Wahabite rite, and do not believe in the divine mission of Mohammed. The mosques are very small.

The island, although flat and without any rivers, is very fertile and beautiful. All the villages and houses are surrounded by gardens and orchards, the farms are well cultivated (armed like fortresses against any possible attack of the nomads), and olive groves flourish in perfection. The island contains 1,300,000 palm trees, 500,000 olive trees, 150,000 fruit trees, and 500,000 vines.

The inhabitants are gentle, active, bright, and industrious, engaged as cultivators of the soil, or in the weaving of loose coats, known as **djerbas**, also of blankets and burnouses. Others are employed in the manufacture of pottery, especially at **Gallala**, others again as sailors and fishermen. A considerable trade is done in sponges, and the island oil, pottery, and woollen articles are exported in large quantities.

The most important ruins are to be found at **El Kantara**, the ancient **Meninx**, once a magnificent city, situated on the larger strait of the inland sea which separates the island from the mainland, and connected therewith by a causeway. The ruins consist of sculptured stones, vases, broken columns, and sarcophagi of various coloured marbles. And recently, M. Sadoux, inspector of antiquities and arts, has discovered several hydraulic installations of an original type, and a large funereal cavern cut in the rock, with an interior colonnade, dating, in all probability, from the Punic period. The plan of a large Christian basilica has also been ascertained.

The means of locomotion in the island are not very comfortable or ample, but carriages may be hired (20f. per day) at Houm-Souk. Saddle mules (5f. a day) are, however, preferable.

The following itinerary will include all the places worth visiting :—

Houm-Souk, Ajim, Kallala, El Kantara, Mahboubine, Midoun, and return to Houm-Souk.

(10) Tunis to Sousse, Gabès and Djerba.

(By Rail, Steamer, etc.)

For travellers who have no desire to take the coast route, the island of Djerba can be visited from Tunis (and return) in five or six days, as under :—

Tunis to Sousse by rail (1.52 p.m.), due Sousse 7.55 p.m. (1 day).

Sousse to El Djem (*see* p. 367) and Sfax (*see* p. 392) by automobile (*see* p. 367) in about 6½ hours (1 day).

Sfax to Gabès by steamer (5 to 6 hours) or train to Graiba, thence diligence (1 day).

Gabès to Djerba by steamer (4 hours).

(Consult railway and steamer time tables so as to connect without loss of time for the return journey.)

(11) Tunis to Tripoli (Barbary).

Although Tripoli is outside the Regency of Tunisia and in a vilayet or province of the same name belonging to the Ottoman Empire, a few particulars of the journey hence from Tunis may not be out of place in the present volume, especially as some tourists may elect to return to Europe *viâ* Tripoli and Malta. Or a circular voyage by sea may be made from Tunis to Tripoli, Malta, and back to Tunis.

The Italian General Navigation Co.'s steamers leave Djerba every Saturday afternoon, reaching Tripoli on Sunday morning (about 13 or 14 hours).

The same Company's steamers leave Tunis for Tripoli (calling at Sousse, Monastir, Mehdia, Sfax, Gabès, and Djerba) every Wednesday evening, returning from Tripoli on Thursdays.

The Cie. de Navigation Mixte (Touache) steamers leave Djerba every Monday evening, due Tripoli Tuesday morning (about 13 hours), and Tunis (calling at above-named intermediate ports) on Friday evening.

From Tripoli one may return to Tunis by the steamers of either of the two above-mentioned Companies, or proceed to Malta by the Italian Navigation Co.'s vessels, leaving Tripoli on Sunday afternoons, due Malta about midday on Monday ; thence to Egypt, Palestine, and various European ports.

Travellers from Tunisia landing at Tripoli should have either a passport *visé* by a Turkish Consul or a simple Consular pass obtained through a "contrôleur civil." Failing either of these, a little baksheesh nearly always smooths away any obstacle on the part of the Turkish officials.

Hotels at Tripoli : Hôtel Transatlantique and Hôtel Minerva. Cook's Coupons, Series R, accepted at both.

For conducted tours from London, including Tunisia, *see* p. 50.

MOROCCO.

Morocco is generally visited from Gibraltar, there being regular services between that place and Tangier, the principal port of Morocco, leaving Gibraltar on Tuesdays, Thursdays, and Saturdays at 11.0 a.m., returning Mondays, Wednesdays, and Fridays at 11.30 a.m.

The *Cie. de Navigation Mixte* have a fortnightly service, leaving Gibraltar on Wednesdays, early morning, and Marseilles in the evening of same day.

From Cadiz or Gibraltar three times a week by the Cie. *Trasatlantica.*

Tangier may also be reached by the Papayanni line from Liverpool (fortnightly) ; German East African line (every three weeks) from Dover, calling at Lisbon ; Oldenburg-Portuguese SS. Co. (twice a month) from Hamburg and Antwerp for Gibraltar and Tangier.

Hotel at Tangier : Hotel Bristol. Cook's Coupons, Series R, accepted.

Consul-General.—Sir G. A. Lowther, K.C.M.G., etc.

Consul.—H. E. White, C.M.G. **Vice-Consul.**—G. Lascelle.

From Tangier there are sailings to Melilla, Tetuan, Ceuta, Laraiche, Rabat, Casablanca, and other Moroccan ports. In the present unsettled state of the country, however, few tourists penetrate into the interior to Fez, Méquinez or Morocco city, mostly confining their visits to Tangier and neighbourhood.

Tetuan.—**Vice-Consul :** W. S. Bewicke.

Morocco City.—**Consular-Agent :** Alan Lennox.

Rabat.—**Vice-Consul :** G. E. Naroutsos.

Laraiche.—**Vice-Consul :** Lewis Forde.

Conducted Excursions to Tangier leave Cook's Office *Waterport Street, Gibraltar, twice a week during the season.*

LIST OF MODERN BOOKS RELATING TO TUNISIA.

Rapport du Résident-Général de France à Tunis.   Annual.

Ashbee (H. S.), Bibliography of Tunisia.   London, 1889.

Bazàban (L.), A travers la Tunisie.   Paris, 1887.

Blanchard (& ors), La Tunisie au debut du XXe siècle.   Paris, 1904.

Boddy (A.), To Kairwân the Holy.   London, 1885.

Broadley (A. M.), Tunis, Past and Present.   London, 1882.

Cagnat & Saladin, Voyage en Tunisie.   Paris, 1887.

Charmes (Gabriel), La Tunisie et la Tripolitaine.   Paris, 1883.

Daubiel (J.), Notes et Impressions sur la Tunisie.   Paris, 1897.

Fage (R.), Vers les Steppes et les Oases.   (Algérie-Tunisie.)   Paris 1906.

Faucon (N.), La Tunisie avant et depuis l'occupation française.   2 vols.   Paris, 1893.

Flaubert (G.), Salammbô.

Gauckler (P.), Les fouilles de Tunisie, et outres ouvrages.   1900-1903.

Graham (A.) and *Ashbee* (H. S.), Travels in Tunisia.   London, 1887.

Guérin (V.), Voyage archéologique dans la Régence de Tunis, etc.   Paris, 1862.

Hesse-Wartegg (Chevalier E. von), Tunis : the Land and the People.   2nd edition.   London, 1899.

Johnston (Sir Harry H.), A History of the Colonisation of Africa.   Cambridge, 1899.

Lapie (P.), Les Civilisations tunisiennes.   Paris, 1897.

Le Nouveau Port de Bizerte, Tunisie.   Paris, 1899.

Leroy-Beaulieu (Paul), L'Algérie et la Tunisie.   2nd edition.   Paris, 1897.

Michel (Léon), Tunis.   2nd edition.   Paris, 1883.

Olivier (L.), La Tunisie.   Paris, 1898.

Perry (Amos), Carthage and Tunis.   New York, 1869.

Salvator (Archiduc L.), Bizerte.   Paris, 1901.

Schoenfield (E. D.), Aus der Staaten der Barbaresken [Tripoli and Tunis].   Berlin, 1902.

Sladen (D.), Carthage and Tunis.   2 vols.   London, 1906.

Smith (R. Bosworth), Carthage and the Carthaginians.   London, 1879.

Tchihatcheff (M.), Algérie et Tunis.   Paris, 1880.

Tissot (Charles), Exploration scientifique de la Tunisie.   2 vols.   Paris, 1884-87.

Vivian (H.), Tunisia and the Modern Barbary Pirates.   London, 1899

(*See* also pp. 285, 320, 324 and 333).

INDEX.

[The main references are printed in heavier type.]

CPSIA information can be obtained at www.ICGtesting.com
Printed in the USA
BVOW06s2251260616

453548BV00015B/170/P

ALGIERS.

Grand Hotel - -
- - de l'Oasis.

BOULEVARD DE LA RÉPUBLIQUE,
. . ALGIERS. . .

Proprietor = = J. JAMAR.

THIS first-class Hotel is the largest and one of the best situated in the town of Algiers, containing over 120 bedrooms and sitting-rooms. It has been completely renovated by its new proprietor, and offers to visitors every desirable comfort. It is within a few minutes' walk of the offices of the principal Shipping Companies, the Railway Station, Banks, Cook's Office, and the English Consulate. Situated on the Boulevard de la République, the principal promenade in Algiers, the view over the Harbour and Bay rivals the famous view over the Bay of Naples, added to which is the magnificent view of the hill slopes of Mustapha, and the plain of the Metidja and Atlas Mountains.

Table d'Hôte and Restaurant à la Carte.
Large and small sitting-rooms for families. •

Choice French Wines and Wines of the Country.
Special arrangements for lengthened stay.

COOK'S COUPONS TAKEN.
Omnibus to meet Steamers and Trains.

Interpreter attached to Hotel, speaking various languages.

ALGIERS.

GRAND HOTEL DE LA RÉGENCE.

FIRST CLASS.

APARTMENTS with BATH and LAVATORY

Only Hotel Facing Full South.

LIFT.   **ELECTRIC LIGHT.**

WINTER GARDEN.   ALL MODERN COMFORTS

RECENTLY ENLARGED.

CLOSE TO THE LANDING STAGE AND RAILWAY STATION.

Bus meets Steamers and Trains.

Telegraphic Address: Régence, Algiers.   NEW PROPRIETORS

BRUGGEMANN and FLUMM,

Swiss Managers, late of Hotel Rigi, Lucerne, & Bear Hotel, Grindelwald

<u>ÁLGIERS.</u>

ALGERIA.

The Hotel Continental,

MUSTAPHA SUPÉRIEUR.

⚜ ⚜

MR. HILDENBRAND, Proprietor and Manager.

⚜ ⚜

THIS FIRST-CLASS HOTEL is the only one at Mustapha Supérieur combining the most splendid view with a full southern exposure, and is therefore unrivalled in its position. It offers every comfort and modern improvement, with most perfect sanitary arrangements. The Continental was considerably enlarged last year, and contains many Spacious Public Rooms, 23 feet high, all warmed by hot air system. Eight acres of Garden, having a frontage to the south of 200 yards. Tennis Court. Electric Tramway to town every five minutes. Hotel Omnibus awaiting Steamers and Trains. Tariff and Prospectus sent on application.

COOK'S TOURS.

INDEPENDENT TICKETS.

COOK's Tickets are available all over the World, either for simple journeys or the most complex tours, and give special facilities with regard to break of journey and conveyance of luggage. Interpreters in uniform are in attendance at principal stations and seaports to render assistance to holders of Cook's Tickets.

INCLUSIVE INDEPENDENT TRAVEL.

The acme of travel without trouble is attained by the above method. By it the traveller journeys with absolute independence, but with every detail arranged beforehand, and practically every expenditure provided for. Write for explanatory prospectus.

SELECT PARTIES.

Select Parties frequently leave London under experienced Conductors (not in uniform) for well-planned tours to the chief countries in Europe, also to America, Palestine, Egypt, Algeria, etc., according to season, at fares which include all necessary expenses.

"POPULAR" HOLIDAY TOURS.

These Tours provide for travel ticket and hotel expenses at moderate and inclusive fares, and are arranged to all parts of Europe. They range from a single Saturday to Monday excursion to holidays of three weeks' duration, and do not tie the tourist to any fixed daily programme.

OCEAN TRAVEL DEPARTMENT.

Saloon and emigrant passage tickets are issued at lowest rates to allparts of the World. The accredited agents equally of every steamship line of repute, THOS. COOK & SON have no special interest to serve, but are in a position to give accurate and absolutely unbiassed information and guidance to their clients.

COOK's OCEAN SAILING LIST is published monthly, and may be had at any of their offices.

PLEASURE CRUISES.

Summer and Winter Cruises by specially appointed steamers of the P. & O., Orient, Royal Mail, and other first-class lines are organised throughout the year.

BANKING, EXCHANGE AND INSURANCE.

Foreign moneys exchanged at most advantageous rates. Circular Notes and Letters of Credit issued for all parts of the World.

Travellers with Cook's Tickets may, for small premiums, insure their baggage against loss. Baggage and goods of every description may be stored or forwarded to any part of the World at lowest rates.

HOTEL COUPONS.

Hotel Coupons are issued from 7/6 to 16/- per day, available at one or more of the principal hotels in each of the chief cities, towns, and places of Tourist resort in Great Britain and on the Continent. Full particulars are given in the "Traveller's Gazette," 3d. monthly, by post 5d.

PLEASURE OR BUSINESS TRAVEL IN GREAT BRITAIN.

Passengers travelling for pleasure or on business in Great Britain or to and from the Continent are informed that, as official Agents to the Midland Railway Company, THOS. COOK & SON issue tickets from and to most of the principal towns and tourist resorts of England, Scotland, and Ireland. The Midland Railway Company's express trains and connections serve most of the places of industrial and tourist interest, and comfortable and expeditious travel is ensured by this route.